Taxation in a Global Economy

In recent years the increasing international mobility of capital, firms and consumers has begun to constrain tax policies in most OECD countries, playing a major role in reforming national tax systems. Haufler uses the theory of international taxation to consider the fundamental forces underlying this process, covering both factor and commodity taxes, as well as their interaction. Topics include a variety of different international tax avoidance strategies – capital flight, profit-shifting in multinational firms and cross-border shopping by consumers. Situations in which tax competition creates conflicting interests between countries are given particular consideration. Haufler addresses the complex issue of coordination in different areas of tax policy, with special emphasis on regional tax harmonisation in the European Union. A detailed introduction to recent theoretical literature is also included.

ANDREAS HAUFLER is Associate Professor of Public Finance and Social Policy in the Department of Economics, University of Göttingen. He is the author of *Commodity Tax Harmonization of the European Community* (1993) and has published articles in journals including *Journal of Public Economics*, *Oxford Economic Papers*, *Scandinavian Journal of Economics*, *Fiscal Studies* and *International Tax and Public Finance*.

Taxation in a Global Economy

Andreas Haufler

University of Göttingen

PUBLISHED BY THE PRESS SYNDICATE OF THE UNIVERSITY OF CAMBRIDGE
The Pitt Building, Trumpington Street, Cambridge, United Kingdom

CAMBRIDGE UNIVERSITY PRESS
The Edinburgh Building, Cambridge CB2 2RU, UK
40 West 20th Street, New York NY 10011–4211, USA
10 Stamford Road, Oakleigh, VIC 3166, Australia
Ruiz de Alarcón 13, 28014 Madrid, Spain
Dock House, The Waterfront, Cape Town 8001, South Africa

http://www.cambridge.org

First published 2001

Printed in the United Kingdom at the University Press, Cambridge

Typeface 10/12 Plantin System 3B2

A catalogue record for this book is available from the British Library

Library of Congress Cataloguing in Publication data

Haufler, Andreas.
Taxation in a global economy / Andreas Haufler.
p. cm.
Includes bibliographical references and index.
ISBN 0 521 78276 7
1. Taxation. 2. Capital movements. 3. Taxation of articles of consumption.
4. Competition, International. 5. Taxation–European Union countries. 6. Capital movements–European Union countries. 7. Taxation of articles of consumption–European countries. I. Title.

HJ2305 .H38 2001
336.2–dc21 2001025239

ISBN 0521 78276 7 hardback

Contents

Part 4 Factor and commodity taxation

Figures

Tables

General symbols used

c_k^i	consumption of good $k \in \{1, 2, 3\}$ in country $i \in \{A, B, C\}$
δ	depreciation rate of capital
f_k^i	production function for good k in country i
F^i	best response function of country i
g^i	public good supply in country i
k^i	capital stock in country i
l^i	labour supply in country i
n	number of identical countries, firms or consumers
p_k^i	producer price of good k in country i
π^i	(pure) profits in country i
q_k^i	consumer price of good k in country i
r^i	gross return to capital in country i
R	world interest rate
σ	elasticity of substitution in consumption
t_k^i	tax rate on activity k in country i
T^i	total tax revenue in country i
τ_k	transaction cost function for activity k
u^i	direct utility function of country i
v^i	indirect utility function of country i
w^i	gross wage rate in country i
ω^i	net wage rate in country i
x_k^i	output or endowment of good k in country i

Preface

International taxation and tax competition have been among the dominant and most rapidly expanding fields in the recent public finance literature. Despite the wealth of analyses, however, there are still only very few books on these subjects which offer a synthesising and integrating treatment of seemingly disparate issues discussed in professional journal articles. This relative lack of broad-based analytically oriented studies in international taxation has been my main motivation to put together the present book. A special feature of this volume is that it covers issues in both international commodity and factor taxation, as well as their interaction. Furthermore, I have made an attempt to extensively compare the results derived with those obtained in related and recent literature.

In many respects this book is a joint research effort. Several chapters draw on joint work with Wolfgang Eggert (chapter 5), Bernd Genser (chapters 9 and 11), Søren Bo Nielsen (chapter 9), Guttorm Schjelderup (chapter 7), Peter Birch Sørensen (chapter 9), and Ian Wooton (chapter 12). I wish to thank all my co-authors for the permission to use these joint results in the present volume, as well as for numerous helpful comments on the chapters in which they were not directly involved. Most of all, I am indebted to Bernd Genser, my academic teacher, who has supported the development of this book in every possible respect. I would also like to thank Friedrich Breyer, Wolfram Richter and Wolfgang Wiegard, who have reviewed a previous version of the entire manuscript of my habilitation thesis in Konstanz. Individual chapters have benefited greatly from the comments and suggestions of a large number of colleagues; in particular I would like to mention Max Albert, Lans Bovenberg, Sam Bucovetsky, Sijbren Cnossen, Michael Devereux, Hans Fehr, Harry Huizinga, Mick Keen, Ben Lockwood, Jürgen Meckl, Jack Mintz, Wolfgang Peters, Günther Schulze and Hans-Werner Sinn.

Most of the research documented in this book was undertaken at the University of Konstanz where I have benefited greatly from the

Sonderforschungsbereich 'Internationalization of the Economy'. I am very grateful to its chairman, Hans-Jürgen Vosgerau, for having provided this stimulating research environment. The groundwork for a substantial part of the analyses was laid, however, when I was a Visiting Scholar at the University of Western Ontario in London, Canada. During this period, the help from John Whalley, Carlo Perroni and Ig Horstmann proved to be critical. Another important stimulus was provided by the meetings of the European Union's Human Capital and Mobility Programme 'Fiscal Implications of European Integration', and I am grateful to Dieter Bös for admitting me to his team. I also thank Barbara Docherty and Ashwin Rattan from Cambridge University Press for their professional and competent help and three anonymous referees who made a number of valuable suggestions to improve the manuscript. The largest debt I owe to my wife Kerstin for all her support, endurance and sacrifice during an intense period of starting both a career and a family at the same time.

Andreas Haufler

1 Introduction

1.1 Market integration

The years since 1980 have seen a worldwide acceleration in the process of integrating the goods and factor markets of different countries. Among the most important factors in this development are the integration of the former Communist countries into the world economy, trade liberalisation and market oriented reforms in many developing countries, and the formation or the strengthening of regional economic groupings such as the European Union (EU), the North American Free Trade Agreement (NAFTA), the Commonwealth of Independent States (CIS), the South American Free Trade Association (MERCOSUR) and the Association of South East Asian Nations (ASEAN). In the European Union, for example, the so-called 'four liberties' (the free flow of goods, services, capital and labour) form the cornerstone of the internal market programme, and NAFTA similarly grants mutual market access to producers and capital owners in the United States, Canada and Mexico.

The increasing degree of market integration has been most visible with respect to capital markets. In the period between 1983 and 1998, the annual flow of outbound foreign direct investment (FDI) has nominally increased by more than 1200 per cent worldwide, rising from less than $50 billion in 1983 to more than $600 billion in 1998. During the same time period, world commodity trade has more than tripled from a total export volume of $1667 billion in 1983 to $5377 billion in 1998 (International Monetary Fund, 1990, 1999). With respect to migration, the increase in mobility is generally less pronounced. In the period between 1981 and 1995 the share of foreigners in the total population increased only slightly in most OECD countries and remained below 10 per cent in all Western European nations, except the small countries Luxembourg and Switzerland (see OECD(SOPEMI), 1994, 1997).

From a trade perspective, the increasing international mobility of commodities and factors is generally seen as an efficiency-enhancing increase in the international division of labour and the utilisation of scarce resources in places where they yield the highest marginal product. From the viewpoint of national tax policy, however, increased mobility constitutes a constraint, since it raises the elasticity of national tax bases and thus the excess burden of the tax system. In principle, the adverse effects of taxation on mobile commodity and factor tax bases could be neutralised by appropriate schemes of international taxation. The destination principle of commodity taxation and the residence principle of factor taxation have long been the dominant international tax principles. Both imply that taxes fall on consumption rather than production and thus they effectively shield national tax systems from international competition in goods and factor markets. Recent developments have made it more difficult, however, to enforce these desirable international tax schemes.

For the taxation of capital income, the growing international investment opportunities and the difficulties in monitoring foreign investment income have put increased reliance on source or withholding taxes levied in the country where capital is invested. A recent example is the switch of several European countries to source-based, flat taxes on capital income, which remain substantially below the top marginal tax rates on wage income. This 'dual income tax' breaks with the tradition of comprehensive, worldwide income taxation under the residence principle and many observers expect similar reforms in other countries as capital market integration proceeds.

At the same time, the increased mobility of consumers makes it more difficult to sustain the destination principle as a general scheme for international commodity taxation. This applies in particular in the European Union, where the abolition of internal border controls has removed most restrictions on private purchases abroad and cross-border shopping introduces elements of origin-based taxation into the overall mix of taxing trade. Cross-border shopping is also important in other parts of the world, for example at the Canada-US or the US-Mexican borders.

If taxes fall at least partly on the production of goods or the employment of factors, they affect the competition in global markets. Therefore, the developments outlined above have raised a complex set of problems for the taxation of international goods and factor flows. Following a traditional categorisation in international taxation, these problems comprise aspects of efficiency, interindividual equity and internation equity (Musgrave and Musgrave, 1989, ch. 33). To give just a few examples of questions that have arisen: first, given that pure destination- or residence-based taxation is no longer feasible, is it preferable to maintain these principles for at least some transactions, or should they be abandoned altogether and be replaced by origin- and source-based taxes? Second, what are the effects of increased mobility of tax bases on the structure and the level of public sectors, the welfare costs of the tax system and the relative weights put on different tax instruments? Further, will these changes be dominated primarily by efficiency concerns, or will there be more complex equity–efficiency trade-offs as market integration simultaneously changes the income distribution within each country? And, finally, is it politically feasible and economically desirable to coordinate national tax policies when countries differ in some critical way and coordination must be restricted to a subgroup of countries while others remain outside the agreement?

All these and many other questions have been addressed over the last decade in a large number of widely diversified contributions, making international taxation and tax competition one of the dominant themes in the recent public finance literature. While the research effort has been – and still is – intense, it is in the nature of a relatively new and rapidly expanding field that the focus is on analytical differences between individual models, rather than on the common elements and close links that exist between alternative settings and approaches. In particular, the analytically oriented literature dichotomises almost completely into models of either commodity or factor taxation and this distinction conceals the close similarities underlying many of the results. Furthermore, on the basis of individual articles with often conflicting results, it is generally quite difficult to draw any reliable policy conclusions for a specific tax competition scenario.

For these reasons, there are some clear advantages that a detailed monograph on international taxation and tax competition has over isolated articles in professional journals; in fact, it is precisely the wealth of articles on this subject that makes an integrated treatment interesting and potentially valuable. To date, there are still only a few monographs in this field which offer a sufficiently broad analytical framework to incorporate a larger share of the literature and the relevant policy issues.[1]

A first and prominent example is Frenkel, Razin and Sadka (1991), who focus on intertemporal aspects of international taxation and dedicate most of their analysis to the taxation of internationally mobile capital. In a two-period 'workhorse model' with endogenous savings and labour supply by a representative agent, they analyse the implications of capital tax competition for the costs of public funds, the optimal

[1] There are also several excellent survey articles, which will be introduced in chapter 3.

structure of capital taxation under conditions of perfect and imperfect capital mobility (when capital controls are permitted) and the desirability of tax harmonisation between a subgroup of countries.

A second monograph is Wellisch (2000), who incorporates household mobility and distinguishes between the mobility of firms and capital. Wellisch's work integrates the local public finance literature with a number of issues that arise equally in a context of international factor taxation. In this study taxes are used to provide public goods, redistribute income between different groups and internalise environmental externalities. The focus of the analysis is on the conditions under which decentralised tax policy leads to an efficient outcome, despite the presence of interjurisdictional tax competition.

Thirdly, Janeba (1997) focuses on game-theoretic aspects of capital income taxation. His analysis covers tax competition for internationally mobile portfolio capital and FDI and also extends to settings where firms operate in oligopolistic markets. A special feature of this work is the detailed modelling of capital tax instruments, in particular different forms of double taxation relief. The questions raised include the existence and efficiency of a non-cooperative tax equilibrium and the possibility to achieve Pareto improvements through various methods of fiscal cooperation.

There are also several policy oriented studies on the same subject. The book by Tanzi (1995) is a prime source in this field, combining theoretical concepts with a detailed discussion of policy experiences and likely further developments. The present book is complementary to Tanzi's work in at least two respects. First, the focus here will be more on theoretical contributions to international taxation, even though policy implications will not be neglected. The second difference is that the policy implications in the present book will be drawn primarily from the perspective of the European Union. This is particularly relevant for commodity taxation, where policy issues in the United States are quite different from those in Europe. Even in the area of capital taxation, however, the European Union is a unique example, since it offers an existing legal framework for trans-national – but geographically restricted – measures of tax harmonisation.

In comparison to the existing theoretical studies, the main distinguishing feature of the present analysis is that it includes a detailed treatment of both commodity and factor taxation. This incorporates the two main strands of the tax competition literature into the scope of our analysis and allows us to establish several links between two otherwise largely separated fields of analysis. We will discuss the interaction of commodity and factor taxation in an open economy context and also draw some policy conclusions for the mix between direct and indirect taxation under conditions of increasing market integration.

A second theme that occurs repeatedly throughout this book is the strategic interaction between two asymmetric players (governments). If all countries were identical, then the implementation of tax coordination measures would be straightforward and tax harmonisation would involve no costs for each individual country. However, tax competition is a policy problem chiefly because countries differ in the level of taxation as well as in the structure of their tax systems. These differences may lead to diverging interests between countries, making it possible that some countries gain from tax competition and hence have no interest in participating in globally welfare improving reforms. Identifying such conflicts of interest is thus a first step in the search for policy solutions that overcome inefficient outcomes of tax competition.

Thirdly, similar to Wellisch (2000) and Janeba (1997) we distinguish between the mobility of capital on the one hand, and the mobility of firms on the other. In the context of this study, the introduction of firm mobility serves two main purposes. First, it makes clear that taxes which are neutral in conventional models of capital mobility – in particular, taxes on pure profits or rents – lead to interregional tax competition when the set of mobility scenarios is extended. Second, the incorporation of firm mobility links the tax competition literature to the new trade theory, where the location decisions of firms operating in imperfectly competitive markets have also become a prominent field of research.

We also emphasise that, unlike Wellisch (2000), the present analysis explicitly addresses international issues, even though links to federally organised nation states will be drawn occasionally. This international focus derives from the mobility scenarios underlying the present study, as well as the specific constraints and policy options analysed. For example, the choice between destination- and origin-based commodity tax principles arises primarily in an international context, since only very few nation states operate decentralised multi-stage commodity tax systems. Similarly, the evasion of capital income taxes is a particularly relevant constraint in an international setting, because all measures to reduce international capital flight require the cooperation of legally independent tax authorities. Furthermore, we ignore labour mobility in the present study, a restriction that is primarily dictated by the need to specialise in a rapidly expanding field. As we have seen above, the assumption of interregional immobility of labour may still be a reasonable approximation in an international context, whereas it is clearly not justified when analysing tax policy in a federal state.

Finally, at least since Brennan and Buchanan's (1980) work on the 'Leviathan' model of government, it is well known that the answers given to almost any public finance issue very much depend on one's view of government behaviour. This is also true for international taxation. Although some progress has been made in defining a more realistic middle ground between the two polar views of completely benevolent and completely selfish government behaviour, most of the literature is still based on either the one or the other view of government. The present book largely works with the assumption of welfare-maximising governments and it does not model the political process in any detail. A complementary work in this respect is Lorz (1997), who analyses the effect that competition for internationally mobile capital has on the decisions made by different interest groups in the economy.

1.2 Plan of the book

The study begins in part 1 with two introductory chapters: in chapter 2 we survey some current policy problems and developments in both international commodity and capital taxation. Most of the discussion will focus on the policy issues in the European Union, but we also take a brief look at developments in other parts of the world. After this policy oriented introduction, chapter 3 gives a brief theoretical introduction to the tax competition literature. The discussion in this chapter focuses on some basic analytical distinctions in tax competition models that are independent of the specific mobility scenario analysed and play an important role in the remainder of the study. The chapter also gives a brief overview of some of the strands in the international tax literature that are not further pursued below.

The main body of the book falls in three parts: part 2 (chapters 4–7) addresses selected issues of factor taxation and part 3 (chapters 8–9) is concerned with isolated models of commodity taxation. Part 4 (chapters 10–12) brings together the different tax instruments and analyses their interaction. Most of the chapters are structured in a similar way: we start out with an introductory section that surveys the fundamental contribution(s) in the particular field. This is followed by our own analysis, where the extensions or modifications of the existing literature are made explicit. Finally, we compare our results with those obtained in related work, with the aim of emphasising analytical links on the one hand and complementary (or conflicting) policy implications on the other.

Part 2 of the book starts out with factor taxation. Chapter 4 gives an overview of some fundamental theoretical results and empirical issues that underlie large parts of the literature on capital tax competition. We first introduce and discuss alternative international principles for the taxation of mobile capital. This is followed by the presentation of two theoretical benchmark results in this literature, the zero taxation of capital income by a small open economy and the underprovision of public goods as a result of symmetric tax competition. Finally, we survey some of the empirical evidence on the development of capital vs. labour taxation since 1980.

Chapter 5 extends and combines the benchmark analyses of chapter 4 to analyse capital tax competition between two countries of different size. We first derive the basic theoretical result that small countries undercut the capital tax rates of their larger neighbours and discuss the parameters that influence the small country's welfare in the Nash equilibrium. This is followed by a numerical specification of the model, which evaluates the conditions under which small countries can be better off in the asymmetric Nash equilibrium, as compared to the case of policy coordination. Finally, we discuss the scope for the regional coordination of capital income taxes when capital flight to third countries can occur.

Chapter 6 introduces distributional motives within each country and analyses the optimal mix of capital and wage taxation when two competing governments maximise the political support from workers and capitalists. In representative consumer models capital market integration leads to an unambiguous shift in the tax structure, reducing the taxation of capital and increasing the tax on wages. In a two-class model it is shown that the opposite can be true in a capital exporting country when income groups try to maintain their net income position and the government is forced to use tax policy to compensate workers for the market-induced fall in gross wages.

In chapter 7 the focus of the analysis shifts from the level to the structure of capital taxation. Corporate tax reforms since the 1980s have combined significant cuts in the tax rate with a broadening of the corporate tax base. A model is set up that explains this pattern of reform as an optimal adjustment to the increased possibilities for multinational firms to shift paper profits between countries. Based on these results we discuss reform measures for the current international system of taxing the profits of multinational corporations.

In part 3 we turn to the analysis of commodity taxation. Chapter 8 analyses asymmetric tax competition under a mixed commodity tax scheme where producer transactions are taxed under the destination principle while cross-border purchases by consumers are taxed under the origin principle. In this setting consumers in high-tax regions have an incentive to shop abroad, creating fiscal externalities that distort commodity tax choices in the Nash equilibrium. Starting from this asymmetric equilibrium we analyse the effects of coordination measures to limit cross-border shopping on the welfare levels in the high-tax and the low-tax region.

Chapter 9 analyses the consequences of switching to a general origin-based system of commodity taxation. This scheme is shown to be equivalent to a general destination principle in the long run, even if capital is mobile internationally. However, the switch in the tax principle will cause anticipation effects that lead to temporary distortions of investment and savings decisions. The discussion identifies several other settings in which origin- and destination-based commodity taxes are equivalent, and where they have differential effects.

The analyses in part 4 incorporate both factor and commodity taxes. Chapter 10 studies the interaction of source-based capital taxes and commodity taxes in a two-good trade model of a small open economy when capital is internationally mobile. Starting from the benchmark case where rents accruing to fixed factors can be taxed by separate instruments, we then introduce both domestic and international constraints on the set of available taxes and study the implications for the optimal tax mix. This analysis forms the starting point for a more detailed discussion of the production efficiency theorem in open economies and for the efficiency of tax competition in models with a broad set of tax instruments.

Chapter 11 simultaneously introduces imperfect international mobility of firms and cross-border shopping by consumers. In this setting a clear-cut efficiency argument against an origin-based commodity tax emerges, since this tax can be duplicated by an appropriate combination of taxes on wages and firms' profits. In contrast, a destination-based commodity tax performs an independent role in the government's tax mix when some capital income escapes direct taxation. The optimal tax mix features a combination of positive taxes on wages, profits and consumption.

Chapter 12 discusses firm mobility in an alternative setting where two countries of different size compete for the location of a single, foreign-owned monopolist. Trade costs for the monopolist's exports introduce a 'home market effect' that gives a location rent to the larger region. In equilibrium, the firm always settles in the large country, reversing the advantage that small countries have in attracting capital in perfectly competitive markets. In the case where both countries dispose of an additional tax on imported goods, it is very likely that the large country can extract a positive profit tax from the monopolist. Policy conclusions are drawn for the need to harmonise corporate taxation in the European Union as a way to capture location rents from foreign firms.

Chapter 13 summarises the results of the study. On the basis of these findings, it evaluates the arguments for tax harmonisation in the European Union in the fields of both commodity and capital income taxation. The chapter concludes with a brief outlook on the optimal mix of direct and indirect taxation in a world characterised by increasingly mobile tax bases.

Part 1

Tax competition: policy and theory

2 Policy issues

The aim of this chapter is to provide a brief overview of the policy issues that have arisen from mobile capital and commodity tax bases. Section 2.1 describes tax reforms and reform proposals in the field of direct taxation, which aim at improving the efficiency and equity of existing income tax systems under conditions of increasing capital mobility. Section 2.2 then focuses on international aspects of indirect taxation and reviews the policy debate with respect to both the choice of an international commodity tax principle and the harmonisation of value-added tax rates. In each section we first survey the developments in the European Union and then briefly look at North America and other parts of the world.

2.1 Direct taxes

2.1.1 Developments in the European Union

This section reviews some general trends in the development of personal and corporate income tax systems in EU member states. Against this background, we then discuss the most important initiatives for harmonising or coordinating capital tax systems in the EU.[1]

Since the 1980s, following the lead of the United States and the United Kingdom, most EU member states have introduced significant changes to their schemes of both personal and corporate income taxation (CIT). While these reforms were clearly motivated, in part, by domestic developments, it is also undisputed that the increasing international

[1] In the literature on international taxation there is no rigorous and generally accepted distinction between the terms 'tax harmonisation' on the one hand, and 'tax coordination' on the other. Supranational legislation that forces individual countries to give up autonomy over national tax rates or tax bases is often classified as 'tax harmonisation', whereas 'tax coordination' refers to multilateral arrangements below this threshold. This is also the practice that will be employed in this book.

Table 2.1 *Taxation of personal capital and labour income in the OECD, 1989 and 1998*

Country	Top personal tax rate on labour income[a] (1989)	Top personal tax rate on labour income[a] (1998)	Top tax rate on interest income (1998)	Interest withholding tax: Domestic investors	Interest withholding tax: Foreign investors
Austria	50	50	25	25	0
Belgium	60	60.8	15	15	0–15[b]
Denmark	69.6	60	60	0[c]	0
Finland	58	55.5	28	28	0
France	56.8	61.6	20.9	10–19.4	0–15[b]
Germany	56	53	53	30	0
Greece	50	45	20	15–20	10–45[b]
Ireland	56	46	27	10 and 26	0–15[b]
Italy	58.1	46	30	12.5–30	0–15[b]
Luxembourg	56	50	50	0	0
Netherlands	72	60	60	0	0
Portugal	40	40	20	20	10–20[b]
Spain	56	56	31	25	0
Sweden	65	56	30	30	0
United Kingdom	40	40	40	20	0
EU average	56.2	52.0	34.0	16.0[d]	1.3[d]
Canada	43.5	44.4	44.4	0[c]	0–25[b]
Japan	65	65	20	20	20
Norway	53	41.7	28	0[c]	0
Switzerland	40.9	42.4	42.4	35	0–35[b]
United States	36.6	46.2	39.8	0[c]	0

Notes:

[a] Combined tax rate at all levels of government.

[b] Withholding tax rates depend on type of interest income and double taxation agreements.

[c] Interest income of domestic residents is reported to tax authorities.

[d] Averages are based on lower bounds for withholding tax rates.

Sources: Genser and Haufler (1999), table 2b; Mennel and Förster (1999); Sørensen (2000), table 1.

mobility of capital has played an important role in this process. Our focus will be on the taxation of personal interest income on the one hand and corporate profits on the other.

Some relevant indicators for the development of personal income taxation are collected in table 2.1. The first two columns show that top personal rates of income taxation were reduced in the 1990s, but the changes remain moderate for most countries and the top personal income tax rate remains above 50 per cent in the EU average. The comparison with important OECD countries outside Europe shows, however, that tax rates have even increased in Canada and the United States (albeit starting from levels significantly below the EU average), and have remained stable at a very high level in Japan.

The third column of table 2.1 reveals the first obvious sign for the effects of international capital mobility on personal income tax systems. It shows that ten out of the fifteen EU member states now apply personal tax rates on interest income that are well below the top marginal tax rates applicable for wage income. This represents a major break from the the long-cherished principle of comprehensive income taxation, according to which all sources of income should be subject to a common tax schedule. The move towards a 'dual income tax' has been an explicit and major reform process in the Scandinavian countries (see Sørensen, 1994 and the contributions in Sørensen, 1998), and a similar reform has also been adopted in Austria. Country studies for Sweden (Mutén, 1996) and Austria (Genser, 1996a) demonstrate clearly that these reforms were prompted by the experience of massive tax evasion in the years prior to the reform, and tax revenues actually rose after statutory tax rates on capital income had been reduced.

An alternative – or complementary – measure to enforce the taxation of interest income is the introduction of withholding taxes. It is shown in the fourth column of table 2.1 that all except three EU member countries (which partly use alternative measures of tax enforcement) levy withholding taxes on the interest income of *domestic* residents. However, as the fifth column shows, this enforcement scheme is not extended to *foreign* investors in most EU states. Presumably, the rationale for this discriminatory tax policy is that foreign investors are more mobile, on average, than domestic investors from the perspective of national governments. This was well documented by the 1989 introduction of a 10 per cent withholding tax in Germany, which applied to both domestic and foreign residents. In anticipation of this tax, German long-term capital exports reached a record level of 85 billion Deutsche Mark in 1988, forcing the government to abolish the withholding tax in July 1989 (cf. Schlesinger, 1990). In 1993, the German government was forced by its Supreme Court to reintroduce a 30 per cent withholding tax on interest income for domestic equity reasons, but foreigners were now excluded from the withholding tax. While the capital outflow was again substantial, the exclusion of foreigners made the withholding tax sustainable, despite its relatively high rate.

Table 2.2 *Statutory corporate tax rates and corporate tax revenue in the OECD, 1980–1999*

	Top corporate tax rate on retained profits[a]			Corporate tax revenue in per cent of total taxes	
	1980	1985	1999	1980	1996
Austria	61.5	61.5	34	3.5	4.7
Belgium	48	45	40.2	5.7	6.8
Denmark	37	50	32	3.2	4.6
Finland		50	28	3.9	5.6
France	50	50	40	5.1	5.2
Germany	61.7	61.7	52.3	5.5	3.8
Greece		49	35	3.8	6.3
Ireland	45	50/10[b]	28/10[b]	4.5	9.5
Italy	36.3	47.8	37	7.8	9.2
Luxembourg	45.5	45.5	37.5	16.4	17.9
Netherlands	46	42	35	6.6	9.5
Portugal	51.2	51.2	34	8.0[c]	9.5
Spain	33	33	35	5.1	5.8
Sweden	40	52	28	2.5	5.6
United Kingdom	52	40	30	8.4	10.7
EU average	46.7	48.6	35.1	6.0	7.6
Canada	42.4	51.6	44.6	11.6	8.9
Japan	52	55.4	48	21.8	16.4
Norway		51	28	13.3	10.5
Switzerland	36.6	35	25	5.8	5.6
United States	49.2	49.5	38	10.8	9.6

Notes:
[a] Including local business taxes and surcharges.
[b] Special rate for manufacturing sector.
[c] 1990.
Sources: Ruding Report (1992), table 8.5; Genser and Haufler (1999), table 2a, OECD (1999), table 13; Sørensen (2000), table 1.

Next, we turn to a brief description of some developments in the field of CIT.[2] Table 2.2 summarises the changes in statutory corporate tax rates and in the revenue earned from CIT as a share of total tax revenue.

[2] In addition to the changes discussed here, many EU countries have reduced the domestic double taxation of corporate profits by adopting partial or full integration schemes with the personal income tax (see Cnossen, 1996, and Genser and Haufler, 1999, for surveys of this development). However, since integration is not extended to foreigners, this measure does not affect the cost of capital from the perspective of a foreign investor (see Boadway and Bruce, 1992). For this reason, this issue is left aside in what follows.

The first three columns in table 2.2 show that the average of statutory corporate tax rates in the EU fell by more than 13 percentage points since the mid-1980s and current tax reforms indicate that this trend may still continue for some time.[3] A similar pattern is followed by non-EU countries. The largest cuts in statutory corporate tax rates have been made by Austria, Ireland and the Scandinavian countries. This is partly linked to the introduction of dual income tax systems in many of these countries, as large tax differentials between tax rates on personal and corporate capital income give rise to tax arbitrage activities. However, it is also noteworthy that all these countries are small and well integrated in world capital markets.

The last two columns in table 2.2 give the development of corporate tax revenues. The figures show that the importance of corporate tax revenues for the overall financing of the public sector is quite limited in the OECD, and particularly in Europe.[4] The interesting observation is, however, that the share of CIT revenues has substantially *increased* in the (unweighted) EU average since the 1980s. This development is not shared by major OECD countries outside Europe. Closer inspection of individual country figures shows again that the most important increases have occurred in small EU countries, often the same ones that have reduced their statutory tax rates substantially.

The fact that corporate tax revenues in the Union have increased, despite substantial reductions in statutory CIT rates, can be attributed to two different factors. On the one hand, the average profitability of firms has risen in the Union during the time period considered, and this has increased the corporate tax base even in the absence of discretionary policy changes. On the other hand, tax bases have also been broadened, in the EU average.[5] The motivation for these 'tax-rate-cut-cum-base-broadening' reforms of corporate tax systems is not entirely clear, however. A domestic motive for this reform is that lower capital tax rates, combined with fewer exemptions from the tax base, reduce the distortions of the capital tax system. A tax competition interpretation is also possible, however, since low statutory tax rates may be used to attract

[3] Germany, which levied the highest statutory corporate tax rate in the Union in 1998, has meanwhile adopted a major reform of the corporation tax. As of 2001, the corporate tax rate on retained profits, including local business taxes, is lowered to roughly 38 per cent while depreciation allowances are simultaneously reduced.

[4] The lower share of corporate tax revenues in the Union, as compared to other OECD countries, primarily reflects higher overall tax levels in Europe. In relation to gross domestic product (GDP), revenues from corporation tax in the EU average are broadly comparable to the figures for the United States, Canada and Japan.

[5] The empirical studies, on which these results are based, are discussed in more detail in section 4.4.

'paper profits' of multinational firms (see Devereux, 1992). The latter interpretation is particularly suggestive in the case of Ireland, which has more than doubled its share of corporate tax revenues while at the same time employing an extremely low statutory corporate tax rate for certain businesses.

These brief remarks may suffice to indicate that national policy reforms can be seen as rational responses to the increasing mobility of capital. These 'optimal' policies from a national perspective imply, however, that the tax burden is systematically shifted from internationally mobile sources of income to internationally immobile (or less mobile) income sources. There is a growing concern in Europe that the burden of taxation is increasingly shifted towards labour, with adverse consequences for employment and growth in the entire Union (see Daveri and Tabellini, 2000). This is the background against which coordinated policy initiatives to raise the effective taxation of capital income have to be seen.

In contrast to indirect taxation, the harmonisation of direct taxes is not explicitly addressed in the EEC treaty, apart from the avoidance of international double taxation (art. 220). Harmonisation measures in the field of capital taxation must therefore be based on the regulations in art. 100 of the EEC Treaty, which gives the Union a general mandate to harmonise national legislation where this is necessary for the functioning of the internal market. Early harmonisation proposals made in the Neumark Report (1963) and the Van den Tempel Report (1971) focused on the harmonisation of corporate tax systems, the first arguing for a split rate system and the second for a classical system with taxation at both the company and the shareholder level. In 1975 the European Commission instead proposed a directive which would have stipulated a partial imputation system and an approximation of corporate tax rates in the range of 30–40 per cent. The directive was never accepted and was formally withdrawn by the Commission in 1990.

In 1990, in response to capital market liberation and the increased role of multinational corporations in the Union, the Council adopted two directives which had already been submitted by the European Commission in the late 1960s. These concerned the tax treatment of mergers within multinational enterprises and the repatriation of profits via dividends from a subsidiary to its parent. Both measures ensured that entrepreneurial transactions between companies operating in different EU states were placed on an equal tax footing with analogous transactions between national companies. The same goal also underlay an 'arbitration convention' which coordinated the transfer pricing rules used by national tax authorities in order to determine the taxable profits of multinational corporations.[6]

With respect to the taxation of interest income, a 1989 initiative by the European Commission to introduce an EU-wide 15 per cent withholding tax failed to receive the support of four EU members (Germany, the Netherlands, Luxembourg and the United Kingdom). One of the main concerns raised by several EU countries was that the withholding tax might have adverse repercussions on the financial sector and lead to increased pre-tax interest rates. Even a rather modest compromise solution, which aimed at improving mutual tax assistance between national tax administrations was rejected by Luxembourg (see Frank, 1991; Huizinga, 1994).

In May 1998 the Commission launched a new initiative to enforce the taxation of interest income in the European Union (European Communities – Commission, 1998a). According to this proposal, each EU member state would be required to levy either a 20 per cent withholding tax rate on all interest paid to EU investors, or issue a notification of the interest payment to the residence country of the EU investor. At the European summit meeting in June 2000, member states agreed to establish an EU-wide notification scheme by the year 2010, conditional upon the simultaneous introduction of a similar scheme in Switzerland and dependent offshore territories of EU member states. However, critics of a common EU tax policy continue to argue that even if these negotiations are successful, there will always remain tax havens for EU interest income worldwide, so that the main effect of a notification scheme could be to drive financial capital out of the Community altogether.

Turning to corporate taxation, the European Commission instituted an expert committee, chaired by Onno Ruding, in order to evaluate the need for greater harmonisation of business taxes within the Community. The Ruding Committee issued its final report in 1992, finding – at that time – no evidence of 'unbridled tax competition' (Ruding Report, 1992, p. 12). Nevertheless it concluded that the existing differences in the pattern of company taxation gave rise to significant distortions in the allocation of capital across countries, and that these distortions could not be reduced sufficiently by unilateral actions of EU member states. As a consequence, the committee proposed an approximation of statutory

[6] Under present international rules for the taxation of multinational firms, the profits of a parent and each subsidiary are determined separately by the different jurisdictions in which the firm operates ('separate accounting'). Therefore transfer prices need to be introduced for transactions within the multinational firm for tax purposes, and these prices must lawfully be chosen as if the transaction had occurred between two unrelated parties ('dealing at arm's length').

corporate tax rates in member states within a range of 30–40 per cent and a harmonisation of tax bases for corporation tax.

The far-reaching harmonisation proposals of the Ruding Committee have met serious reservations among EU member states. As a consequence, none of the proposals has so far been taken up by the European Commission. Instead, the focus of political attention shifted to the increasing use of discriminatory tax breaks for multinational firms both within and outside the Union. The Ecofin Council (European Communities – Council, 1998) has adopted a 'Code of Conduct' for business taxation, which is targeted at what is labelled 'unfair' tax competition. Under this code, the member countries of the EU commit themselves to refrain from:

1. Tax preferences which are accorded only to non-residents
2. Tax advantages granted to firms with no real economic activity in the country
3. Rules for profit determination that depart from internationally accepted principles
4. Non-transparent administrative practices in enforcing tax measures.

This focus on the issue of non-discrimination follows the earlier pattern of EU harmonisation measures in the field of direct taxation and is closely related to the general policy goal of preventing distortions of competition in the internal market. At the same time, a parallel initiative to prevent discriminatory corporate tax policies worldwide has been undertaken by the OECD (1998a). The OECD (2000) has also taken the first steps to enforce adherence to the standards of 'fair' competition by identifying 35 countries – exclusively very small countries and territories, mostly located in Europe and the Caribbean – that violated these criteria at the time of the OECD (2000) report.

2.1.2 Developments in the United States and Eastern Europe

In the United States, the 1986 income tax reform significantly reduced statutory tax rates on personal and corporate income while at the same time increasing the tax base. For the corporate income tax, an important measure was the partial abolition of the accelerated depreciation allowances that had been introduced in 1981. This 'tax-rate-cut-cum-base-broadening' reform of the income tax system was widely acclaimed both at home and abroad and served as the model for similar tax reforms in many EU countries shortly thereafter (see subsection 2.1.1). The goals of the reform were partly compromised, however, by subsequent increases in tax rates to lower the federal budget deficit. Another frequently raised point of criticism was the continuously growing complexity of the income tax code.[7]

For these reasons, and in order to foster national savings and increase growth, a lively debate on a more fundamental tax reform continued throughout the 1990s. This debate focused on a switch of both the personal and the corporate income tax in the United States to a consumption oriented tax system. It received an important stimulus through the so-called 'flat tax' proposed by Hall and Rabushka (1985). They suggest a tax system composed of a cash-flow business income tax, which allows a full deduction for investment expenditures in the year of purchase, and a linear tax on wage income. According to this proposal some (indirect) progressivity would be built into the wage tax by allowing for personal exemptions, whereas private capital income remains completely untaxed. Furthermore, the rates of the business tax and the tax on wage income would be the same (and should be low). Modifications to the Hall–Rabushka flat tax, such as the so-called 'USA' tax (for 'unlimited savings allowance'), also retain the basic feature of abolishing all taxes on the normal return to capital for both corporations and individuals. While these reform proposals have been seriously discussed in policy circles in the United States, none of them has so far been brought before Congress.[8]

In many Eastern European countries, taxes of the cash-flow type have also been proposed for the dual reason of fostering economic growth and ensuring administrative simplicity. One of the best-known proposals for tax reform in transitional economies is the 'simplified alternative tax' (SAT) advanced by McLure (1991). Similar to the proposals made in the United States, McLure suggests a graduated tax on labour income, whereas all private capital income should remain tax-free. At the corporate level, all business purchases including capital goods should be deductible in the year of purchase, leaving only above-normal returns to investment subject to the tax. According to McLure, exempting the normal return to investment from tax is the best and least costly way to attract investment, minimising the temptation to introduce selective and thus inefficient investment incentives.[9]

Among the most far-reaching reforms with respect to a move towards consumption taxes is the Croatian tax reform adopted in 1994. Along with interest payments on debt, companies can deduct a 'protective inter-

[7] For a detailed review of the 1986 Tax Reform Act, see Auerbach and Slemrod (1997).

[8] For a thorough discussion of the different alternatives and an evaluation of their effects, see the contributions in Boskin (1996).

[9] For a critical evaluation of the simplified alternative tax, and a general survey of tax reform issues in transitional economies, see Holzmann (1992).

est' on their equity capital from the corporate tax base, which attempts to approximate the normal return to capital (or the market interest rate). This 'interest-adjusted income tax' is thus very similar to a cash-flow corporate tax that falls only on pure profits. A similar treatment applies to the taxation of interest income under personal income tax, where a normal return to savings can also be deducted from the tax base.[10]

Summarising the developments and the more far-reaching reform proposals both inside and outside the Union, it should be obvious that capital taxation is undergoing a period of important change worldwide. Furthermore, it is probably legitimate to conclude that the ideal of comprehensive income taxation is slowly giving way to schemes that reduce or even eliminate taxes on the normal return to capital. While the calls for more consumption oriented income tax systems are by no means new, the novel element is that domestic arguments for such a change are now backed by the forces of international tax competition. These developments, and the policy conclusions following from it, underlie our analysis in parts 2 and 4 of the book.

2.2 Indirect taxes

2.2.1 Policy issues in the European Union

At the time of its foundation in 1957, the primary concern of the European Economic Community (EEC) was with commodity rather than factor trade. This is reflected in an explicit legal base for indirect tax harmonisation (art. 99 EEC treaty) and in intense debates on the taxation of intra-Community trade in the 1950s and 1960s. The first relevant document, the Tinbergen Report (1953) even dates back to the time of the European Coal and Steel Community (ECSC). The Tinbergen Committee emphasised the equivalence of value-added taxes levied either in the country of consumption (*destination principle*) or in the country of production (*origin principle*), as long as the tax was levied on all goods at the same rate. However, since the destination principle was generally employed for international trade and the competence of the Community was then confined to the coal and steel sector,

[10] See Rose and Wiswesser (1998) for a detailed account of the Croatian tax reform and Cnossen (1996, pp. 84–5) for a short summary. A partial deduction for the interest cost of equity capital was also introduced in the 1998 corporate income tax reform in Italy (see Bordignon, Giannini and Panteghini, 1999) and in the Austrian corporate tax reform of 2000. These reforms, however, do not fully eliminate the differential tax treatment of alternative financing sources.

the committee recommended to the High Authority that trade in this sector should also follow the destination principle.

The second major report in the early days of the Community was the Neumark Report (1963). It recommended replacing the gross turnover taxes, existing in most EEC members states at that time, by the net turnover or value-added tax (VAT) that was already in place in France. The report also emphasised the importance of removing all 'tax frontiers' within the Community and thus suggested switching from the destination principle, which requires border tax adjustments for its implementation, to the origin principle. The Community followed the recommendations with respect to the introduction of VAT (1967), but decided to maintain the destination principle as the commodity tax scheme governing intra-Community trade.[11]

The European Community's programme to complete the internal market by 1992 affected value-added taxation through the abolition of internal border controls between member states. The European Commission feared a massive increase in private cross-border shopping, as well as the possibility of illegal arbitrage activities for commercial purposes. It therefore proposed the approximation of VAT rates within a band of 14–20 per cent for the standard rate and 4–9 per cent for the reduced rate, as well as the complete harmonisation of all excise taxes. At the same time, the scheme of taxing intra-Community trade had to be changed in the absence of border controls. The Commission proposed to switch to an international tax credit method for VAT, under which taxes would be pre-paid in the exporting country but the importer received a full tax credit for all taxes paid abroad. This scheme was to be accompanied by a clearing mechanism in order to restore as closely as possible the previous (i.e. destination-based) distribution of tax revenues between member states.

EU member states rejected most of these proposals, however, fearing a loss of national control over both the setting of indirect tax rates and the tax base of VAT. Instead, they decided to maintain border tax adjustments for all intra-union purchases by registered traders. The way of implementing this so-called 'transitional system' in the absence of border controls was to require exporters to report the VAT identification number of their customer when claiming the rebate, while demanding that all traders declare the value of imported goods in their next periodic tax return (European Communities, 1991). Observers differ in their evalua-

[11] For a brief introduction to value-added taxation in the European Union see, e.g., Keen and Smith (1996). The reader interested in a more detailed treatment of alternative schemes of value-added taxation is referred to Fehr, Rosenberg and Wiegard (1995, chs. 1–2).

tion of the current transitional system, in particular with respect to its administrative and compliance costs and its ability to prevent fraudulent claims for tax rebates by exporters in the Union.

The European Commission still sticks to its original plans to switch to a 'definitive regime' based on the international tax credit-cum-clearing mechanism (European Communities – Commission, 1996). An alternative proposal, labelled a 'viable integrated value-added tax' (VIVAT), has been advanced by Keen and Smith (1996). This system combines a harmonised tax rate on intermediate transactions – which essentially acts as a withholding device to minimise tax evasion – with nationally chosen tax rates for final sales to consumers. It would thus make value-added taxation in the Union similar to the two-tier system currently in place in Canada (see Bird and Gendron, 1998). This scheme treats domestic and intra-EU transactions alike for VAT purposes, and the common tax rate on intermediate goods would facilitate the politically sensitive clearing mechanism. On the other hand, the scheme requires that all *domestic* sales to registered traders must also be accompanied by a VAT identification number, in order to avoid payment of the sales tax for final consumer purchases.

With respect to tax rates, EU member states found the Community-wide imposition of upper bounds on VAT rates and the complete harmonisation of excises unnecessarily restrictive. Instead, minimum VAT rates of 15 per cent (standard rate) and 5 per cent (reduced rate) were agreed upon, and minimum rates were also set for most excises (European Communities, 1992). In addition, special schemes were introduced for certain transactions that were regarded as particularly vulnerable to tax arbitrage. One of these special schemes concerns the purchase of new cars, for which tax has to be paid when the car is registered in the home country of the customer. A more controversial measure was to require mail-order firms whose annual turnover exceeded a certain threshold to have a local representative in each country where they served customers, and charge VAT according to the rates of the importing country. This imposes extra compliance costs on all traders that operate beyond national borders, and there is already initial evidence that some smaller mail-order firms have withdrawn from serving foreign markets.

After the opening of internal borders in 1992, a convergence of VAT rates towards the Community-wide floor could have resulted from unilateral adjustments by individual member states. This, however, has not happened so far. Table 2.3 shows that there is no general downward trend in the pattern of EU value-added taxation, and the average standard rate has even increased since 1987. While this average includes the

Table 2.3 *VAT rates in the European Union, 1987 and 1998*

Country	1987 (per cent)		1998 (per cent)	
	Standard	Reduced	Standard	Reduced
Austria[a]	20	10	20	10
Belgium	19	1, 6, 17	21	1, 6, 12
Denmark	22	–	25	–
Finland[a]	19.5[b]	–	22	8, 17
France	18.6	2.1, 4, 5.5, 7	20.6	2.1, 5.5
Germany	14	7	16	7
Greece	18	6	18	4, 8
Ireland[c]	25	2.5, 10	2	3.6, 12.5
Italy	18	2, 9	20	4, 10
Luxembourg	12	3, 6	15	3, 6, 12
Netherlands	20	6	17.5	6
Portugal	16	8	17	5, 12
Spain	12	6	16	4, 7
Sweden[a]	23.5[d]	–	25	6, 12
United Kingdom[c]	15	–	17.5	2.5, 8
EU average	18.2		19.4	

Notes:
[a] EU member since 1995.
[b] Effective tax rate on imported goods (gross turnover tax for domestic goods).
[c] Zero rate on certain necessities (food, children's clothing).
[d] Effective tax rate.
Sources: European Communities (1988), Table 3.5.1; Coopers & Lybrand (1988); International Bureau of Fiscal Documentation (1998), pp. 14–15.

mandatory tax increases in Spain, Luxembourg and Germany, even high-tax countries such as Denmark have increased their VAT rates in the internal market in order to make up for the revenue losses incurred from the reform of the income tax system. These developments notwithstanding, the European Commission still aims at a complete harmonisation of member states' VAT rates as a long-term goal (European Communities – Commission, 1996).

One important challenge for the present system of commodity taxation in the Union (and elsewhere) arises from the growth of electronic commerce. There is general agreement within both the Union and the OECD that there should be no tax discrimination between transactions carried out through the Internet and more conventional forms of commodity trade (European Communities – Commission, 1998b; OECD, 1998b). For trade in tangible goods that are ordered, but not delivered, through the Internet the issues are similar, in principle, to those arising under mail-ordering. Given the projected high growth rates of Internet trade this implies, however, that the social costs of enforcing the destination principle by means of the 'local representation' requirement can be expected to rise in the future.

Qualitatively new problems arise from trade in digital products, where the entire transaction is carried out in the Internet.[12] The EU Commission has proposed a Council directive that extends the general rules for commodity taxation in the Union to services supplied by electronic means (European Communities – Commission, 2000). However, the problems of enforcing the destination principle for digital electronic commerce are generally considered to be severe, and special rules and increased intergovernmental cooperation are likely to be required (Hinnekens, 1998; McLure, 1999).

These new developments show that challenges for the system of destination-based commodity taxation arise not only from the European internal market, but also from technological innovations. The volume of cross-border shopping could grow considerably in an increasingly frictionless market, where remote sales through the Internet and conventional mail-ordering are expected to play an increasing role. This could lead to a far more severe erosion of the destination-based commodity tax base than is currently observed. These shortcomings of the present system, and the potential loss of member states' autonomy over VAT rates, form the basis of our discussion in parts 3 and 4 of the book.

2.2.2 *Worldwide perspectives*

While the debates and developments reviewed above are specific to the European Union, the underlying policy issues are not. The problem of cross-border shopping, for example, arises between any independent tax jurisdictions that do not enforce the destination principle between them. This is the case, for example, in the United States, where states levy independent sales taxes ranging from zero to 9 per cent, as well as widely diverging excise taxes (Due and Mikesell, 1994). The main issues of concern in the United States have been mail-ordering and, more recently, electronic commerce. Early estimates by the Advisory Commission on Intergovernmental Relations (ACIR, 1994) put the share of remote sales as a fraction of total retail sales at up to 25 per

[12] Legally, these are generally classified as 'services'. Examples are software and computer services as well as information, educational and entertainment services delivered through the Internet.

cent, and these estimates have even been adjusted upward by the growth of Internet trade. In principle, remote sellers can be required to levy a so-called 'use tax' on their sales and remit the revenue to the state in which the purchaser resides. At present, however, the use tax is widely evaded, not least because of restrictive rulings by the US Supreme Court.

These structural weaknesses are revealed very clearly by the recent growth of Internet trade. Empirical work based on a large sample of online users shows that residents of states with high sales taxes are significantly more likely to buy in the Internet, if other factors are controlled for (Goolsbee, 2000). Goolsbee estimates that enforcing existing sales taxes for Internet commerce could reduce online purchases by as much as 24 per cent. Against this background, it is argued that the reform of the complex and outdated rules for taxing interstate commerce in the United States is one of the most pressing policy questions in the area of state sales taxation (McLure, 1999).

In an international context, national tax autonomy was an important issue when Canada was forced in 1994 to reverse its high-tax policy for cigarettes, which proved unsustainable in view of the large tax differential with the United States. Canadian tobacco manufacturers exported their products net of tax with the United States from where they illegally re-entered the Canadian market, circumventing existing rules of destination. According to estimates by the government of Quebec, two-thirds of all cigarettes consumed in the province were bought illegally before tobacco tax reductions took effect in February 1994 (*Globe and Mail*, January 29, 1994). This demonstrates that infringements of national tax autonomy may arise even when the destination principle is technically in place for consumer purchases.

A second and distinct issue concerns the scheme of taxing international trade under a multi-stage tax like VAT. In 1997, the VAT was the main form of indirect taxation in more than one hundred countries worldwide, and more than half of these countries adopted VAT only during the 1990s (Cnossen, 1998). The use of VAT has grown particularly fast in Eastern Europe and in the Commonwealth of Independent States (CIS), but many countries in the Caribbean, Asia and parts of Africa have also switched to this form of indirect taxation in recent years. Clearly, the VAT-related policy issues that currently arise in the European Union are of direct relevance for those other regions of the world where independent countries are considering closer integration and – possibly – the formation of a tax union.

Furthermore, there are analogies to value-added taxation in a federal country, if the states (provinces, cantons) levy their own, independent VAT. At present, this is the case only in Brazil whereas countries such as

Canada or Switzerland, which generally have a very decentralised tax system, levy only a national VAT.[13] Since there are no 'border' tax adjustments between Brazilian states, the state VAT is effectively levied under the origin principle as far as the distribution of revenues is concerned. Longo (1990) emphasises the distributional issues that arise from trade imbalances between the Brazilian states under the present scheme, and recommends a switch to the destination principle for the state VAT by zero-rating interstate exports. As the EU experience with the current 'transitional system' shows, however, this would require that tax authorities keep track of all domestic transactions in order to detect fraudulent claims for zero-rated sales. A similar trade-off between a 'fair' distribution of revenues on the one hand and the additional costs of administering the destination principle for inter-state transactions on the other would also arise in India, where a VAT at the state level has been proposed to replace the present system of sales taxation by Indian states (Burgess, Howes and Stern, 1995).

[13] However, the Canadian provinces levy independent sales taxes in addition to the federal VAT.

3 A first look at the literature

The roots of the recent literature on international tax competition and optimal taxation with internationally mobile tax bases seem to be twofold. The first predecessor is the theory of international trade policy with the classic analysis of the optimal tariff.[1] The case of retaliatory tariff-setting as a first game-theoretic analysis of non-cooperative government decision-making had already been analysed in the 1950s (Johnson, 1953/4). The links between optimal tariff theory and the strategic setting of domestic taxes in an open economy context have also long been understood (Friedlaender and Vandendorpe, 1968). However, despite the close analytical links that exist between international trade policy and open economy public finance (see Dixit, 1985), the two fields have remained quite far apart and the tax competition literature did not develop as an extension of the classical 'tariff-war' analysis.

The immediate roots of the literature on international tax competition can instead be found in the local public finance tradition. The early literature on fiscal federalism (Oates, 1972) emphasised the trade-off between the ability of lower levels of government to account for local and heterogeneous preferences on the one hand, and the potentially distortive effects of interjurisdictional competition for mobile tax bases on the other.[2] Based on these arguments, the first general equilibrium models of tax exporting and tax competition were developed in the late 1970s and early 1980s (see Wildasin, 1986, ch. 6, for a survey of this early literature). It is clearly no coincidence that the papers that initiated the (capital) tax competition literature in a more direct sense (Wilson, 1986; Zodrow and Mieszkowski, 1986) were both published in local public finance journals. While the independent taxing powers of lower

[1] See Chipman (1987) for a detailed account of the development of optimal tariff theory.

[2] The latter result conflicts directly with the implications of the influential analysis by Tiebout (1956), where competition between regional governments is efficiency-enhancing. As subsequent research has pointed out, however, the Tiebout result depends on a highly restrictive set of assumptions (see Bewley, 1981).

levels of government are a typical feature of fiscal federalism in the United States, the potentially distortive effects of decentralised fiscal decision-making were also studied early on in other federal countries, such as Germany (Wiegard, 1980).

Within the local public finance tradition, an early work by Gordon (1983) has been particularly influential in systematically describing the externalities that can arise between independent jurisdictions. These include, among others: (i) changes in the tax base of another jurisdiction; (ii) residents of another jurisdiction paying some of the taxes collected in the home country; (iii) changes in the prices of factors or commodities purchased by non-residents; (iv) non-residents receiving some of the benefits from public good supply; (v) changes in the congestion costs or resource costs for public services faced by non-residents. Gordon's analysis provides a common framework for many of the more detailed analyses, which have subsequently discussed these externalities in isolation.[3]

From these beginnings, a large and widely diversified literature on tax competition has developed in the past ten–fifteen years. Alternative classifications of this literature can either focus on the underlying mobility scenario (internationally mobile consumers, capital, and workers or households), or on the instruments of tax competition (commodity taxes, capital taxes, wage or social security taxes). Perhaps the most comprehensive survey of this literature to date is Wilson (1999), who covers capital and commodity tax competition and also includes several recent developments in the literature, such as imperfectly competitive market structures, government commitment problems and political economy considerations. An earlier synthesis focusing on the welfare implications of cooperative and non-cooperative tax policy for both capital and commodity taxation is Keen (1993a). Cremer *et al.*(1996) survey the literature on redistributive government policies in open economies, covering both capital and labour mobility. The fundamental implications of international mobility of commodities, capital and labour are compared in Christiansen, Hagen and Sandmo (1994). Sinn (1997) analyses market failures in three related settings, comparing fiscal competition for the provision of impure public goods, redistributive taxation and quality regulation. Finally, Gordon (2000) provides a comprehensive overview of theoretical arguments for the taxation of labour vs. capital income that also incorporates aspects of indirect taxation.

[3] Gordon's framework has been extended by Inman and Rubinfeld (1996) to cover political economy aspects as well.

In addition, there are several specialised surveys that focus on either commodity or capital taxation.[4] A comprehensive synthesis of the theoretical literature on commodity tax competition and tax coordination is given by Lockwood (1998a). Policy oriented surveys on commodity taxation that also incorporate parts of the theoretical literature are Smith (1993) and Keen and Smith (1996). For capital taxation, Mintz (1994) gives a systematic summary of the different fiscal externalities involved. A critical review of the theoretical literature on capital tax competition can be found in Koch and Schulze (1998).

The present work focuses on mobile consumers, capital and firms, leaving aside the issues raised by labour mobility. On the other hand, an important goal of our analysis is to emphasise the links that exist between the different strands in the literature on commodity and capital tax competition. We thus postpone a review of the specific issues that arise in each of these fields to later chapters, and instead emphasise some basic analytical distinctions in tax competition models that are independent of the specific mobility scenario analysed. Sections 3.1.-3.5 collect those general issues in tax competition models that will be discussed further in the present work. Section 3.6 then briefly mentions some aspects of tax competition and international taxation that are not taken up in later chapters.

3.1 Three important fiscal externalities

Of the various externalities analysed by Gordon (1983), three play an important role in the literature to be discussed here.

(i) The *tax base externality* is the central fiscal externality in the tax competition literature. It describes the effect that a tax levied in one jurisdiction will drive some part of an internationally mobile tax base out of the jurisdiction levying (or increasing) the tax, and into a neighbouring jurisdiction. For example, a tax on internationally mobile capital in country *A* will reduce the net return to capital in this country and cause it to move to jurisdiction *B*, where the tax (and thus the net return) is unchanged. Thus the imposition of the tax in country *A* causes a *positive* fiscal externality for country *B*.[5] The same positive externality is caused by a commodity tax increase in country *A*. This will make the product more expensive for consumers shopping in country *A* and will cause some of them to move

[4] For further literature on wage and social security taxation, see subsection 3.6.1.

[5] The effect sketched here depends on the tax principle that is in operation for international capital transactions. This will be discussed in detail in section 4.1 below.

instead to country B. As is well known from the general theory of externalities, activities that cause positive externalities for others will be undersupplied in a non-coordinated equilibrium. For the tax competition literature this implies that the tax base externality will generally cause taxes on an internationally mobile factor or commodity to fall *below* their levels in a global welfare optimum.

In simple models of tax competition, where other externalities are excluded, the effects of non-cooperative tax setting are thus unambiguous. The early model of Zodrow and Mieszkowski (1986) demonstrates the basic mechanism of tax base competition in the simplest possible way, and thus has become a benchmark analysis for much of the later work. In this model the assumption of small, identical jurisdictions ensures that terms of trade considerations will be absent from optimal tax policy. Furthermore, all rent income accrue to domestic residents so that a strategic motive to tax these rents is also absent. In this model, non-coordinated tax policy therefore leads to capital tax rates and levels of public good supply that are unambiguously lower than in a cooperative equilibrium. A formal analysis of this model – in a somewhat generalised form – will be given in chapter 4. The tax base externality is also present, however, in all more complex models that incorporate further fiscal externalities.

(ii) A *tax exporting externality* occurs when foreigners earn some rents in the home country. Non-coordinated policy will then use taxes to shift some of these rents from foreigners to the home treasury. By reducing the rent income accruing to foreigners this causes a *negative* fiscal externality for the neighbouring country. Hence the tax exportation motive will tend to raise tax levels *above* their globally optimal levels. In conjunction with the presence of strategic tax base effects, tax rates and levels of public good supply can thus either be 'too high', or 'too low', depending on which of the two effects dominates.

In the tax competition literature, the tax exportation effect has been mainly analysed in models of capital income taxation. Two widely quoted analyses in which this effect plays a central role are Mintz and Tulkens (1996) and Huizinga and Nielsen (1997a). Both papers consider small countries, demonstrating that the tax exportation effect is present even if countries have no power to change world market prices (and thus *competitive* returns to factors of production). In the present book, the tax exportation externality is explicitly introduced in the model of chapter 7, but we will also encounter it in several other cases, including models of commodity taxation.

(iii) The final important effect is the *terms of trade externality* familiar from the theory of international trade policy. In a similar way as tariffs, national commodity taxes can be used to shift international commodity prices in favour of the home country, at the expense of foreigners (Friedlaender and Vandendorpe, 1968; Keen, 1989). In a completely analogous way, countries can impose domestic taxes on capital in order to influence the world rate of return, i.e., the intertemporal terms of trade (Hamada, 1966; Sørensen, 1991). In both cases, however, this externality will arise only if the taxing country is sufficiently large in the world economy.

As is well known, the trade pattern is crucial to determining the direction of terms of trade effects. If a large country levies, say, a tax on capital that reduces domestic demand, then world demand for capital and the world interest rate will both fall. This improves the domestic terms of trade if the taxing country is a capital importer, but worsens them in the opposite case. Hence, a capital importer has an incentive to strategically raise its capital tax rate while the exporter will lower it. The terms of trade externality will thus reinforce the fundamental tax base externality for a capital exporter, whose tax rate will be unambiguously 'too low' if the tax exportation effect is absent. For the capital importing country the terms of trade and the tax base externality work in opposite directions, however, and the capital tax rate can be above or below the coordinated level (see, e.g., Bucovetsky, 1991). A similar pattern occurs under commodity taxation where the net effect of fiscal externalities will be unambiguous for one of the taxing countries, but ambiguous for the other (Mintz and Tulkens, 1986; Lockwood, 1993). In the present book, the terms of trade externality will be of particular relevance in our discussion of commodity tax competition in chapter 8, but it will also occur in some of our models on capital taxation (chapters 5 and 6).

3.2 Symmetric vs. asymmetric countries

The benchmark model of symmetric capital tax competition between a large number of small jurisdictions – the analysis by Zodrow and Mieszkowski (1986) – has been introduced above. A generalisation of this model treats the number of identical jurisdictions (n) parametrically. This specification includes as benchmarks the autarky case ($n = 1$) on the one hand, and the small open economy setting ($n \to \infty$) on the other. It thus allows us to link the degree of underprovision of the public good, or the level of tax rates, to the number of competing jurisdictions n. Clear expositions of this are found in Hoyt (1991) and Bucovetsky and Wilson (1991). An introductory formal analysis of this scenario will be given in chapter 4.

Apart from the fact that symmetric models of tax competition eliminate terms of trade effects (see section 3.1), a more general implication of this framework is that conflicts of interest between the competing jurisdictions cannot arise. To incorporate real-world heterogeneity, several models concentrate on specific sources of asymmetries between countries and link the outcome of tax competition to the isolated difference in this characteristic. One popular framework is that countries are identical in all structural respects, but all variables in one country are a multiple of the corresponding values in the other. This setting with differences in 'country size' has been studied by Bucovetsky (1991) and Wilson (1991) for capital taxation, and by Kanbur and Keen (1993) for commodity taxation. A general result in this literature is that the small country faces the more elastic tax base and consequently undercuts the large country in the asymmetric Nash equilibrium. This implies that the tax base of the small country will be larger than in autarky and hence opens up the possibility that the small country gains from tax competition. This issue is at the heart of our analysis in chapter 5. Differences in country size are considered again in chapter 12, where we introduce transport costs for goods and thus a home market effect that works in favour of the larger country.

In models focusing on distributional policies *within* a country, asymmetric tax competition often takes the form that one country has a stronger preference for income redistribution than the other (see Persson and Tabellini, 1992, Lejour and Verbon, 1996, and the papers surveyed by Cremer *et al.*, 1996). In this framework exogenous shocks affect the countries in different ways, opening up the possibility that tax responses to exogenous changes in the environment are qualitatively different in the two countries analysed. A frequently analysed shock is given by an exogenous change in the degree of market integration. We will study this scenario in chapter 6 to show that market integration can have unexpected results when the optimal mix of wage and capital taxation varies across countries as a result of differences in the relative strengths of interest groups. In chapter 8, a similar analysis is carried out in the context of commodity tax competition when countries differ with respect to their preferences for public good supply.

3.3 The set of tax instruments

It is a general lesson from the optimal taxation literature that model results depend critically on the set of available tax instruments. This is explicit, for example, in the conditions that are required for the well-known production efficiency theorem of Diamond and Mirrlees (1971). This theorem states that, provided that there are no pure profits and a full set of consumption taxes exists, taxes on production will not be used in the optimum and the economy operates on its production possibility frontier (PPF). In the presence of inelastically supplied factors the conditions underlying the theorem imply, however, that all rents can be taxed away by a separate (lump-sum) instrument. If this were not the case, a tax on production would be able to act as a partial substitute for the 'missing' lump-sum tax, and would thus not be zero in the optimum. Similarly, the condition that there is a separate tax instrument for each margin of substitution in the agent's utility function (see Munk, 1980) ensures that the production tax cannot act as a substitute for a 'missing' consumption tax.

Similarly, the set of available tax instruments is critical for optimal taxation in an international setting. Open economy extensions of the production efficiency theorem state that neither source-based taxes on capital nor origin-based taxes on production should be used in the optimum, if a complete set of consumption taxes exists and there are no pure profits. A special case of this is a small open economy that also has a wage tax at its disposal. The result that the optimal source tax on capital is zero in this case (Gordon, 1986) will be derived and discussed in chapter 4. The corresponding result for an origin-based production tax is derived in chapter 10. These taxes will, however, be used even by small countries and in the presence of a wage tax, if there are untaxed profits (Mintz and Tulkens, 1996; Huizinga and Nielsen, 1997a; Keen and Piekkola, 1997).

A related question is whether non-coordinated tax policy decisions can lead to an efficient outcome, in the sense that coordinating the *given* set of tax instruments between the competing regions yields no welfare gains. The answer to this question depends partly on the collective size of the coordinating countries, relative to the world economy, but also on the taxes with which regions are competing against each other (Razin and Sadka, 1991a; Bucovetsky and Wilson, 1991). This issue will be addressed in chapter 4 for the case of isolated capital taxation and in chapter 10 for an extended setting where factor and commodity taxes are considered simultaneously.

A final case where the set of available tax instruments is critical arises when one tax can be duplicated by a set of other taxes. In particular, there are important equivalence relations between linear taxes on factor incomes and taxes on commodities (see Frenkel, Razin and Sadka, 1991, ch. 4). In the context of the present study, one important equivalence is between an origin-based consumption tax on the one hand, and the combination of a wage tax and a cash-flow tax on pure profits on the other. This has two implications. First, the dynamic effects of introducing an origin-based consumption tax are similar to those of a cash-flow corporate tax (cf. Bovenberg, 1994; Bradford, 1996). This similarity will be used in our analysis of a switch to the origin principle in chapter 9. Second, when countries can levy both direct and indirect taxes, then an origin-based commodity tax can be replicated by a set of factor taxes. The implications of this basic property for the choice of a commodity tax scheme in the European Union are the subject of chapter 11.

3.4 Firm mobility and imperfect competition

Many models of tax competition assume that firms are price-takers and operate under a constant returns to scale technology, thus making zero profits in equilibrium. The firm as an independent production unit is then irrelevant for tax policy and the analysis concentrates on the taxation of the (normal) return to the production factor capital. The easiest way to depart from this framework is to model a fixed factor that is not remunerated independently and hence represents a source of pure profits (Mintz and Tulkens, 1996; Huizinga and Nielsen, 1997a, 1997b). We will introduce this model element in chapter 7. Its implications for the optimal level of source-based tax instruments have already been summarised in section 3.3.

A further step is to assume that profit-making firms are mobile across jurisdictions while profits still derive from a fixed, unremunerated factor (e.g. public infrastructure). Firm mobility then introduces the international arbitrage condition that net profits – rather than net returns to capital – must be equal across jurisdictions. This difference has important implications for tax competition when cash-flow profit taxes or origin-based consumption taxes are considered. While these taxes do not affect the return to capital, they do affect net profits and thus cause firms to move to neighbouring jurisdictions (Richter, 1994; Richter and Wellisch, 1996; Wellisch, 2000). We will use this setting in our comparison of destination- and origin-based commodity taxation under firm mobility in chapter 11.

Other models explicitly introduce imperfectly competitive behaviour by firms, but do not consider firm mobility. In this case, tax competition can act as a constraint on the firm's price-setting power in national markets. This yields second-best results in favour of tax competition (Trandel, 1992) or for the imposition of production-based – rather than consumption-based – commodity taxes (Keen and Lahiri, 1998).

Finally, several models in the tradition of the new international trade theory combine imperfect competition and international mobility of firms. In this setting, subsidy competition between potential host countries can arise for the location of an internationally mobile firm, if the investment is associated with positive agglomeration externalities, savings in trade costs or the alleviation of domestic distortions (Black and Hoyt, 1989; Haaparanta, 1996). On the other hand, location-specific rents arise for an internationally mobile firm, if the investment in one country is associated with higher profits as compared to alternative investment opportunities. The existence of such rents allows the host country to extract positive taxes even from an internationally mobile firm. A similar framework, where two countries of different size compete for a foreign-owned monopolist, underlies our analysis in chapter 12.

3.5 Political economy aspects and alternative government objectives

Diverging views on the behaviour of governments are as relevant in the field of international taxation as they are in other areas of public policy. While most of the tax competition literature follows a conventional, benevolent dictator model of government, others adopt a Leviathan approach (Brennan and Buchanan, 1980) which holds that governments are interested solely in the maximisation of tax revenues. This has given rise to a fundamental controversy as to whether tax competition leads to harmful distortions of otherwise efficient tax choices, or may instead act as a desirable means to discipline wasteful national governments. Arguments for institutional competition between governments are given, for example in S. Sinn (1992), Siebert and Koop (1993) and Vanberg (2000). In general, the 'economic externalities' emphasised in the welfare-theoretic literature surveyed above, and 'political externalities' arising from imperfectly responsive governments, will both be present simultaneously, so that the core issue is which of the two types of externalities will dominate (Frey, 1990).

This trade-off between political efficiency gains and economic efficiency losses from tax competition has been addressed in a number of formal analyses. One of the first models of international tax competition which incorporates political externalities is Oates and Schwab (1988). They model a government whose objective function is defined over tax revenues and the utility of a representative voter, thus incorporating the pure Leviathan hypothesis and the benevolent dictator view of government as special cases. In this framework, governments will set a positive tax rate on capital in order to increase tax revenue, even though the efficient tax rate from the perspective of the consumer is zero in this model.

Edwards and Keen (1996) set up a model that explicitly aims at incorporating the arguments for and against tax competition in a common analytical framework. Their government objective function includes the utility of the representative consumer, but also some 'wasteful' government expenditures that do not benefit the representative citizen. The economic model underlying their analysis is an extended version of the symmetric Zodrow and Mieszkowski (1986) framework described above. Edwards and Keen show that the welfare gains from tax coordination can be approximated by the marginal excess burden of the tax system, whereas the welfare losses from coordination are given by the policy-maker's 'propensity to waste'. Hence, if the former exceeds the latter, then a coordinated increase in the tax rate on mobile capital raises the utility of the representative consumer, despite the existence of political externalities.

Another political economy aspect is the emphasis on the redistributive effects of tax policy in a model with heterogeneous agents. Most models in this group confine themselves to a positive analysis, using either a median voter approach (e.g. Persson and Tabellini, 1992; Gabszewicz and van Ypersele, 1996) or an interest group model with two classes of individuals – usually workers vs. capitalists (e.g. Lejour and Verbon, 1996). However, there are close formal analogies between a political support function based on an interest group approach, and a conventional social welfare function (e.g. Lopez, Marchand and Pestieau, 1998). The novel aspect arising from the heterogeneity of individuals is that increased economic integration now has two effects: it raises the efficiency costs of taxation, but at the same time affects the political equilibrium through the induced changes in the distribution of factor incomes. The distributional repercussions arising in a model where the government maximises a political support function will be the subject of our analysis in chapter 6.

Finally, several analyses consider the case of revenue-maximising governments, but identify Pareto efficiency with the objective of maximising tax revenue (e.g. Kanbur and Keen, 1993; Janeba and Peters, 1999). Hence there is no conflict between the interests of the government and the interests of the population in these models, despite the use of a 'Leviathan' objective. This is made very explicit by Kanbur and Keen:

> The analysis can thus be viewed either as providing a public choice perspective on strategic aspects of tax setting in an international context or – our preferred interpretation – as a conventional welfarist treatment of such issues for the case in which consumers place a very high marginal valuation on some public good which tax revenue goes to finance. (Kanbur and Keen, 1993, p. 878)

Essentially, the assumption of revenue maximisation in these models serves as a simplifying analytical device. One core implication is that terms of trade effects become irrelevant under this objective, since they affect private income but not tax revenue. Therefore the ambiguity arising from simultaneous tax base and terms of trade externalities in models of asymmetric tax competition (cf. section 3.1) disappears under the assumption of revenue maximisation. Of course, this raises the question whether the results obtained in these models are sensitive to the simplified specification of the government objective. For the analysis of Kanbur and Keen, Trandel (1994) has demonstrated that one core result – the small country undercutting the large one in the Nash equilibrium – generalises to the case where governments maximise a standard utility function defined over both private and public consumption. In chapter 8 we will argue, however, that the specification of the government objective function is critical for the results of the Kanbur and Keen model with respect to the welfare effects of tax coordination measures.

3.6 Further issues

The following section briefly collects some issues and fields of analysis which will not be further analysed in this book. While it is obvious that this overview must be far from complete, the purpose of this section is to give at least some indication of the wide range of policy areas that have been discussed in the recent literature on international taxation and interjurisdictional tax competition.

3.6.1 Household mobility and tax competition in federations

Some aspects of tax competition in the presence of labour and household mobility run largely parallel to the literature on capital tax competition. For example, capital mobility raises similar problems for the pursuit of redistributive tax policies as labour mobility does in a framework with heterogeneous workers differing in their earning abilities (see the survey by Cremer *et al.*, 1996, or Wildasin, 1997). However, given that labour and household mobility is still limited at an international level, analyses which do make this assumption are often applied to a federal state. One of the differences to the literature on international tax competition is that federal and local governments have independent taxing powers, and transfers from the federal to local levels of governments are an important instrument in many analyses. Recent papers in this area have incorporated informational asymmetries between the federal and local levels of government, and have analysed the implications for the optimal design of redistributive grants (e.g. Bordignon, Manasse and Tabellini, 1996; Bucovetsky, Marchand and Pestieau, 1997; Raff and Wilson, 1997; Lockwood, 1999). Even in models with a single level of government, perfect household mobility may induce jurisdictions to give an unconditional transfer to the other region, as utility levels obtained in different jurisdictions must be equal in the arbitrage equilibrium (Myers, 1990). This interregional arbitrage condition for mobile households has played an important role in the recent literature on local public finance, which has studied the efficiency of decentralised tax policy in a variety of different settings. For a detailed and up-to-date account of these issues, see Wellisch (2000).

A further feature of tax competition in federations is that higher and lower levels of government often share the same tax base ('tax base overlap'), giving rise to 'vertical' fiscal externalities. The essential difference to 'horizontal' tax competition, on which the international strand in the tax competition literature is focused, is that the tax base externality is here a negative one. Intuitively, if different jurisdictions share a common tax base then a tax levied by one level of government will simultaneously reduce the tax base of other levels of government in the same country. Vertical tax competition alone therefore leads to tax rates that are inefficiently high, calling for revenue sharing agreements between different levels of government (Flowers, 1988; Dahlby, 1996). When vertical and horizontal externalities are combined, then the outcome of non-cooperative tax setting is unclear *a priori*, but there are plausible settings in which the vertical externality must dominate (Wrede, 1996; Keen, 1997). Therefore, when several levels of government share taxing powers over the same tax base, then the conventional modelling of monolithic national governments engaged in tax competition may yield misleading results.[6]

[6] In an extension of this literature, Boadway, Marchand and Vigneault (1998) study the implications of tax base overlap on redistributive income tax schedules set independently by the federal and state governments. Wrede (2000) considers tax competition when different levels of governments share both tax sources and public expenditures.

Finally, the analysis of income redistribution in the presence of household mobility is closely linked to the emerging literature on the harmonisation of social policies and social insurance systems in integrating countries. These issues are summarised in the survey by Breyer and Kolmar (1996) and are treated in more detail in the monographs of Lejour (1995) and Kolmar (1999). To the extent that the social security system involves an intra-period redistribution between heterogeneous agents (unemployment insurance, social welfare), there are again direct links to the literature on redistributive capital and labour taxation. Distinct issues are raised, however, by those branches of the social security system that have redistributive intergenerational effects, such as old-age insurance.

3.6.2 *Environmental externalities*

As in the case of labour mobility, the literature on environmental tax competition has grown rapidly in recent years, and no attempt will be made here to survey even the most important works. Instead, we will confine ourselves to a few remarks that emphasise the similarities and one critical difference to the issues discussed so far. One of the first analyses in this field is again Oates and Schwab (1988), who focus on the interaction between source-based capital taxes and environmental standards and show that both have similar (negative) effects on the employment of capital in the taxing region. The new element that arises in this literature is that there are counteracting effects for a country which attracts internationally mobile capital or firms: it receives tax revenue and/or benefits from the increased productivity of its immobile factors, but at the same time suffers a welfare loss from increased pollution tied to the local production of the firm. Hence, there are two possible outcomes in the non-cooperative Nash equilibrium: environmental taxes may either be set inefficiently low, as in the standard model of (source-based) capital tax competition. This case is often referred to as 'ecological dumping'. Alternatively, taxes may also be set inefficiently high if the representative agent is sufficiently averse to pollution, and this is referred to as the 'not-in-my-backyard' (NIMBY) scenario. Analyses that demonstrate the possibility of these alternative outcomes in models of imperfect competition include Markusen, Morey and Olewiler (1995), Rauscher (1995) and Hoel (1997a). Implications for the coordination of environmental taxes are summarised in Hoel (1997b).

Another large branch in this literature has aimed at defining environmental tax reforms which yield a 'double dividend' by alleviating existing tax distortions or reducing involuntary unemployment, in addition to the internalisation of environmental externalities. Many of these contributions are carried out in an open economy framework and thus – where the taxation of energy as a production input is analysed – have close parallels to the analysis of source-based capital taxation. Comprehensive surveys of this literature, which generally end with a sceptical note on the existence of a 'double dividend' for environmental tax reforms, are found in Goulder (1995) and Bovenberg (1999).

3.6.3 Competition through public expenditures

Our overview so far has concentrated on taxes as the strategic variables in models of tax competition, with the level of public expenditures adjusting passively through the government budget constraint. Wildasin (1988) has pointed out that there is a 'dual' formulation of the basic problem, where countries compete instead through the supply of residential public goods. He shows that the results of the two alternative problems do not coincide; instead, competition in public expenditures is 'more intense' than competition in tax rates, in the sense that it leads to a more severe undersupply of public goods in the Nash equilibrium. Based on this result, Wildasin (1991) further shows that tax rate competition is the dominant strategy if the two countries can, in a first stage of the game, decide on the strategic variable to be used.

While these results can provide a justification for the emphasis on tax competition in most of the literature, matters are quite different when the public good serves as an input in the production process. In this setting, first analysed in Zodrow and Mieszkowski (1986), public services may be overprovided in equilibrium as a way to attract mobile capital when tax rates are not available as a strategic variable (Fuest, 1995; Bayindir-Upmann, 1998). Furthermore, when both residential public goods and public inputs are provided by the government, then non-cooperative fiscal policy leads to a systematic bias in the pattern of public spending towards the provision of business inputs (Keen and Marchand, 1997). In some ways, this new emphasis on the public expenditure side takes up in formal models the idea that it is the *net fiscal burden* which is responsible for international distortions (Shoup, 1969, p. 648). The important implication from this work is that the harmonisation of tax rates alone may not be sufficient to prevent prisoner's dilemma situations, as countries may turn to expenditure competition in order to pursue beggar-thy-neighbour policies.

3.6.4 *Growth effects of capital taxation*

A final point to be included here concerns the dynamic effects of capital taxation. A core result in this field, obtained for a closed economy and an exogenously given growth rate, is that capital should not be taxed in the steady state if consumers are infinitely lived (Chamley, 1986). Frenkel, Razin and Yuen (1996, ch. 14) show that this finding also applies in a small open economy, and it can be linked to results that are obtained in a simpler two-period model of capital taxation. A detailed dynamic analysis of capital taxation in an open economy model of exogenous growth is carried out in Nielsen and Sørensen (1991).[7]

The effects of capital taxation in open economies have also been analysed in models of endogenous growth. One example is Razin and Yuen (1996), who introduce international capital mobility and endogenous population growth to Lucas' (1990) framework of human capital accumulation. They calibrate their model for the G-7 nations and show that the combination of cross-country capital flows and endogenous population growth may lead to large effects of capital tax reform on the growth rate. Capital tax competition in a two-country model of endogenous growth is analysed by Lejour and Verbon (1997), who show that capital taxation in one country may have a negative effect on the growth rate of the other region, counteracting the positive fiscal externality that works through the static tax base effect (cf. section 3.1). As a result, taxes may be inefficiently high in the steady-state Nash equilibrium. While these growth effects are clearly important for an overall evaluation of capital taxation and tax competition in open economies, it is a general feature of this literature that results tend to be highly dependent on the exact specification of the growth channel. Hence any rigorous treatment requires a detailed evaluation of alternative models of economic growth that is beyond the scope of the present analysis. For a recent summary of the theoretical and the empirical literature on the growth effects of taxation, see Myles (2000).

[7] Some links to this literature will be drawn from our analysis of the dynamic effects of a switch in the commodity tax principle (chapter 9) and the discussion of production efficiency in an open economy (section 10.5).

Part 2

Factor taxation

4 An introduction to capital tax competition

Part 2 of this book studies the implications of capital mobility for the taxation of factor incomes in open economies. The literature on this subject is so vast that the issues studied in detail in this part necessarily reflect a highly selective choice. Nevertheless, an attempt will be made to deal with some of the key positive and normative issues in the area of capital taxation. On the one hand we will offer explanations for some important stylised facts, such as the low capital tax rates levied by small countries, the 'tax-rate-cut-cum-base-broadening' structure of income tax reform, and the observation of rising effective capital tax rates in some countries, against the general trend. On the other hand, we also address some important policy issues raised in section 2.1, in particular the enforcement of taxes on international interest income and the taxation of profits accruing to multinational corporations.

Chapter 4 introduces some of the fundamental theoretical results in the area of capital taxation, and also provides an empirical overview of the changes in the structure and level of factor taxation since the 1980s. Chapter 5 focuses on issues of *international* redistribution in a model of capital tax competition between countries of different size. Chapter 6 is instead concerned with *interpersonal* distribution within each country, and studies the optimal mix of capital and labour taxes under conditions of increasing capital mobility. Finally, chapter 7 deals with the optimal structure of corporation tax in the presence of multinational firms and cross-country profit-shifting.

The purpose of chapter 4 is to give an overview of the theoretical and empirical issues that underlie much of the discussion on the taxation of factor incomes under increasing capital mobility. In section 4.1 we introduce the basic principles of international factor taxation, the *residence principle* and the *source principle*, and argue that the latter is the more relevant in practice. Based on this finding, the ensuing sections focus on source-based capital taxes only. In section 4.2 we discuss the choice between labour and capital taxes in a small open economy that is perfectly integrated in world markets. Section 4.3 then provides a simple analysis of symmetric, source-based capital tax competition and its effect on the provision of public consumption goods. Finally, section 4.4 takes a brief look at the empirical evidence on the development of effective tax rates on capital vs. labour income, and at the overall level of taxation under conditions of increasing economic integration.

4.1 Residence- vs. source-based capital taxation

4.1.1 Principles of capital taxation and international production efficiency

International factor flows can either be taxed in the country where the income originates (*source principle*), or in the country where the factor owner resides (*residence principle*). In principle, this distinction applies to both labour and capital income. However, since we assume throughout this book that labour is not mobile internationally, the discussion will be focused on capital taxation only. In the following, we compare the basic properties of residence-based vs. source-based capital taxation and introduce a theoretical criterion that allows a welfare ranking between them.[1]

Residence principle

Under the residence principle, capital income is taxed in the country where the investor resides, irrespective of where the capital income has originated. Let the gross returns to capital in two countries $i \in \{A, B\}$ be denoted by r^i. A capital owner in country A comparing the net returns from domestic and foreign investments thus faces the international arbitrage condition

$$r^A(1 - t^A) = r^B(1 - t^A) \quad \Longrightarrow r^A = r^B. \tag{4.1}$$

Arbitrage by capital owners will thus equalise gross-of-tax returns across countries. From the profit-maximising input choices of competitive producers, the gross return to capital will equal the marginal productivity of capital $(\partial f^i / \partial k^i)$ in each country. Hence we have

$$\frac{\partial f^A}{\partial k^A} = r^A = r^B = \frac{\partial f^B}{\partial k^B}, \tag{4.2}$$

so that marginal productivities of capital are equated across countries. This leads to an efficient allocation of investment worldwide and is also referred to as *capital export neutrality*. At the same time, the net returns to capital will differ across countries when $t^A \neq t^B$. By the consumers'

[1] For a more detailed introduction to the properties of international principles of capital taxation, see Frenkel, Razin and Sadka (1991, ch. 2).

intertemporal optimisation, the net return to capital will equal the marginal rate of substitution between consumption today (c_0) and consumption tomorrow (c_1), so that

$$\frac{\partial u^A/\partial c_0^A}{\partial u^A/\partial c_1^A} = 1 + r^A(1 - t^A) \neq 1 + r^B(1 - t^B)$$
$$= \frac{\partial u^B/\partial c_0^B}{\partial u^B/\partial c_1^B} \qquad \text{if } t^A \neq t^B.$$

Hence, when tax rates differ across countries, an inefficient allocation of world savings will result under the residence principle.

Source principle

Under the source principle, capital incomes are taxed in the country where the investment takes place, irrespective of the nationality of the investor. This will occur either if the residence country of the investor exempts the foreign-earned income from tax, or if it grants a limited tax credit, and the tax rate in the host country exceeds the tax rate in the residence country of the investor (see below). The international arbitrage condition for capital owners in each country is then given by

$$r^A(1 - t^A) = r^B(1 - t^B) \tag{4.3}$$

When tax rates differ across countries, gross-of-tax returns and hence marginal productivities of capital will thus differ internationally and investment decisions are distorted:

$$\frac{\partial f^A}{\partial k^A} = r^A \neq r^B = \frac{\partial f^B}{\partial k^B} \qquad \textit{if } t^A \neq t^B. \tag{4.4}$$

At the same time, net returns to capital are equalised across countries. This property is also known as *capital import neutrality*, since taxes levied do not depend on the country from which the capital is imported. Equating net returns to the marginal rate of intertemporal substitution shows that the allocation of world savings is efficient:

$$\frac{\partial u^A/\partial c_0^A}{\partial u^A/\partial c_1^A} = 1 + r^A(1 - t^A) = 1 + r^B(1 - t^B) = \frac{\partial u^B/\partial c_0^B}{\partial u^B/\partial c_1^B}.$$

It is immediately clear from our above discussion that internationally efficient investment *and* savings decisions can be expected only when tax rates are equalised across countries. This forms one of the basic efficiency reasons for the international harmonisation of tax rates on capital. It is equally clear, however, that tax rate harmonisation will impose substantial costs on countries with diverse structures and levels of capital taxation. Taking different national capital tax rates as given, the theoretical comparison between the residence and the source principle of capital taxation reduces to the question of which principle implies the lower welfare costs of international tax rate diversity.

In a partial equilibrium framework, this question was first addressed by Horst (1980). Horst assumed that both taxes can be used simultaneously and argued from standard optimal tax reasoning that the residence-based tax should be high, relative to the source-based tax, when the elasticity of the supply of capital (i.e. savings) is lower than the elasticity of capital demand. He also discussed the special case of fixed domestic savings and thus a fixed domestic capital supply, where only the residence-based tax is used in the optimum. The other limiting case leading to the same result arises when the taxing country faces a perfectly elastic capital demand.

Later work has shown that there is a more general theoretical basis for the superiority of residence-based capital taxation, which is closely linked to the fundamental *production efficiency theorem* in optimal tax theory (Diamond and Mirrlees, 1971). In a closed economy setting, this theorem postulates that if a full set of tax instruments exists and there are no untaxed profits, then production decisions should not be distorted in a tax optimum. Applied to an open economy context, this requires that marginal productivities of capital are equalised across countries. It can be seen from (4.2) that this condition is always fulfilled under the residence principle, even if tax rates differ across countries. In contrast, (4.4) shows that the same is true under the origin principle if and only if tax rates are equal in the trading countries.[2] Homburg (1999) has labelled this result the *international* production efficiency theorem, in order to differentiate it from the optimal taxation of capital income from the perspective of a single country. The latter will be analysed in detail in section 4.2 below.

Keen and Wildasin (2000) have raised an important caveat, however, by showing that international production efficiency cannot generally be equated with (international) Pareto efficiency, even if the conditions of

[2] See Frenkel, Razin and Sadka (1991, ch. 5) for a detailed analysis in the small country case and Homburg (1999, proposition 2) for an exposition in the case of large countries. Keen and Piekkola (1997) consider the optimal taxation of international capital income in a more general framework where untaxed profits are permitted and link their results to the optimal tax rules derived by Horst (1980). They show in a two-country general equilibrium model that if profits are incompletely taxed, then the globally optimal mix of residence- and source-based capital taxation depends – as in Horst's analysis – on the elasticities of the demand for capital and the supply of savings. If profits can be fully taxed, however, the Horst rule loses its relevance and source taxes are zero, in accordance with the production efficiency theorem.

the Diamond and Mirrlees theorem in the closed economy are met. The additional difficulty that arises in an international context is that countries face distinct national budget constraints. Hence, if the shadow price of public revenues differs between countries, and lump-sum transfers or equivalent policy tools are absent, then it will be globally welfare improving to sacrifice production efficiency in order to redistribute tax revenues to the country with the greater need for government funds.

4.1.2 *Problems of enforcing the residence principle*

Despite the caveat just mentioned, it is widely accepted that international production efficiency is desirable and hence the taxation of capital income should follow the residence rather than the source principle. This contrasts, however, with recent tax reforms in several countries towards a source-based system of capital taxation (see section 2.1). In this subsection we therefore critically discuss the feasibility of residence-based capital taxation.

International tax relations are governed by a comprehensive net of bilateral double taxation treaties, based on the recommendations of the OECD model double taxation convention (OECD, 1977). This model convention generally grants the host country of an investment the right to tax incomes that originate within its territory, but leaves the home country of the investor two different options to avoid international double taxation: it can either exempt the foreign-earned income from domestic tax, or it can grant a tax credit for the taxes paid in the source country.

When the residence country exempts foreign-earned income from tax, then a pure source principle applies for international factor flows. With a tax credit matters are more complicated since residence countries generally do not offer a tax refund if the tax payment in the source country exceeds the tax liability on the same income in the country of residence. Therefore, two cases must be distinguished: if the tax rate of the source country is higher, then a pure source principle also applies under the tax credit method. In contrast, if the tax rate in the residence country is the higher one, then tax revenues are shared between the two countries but the tax rate of the residence country is relevant from the perspective of the international investor.

The fact that the residence principle must generally be implemented by means of a (limited) tax credit already points to a fundamental theoretical problem faced by residence-based capital taxation. In a non-cooperative game between host and residence countries the host country always has an incentive to set its tax rate at least as high as the tax rate in the residence country. The reason is that this will allow the host country to appropriate the maximum amount of tax revenue without adversely affecting investment decisions in its territory. A situation of equal tax rates can, however, clearly not be optimal for the residence country, whose tax revenues will then be zero. Hence, depending on the exact specification of the model, there exists either no Nash equilibrium at all (Gordon, 1992), a Nash equilibrium that eliminates all trade in capital (Bond and Samuelson, 1989), or the residence country endogenously chooses a zero tax rate on capital and thus eliminates the tax credit (Janeba, 1995; Wagener, 1996).[3]

Despite the problem that tax credits may give rise to strategic behaviour by source countries, tax credits are widely used in existing double taxation arrangements.[4] However, existing tax credits lose much of their importance when institutional arrangements are considered in more detail. This will be shown below for the case of corporate taxation on the one hand, and interest income taxation on the other.

Turning first to corporation tax, the principal problem of enforcing residence-based corporate income taxes is the possibility of deferring taxation in the residence country through the retention of profits. This strategy will be attractive whenever tax rates in the residence country are higher than in the source country. In the opposite case, however, residence-based taxation is also precluded because the limitation of the tax credit to the tax rate of the residence country will then be binding.

It then follows that residence-based corporate taxation can be ensured only if (i) unlimited tax credits are granted in the residence country, thus allowing for tax rebates; (ii) corporate profits of a foreign subsidiary are taxed in the residence country of the parent upon accrual, even if these profits are not distributed and repatriated. Condition (i) would further increase the above-mentioned incentive for host countries to push source

[3] A related and well-known result is that a small capital exporting country that unilaterally decides on the method of double taxation relief should allow taxes paid in the source country to be deducted from the domestic tax base, but will not find it optimal to grant a full tax credit. From the perspective of the capital exporting country, this *deduction method* (P. Musgrave, 1969; R. and P. Musgrave, 1989, pp. 571–2) equates the social return to a unit of capital invested at home and abroad, but grants only partial double taxation relief to the investor.

[4] One explanation for this 'tax credit puzzle' has been advanced by Gordon (1992). He shows that a capital exporter, acting as a Stackelberg leader, may offer a tax credit to induce the capital importing country to set a positive source tax on capital rather than behave as a tax haven. This in turn allows the capital exporting country to raise its tax on domestic capital income, with less fear of inducing capital flight. Janeba (1995) offers an alternative explanation that is based on cooperative tax setting. He shows that the tax credit is the only method of double taxation relief which allows policy-makers to implement all efficient outcomes without restraining countries in the choice of capital tax rates.

taxes on foreign corporations upward and 'exploit' the tax crediting arrangement. Most likely, such a scenario would be feasible only in the presence of a clearing mechanism that allocated tax revenue between source and residence countries. Condition (ii) is not compatible with current international law, which regards the foreign subsidiary as an independent legal entity. It implicitly assumes a pure 'conduit system' under which corporation tax is a withholding tax only for personal income tax. It should be obvious even from this brief discussion that the *de facto* taxation of corporate profits in the residence country of the investor is impossible without a fundamental reform of the entire present system of corporate taxation.

In the case of interest income taxation, all countries legally adhere to the residence principle with tax credits for foreign source taxes. However, institutional investors such as pension funds, life insurance companies and social security funds are often tax-exempt in the residence country so that the source principle is effectively in place for these incomes. For the remaining part of private savings, which is taxable under national law, the core problem is the enforcement of taxes on income earned abroad. Widespread evasion of residence-based capital taxes was the primary reason for the reforms towards a dual income tax in Scandinavia and Austria. Even a country such as Germany, which still nominally maintains a comprehensive, residence-based personal income tax, has been forced by a Supreme Court ruling to raise the allowance for personal interest income by a factor of ten, thus exempting roughly 80 per cent of private interest income from tax (Genser, 1996a, pp. 76–7). The decision of the Supreme Court was motivated explicitly by the inequities caused by widespread evasion of capital income taxes, which were estimated to substantially exceed 50 per cent of total taxable interest income.

The existing econometric evidence also points very strongly in the direction of large-scale evasion of interest income. This work has estimated the effect that the introduction of a withholding tax on interest income has on the pre-tax rate of return required by investors. The underlying idea is that withholding taxes should have no effect on the gross-of-tax interest rate, if investors use the tax credit offered by their country of residence, and hence subject their interest income to the legally stipulated residence principle of taxation. With respect to the (temporary) introduction of a withholding tax on interest income in Germany in 1989 (cf. subsection 2.1.1), Nöhrbaß and Raab (1990) have found, however, that the gross interest rate has risen by the full amount of the tax, indicating that tax credits are irrelevant from the perspective of international investors. A study by Eijffinger, Huizinga and Lemmen (1998) confirms this result for a broader sample of countries that impose interest withholding taxes on either US or Japanese investors. Here again, the estimates from the pooled cross-section, time-series regressions indicate that pre-tax returns must rise by the full amount of the tax, implying that none of the tax is borne by international investors. Together these results strongly suggest that withholding taxes are largely seen as final taxes by internationally mobile investors, implying that the legally applicable residence principle plays only a very limited role for the international taxation of capital income.

For these reasons, most of our analysis below will assume that capital taxes are levied under the source principle. For the case of interest income taxation, the possibility of enforcing residence-based taxation through international information exchange is discussed in section 5.5.

4.2 Capital and labour taxes in a small open economy

4.2.1 The benchmark: zero source taxes on capital

One benchmark scenario in the literature on international factor taxation is the case of a small open economy that disposes of a source-based capital tax and a tax on wage income. Capital is perfectly mobile internationally so that the small country faces a fixed world interest rate R. Labour is internationally immobile but the supply is elastic within the small country, so that the wage tax is distortive.

Given a fixed world interest rate, the source tax on capital must raise the gross return to capital by the full amount of the tax, in order for the small country to attract any capital in the integrated world capital market. For notational simplicity, we model all factor taxes as unit taxes; in a setting with perfectly competitive producers this can be done without changing any of the results.[5] Hence

$$r = R + t_k. \tag{4.5}$$

Similarly, the wage tax drives a wedge between the gross return to labour w and the net wage ω

$$\omega = w - t_w. \tag{4.6}$$

[5] In contrast, the difference between *ad valorem* and specific taxation is important in oligopolistic markets. For analyses of this issue, see Delipalla and Keen (1992) and Myles (1996).

Consumption

The standard model assumes a representative household in the small open economy, which supplies all factors and consumes all goods. The utility function of this household depends positively on her aggregate consumption level c, and negatively on labour supply l

$$u = u(c, l), \quad \frac{\partial u}{\partial c} > 0, \quad \frac{\partial u}{\partial l} < 0.$$

In addition, the representative household disposes of a fixed capital endowment $\bar{k}$. The price of the aggregate commodity is normalised to unity so that the budget constraint of the individual is given by

$$c = \omega l + R\,\bar{k}, \tag{4.7}$$

where capital income is a lump sum since both the endowment and the world interest rate are given.

Utility maximisation subject to the budget constraint (4.7) yields the following optimisation problem for the individual

$$\mathcal{L}^I(c, l, \lambda) = u(c, l) + \lambda\left(\omega l + R\,\bar{k} - c\right).$$

Maximisation with respect to c and l leads to the first-order condition

$$\frac{\partial u/\partial c}{\partial u/\partial l} = -\frac{1}{\omega}.$$

Substituting this into the budget constraint gives the consumption function $c(\omega, I)$ and the labour supply function $l(\omega, I)$, where ω is the relative price of leisure and $I \equiv R\bar{k}$ is the exogenous income.

Substituting the consumption and labour supply functions back into the direct utility function yields the individual's indirect utility function

$$v(\omega, I) \equiv u[c(\omega, I), l(\omega, I)]. \tag{4.8}$$

Using Roy's theorem, we can differentiate the indirect utility function with respect to the only endogenous price, the net wage ω. Furthermore, to save notation and with no loss of generality, we can normalise the marginal utility of income to unity. In this case, the gain in indirect utility following a rise in the net wage simply equals the equilibrium labour supply

$$\frac{\partial v}{\partial \omega} = l(\omega, I). \tag{4.9}$$

Production

Output (x) is produced using labour (l) and capital (k). Production occurs under conditions of perfect competition, ensuring that revenue equals total factor payments and profits are zero. The demand for factor inputs depends on the gross factor prices w and r

$$x[k(w,r),l(w,r)] - rk(w,r) - w(r)l(r) = 0. \tag{4.10}$$

We differentiate (4.10) with respect to r and use the optimality conditions for the firm's factor demands

$$\frac{\partial x}{\partial k} = r, \quad \frac{\partial x}{\partial l} = w.$$

This yields the negatively sloped factor price frontier

$$\frac{\partial w}{\partial r} = -\frac{k}{l} < 0. \tag{4.11}$$

In the following, we will also use the derivative of the factor price frontier with respect to r. Under the standard assumption that capital and labour are complements in production, this is given by

$$\frac{\partial^2 w}{\partial r^2} = -\frac{\partial(k/n)}{\partial r} > 0. \tag{4.12}$$

Government

The government faces the standard Ramsey optimal tax problem of maximising the indirect utility function (4.8) subject to the constraint that a fixed amount of tax revenue $\bar{T}$ must be collected. Given the two taxes permitted in this setting, the government's budget constraint is

$$\bar{T} = t_w l + t_k k.$$

Substituting (4.11) and the labour supply function into the government's budget constraint yields the government's Lagrange problem

$$\mathcal{L}^G = v(\omega, I) + \mu\left[\left(t_w - \frac{\partial w}{\partial r}t_k\right)l(\omega, I) - \bar{T}\right].$$

It is now straightforward to differentiate the Lagrangian with respect to the two tax instruments t_w and t_k. Using Roy's theorem and the net wage effects $\partial\omega/\partial t_w = -1$ and $\partial\omega/\partial t_k = \partial w/\partial r$ from (4.5), (4.6) and (4.11) this yields

$$\frac{\partial \mathcal{L}}{\partial t_w} = -l + \mu\left[l - \left(t_w - \frac{\partial w}{\partial r}t_k\right)\frac{\partial l}{\partial \omega}\right] = 0, \tag{4.13}$$

$$\begin{aligned}\frac{\partial L}{\partial t_k} &= -\frac{\partial w}{\partial r}\left\{-l + \mu\left[l - \left(t_w - \frac{\partial w}{\partial r}t_k\right)\frac{\partial l}{\partial \omega}\right]\right\} - \mu t_k l\frac{\partial^2 w}{\partial r^2} \\ &= -\frac{\partial w}{\partial r}\frac{\partial \mathcal{L}}{\partial t_w} - \mu t_k l\frac{\partial^2 w}{\partial r^2} = 0.\end{aligned} \tag{4.14}$$

The core result is that the first-order condition for the capital tax rate t_k includes the complete first-order condition for the wage tax, but also contains an additional term. If the wage tax is optimised then the first term in the second line of (4.14) is zero and only the second term remains. But since $\partial^2 w/\partial r^2 \neq 0$ from (4.12), (4.14) can be zero only for $t_k = 0$. Hence, the optimality conditions (4.13) and (4.14) jointly imply that a small open economy should not levy source-based taxes on capital and instead should rely exclusively on (distortive) wage taxation.

Intuitively, if capital is perfectly mobile internationally then a source-based tax on capital will be borne exclusively by labour. While the wage tax directly reduces the net wage, the capital tax reduces the marginal productivity of labour and hence the gross wage by driving out capital from the small open economy. Hence the incidence of the capital and the wage tax is identical in this setting and both taxes distort the consumption–leisure decision of the representative household. However, the capital tax causes an *additional* distortion by raising the gross return of capital above the opportunity cost of capital in the world market. Hence there is 'too little' capital in the small open economy and production is inefficient.

Importantly, this efficiency argument is independent of distributional considerations, since all efficiency losses will also be borne exclusively by workers when capital is fully mobile internationally. Hence, even if heterogeneous individuals were allowed in the setting above and only the welfare of workers mattered for optimal tax policy, the source-based capital tax would still be strictly dominated by a direct tax on labour.

The result that a small open economy should not levy any source-based taxes on capital was first derived in a general equilibrium model by Gordon (1986), *en route* to other findings. Later contributions by Razin and Sadka (1991a) and Bucovetsky and Wilson (1991) have explicitly focused on this result and linked it to what can be called a *national production efficiency theorem* (Homburg, 1999). From the perspective of a small country, the world capital market line (with the slope $1 + R$) is the relevant PPF, and the small country will produce on this frontier only if r is also its domestic gross return to capital.[6]

The result can also be illustrated graphically in a simple partial equilibrium framework. Figure 4.1 shows how the imposition of a source-based capital tax raises the marginal productivity of capital (*MPK*) and hence the gross return to capital in the small open economy. In equilibrium, this reduces investment in the small country from k^0 to k^1 and results in a deadweight loss (*DWL*) from the production inefficiency that would not occur if a labour tax were used instead.

We summarise our analysis in this section as follows:

Proposition 4.1 (Gordon, National Production Efficiency Theorem)
For a small open economy, the optimal source-based capital tax is zero, if it simultaneously disposes of a (distortive) wage tax and worldwide capital mobility is perfect.

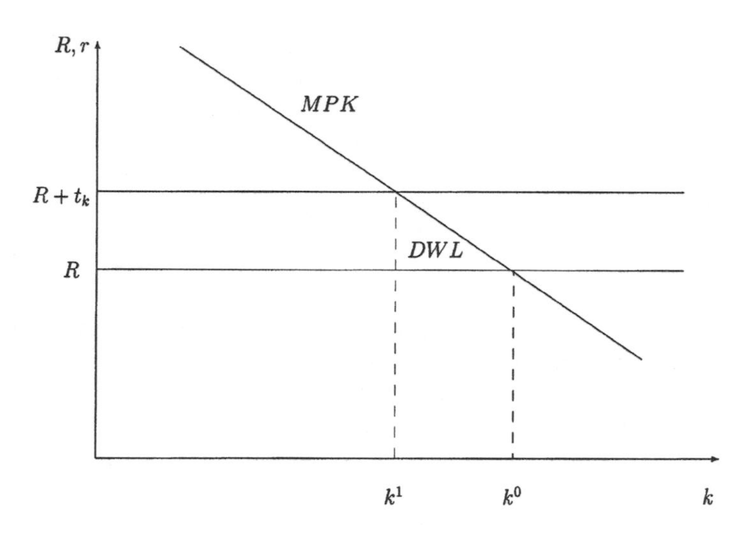

Figure 4.1 Source-based capital taxation in a small open economy

[6] It should be noted, however, that the small open economy setting analysed here represents only a special case of the more general (national) production efficiency theorem. This further discussion is postponed to chapter 10, where we analyse production efficiency in a more general context that also incorporates commodity taxes.

4.2.2 *Reasons for positive source taxes*

The above analysis suggests that small open economies should completely exempt capital income from tax, if they cannot enforce residence-based taxation of the relevant income source. Furthermore, while large countries may be able to improve their intertemporal terms of trade by taxing capital at source (cf. section 3.1), this argument leads to a positive source-based tax only if the country is a net capital importer. In contrast, capital exporters should offer an investment *subsidy* in order to raise world demand and thus the world return to capital (MacDougall, 1960; Kemp, 1962). This terms of trade argument implies in particular that the optimal capital tax rate changes its sign when the country switches from being a net capital importer to being a capital exporter – a prediction that is clearly at odds with empirical evidence (see Gordon, 1992).

Our policy overview in section 2.1 has shown, however, that most countries continue to levy positive source-based taxes on most forms of capital income. In the following we therefore discuss some possible reasons for maintaining positive taxes on capital in integrated economies.

A frequently raised argument is that capital may not be perfectly mobile across countries. This argument is generally based on the influential study by Feldstein and Horioka (1980), who find a surprisingly high correlation between domestic savings and domestic investment, whereas there should be no correlation at all for a small open economy operating in perfectly integrated capital markets. The high saving–investment correlations found by Feldstein and Horioka have been confirmed in many subsequent studies cited, for example, in Gordon and Bovenberg (1996).

However, several authors have argued that the correlation need not indicate capital immobility, but may instead derive from underlying macroeconomic factors which simultaneously affect both savings and investment. For example, Baxter and Crucini (1993) set up a two-country stochastic growth model with random productivity shocks and assume perfect capital mobility between countries. Their model generates correlation coefficients in the range of 0.85 (for a small country) to 0.95 (for two countries of equal size). The explanation for this high correlation is that, say, a positive productivity shock simultaneously raises investment and temporarily increases aggregate factor incomes, which in turn leads to increased savings in a model of lifetime consumption.

Recent econometric work has used refined techniques to overcome such ambiguities and has yielded some results which conflict with the findings of Feldstein and Horioka. Jansen and Schulze (1996) use an error correction model that allows for structural breaks and apply this model to Norway. They find a high correlation between savings and investment for the period before capital market liberalisation took place in the mid-1970s, whereas the coefficient is zero for the period thereafter. These empirical results fully conform to the theory of a small open economy operating under imperfect and perfect capital mobility, respectively. Hussein (1998) uses a dynamic OLS estimation technique to account for the possible endogeneity problem between savings and investment. He finds that the correlation between savings and investment is significantly different from unity for eighteen out of twenty-three OECD countries in his sample, suggesting substantial capital mobility over the last decades.

In sum, the empirical evidence on the extent of capital mobility is not fully conclusive. For this reason, some researchers use models of perfect capital mobility whereas others introduce some frictions in world capital markets by specifying mobility costs for international capital movements. These mobility costs can be regarded as a simple instrument to capture all extra complications of foreign investment, including those associated with uncertainty and country-specific risk. It is shown by Gordon and Varian (1989) that when national securities are not perfect substitutes and investors wish to diversify their portfolios, then even a small country will impose a positive tax on dividends, part of which is borne by foreigners.[7] An important implication is that distributive arguments are no longer irrelevant when capital mobility is imperfect, since it will then be possible to shift at least part of the burden of the capital tax to the owners of this factor. A setting with imperfect capital mobility and redistributive concerns by governments underlies our analysis in chapter 6.

There are also two further efficiency reasons for positive source taxes on capital, even if capital mobility is perfect. The first argument goes back to R. A. Musgrave (1959), who argued that the corporation tax rate should be set at a similar rate as the top rate on labour income in order to avoid highly taxed labour income being shifted into profit income. This argument has been formalised by Gordon and MacKie-Mason (1995) in

[7] Note, however, that an explicit modelling of the underlying source of capital market imperfections may sometimes lead to different conclusions. For example, Gordon and Bovenberg (1996) set up a model with asymmetric information, arguing that investors operating in foreign countries have informational disadvantages with respect to the prospects of specific firms as well as local demand, contract law, or customs governing labour relations. They show that this may lead to foreign investors being overcharged when they acquire a firm or purchase inputs and services. In this case the optimal tax policy of a small capital importing country calls for a *negative* source tax on capital, in order to compensate for the information problems encountered by foreigners.

a setting where an individual can work either as an employee or as an entrepreneur. The authors show that the optimal tax on corporate profits then trades off the distortion in the individual's decision where to work against any international distortions caused by a positive profit tax. The optimal profit tax will thus be unambiguously positive, serving as a 'backstop' for the labour income tax. The policy relevance of this argument is stressed, among others, by Sørensen (1995) and Cnossen (1999).

A second efficiency reason for source-based capital taxes is that even small countries are able to tax country-specific rents. These are modelled as country-specific fixed factors which do not have to be remunerated by the firm and may represent, for example, entrepreneurial skills. If it is impossible to isolate pure economic profits and tax them by a non-distortive instrument, then there is an efficiency argument for positive source-based taxes on capital.[8] In this case, the conditions of the production efficiency theorem will be violated and the source tax on capital serves as a second-best substitute for the missing direct tax on rents. This setting is used by a number of different authors (e.g. Mintz and Tulkens, 1996; Huizinga and Nielsen, 1997a) and it underlies our analyses in chapters 7 and 10.

4.3 Tax competition with source-based capital taxes

4.3.1 *The undersupply of public goods*

This section introduces another fundamental result of capital tax competition, the 'underprovision' of public (consumption) goods. The seminal contribution on symmetric tax competition between *small* countries is Zodrow and Mieszkowski (1986). The analysis in this section follows the somewhat more general framework of Hoyt (1991), which allows for tax competition between any number of symmetric countries.[9]

Consider a static model of n identical countries, where $n \in \{1, \ldots \infty\}$. Hence the share of each country in the world population is $1/n$. Each individual in each jurisdiction supplies one unit of labour and owns $\bar{k}$ units of capital. Capital is perfectly mobile between countries whereas

[8] One reason why non-distortive taxes on 'pure economic rents' may not be available is that entrepreneurial effort (and risk-taking) is endogenous and will be adversely affected by taxes on its return (see Haaparanta and Piekkola, 1998). Another reason is that not only capital, but also firms and their profits may be mobile internationally. This will be discussed further in part 4.

[9] Wildasin (1991) gives a brief overview of the use of this model in analyses of tax incidence and fiscal competition.

labour is immobile. Denoting the amount of capital employed in each region by k^i, capital market clearing implies

$$\sum_{i=1}^{n} k^i = \sum_{i=1}^{n} \bar{k} \equiv \bar{K}. \quad (4.15)$$

All countries produce a single, homogeneous output good whose price is normalised to unity. The production function is identical across countries and is given by $f(k^i)$ where the fixed labour input is suppressed. It is twice differentiable in k^i, with the usual properties $f'(k^i) > 0$, $f''(k^i) < 0$. Output and factor markets are perfectly competitive.

As before, each country levies a source tax at rate t^i on each unit of capital employed in its jurisdiction. Arbitrage by investors is based on a comparison of net-of-tax returns, $f'(k^i) - t^i$, across countries. From the perspective of a typical country i, the arbitrage condition is

$$f'(k^i) - t^i = R(t^i) \quad \forall \quad i \in \{1, ..., n\}, \quad (4.16)$$

where R is the net interest rate, which is equalised worldwide. It is a function of t^i whenever country i is not small in the world economy (i.e. when n is finite).

From the arbitrage condition (4.16) we get through implicit differentiation

$$\frac{\partial k^i}{\partial t^i} = \frac{1 + (\partial R/\partial t^i)}{f''(k^i)}, \quad \frac{\partial k^j}{\partial t^i} = \frac{(\partial R/\partial t^i)}{f''(k^j)} \quad \forall \quad i, j, i \neq j. \quad (4.17)$$

We now adopt the perspective of one particular country i. Differentiating the capital market clearing condition (4.15) and using the assumption that all other countries j are identical, we get

$$\frac{\partial k^i}{\partial t^i} + (n-1)\,\frac{\partial k^j}{\partial t^i} = 0 \quad \forall \quad i, j, i \neq j. \quad (4.18)$$

Substituting (4.17) in (4.18) and rearranging yields the effect of a change in country i's tax rate on the world interest rate:

$$\frac{\partial R}{\partial t^i} = \frac{-1}{n} \quad \forall \quad i. \quad (4.19)$$

Hence, by reducing the domestic demand for capital, a tax increase in country i will also lower the world interest rate. Given the assumption that all countries (including country i) are identical, this effect will be the stronger, the fewer countries there are in the world economy.

Finally, substituting (4.19) in (4.17) gives the effect of a change in t^i on country i's equilibrium capital stock, and hence its tax base:

$$\frac{\partial k^i}{\partial t^i} = \frac{[1 - (1/n)]}{f''(k^i)} \quad \forall \quad i. \tag{4.20}$$

The effect of a change in t^i on country i's tax base is the mirror image of the effect on the world interest rate: if n is large, then the world interest rate will fall only slightly and the tax increase will primarily raise the gross-of-tax return in country i. This implies a large reduction in country i's capital stock and hence a large elasticity of the domestic tax base.

We can now turn to the determination of the optimal capital tax rate. Each government maximises the (identical) utility function $u(c^i, g^i)$ of a representative individual in its jurisdiction, where c^i and g^i denote private and public consumption, respectively. The private and the public good represent different uses of the same output so that the marginal rate of transformation between c^i and g^i is equal to one.

The government budget constraint of each country is

$$g^i = t^i k^i \quad \forall \quad i. \tag{4.21}$$

The representative resident in each country receives rent income (the value of production, less the payments for the mobile factor capital) plus the net return R on her capital endowment:

$$c^i = f(k^i) - f'(k^i)k^i + R\bar{k} \quad \forall \quad i. \tag{4.22}$$

Each government takes the tax rate in the other regions as given and the first-order conditions for the optimal source tax on capital are determined by

$$\frac{\partial u}{\partial t^i} = \frac{\partial c^i}{\partial t^i} + m^i(c^i, g^i)\,\frac{\partial g^i}{\partial t^i} = 0 \quad \forall \quad i, \tag{4.23}$$

where we have inserted the marginal rate of substitution

$$m^i(c^i, g^i) = \frac{\partial u / \partial g^i}{\partial u / \partial c^i}.$$

Differentiating (4.21)–(4.22) with respect to t^i, substituting the results along with (4.20) into the first-order condition (4.23), and using again the symmetry assumption gives the best-response function of each government[10]

$$\bar{k}(m^i - 1) + m^i t^i\,\frac{[1 - (1/n)]}{f''(\bar{k})} = 0 \quad \forall \quad i. \tag{4.24}$$

Under the usual assumptions that the second-order conditions are ful-

[10] Note that from the symmetry assumption $k^i = \bar{k}\ \forall\ i$ in the Nash equilibrium.

filled and that reaction functions are continuous, (4.24) describes a symmetric Nash equilibrium in capital tax rates.

As a benchmark, let us first consider the case of a closed economy ($n = 1$). In this case the second term in (4.24) is zero and the first-order condition (4.24) reduces to $m^i = 1$. This implies that the marginal rate of substitution between the private and the public good equals the marginal rate of transformation and public goods will be efficiently provided in this case. For $n > 1$, the second term in (4.24) will be negative, hence $m^i > 1$ must hold in the Nash equilibrium. This is the fundamental result that tax competition leads to an *underprovision of public goods*, relative to an autarky situation where the capital tax base is immobile.

As n is continuously raised, the fraction in the second term becomes larger in absolute terms, indicating that the domestic tax base becomes more elastic from the perspective of each competing government. The first-order condition is maintained by a combination of an increase in m^i (which makes both the first and the second term larger in absolute value) and a reduction in t^i (which reduces the absolute value of the second term). Clearly, this is consistent with the budget constraint (4.21) since an underprovision of public goods must be accompanied by an 'under-taxation' of capital, relative to the closed economy benchmark.

Finally, it is straightforward to show that tax coordination is beneficial for all countries in this setting. A coordinated, simultaneous increase in the tax rate on capital is a lump-sum instrument, since the overall capital supply is fixed at $\sum_{i=1}^{n} \bar{k} \equiv \bar{K}$. Hence, acting collectively, the countries can exchange one unit of private consumption in each country against one unit of the public consumption good. This must be welfare increasing since the marginal rate of substitution between these two goods exceeds unity in the tax competition equilibrium. In fact, the coordinated tax equilibrium replicates the closed economy case in this symmetric setting.

Figure 2 illustrates this result. The PPF is given by a straight line with slope -1. In a closed economy, or with coordinated tax-setting, this is also the relative price of public vs. private consumption from the perspective of each regional government. Hence, the equilibrium will be in E^0, with the level of public consumption g^0 and the corresponding utility level u^0. With non-coordinated tax-setting, however, each regional government will perceive an increased price of public good supply, as represented by the steeper budget line with slope $-b$. Hence the tax competition equilibrium is at E^1, with the lower public good level g^1 and the lower utility level u^1. We can summarise the results in this section as follows:

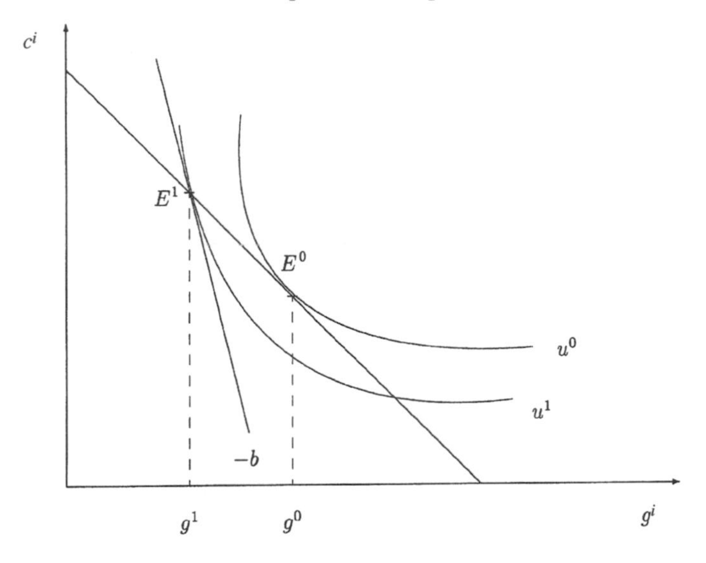

Figure 4.2 Undersupply of public goods through tax competition

Proposition 4.2 (Zodrow and Mieszkowski)
Symmetric tax competition with source-based capital taxes leads to inefficiently low capital tax rates and levels of public good supply in each country, relative to a situation where tax rates are coordinated.

4.3.2 *Constrained-efficient tax competition*

While the welfare gains from tax coordination are obvious in the simple model just discussed, the same need not be true in other models of tax competition where the set of tax instruments is expanded or the number of coordinating countries is restricted. This issue is systematically explored in several contributions that analyse the conditions under which decentralised decision-making by governments is *constrained efficient*, i.e., it produces a globally efficient outcome for the given set of tax instruments. If this is the case, the important policy implication is that international coordination or harmonisation of the available tax instruments will not yield any welfare gains for the competing countries.

In a well-known paper, Razin and Sadka (1991a) have analysed tax competition between two small countries that have an additional wage tax instrument at their disposal, but cannot enforce residence-based capital taxation worldwide. In this setting they find that tax competition is constrained efficient, in the sense that coordination between the two *infinitely small* countries cannot improve upon the non-cooperative outcome. This result is easy to understand from our earlier analysis in section 4.2. As stated in proposition 4.1, a small open economy that also disposes of a wage tax will set the source-based capital tax equal to zero. If coordination is confined to two (infinitely) small countries, then the optimal coordinated source tax on capital is still zero, and hence offers no welfare gains. Furthermore, if the residence principle can be enforced in the union, but not with the rest of the world, then the internal coordination possibility is irrelevant. Hence, the optimal residence-based tax is equally zero for the union of small open economies.

Bucovetsky and Wilson (1991) have extended this analysis by considering tax competition between a finite number of identical jurisdictions, similar to the analysis above. In contrast to Razin and Sadka (1991a), the coordinating countries no longer face a fixed interest rate in this model. Hence, if governments dispose of a wage tax and a source-based capital tax, they can collectively impose a lump-sum tax on capital, and there is a similar welfare argument for tax harmonisation as in the basic one-instrument case summarised in proposition 4.2.

In contrast, tax competition between symmetric countries with some market power will be efficient if countries dispose of a residence- and a source-based capital tax, but not a wage tax (Bucovetsky and Wilson, 1991, proposition 3). With one instrument controlling the supply of capital (the residence-based tax) and one instrument controlling the demand (the source-based tax), each country is able to insulate itself from changes in the world interest rate. Hence, as in the case of infinitely small countries, there are no fiscal externalities associated with the capital tax policies of each region and competition is efficient.

The last result is of limited policy relevance, however, because residence-based capital taxation is very difficult to enforce (cf. subsection 4.1.2). Furthermore, if *both* residence- and source-based taxes are levied in equilibrium, then there will be double taxation of international capital income, violating production efficiency. The implication of this literature is thus that for a 'realistic' set of tax instruments (wage taxes and source-based capital taxes) tax coordination can be welfare improving, if the coordinating countries are large enough to influence the world interest rate. This result will be used in our discussion of an EU-wide interest withholding tax in section 5.5. The theoretical discussion on constrained-efficient tax competition will be extended in section 10.5 where we simultaneously incorporate commodity taxes.

4.4 Capital tax competition: empirical evidence

The theoretical results presented above suggest that increased capital mobility should lead to (i) a change in the *structure* of direct taxation away from capital and towards labour taxes, and (ii) an overall reduction in the *level* of the public budget resulting from an increase in the excess burden of taxation. In the final section of this introductory chapter, we survey some of the empirical evidence on both of these issues.

4.4.1 Developments in the tax structure

We have argued in chapter 2 that the reform of personal and corporate income taxation since the 1980s has generally followed a pattern of 'tax-rate-cut-cum-base-broadening'. To analyse the effect of these reforms on the overall tax burden on capital in more detail, two different measures have been used in the literature. The *effective marginal tax rate* (EMTR) measures how a marginal adjustment to the capital stock in a given country is taxed, taking into account both the nominal tax rate and the definition of the tax base (e.g. depreciation rules). It is generally calculated at the firm level, using weighted averages of different investment projects and financing methods.[11] In contrast, the *effective average tax rate* (EATR) measures total taxes paid, as a fraction of the relevant tax base (capital income or corporate profits). It thus includes lump-sum taxes or subsidies that leave marginal additions to the capital stock untaxed. It is based on macroeconomic data on tax revenues on the one hand, and national accounts aggregates on the other.

Empirical evidence on the development of effective marginal tax rates on corporate profits is provided by Chennells and Griffith (1997). They calculate EMTRs for ten OECD countries – among them six EU members – during the period 1979–94.[12] Their results show (1997, table 4.1, p. 44) that EMTRs for domestic investment in these countries converged visibly in the time period analysed, implying significant reductions in EMTRs for Australia, Germany and France, whereas EMTRs rose considerably in the United Kingdom and Italy. The average of domestic EMTRs in the ten countries of their sample fell moderately from 21.7 per cent to 20.5 per cent during the period 1979–94. Since this reduction is much smaller than the fall in statutory corporate tax rates (cf. table 2.2), it indicates that tax bases have indeed been broa-

[11] The fundamental contribution applying this method to a cross-country comparison of capital income taxation is King and Fullerton (1984).

[12] The countries are Australia, Canada, France, Germany, Ireland, Italy, Japan, Spain, the United Kingdom and the United States.

dened, on average, in the countries analysed. This result is confirmed by calculating the net present value of depreciation allowances for plant and machinery, which has been reduced in most countries of the sample since the 1980s (Chennells and Griffith, 1997, figure 2.2, p. 29).

Largely comparable results are obtained by Schaden (1995), who calculates EMTRs for most EU countries and Switzerland during the period 1981–91. Schaden also finds a clear downward trend in the EMTR for domestic investment in Germany, but an upward trend in Italy and the United Kingdom (1995, table 5.9, p. 106). Furthermore Schaden's analysis supports the conclusion that the variation of individual countries' EMTRs fell significantly during the 1980s. The average of domestic EMTRs in her sample even increased from 24.6 per cent to 28.4 per cent, whereas the EMTRs for German direct investment in other EU countries remained virtually constant around 24 per cent. These averages cannot be directly compared to those calculated by Chennells and Griffith (1997), however, because both the country sample and the time period covered differ in the two analyses. Nevertheless, these detailed studies give clear evidence of a 'tax-rate-cut-cum-base-broadening' pattern of tax reform that has led to reduced variability but an almost stable average of EMTRs in the EU and OECD countries.

This pattern is roughly consistent with empirical evidence on average effective tax rates. Mendoza, Razin and Tesar (1994) cover the G-7 countries during the time period 1965–88 and find wide country-specific fluctuations for both corporate income tax and a more general measure of capital income taxation that includes the taxation of interest, dividends and capital gains accruing to individuals.[13] In the G-7 average, EATRs on corporate and capital income generally increased through the 1970s and remained roughly constant during the 1980s. In contrast, effective average tax rates on labour income rose throughout the time period analysed.

Volkerink and de Haan (2000) and Hettich and Schmidt (2001) have updated and extended the EATR calculations in Mendoza, Razin and Tesar (1994), using refined techniques to separate capital from labour income (see n. 13). The study by Volkering and de Haan covers eighteen OECD countries during the period 1965–96 while Hettich and Schmidt

[13] The taxation of capital income at the level of individuals is generally incorporated in personal income tax. While withholding taxes on certain capital incomes can be isolated in the tax statistics, these need not be a close approximation for the final taxation of this capital income. Therefore, a core problem for the calculation of effective average tax rates on capital vs. labour income is the decomposition of tax revenue from personal income tax.

consider fourteen OECD countries and the period 1980–96. Both studies confirm the existence of large fluctuations in the EATRs of many countries studied. Furthermore, for the years since 1980, they both find significant reductions in effective average tax rates on corporations for France, Germany and the United Kingdom, whereas the trend in Italy goes in the opposite direction. EATRs on all capital income are generally lower than EATRs on corporate income, reflecting the fact that at least some part of personal capital income is either taxed at reduced rates (capital gains) or evades taxation (interest income). Nevertheless, EATRs on capital income follow a similar pattern as EATRs on corporate income in most of the countries analysed. Finally, both studies find that EATRs on labour income (including social security contributions) have continued to rise in most countries during the 1990s, with the notable exception of the United Kingdom.

To sum up, EMTR and EATR calculations yield different average tax levels and there are also isolated countries, in particular the United Kingdom, where the *changes* in EMTR and EATR measures point in different directions. Nevertheless, there seems to be a general agreement in the relevant literature that the two measures lead to broadly similar conclusions with respect to the development of capital taxation since the 1980s. Table 4.1 summarises the development of effective average tax rates on labour and capital income, using averages of annual data in the first half of the 1980s and the 1990s, respectively. The table is based on effective average tax calculations in Volkerink and de Haan (2000) and Daveri and Tabellini (2000), as put together by Sorensen (2000, table 2).

Table 4.1 shows that a substantial gap between the average tax rates on labour and capital income already existed in the early 1980s, if consumption taxes are included in the total effective tax rate on labour.[14] In the average of the twelve EU countries covered by table 4.1, this gap has widened further – though not dramatically – as effective tax rates on labour income rose in the following decade while the effective tax rate on capital income fell slightly. On average, the calculations of effective tax rates on capital vs. labour income thus support the predictions of theoretical models that increasing capital mobility leads to a shift in the tax mix away from the taxation of capital and towards the taxation of wages. At the same time, however, table 4.1 also shows that EATRs on capital income have risen in several countries inside and outside the European Union since the 1980s, demon-

[14] Note that consumption taxes reduce the real wage rate by increasing the price level. In contrast, they do not affect the real interest rate, if tax rates are constant over time.

Table 4.1 *Effective average tax rates on labour and capital in the OECD, 1981–1995*

	Total effective tax rate on labour income (per cent)[a]		Effective tax rate on capital income (per cent)	
	1981–5	1991–5	1981–5	1991–5
Austria	54.6	55.7	21.5	22.7
Belgium	52.9	54.7	39.5	36.0
Denmark[b]	55.6	59.7	47.8	40.0
Finland	45.2	49.5	35.2	45.2
France	52.5	57.0	28.4	24.8
Germany	47.1	50.2	31.0	26.5
Ireland	45.3	45.7[c]	11.4	11.1[c]
Italy	43.8	52.8	25.3	34.5
Netherlands[b]	57.3	59.8	29.7	31.9
Spain	37.7	40.9	13.9	20.3
Sweden[b]	57.4	59.8	47.4	53.1
United Kingdom	37.5	35.6	66.5	45.3
EU average	48.9	51.8	33.1	32.6
Japan	27.9	31.7	39.7	43.9
Norway	53.8	54.1	42.6	30.3
Switzerland	30.7[d]	30.7[c]	29.5	36.5
United States	32.1	31.1	40.9	41.1

Notes:
[a] Includes taxes on consumption.
[b] Effective tax rates on labour and capital income include personal income taxes on public transfers.
[c] 1991.
[d] 1985.
Sources: Sørensen (2000), table 2, based on computations in Volkerink and de Haan (2000) and Daveri and Tabellini (2000).

strating that the trend towards reduced taxation of capital income is by no means universal.[15]

There are also some econometric analyses that try to link changes in the observed tax mix to the increasing liberalisation of capital markets while controlling for changes in other relevant variables. Rodrik (1997) performs a pooled cross-section, time-series analysis based on the effective average tax rates calculated by Mendoza, Razin and Tesar (1994),

[15] Note also that the rise in the effective taxation of labour is due primarily to increasing social security contributions. This increase, in turn, is caused mainly by demographic changes and medical progress, and hence may have little connection with international developments.

but uses an extended data set that incorporates developments in eighteen OECD countries during the period 1965–92. Effective capital and labour tax rates are regressed on a trade-related variable for the 'openness' of the economy and *per capita* GDP. In his main regression, Rodrik obtains the result that the 'openness' variable has a positive and statistically significant effect on the labour tax rate, but a negative and also significant effect on the capital tax rate. Hence his findings lend additional support to the theoretical result predicting a shift in the tax structure from capital to wage taxation.

Other econometric analyses by political scientists seem to find directly opposing evidence that the liberalisation of capital markets is associated with an *increase* in capital taxation (Garrett, 1995; Quinn, 1997). Garrett interprets this result as showing that governments do not choose tax levels so as to minimise the excess burden of taxation (what is called the 'efficiency hypothesis') but rather set taxes so as to compensate those who lose from increased market integration (the 'compensation hypothesis'). However, the dependent variable in these studies is corporate tax *revenue*, in relation either to GDP or to some other tax measure. Since the share of operating profits in GDP has risen since the early 1980s (cf. section 2.1 and Ruding Report, 1992, p. 154), this finding need not contradict the evidence for decreasing effective corporate tax *rates*.[16] It is demonstrated by Bretschger and Hettich (2000) that the conflicting results between the studies of Garrett and Quinn on the one hand and Rodrik on the other can be explained by the different ways of measuring the dependent variable. Hence, the 'efficiency hypothesis' derived from the literature on capital tax competition is not refuted by the empirical work of Garrett and Quinn.

4.4.2 *Developments in tax and expenditure levels*

Empirical interest in the link between tax competition and the overall size of government dates back to the 1980s. The initial contribution by Oates (1985) tested whether various measures of fiscal decentralisation are associated, on average, with reduced government expenditures. This work sparked a vivid debate that has run largely under the label of testing the 'Leviathan hypothesis' of government behaviour. However, as later observers have pointed out, the empirical results cannot be used to discriminate between alternative models of government. Instead, they test the *effectiveness* of tax competition in reducing expenditures under any

[16] For a more detailed evaluation of the econometric literature on this issue, see Schulze and Ursprung (1999, pp. 312–17).

form of government behaviour. As summarised by Oates (1989) this literature has provided some evidence that tax competition between local governments in the United States has reduced the combined level of expenditure by local and state governments. For the international samples, however, there is no systematic evidence that decentralised ('federal') countries have lower overall levels of taxation as a share of national GDP.[17] This result is confirmed by Anderson and van den Berg (1998), who broaden the measure of total economic activity in each country by adding household production and the informal sector. It is important to emphasise, however, that all these analyses are based on cross-section data for large samples covering both developed and developing countries and the focus of the empirical analysis is on tax competition *within* each individual country.

More recently, a different set of studies has analysed the relationship between the 'openness' of an economy and the size of government spending. In these analyses the focus is thus on tax competition *between* different countries. In two cross-section studies based on large samples of countries, Quinn (1997) and Rodrik (1998) find a *positive* correlation between capital mobility or trade integration on the one hand, and government spending on the other. Rodrik (1998) furthermore shows that this positive relationship applies to most types of government spending. Hence, the findings of these studies seem to directly contradict the theoretical result that tax competition should reduce the supply of public goods. Instead, they offer empirical support for the 'compensation hypothesis', which argues that market integration increases the volatility of private earnings and hence calls for increased government involvement in the economy. However, in a simple regression analysis that is confined to the OECD countries, Rodrik (1997) obtains the opposite result and finds a *negative* correlation between openness and government expenditures on social security and welfare.[18]

The conflicting results of Rodrik's (1997, 1998) analyses suggest that the composition of the international sample does matter, and that tax competition between the OECD countries – where economic integration has proceeded furthest – has indeed had a negative effect on overall tax

[17] Examples of countries with highly decentralised fiscal decision-making and low overall levels of taxation are Switzerland and the United States. Even for Switzerland, however, a study by Kirchgässner and Pommerehne (1996) finds no evidence that tax competition between cantons reduces public good supply or income redistribution. One possible reason for this result is suggested by empirical evidence that Switzerland's system of direct democracy increases the loyalty of households with their canton of residence and thus mediates tax competition (Feld, 1997).

[18] For a detailed review of this empirical literature, see Schulze and Ursprung (1999, pp. 330-44).

and expenditure levels. At the same time, it should not be too surprising that the negative relation between globalisation and the level of government expenditures is not too robust. First, important determinants of government growth – in particular expenditures on health care and old-age insurance – have little systematic relationship with the internationalisation of the economy (cf. n. 15).[19] Furthermore, given that tax competition is strongest in the area of capital taxation, but revenues from this source finance only a minor fraction of total government expenditures, it seems quite intuitive that changes in the structure of taxation should be more pronounced as a result of increasing capital mobility as compared to changes in the overall tax level.

[19] In fact, if social security contributions are excluded from the measure of tax revenue, then a statistically significant negative effect of fiscal decentralisation on government size emerges in a simple cross-section analysis for the OECD countries. See Keen (1993b, ch. 6).

5 Capital tax competition and country size

The two benchmark analyses presented in chapter 4 focused on special cases with respect to the size of the countries involved in tax competition. The first case (section 4.2) showed that the optimal capital tax rate for a small open economy is zero. In other words, if a country cannot influence the international interest rate, then it is rational from a national welfare perspective to play the role of a 'tax haven'. The other benchmark analysis has focused on the case of symmetric tax competition between identical regions (section 4.3). In this model, the symmetry of regions precluded any potential conflict of interests between them, and tax coordination could simultaneously benefit *each* of the competing countries. The analysis in the present chapter combines and extends each of these benchmark models by considering two countries of different size which both have some effect on world market prices. The core question is whether, and under which conditions, the smaller of the two countries may benefit from tax competition.

Some evidence on the relationship between country size and rates of capital taxation has already been discussed in chapter 2. We have seen there that the countries which have enacted the most severe cuts in standard nominal rates of corporate taxation are all small open economies. This applies in particular to Ireland, which levies a very low tax rate on manufacturing and financial services companies and has experienced a large increase in corporate tax revenues (cf. table 2.2). A similar pattern also obtains for personal income tax. A special position is here taken by Luxembourg, which formally taxes capital income at high rates, but levies no withholding taxes on either domestic or foreign investors (cf. table 2.1). While Luxembourg is not the only EU country that currently exempts foreign interest income from withholding tax, it plays a dominant role, for example, for German portfolio investors. Schaden (1995, pp. 14–17) reports that more than 90 per cent of the portfolio capital that fled Germany in anticipation of the withholding tax on German interest income on 1 January 1993, was invested in Luxembourg. These small

EU countries are thus likely to be beneficiaries of tax competition for internationally mobile capital.[1]

The potentially conflicting interests of large and small countries with respect to capital tax competition and tax coordination are the subject of the present chapter. Section 5.1 introduces the basic model of capital tax competition between two countries of different size. Section 5.2 extends this model by introducing an additional wage tax instrument. These two sections provide the theoretical basis for the simulation analysis in section 5.3, which tries to assess the likelihood that the small country benefits from capital tax competition. Section 5.4 briefly compares our analysis with the international trade literature on retaliatory tariff-setting between asymmetric countries. Finally, section 5.5 addresses the welfare effects of a regional coordination of capital income taxes in the presence of worldwide capital mobility.

5.1 A basic model of asymmetric capital tax competition

The fundamental contributions on tax competition between countries of different size are Bucovetsky (1991) and Wilson (1991). This section develops an intuitive understanding for the basic results derived in their analyses.[2]

The analysis considers a static model of two countries $i \in \{A, B\}$ which are identical in all respects except for population size. In the basic model of this section, each individual in either jurisdiction exogenously supplies one unit of labour and k^* units of capital. Thus k^* is also the average capital–labour ratio in the world. Capital is perfectly mobile between countries whereas labour is immobile. In the presence of international capital flows, the capital–labour ratio employed in each country differs from the world average. In this chapter, we denote the *per capita* level of capital by k^i, and s^i is the exogenous share of country i in the world population. The worldwide capital market clearing condition is then given by[3]

[1] Similarly, the existence of tax havens in the Caribbean has long been a problem for the United States' tax policy. Papke (2000) gives a detailed account how a special double taxation treaty between the United States and the Netherlands Antilles eroded the base of the US withholding tax on interest paid to foreigners, eventually leading to the abolition of this tax in 1984.

[2] Sections 5.1–5.3 are a revised and simplified version of Eggert and Haufler (1998).

[3] To derive this *per capita* formulation, let $K^* = K^A + K^B$ denote the more conventional full employment condition in levels. Dividing through by the world labour endowment, L^*, and using the definitions $s^i = L^i/L^*$ for the shares of each country's population size gives (5.1).

$$s^A k^A + s^B k^B = k^*, \qquad s^A + s^B = 1. \tag{5.1}$$

Both countries produce a single, homogeneous output good whose price is normalised to unity. The production function is identical across countries and exhibits constant returns to scale; hence it can be written as $f(k^i)$. It is twice differentiable, with the usual properties $f'(k^i) > 0$, $f''(k^i) < 0$. Output and factor markets are perfectly competitive.

Each country levies a source tax at rate t^i on each unit of capital employed in its jurisdiction. Since *per capita* endowments, technologies and preferences are identical, capital movements will occur in equilibrium only if tax rates differ between countries. We assume, without loss of generality, that $t^A \geq t^B$. Then, if capital flows occur in equilibrium, the high-tax region A exports capital to country B.

Producer profit maximisation implies that the gross return to capital equals its marginal product. Arbitrage by investors equates the net-of-tax returns, $f'(k^i) - t^i$, across countries

$$f'(k^A) - t^A = f'(k^B) - t^B \equiv R. \tag{5.2}$$

Solving (5.1) for k^A and k^B, respectively, substituting in (5.2) and implicitly differentiating gives the change in each country's *per capita* capital stock in response to a domestic tax increase

$$\frac{\partial k^i}{\partial t^i} = \frac{(1 - s^i)}{(1 - s^i)f''(k^i) + s^i f''(k^j)} < 0 \quad \forall \quad i, \; i \neq j. \tag{5.3}$$

It can be seen from (5.3) that the numerator is larger for the small country, and this effect must dominate any difference in the denominator.[4] Hence the small country faces the larger reduction in its *per capita* capital stock following a domestic tax increase. This is the crucial effect for the asymmetric incentives that exist in a model where countries of different size engage in capital tax competition.

Each government maximises the (identical) utility function of a representative individual in its jurisdiction, $u(c^i, g^i)$, where c^i and g^i denote private and public consumption *per capita*. Thus the public good considered here is a quasi-private good and there are no economies of scale in its consumption (cf. Wilson, 1991, p. 426). As in section 4.3, the private and the public good represent different uses of the same output, so that the marginal rate of transformation between c^i and g^i is equal to

[4] This is most easily seen for the case of quadratic production functions, where $f'' = \text{const}$ and the denominator is the same for both countries.

one. In the benchmark model the only tax instrument available to the government is a source tax on the capital employed in its jurisdiction. The government budget constraint of each country is then simply

$$g^i = t^i k^i \quad \forall \quad i. \tag{5.4}$$

In each of the two countries, the *per capita* private budget constraint of a representative individual is given by

$$c^i = f(k^i) - f'(k^i)k^i + Rk^*. \tag{5.5}$$

Each government takes the tax rate in the other region as given and the first-order conditions for the optimal source tax on capital are determined by

$$\frac{\partial u}{\partial t^i} = \frac{\partial c^i}{\partial t^i} + m^i(c^i, g^i)\,\frac{\partial g^i}{\partial t^i} = 0 \quad \forall \quad i, \tag{5.6}$$

where the marginal rate of substitution $m^i(c^i, g^i) = (\partial u/\partial g^i)/(\partial u/\partial c^i)$ is non-decreasing in c^i and non-increasing in g^i. Differentiating (5.4)–(5.5) with respect to t^i and substituting in (5.6) gives the best-response function (cf. Bucovetsky, 1991, 8)

$$f''(k^i)\frac{\partial k^i}{\partial t^i}(k^* - k^i) - k^* + m^i\left(k^i + t^i\frac{\partial k^i}{\partial t^i}\right) = 0 \quad \forall \quad i, \tag{5.7}$$

where the partial derivatives $\partial k^i/\partial t^i$ must be inserted from (5.3).

The first of the three terms in (5.7) is positive for a capital exporting country, but negative for a capital importer. The second term is always negative and identical for both countries, while the third term must be positive in each country under an optimal tax policy. Assume now that even though the derivative $\partial k^i/\partial t^i$ differs for the small and the large country, both set the same tax rate and have the same capital–labour ratio in equilibrium. In this case the first terms in (5.7) drop out for both countries, but the third term will be unambiguously smaller in the small country. Hence this cannot be an equilibrium, given that the second terms are identical in both countries. The only possible adjustment is for the small country to reduce its tax rate. This will raise the capital–labour ratio in this country from the arbitrage condition (5.2) and increases the third term. This is, of course, fully compatible with a standard inverse-elasticity reasoning, since we have seen in our discussion of (5.3) that the small country faces the more elastic tax base.

Given that *per capita* endowments in both countries are equal, it is then only a small step to establish that *per capita* utility in the Nash equilibrium must be higher in the small country as compared to the large region. Since the low-tax country always has the higher capital–labour ratio in this model, the small country must also have the higher wage rate in equilibrium. At the same time, the return to the capital endowment is equalised across countries by investor arbitrage. Hence the total value of the *per capita* endowment in the small country exceeds *per capita* income in the large region.

The results which have been intuitively derived here have been proven more formally in the analyses of Bucovetsky (1991) and Wilson (1991). While Bucovetsky was able to demonstrate these results only for the case of quadratic production functions (theorems 1 and 2), Wilson has shown that the proof carries over to more general production functions (propositions 1 and 2). For later reference, we summarise these results in

Proposition 5.1 (Bucovetsky, Wilson)
If two countries differ only in size, then the smaller country levies the lower capital tax rate and has the higher per capita *utility level in the asymmetric Nash equilibrium.*

Proposition 5.1 compares the *per capita* utility levels in the two competing countries in the Nash equilibrium. It does not, however, compare the utility level of the small country in the Nash equilibrium to this country's utility level under tax coordination. Nevertheless, this comparison can also be easily deduced from the simple analysis carried out above.

To evaluate under which conditions a small country can gain from capital tax competition, let us first consider the reference case of full coordination. Importantly, there is no motive for trade in a model with identical *per capita* endowments so that – as in our analysis of section 4.3 – a coordinated policy can at best replicate the closed economy equilibrium. In the absence of capital mobility we have $\partial k^i/\partial t^i = 0$ and $k^A = k^B = k^*$. It is then seen immediately that both first-order conditions (5.7) reduce to $m^i = 1$, which is the condition for an efficient provision of the public good. If we open the economies to trade, global efficiency requires that optimal tax rates are the same in both countries, equalising the marginal product of capital across countries from (5.2). Identical technologies then imply $k^A = k^B = k^*$ and there are no capital movements between countries of different size in the coordinated open economy equilibrium. Furthermore no country needs to fear a capital outflow from a *coordinated* tax increase and $m^i = 1$ will again be attained. From a global perspective the capital tax is a lump-sum instrument, allowing each country to redistribute purchasing power from the private to the public sector at no extra cost.

Against this coordination scenario, we can now discuss two special cases of tax competition. The first is the case where both countries are of equal size. In the second case the small country's share in the world population approaches zero.

1. The first scenario is the symmetric case, $s^A = s^B = 0.5$, which implies that the first-order conditions (5.7) are identical for the two countries and a Nash equilibrium with equal tax rates exists. Hence there will again be no capital movements in equilibrium. However the partial derivatives $\partial k^i/\partial t^i$ in (5.3) are negative in the case of symmetric tax competition, since each country perceives a capital outflow in response to a domestic tax increase, conjecturing a *constant* tax rate in the other region. Substituting (5.3) and $k^A = k^B = k^*$ into the best-response functions (5.7) gives

$$m^i = 1 \bigg/ \left(1 + \frac{t^i}{2f''(k^*)}\right) > 1 \quad \forall \quad i \tag{5.8}$$

   in the symmetric Nash equilibrium. Since no country can influence the international distribution of income to its own advantage, the only effect of opening the economies to trade is a reduction in the level of public good provision below its efficient level. Hence welfare in both countries must be unambiguously lower than in the coordinated case. This, of course, replicates our discussion in section 4.3.
2. The other special case arises when the share of the (by convention) large country A in the overall population approaches one. From (5.3) the derivative $\partial k^A/\partial t^A$ then approaches zero and country A will choose the same tax rate as in the coordinated case (or in the closed economy). For the small country B this implies that the utility level under coordination can always be attained by also setting its tax rate equal to the closed economy level. However (5.7) shows that this cannot be optimal since the derivative $\partial k^B/\partial t^B$ is non-zero for this country. By a revealed preference argument the welfare level of an *infinitesimally small* country must therefore necessarily be higher than under coordination.

It follows from these two cases that there must be a critical level of s^B, where the smaller country is just indifferent between coordination and the non-cooperative Nash equilibrium. At this critical level of relative country sizes, the net benefits from non-cooperation turn positive for the smaller country. In contrast, it is clear that the larger country must always lose from asymmetric tax competition, because it underprovides the public good and at the same time loses tax revenue to its small trading partner.

The result that a *sufficiently* small country can gain from tax competition is also discussed in the analyses of Bucovetsky (1991) and Wilson (1991). Since this finding is critical for our further discussion in this chapter, we summarise it in

Proposition 5.2 (Bucovetsky, Wilson)
If differences in country size between two otherwise identical jurisdictions are continuously increased, there must be a critical distribution of the world population where the smaller country has a higher per capita *utility level in the non-cooperative Nash equilibrium, as compared to the equilibrium with coordinated tax rates.*

In our numerical analysis below, we will examine how realistic the possibility raised by proposition 5.2 is for a set of 'plausible' parameter values. Before this is done, however, it is important to be aware of the limitations of the theoretical model used so far. For this reason, the following section analyses an important model extension – the availability of an additional wage tax instrument – and asks whether this is likely to affect the possibility of the small country to gain from tax competition.

5.2 Asymmetric capital tax competition with two tax instruments

The case where governments of different size simultaneously dispose of a source-based labour tax and a distortionary tax on wage income is analysed by Wilson (1991, section 6). However, Wilson's treatment uses a fixed revenue constraint so that effectively only one of the two tax instruments can be endogenously chosen. This implies, however, that there can be no undersupply of public goods and hence no potential losses from tax competition for the small country. Since our purpose here is only to prepare the simulation analysis in the following section and derive first-order conditions for the optimal capital tax rates that are comparable to (5.7), we can extend Wilson's framework and allow for an endogenous supply of the public good. At the same time, our treatment in this section extends the analysis of optimal factor taxation in a small open economy (section 4.2), as the world price of capital will generally be affected by tax policies in the two countries.

To prevent the wage tax from being a lump-sum instrument, the standard model of asymmetric capital tax competition is modified to allow for an endogenous labour supply. The *per capita* production function of country i is then given by $f(k^i, l^i)$, where l^i is the endogenous labour supply of each individual. The gross wage and the gross return to capital in each country are given by w^i and r^i, respectively. Producer profit maximisation implies $\partial f/\partial l^i = w^i$ and $\partial f/\partial k^i = r^i$. Assuming that the production function exhibits constant returns to scale, the zero profit condition can be written as

$$f[k(w^i, r^i), l(w^i, r^i)] - r^i k(w^i, r^i) - w^i l(w^i, r^i) = 0,$$

where we note again that all functional relationships are identical across countries. Implicitly differentiating and using the conditions for producer profit maximisation links the capital–labour ratio to the slope of the factor price frontier $w^i(r^i)$ (cf. (4.11))

$$\frac{\partial w^i}{\partial r^i} = -\frac{k^i}{l^i}\,. \tag{5.9}$$

In addition to the capital tax rate t^i the government disposes of a labour tax instrument, denoted by t^i_w. If both taxes are unit taxes, the net returns to each factor are defined by

$$\omega^i = w^i - t^i_w \quad \forall\ i, \tag{5.10}$$

$$R = r^i - t^i \quad \forall\ i, \tag{5.11}$$

where ω^i is the net wage in country i and R is the endogenous world (net) return to capital, which must be equal in the two countries (cf. (5.2)). Of course, the government budget constraint (5.4) also changes to

$$g^i = t^i k^i + t^i_w l^i. \tag{5.12}$$

For simplicity, we assume that the representative individual in each country maximises an additively separable utility function $u = u_1(c^i, l^i) + u_2(g^i)$. The budget constraint of a typical individual in each country is given by

$$c^i = \omega^i l^i + Rk^* \quad \forall\ i. \tag{5.13}$$

Solving the household's maximisation problem determines the *per capita* labour supply function $l(\omega^i, R)$. Note that, owing to the separability of the direct utility function, labour supply is independent of g^i. However, the level of the public good enters the indirect utility function $v(\omega^i, R, g^i)$. The government's problem is then to maximise v subject to its budget constraint (5.12). Using (5.9)–(5.11) and introducing the arguments of $v(.)$ and $l(.)$ to facilitate the derivations below, gives the Lagrangians

$$\mathcal{L}^i = v(w[R+t^i] - t_w^i, R, g^i) + \lambda\left\{\left(t_w^i - t^i\frac{\partial w}{\partial r^i}[R+t^i]\right)l^i(w[R+t^i] - t_w^i, R) - g^i\right\}. \tag{5.14}$$

Note that $R(t^i)$ is a function of each country's capital tax rate in this model. Expressing the capital stock in each country as a function of the domestic return to capital, we can re-write the capital market clearing condition (5.1) as

$$s^i k(R+t^i) + s^j k(R+t^j) - k^* = 0,$$

where $k(.)$ denotes a functional argument. Implicitly differentiating the capital market clearing condition gives in a first step

$$\frac{\partial R}{\partial t^i} = \frac{-s^i(\partial k/\partial r^i)}{s^i(\partial k/\partial r^i) + (1-s^i)(\partial k/\partial r^j)} \quad \forall\ i,j,\ i \neq j.$$

This expression can be further reduced if we implicitly differentiate the profit maximisation condition $\partial f/\partial k^i(k^i) = r^i$ to get $\partial k/\partial r^i = 1/(\partial^2 f/\partial k^{i2}) < 0$. Substituting this and performing straightforward manipulations gives the final equation for the tax-induced change in the world return to capital

$$\frac{\partial R}{\partial t^i} = \frac{-s^i(\partial^2 f/\partial k^{j2})}{s^i(\partial^2 f/\partial k^{j2}) + (1-s^i)(\partial^2 f/\partial k^{i2})} < 0 \quad \forall\ i,j,\ i \neq j. \tag{5.15}$$

Hence a source tax on capital imposed by either country reduces the overall demand for capital and lowers the world interest rate. Furthermore, it is seen from the numerator in (5.15) that this effect will be the stronger, the larger is the country that imposes the tax. Focusing on the differential effects that domestic capital taxes have on the world interest rate – rather than deriving the change in the domestic *per capita* capital stock, as in (5.3) – is thus simply an alternative way of showing the asymmetric strategic incentives that exist for the small and the large country.

Capital's gross-of-tax return, $r^i = R + t^i$, is determined by

$$\frac{\partial r^i}{\partial t^i} = \frac{\partial R}{\partial t^i} + 1 = \frac{(1-s^i)(\partial^2 f/\partial k^{i2})}{s^i(\partial^2 f/\partial k^{j2}) + (1-s^i)(\partial^2 f/\partial k^{i2})} > 0 \quad \forall\ i,j,\ i \neq j, \tag{5.16}$$

which shows that the capital tax is only partly shifted into lower world prices and will also raise the gross return to capital in the taxing country.

We can now differentiate the Lagrange function (5.14) with respect to the two tax instruments and the level of public good supply, employing $\partial v/\partial \omega^i = (\partial v/\partial c^i) l^i$ from Roy's identity and $\partial v/\partial R = (\partial v/\partial c^i) k^*$ from (5.13). Further using (5.9) and (5.16) in the first-order condition for the capital tax rate gives

$$\frac{\partial \mathcal{L}}{\partial t_w^i} = -l^i \frac{\partial v}{\partial c^i} + \lambda^i \left\{ l^i - \left[t_w^i - t^i \frac{\partial w}{\partial r^i} \right] \frac{\partial l}{\partial w^i} \right\} = 0, \tag{5.17}$$

$$\begin{aligned} \frac{\partial \mathcal{L}}{\partial t^i} = & \left[-k^i + (k^* - k^i) \frac{\partial R}{\partial t^i} \right] \frac{\partial v}{\partial c^i} + \lambda^i \left\{ k^i - t^i \frac{\partial^2 w}{\partial r^{i2}} l^i \left(\frac{\partial R}{\partial t^i} + 1 \right) \right. \\ & \left. + \left[t_w^i - t^i \frac{\partial w}{\partial r^i} \right] \left[\frac{\partial w}{\partial r^i} \frac{\partial l}{\partial w^i} \left(\frac{\partial R}{\partial t^i} + 1 \right) + \frac{\partial l}{\partial R} \frac{\partial R}{\partial t^i} \right] \right\} = 0, \end{aligned} \tag{5.18}$$

$$\frac{\partial \mathcal{L}}{\partial g^i} = \frac{\partial v}{\partial g^i} - \lambda^i = 0. \tag{5.19}$$

Since the wage tax is set optimally we can multiply (5.17) by $(-k^i/l^i)$ and add the resulting equation to (5.18). Furthermore, assuming complementarity between capital and labour in the production function, we can differentiate (5.9) with respect to r^i to get

$$\frac{\partial^2 w}{\partial r^{i2}} = -\frac{\partial (k^i/l^i)}{\partial r^i} > 0, \tag{5.20}$$

which corresponds to (4.12) in chapter 4. Further using (5.19) to eliminate the Lagrange multiplier λ^i, dividing by $(\partial v/\partial c^i)$ and introducing the marginal rate of substitution, m^i, gives

$$\begin{aligned} (k^* - k^i) \frac{\partial R}{\partial t^i} + m^i & \left\{ t^i l^i \frac{\partial (k^i/l^i)}{\partial r^i} \left(\frac{\partial R}{\partial t^i} + 1 \right) \right. , \\ & \left. + \left(t_w^i + t^i \frac{k^i}{l^i} \right) \left(\frac{\partial l^i}{\partial R} - \frac{k^i}{l^i} \frac{\partial l^i}{\partial \omega^i} \right) \frac{\partial R}{\partial t^i} \right\} = 0. \end{aligned} \tag{5.21}$$

Equation (5.21) is the first-order condition for the capital tax in the presence of a simultaneous wage tax instrument and thus corresponds to the optimality conditions (5.7) in section 5.1. The important difference is that the optimal use of the labour tax instrument is incorporated in

(5.21). The condition therefore isolates those effects of the capital tax instrument that cannot be duplicated by a direct tax on wages.

The first term in (5.21) is a terms of trade effect that derives from the fall in the world price of capital in response to a domestic tax. This term is positive for the capital importer, but negative for the capital exporter. The second effect – the first effect in the curly bracket – gives the change in the capital–labour ratio induced by the tax and captures the distortion in the international allocation of capital. Using (5.16) and (5.20) shows that this effect is negative for a positive tax rate on capital. Finally, the third effect in (5.21) gives the increase in labour supply that is feasible for any given level of g^i when some of the tax burden falls on capital. This effect must be positive when the labour supply curve is upward sloping ($\partial l^i/\partial \omega^i > 0$) and leisure is a normal good so that income effects from changes in the return to the capital endowment reduce labour supply ($\partial l^i/\partial R < 0$).

If country B is infinitesimally small ($s^B = 0$), it follows from (5.15) that $\partial R/\partial t^B = 0$. In this case, only the second effect in (5.21) remains and only $t^i = 0$ satisfies the optimality condition. In this case, the capital tax falls entirely on labour and is thus dominated by a direct tax on wages. Hence, the optimality of a zero source tax on capital in a (infinitesimally) small open economy (proposition 4.1) is included in the present analysis as a special case.

Correspondingly, the first-order condition for the optimal capital tax rate will also simplify for a very large country ($s^A \to 1$). Note first from (5.15) and (5.16) that $\partial R/\partial t^A = -1$ and $\partial r^A/\partial t^A = 0$ in this case. Substituting this in (5.18), using (5.9) and (5.19) and introducing m^i gives

$$\begin{aligned} \frac{\partial \mathcal{L}}{\partial t^A} &= -k^* + m^A \left\{ k^A - \left[t_w^A + t^A \frac{k^A}{l^A} \right] \frac{\partial l^A}{\partial R} \right\} \\ &= k^A(m^A - 1) - m^A \left[t_w^A + t^A \frac{k^A}{l^A} \right] \frac{\partial l^A}{\partial R} = 0. \end{aligned} \tag{5.22}$$

The second line in this equation has used the fact that $k^* = k^A$ must hold for a very large country which, in the limiting case, becomes a closed economy. It can be seen from (5.22) that the shadow price of public consumption will then be less than one (i.e. the first term in the second line must be negative), because the income losses caused by the reduction in the net return to capital will have a positive effect on work effort and thus tax revenues (so that the second term in the second line is positive).[5] Clearly, since the capital tax represents a lump-sum instrument in the closed economy, it will dominate the distortive labour tax from the perspective of a very large country.

It follows from this discussion that an infinitesimally small country must gain even more from tax competition in the presence of an additional wage tax instrument than it does in the standard model discussed in section 5.1. Since the large country does not use the wage tax instrument, it will choose the same capital tax rate as before. The small country, however, chooses a capital tax rate of zero if it can also tax labour income. By a similar revealed preference argument as above, the zero tax on capital therefore not only dominates the cooperative solution from the perspective of the (very) small country, but it also dominates the positive tax rate that the small country has set in the benchmark with only one tax instrument.

More generally, however, both countries face finite elasticities for the capital and labour tax bases and will choose some combination of the two distortive instruments. The third term in (5.21) is then positive under the assumptions on income effects made above, reflecting the fact that the base of the capital tax is less than perfectly elastic. Hence, the capital importer (for whom the first term is also positive) will unambiguously set a positive tax rate on capital. For the capital exporter, the terms of trade effect is negative, however, so that no unambiguous result emerges for t^i on the basis of our (5.21). For the case of a fixed government budget, Wilson (1991, proposition 4) is able to demonstrate that both tax rates must be positive in both countries in the optimum. Hence, the reduced reliance on capital taxation in the large country will lower the redistributive gains to its small, low-tax neighbour.

However, when public good supply is endogenous, the existence of the second tax instrument may also allow the small country to reduce the excess burden of taxation and increase public good supply towards its efficient level. Hence, it cannot be concluded in general that adding a wage tax instrument to the model of asymmetric capital tax competition will always reduce the possibilities of the smaller country to gain from tax competition. In the following section, we will therefore set up a numerical specification of the model that allows us to weigh the gains from the inflow of foreign capital to the smaller country against the inefficiencies caused in the domestic supply of public goods.

[5] It is well known that the marginal costs of public funds can be less than one when tax revenues are not redistributed lump-sum to the representative consumer, and the tax base increases as a result of the income effect caused by the tax. See Ballard and Fullerton (1992) for a detailed discussion.

5.3 Numerical analysis

5.3.1 *Model specification and elasticity estimates*

The model that underlies our numerical analysis includes an endogenous labour supply decision, as described in section 5.2. To specify the numerical model we use literature estimates for substitution elasticities and share parameters in the production and utility functions. These are summarised in table 5.1 and are described below.

Turning first to production, elasticities of substitution between capital and labour are discussed in a large-scale tax reform model for the United States (Ballard *et al.*, 1985, pp. 132–4). For many industries these estimates are relatively close to unity, at least for cross-section analyses. For the purposes of our aggregate (*per capita*) production function we thus assume a Cobb–Douglas specification given by

$$f(k^i, l^i) = (k^i)^{\alpha}\ (l^i)^{(1-\alpha)}, \quad 0 < \alpha < 1, \tag{5.23}$$

where technologies are identical across countries and the share of capital has been set at $\alpha = 0.25$. This is in accordance with the distribution of national income in most OECD countries, where capital income ('operating surplus') accounts for roughly one-third of wage income (United Nations, 1996).

The utility function of the representative individual is of the nested constant elasticity of substitution (CES) form. As is well known, CES functions allow us to specify any substitution elasticity between zero (implying that goods are demanded in fixed proportions) and infinity

Table 5.1 *Summary of parameter specifications*

Symbol	Value	Description	Literature sources
–	1	Elasticity of factor substitution in production	Ballard *et al.* (1985)
α	0.25	Share of capital in production	United Nations (1996)
φ_x/φ_h	4	Ratio of expenditure shares: private consumption good to leisure	Ballard *et al.* (1985)
θ_z/θ_g	4	Ratio of expenditure shares: private composite good to public good	OECD (1996)
ε	0.5	Elasticity of substitution between leisure and private consumption good	Ballard *et al.* (1985); Hausman (1985)
σ	0.25 – 2.0	Elasticity of substitution between public good and private composite good	Whalley and Trela (1986); Rubinfeld (1987)

(implying that demands respond infinitely elastically to changes in relative prices). In the lower nest, leisure is denoted by h and is aggregated with the private consumption good (c) to a private composite good, denoted by z. In the top nest, the private composite good (z) and the public good (g) are then aggregated to give the overall utility index. Using a nested CES specification has the advantage that the elasticities of substitution in the upper and the lower nest can be specified independently. The utility function in each country is given by

$$u^i(c^i, h^i, g^i) = \left[\theta_z^{1/\sigma} \left(\varphi_c^{1/\varepsilon} (c^i)^{\frac{\varepsilon-1}{\varepsilon}} + \varphi_h^{1/\varepsilon} (h^i)^{\frac{\varepsilon-1}{\varepsilon}} \right)^{\frac{\varepsilon(\sigma-1)}{(\varepsilon-1)\sigma}} + \theta_g^{1/\sigma} (g^i)^{\frac{\sigma-1}{\sigma}} \right]^{\frac{\sigma}{\sigma-1}},$$

where the parameters φ denote the shares of private commodity consumption and leisure in the lower nest, whereas θ gives the shares of the private composite good and the public good in the top nest. All share parameters and substitution elasticities are assumed to be equal across countries. For CES functions the adding-up restriction on the shares in each nest implies $\theta_z^{1/\sigma} + \theta_g^{1/\sigma} = 1$ and $\varphi_x^{1/\varepsilon} + \varphi_h^{1/\varepsilon} = 1$. This leaves one degree of freedom to choose the *ratio* of the shares in each nest.

Our specification assumes that $\varphi_x/\varphi_h = 4$ and $\theta_z/\theta_g = 4$. The first ratio roughly corresponds to the weights calibrated by Ballard *et al.* (1985, p. 130). The latter choice reflects the fact that the ratio of government expenditures (excluding social security) in GDP is within a range of 20–30 per cent in many OECD countries (OECD, 1996). Sensitivity analyses show that our results are quite robust with respect to the choice of share parameters in both the production and utility functions.

In contrast, elasticities of substitution are clearly critical for the results. The elasticity of substitution between leisure and private commodity consumption in the lower nest, ε, is important for the counterfactual scenario in which the wage tax is introduced. When the share of leisure consumption in the individual's utility function is very small, then this elasticity is approximately equal to the uncompensated labour supply elasticity, but it will exceed the latter as the consumption of leisure grows. The numerical study by Ballard *et al.* (1985, pp. 125–30) assumes an uncompensated labour supply elasticity of -0.15, an estimate that is supported by most econometric work (cf. Hausman, 1985). Furthermore for their benchmark data set this labour supply elasticity corresponds to a substitution elasticity of about 0.5, and this is the value of ε chosen here. However, we will perform a sensitivity analysis with respect to this parameter by considering a high-elasticity scenario with $\varepsilon = 1$.

For the issue of whether a small country can gain from tax competition, the most important role is played by the elasticity of substitution between public and private consumption. To see this consider once again the first-order condition in the case of two identical countries, as given by (5.8). Since tax competition raises the shadow price of the public good above unity, the marginal rate of substitution (of c^i for g^i) must also rise in the optimum. For any given increase in m^i, the reduction in the level of public good supply will be the more pronounced, the higher is the elasticity of substitution in consumption

$$\sigma = \frac{d(c^i/g^i)}{dm^i} \frac{m^i}{c^i/g^i} \quad \forall \ i.$$

By the standard optimal tax intuition, a high level of σ implies an elastic response to the (perceived) change in the relative price of public vs. private consumption, leading to a high excess burden imposed by capital tax competition. Thus while the relative size parameter s^B is an indicator of the potential gains that a small country can reap through tax competition, the substitution elasticity σ is a quantitative indicator of the welfare losses incurred by non-cooperation.

Unfortunately, it is very difficult to obtain precise estimates for the value of the elasticity σ. Whalley and Trela (1986, p. 136) set this elasticity equal to 0.5, which is roughly consistent with own-price elasticities in the range of -0.2 to -0.4, as summarised in Rubinfeld (1987, p. 608). However, both sources emphasise the considerable measurement problems involved in estimating this parameter. In presenting our simulation results, we will therefore consider alternative values for σ in the range of 0.25–2.0 and focus on the range of (s^B, σ)-combinations under which the small country gains from tax competition.

5.3.2 *Simulation results*

In presenting our simulation results, we first consider the benchmark case, in which only a source-based capital tax is available. We then turn to the scenario where governments simultaneously dispose of a tax on wage income.[6]

The benchmark case

Figure 5.1 presents the results for the benchmark scenario without the labour tax instrument. The line dividing the graph shows the locus of all

[6] All simulations are carried out using the GAMS (General Algebraic Modelling System) software developed at the World Bank (see Brooke, Kendrick and Meeraus, 1992).

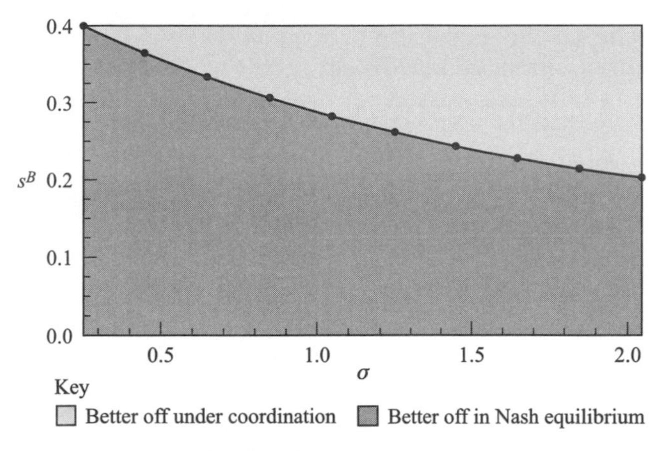

Figure 5.1 The benchmark case

combinations of substitution elasticities σ and relative size parameters s^B for which the small country attains exactly the same utility level under tax competition as it would obtain under full coordination. At any point *on* the curve the smaller country is thus indifferent between an international agreement which ensures coordinated capital tax rates, and the non-cooperative equilibrium with diverging tax rates.[7] In the heavily shaded area below this curve, the small country is better off in the Nash equilibrium as compared to the cooperative case, whereas the small country loses from tax competition in the lightly shaded area above the curve.

The intuition for the negative slope of the indifference locus should be obvious from our earlier discussion. The higher is the elasticity of substitution, the larger is the reduction of public good supply and thus the inefficiencies caused by tax competition. Hence for any given distribution of the world's population, a higher σ makes it more difficult for the small country to gain from tax competition. On the other hand, for any given substitution elasticity σ, the small country is the more likely to gain, the larger is the difference in relative country size.

Figure 5.1 shows that in the benchmark case the chances of country B to gain from tax competition – as measured by the size of the area below the indifference locus – are rather high. If the substitution elasticity between private and public consumption is sufficiently low, then even

[7] Consumption patterns differ in both situations, however, since the representative individual of a country which is engaged in tax competition consumes more private and fewer public goods than under coordination.

Table 5.2 *Percentage change in* per capita *utility in the small country: Nash equilibrium vs. coordinated equilibrium*

			Labour tax	
σ (1)	s^B (2)	Benchmark (3)	$\epsilon = 0.5$ (4)	$\epsilon = 1.0$ (5)
	0.05	6.377	0.214	0.728
0.25	0.10	4.530	−0.068	0.098
	0.25	1.562	−0.217	−0.349
	0.05	8.102	0.240	0.844
0.50	0.10	5.188	−0.078	0.108
	0.25	1.345	−0.249	−0.421
	0.05	8.996	0.368	1.382
1.50	0.10	4.552	−0.131	0.116
	0.25	−0.136	−0.418	−0.850

a small difference in relative size is sufficient for the smaller country to gain. Since most estimates of this elasticity point to rather rigid tax revenue requirements (see the discussion above) we can conclude that small countries stand a good chance of winning a 'tax war' in the standard two-country, one-instrument, perfect-mobility model of capital tax competition.

Table 5.2 quantifies the possible welfare increases that the smaller country can achieve over the coordinated equilibrium by engaging in capital tax competition. It measures the percentage utility increase (or decrease) *per capita* in the Nash equilibrium *vis-à-vis* the utility level obtained in the case of full coordination. Since the CES utility function used in our simulations is homogeneous of degree one, this relative utility change corresponds to the equivalent variation (EV) when *per capita* income in the reference equilibrium with coordinated tax policy is normalised to unity (see Shoven and Whalley, 1992, pp. 123–8). Percentage utility changes are given for different values of σ (column (1)), and for different world market shares s^B of the small country's population (column (2)). For the benchmark model of capital tax competition, the results in column (3) indicate, for example, that for $s^B = 0.1$ *per capita* utility increases of approximately 5 per cent are feasible over the coordinated equilibrium. If the small country's population is only 5 per cent of the world total, then *per capita* utility increases over the case of tax coordination are even higher and are in the range 6–9 per cent. The conclusion is thus that the utility increase that the small country can

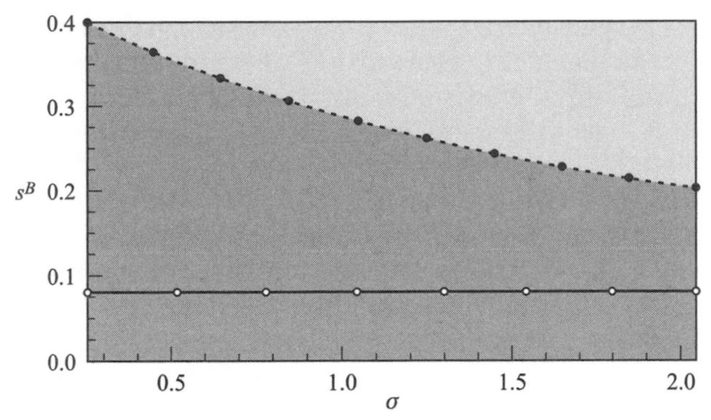

Figure 5.2 The benchmark case •- - - •- - - • and labour tax case ○—○—○

obtain through capital tax competition is quantitatively significant in the benchmark model.

The counterfactual with two tax instruments

We now relax the assumption that the governments of both countries have to rely exclusively on the source tax on capital in order to supply public goods. A wage tax is introduced which distorts each individual's labour–leisure choice, and governments now optimise simultaneously over two independent tax instruments. Figure 5.2 gives the effects of this model extension.

Our theoretical discussion in section 5.2 has suggested that the new tax instrument reduces both the redistributive gains and the efficiency losses of taxation from the perspective of the small country. The theoretical ambiguity is confirmed in our simulation analyses, but the indifference loci for the benchmark and the wage tax scenario intersect only at an unrealistically high level of $\sigma \approx 6$. In the relevant parameter range for σ, the reduced gains from undercutting the large country's capital tax rate emerge as the dominant effect and the introduction of an additional wage tax instrument unambiguously and strongly reduces the likelihood that the small country gains from tax competition. It can be immediately seen from figure 5.2 that if the small country has a size of 10 per cent or more in the world population, then it will be worse off in the Nash equilibrium as compared to full coordination.

Figure 5.2 also shows that with an additional labour tax instrument, the small country's indifference locus in this range is almost independent of σ. This is explained by the fact that both the reliance on capital taxation and the efficiency costs of capital tax competition are relatively low in the optimum under the assumed low elasticity of substitution between leisure and private consumption ($\varepsilon = 0.5$). Column (4) of table 5.2 confirms that the quantitative gains from non-cooperation remain well below 0.5 per cent under this extension, even for the small size parameter $s^B = 0.05$.

It is then also obvious how changes in the assumed level of ε will influence the results. A continuous increase in ε (representing a more elastic labour supply) leads to a convergence of the indifference loci in the benchmark and in the wage tax scenarios. In column (5) of table 5.2 we have increased the substitution elasticity between leisure and commodity consumption to $\varepsilon = 1$. Even with this (perhaps unrealistically) high estimate, the gains from tax competition for a country with a share of 10 per cent in the world population remain negligible (around 0.1 per cent), and for $s^B = 0.05$ the gains exceed 1 per cent only in the case where the elasticity of substitution between private and public consumption is also very high ($\sigma = 1.5$). On the other hand, if the labour–leisure distortion is further reduced ($\varepsilon \rightarrow 0$), only wage taxes are employed in equilibrium and capital tax competition becomes irrelevant.

Summing up, the simulation results reported in this section indicate some more clear-cut answers to the question whether small countries can gain from tax competition than the theoretical analysis has been able to provide. While the gains from non-cooperation are potentially large for a small country in the standard one-instrument model of source-based capital tax competition, they are significantly reduced when a second (wage) tax instrument is introduced. Given this more realistic set of tax instruments, moderate differences in country size no longer lead to conflicting interests with respect to tax coordination. Consistent with the examples given at the beginning of this chapter it is still possible, however, that a single very small country can gain from non-cooperation.

5.4 Asymmetric tariff competition

It may be interesting to briefly point out the parallels between our analysis of 'tax wars' in the present chapter and the international trade literature on retaliatory tariff-setting. The crucial difference is that, in the case of tariffs, it is a negative terms of trade externality rather than a positive tax base effect that underlies the incentive to deviate from the cooperative equilibrium. Hence, while the larger country will again have the higher tax (tariff) rate in the Nash equilibrium, it is now the large rather than the small country that may benefit from non-cooperation.

The pioneering analysis of this issue is Johnson (1953/4) who already delineates different regimes, depending on whether both countries lose or one country gains from tariff competition. His analysis is cast in terms of elasticities of import demand rather than differences in country size, but we have seen above that the two are directly linked to each other if other differences between countries are absent.

Johnson's analysis has been taken up by Kennan and Riezman (1988), who set up a simple exchange model of tariff competition with identical Cobb–Douglas preferences in both countries. In this model, 'size' is determined by the distribution of the world endowment in the two traded goods between the two countries. This framework allows us to link the existence of different regimes directly to the distribution of initial endowments. Kennan and Riezman derive areas where non-cooperation benefits one of the competing countries, similar to figure 5.1 above, and conclude from their model that 'the possibility that one side or the other could win a tariff war is by no means remote' (1988, p. 84).

More detailed computable general equilibrium analyses of tariff competition between the United States and Canada show that the precise modelling of the production side is crucial for the possibility of the large country (the United States) to gain from non-cooperation. Markusen and Wigle (1989) incorporate two extensions of the standard optimal tariff model, given by scale economies and imperfect competition on the one hand, and capital mobility on the other. Consistent with the theoretical predictions, the simulation results demonstrate that Nash equilibrium tariff rates are much smaller than those derived from the standard competitive trade model, and approach values that can be observed empirically. In this model, even if the United States is ten times as large as Canada (as measured by GDP), it loses slightly from tariff competition (ca. 0.02 per cent of GDP), whereas the losses for Canada are much larger (ca. 2 per cent of GDP).

Perroni and Whalley (2000) calculate Nash equilibrium tariffs in a seven-region model with trade in differentiated products. Their focus is on the insurance function that regional trade agreements offer to small countries, by increasing their market power towards third states. Applied to the US-Canadian free trade agreement (CUFTA), Perroni and Whalley calculate that the insurance value of this agreement was large for Canada, whereas it reduced welfare in the United States, relative to the non-cooperative equilibrium. From these results they argue that the implicit side payments made by Canada in this agreement can be seen as a compensation to the United States for giving up its monopoly power *vis-à-vis* its small neighbour.

5.5 The 'third country problem' and the regional coordination of capital income taxes

Our analysis in this chapter has focused on the potential for conflicting interests with respect to capital tax coordination within a tax union like the European Union. While the results from the highly stylised model of asymmetric capital tax competition can clearly not claim any direct policy relevance, they nevertheless suggest that the chances for realising policy agreements on capital tax policy within the European Union should not be underestimated. The most recent developments indicate that a broad political consensus exists in the Union for coordination measures in the area of interest income taxation, and an internal political agreement on these issues may indeed be possible (cf. subsection 2.1.1).

At the same time, the focus of attention has shifted to a fundamental weakness of *regional* tax coordination, since capital flight may also occur to third countries. This issue has been left out in the discussion of this chapter so far, and will now be addressed.

One response to the 'third-country problem' is to aim for global tax coordination, embodied in an institution like a World Tax Organisation (cf. Tanzi, 1999). At this point, however, there are few signs suggesting that a worldwide solution to the problem of capital flight is a feasible option. For this reason, regional trading blocs like the European Union face the issue whether internal coordination measures can be welfare improving, given that coordination measures with the rest of the world cannot be enacted.

A systematic approach to address this question can be based on our discussion of constrained-efficient tax competition in subsection 4.3.2. We have seen there that the scope for the regional coordination of capital income taxes is determined by the polar cases of the small country analysis in Razin and Sadka (1991a) on the one hand, and the analysis of worldwide coordination in Bucovetsky and Wilson (1991) on the other. It is clear from these analyses that the size of the integrating region in the world economy, and hence its influence on the world interest rate, is of crucial importance for the question whether tax coordination can be welfare improving. Another determinant, not covered in the analyses above, concerns the degree of international capital mobility. We have already discussed empirical evidence suggesting that capital may not be perfectly mobile worldwide (see subsection 4.2.2). Imperfect mobility of portfolio capital may explain, for example, why many EU countries levy no withholding taxes on the interest income earned by foreigners, even if there is a withholding tax on such income for domestic residents (cf. table 2.1). It has been shown by Janeba and Peters (1999) that this discriminatory tax treatment is rational from the perspective of each country, as it allows to tax the interest income of a risk-averse segment of the domestic population while at the same time competing for internationally mobile financial capital.

Under such conditions there remains some scope for a coordinated tax policy in a relatively large trading bloc like the European Union, even if the effectiveness of any regional coordination measure is reduced by the possibility of capital flight to third countries. In principle, there are then two alternative ways to enforce the taxation of interest income within the tax union. One is to levy withholding taxes on all interest payments to EU residents; this method effectively relies on the source principle of capital taxation. Alternatively, banks or governments in one member state can notify the tax authorities in other member states of cross-country interest payments made; this type of information exchange would aim at enforcing the residence principle of capital income taxation (cf. subsection 4.1.2).[8]

We first turn to residence-based solutions to tax international interest income. There are two different schemes to improve international information exchange. The less demanding, but also less effective alternative is the exchange of information between tax authorities. An attempt in this direction has been made in the Union after the failure to impose a common withholding tax on interest income in 1989. However, even this relatively modest proposal did not meet unanimous approval in the Union, Luxembourg being the country that voted against it. Furthermore, the effectiveness of such a policy is limited when tax administrators do not have independent information on the interest payments that domestic banks make to foreigners (Frank, 1991). The more effective, but also more demanding scheme implies an automatic notification of the foreign tax authorities by the bank that pays out the interest income. The main drawback of this solution is that it meets serious obstacles in those countries where bank secrecy laws have a long-standing tradition.

The degree of voluntary information transmission between governments was first modelled by Bacchetta and Espinosa (1995). They consider a two-country model where each government has complete information over domestic investments, but is fully dependent on information supplied by the foreign government if it wants to tax the foreign-source earnings of its residents. Governments play a static two-stage game: they decide first on the level of information transmitted to the

[8] Recall from section 2.1.1 that the 1998 proposal of the European Commission to enforce the taxation of interest income in Europe (European Communities – Commission, 1998a) gave each member country a choice between these two alternatives.

other government, and then on the domestic tax rate. The analysis of Bacchetta and Espinosa (1995) shows that in a static one-shot game there is no incentive for voluntary information transmission if a pure residence principle applies to the taxation of capital income. In the presence of source taxes, however, governments may have an incentive to transmit information, as this will tend to increase the optimal source tax levied by their neighbours and thus reduce capital flight from the domestic economy. Furthermore, if the analysis is extended to allow for repeated interaction between governments, then a positive level of information transmission may be an equilibrium outcome even under purely residence-based capital taxation (Bacchetta and Espinosa, 2000).

Turning now to the analysis of source-based withholding taxes on interest income, the argument for a positive coordinated tax rate can be based on differential transaction costs within and outside the Union. For example, if exchange rate risk is an important factor determining the mobility of portfolio capital, then the mobility of international capital flows should be much greater within the Union as compared to investments in third countries. There is indeed empirical evidence for this proposition both under the European Monetary System (EMS) (Bhandari and Mayer, 1990) and, more recently, in the European Monetary Union (EMU) (Portes and Rey, 2000). When EU bonds are virtually perfect substitutes it is straightforward to show that small EU members will not be able to tax either foreigners or domestic residents on their interest income. For the Union as a whole, however, the optimal *common* withholding tax will be positive, since transaction costs and exchange rate risk limit capital flows to third countries (Genser and Haufler, 1996a).

A more detailed three-country model of interest withholding taxation is set up by Huizinga and Nielsen (2000a), who consider a large EU country facing competition from both a small EU country and an outside tax haven. Under the assumption that transaction costs within Europe are lower than for portfolio investments in the rest of the world, they show that the Nash equilibrium features positive withholding tax rates in both EU countries. Furthermore, a forced increase in the tax rate of the small EU country will generally benefit the larger EU member.

Even in the absence of transaction costs, the coordination of withholding taxes in a regional tax union is welfare improving, if the union is not small in the world economy. Konrad and Schjelderup (1999) consider a set of identical countries, a subgroup of which coordinates their source taxes on capital. They show that this measure will improve welfare within *and* outside the tax union, provided that tax rates in the initial non-cooperative Nash equilibrium are strategic complements. In this case, the coordinated increase in the capital tax rate of the union countries will cause the non-union countries to respond by increasing their own tax rates. This in turn relaxes the constraint of external capital flight faced by the union countries and reinforces the welfare gains that they can reap from the internal coordination measure.

The discussion so far has shown that both information exchange and withholding taxation are possible – though only partial – solutions for a tax union, provided that it either has some influence in world capital markets or is able to partially shield itself from capital flight to third countries through the existence of positive transaction costs. A relevant policy question is then whether the Union should prefer a source-based withholding scheme or a residence-based system of information exchange to secure a partial taxation of capital income. This issue is addressed by Huizinga and Nielsen (2000b). Their model features a repeated game between governments, an independent banking sector and positive transaction costs. Hence the model captures the arguments for positive levels of both information exchange and withholding taxation. The analytical results of Huizinga and Nielsen (2000b) show that the comparison between the two policy alternatives depends crucially on the level of bank profits on the one hand, and the marginal costs of public funds on the other. Furthermore, simulation results for countries of different size demonstrate the interesting possibility that the larger country selects an information exchange system while the smaller country opts for a withholding tax. The intuition for this result in a repeated game setting is that the information exchange system allows the large country to punish the small country severely (by withholding all information), if the latter adopts an 'aggressive' policy of choosing a low withholding tax rate.

A crucial question is then how large the welfare gains are that can be expected from capital tax coordination. A first attempt to answer this issue is made in Sørensen (2000), who uses a multi-country general equilibrium model that allows for the interaction of national tax policies. An important feature of this model is that there are two counteracting incentives for strategic tax policies. On the one hand, there is the usual tax base externality, which tends to reduce non-coordinated capital tax rates below their globally optimal levels. On the other hand, the model includes pure profits which partly accrue to foreigners. As discussed in section 3.1, this introduces a negative fiscal externality and may lead to non-coordinated capital taxes exceeding their coordinated levels. Hence, global or regional tax coordination in this model may generally raise or lower Nash equilibrium taxes, depending on which of the two fiscal externalities dominates.

Simulation results with this model indicate that *global* coordination of capital taxes among symmetric countries achieves welfare gains in the range of 1 per cent of GDP. *Regional* coordination among the EU countries (which are assumed in the model to comprise 40 per cent of the world population) is far less effective, however. With perfect capital mobility, the gains from either a regional residence principle or a regional withholding tax remain below 0.1 per cent of GDP. If imperfect capital mobility is introduced, using a nested CES function (cf. section 5.3) with a substitution elasticity of $\sigma = 4$ between union and non-union assets, then the gains from regional tax coordination increase to roughly 0.5 per cent of GDP. Nevertheless, as Sørensen (2000) concludes, the overall efficiency gains from a regional coordination of capital income taxes are likely to be modest.

This conclusion is reinforced if other tax avoidance strategies are taken into account. As emphasised by Alworth (1998), the recent growth of financial derivative instruments constitutes an additional and serious problem for a coordinated EU tax on interest income. Financial derivatives allow us to duplicate risk-free portfolio investments by a combination of other instruments that are difficult to tax in a consistent manner. This will give large investors, in particular, a further possibility to circumvent taxes on the returns from government bonds or other forms of interest income.

The final issue concerns the equity effects of a regionally coordinated tax on interest income. Sørensen (2000) simulates a scenario where the population of each union country is broken up into different income groups and finds that the distributive effects of regional tax coordination are both substantial and progressive (i.e. redistributing from richer to poorer households). Sørensen's simulation does not, however, include differential transaction costs for different groups of savers. For the incidence of a regionally coordinated tax on interest income a critical issue is which groups have sufficiently low personal transaction costs of investing in *third* countries, in order to avoid the tax. This group is likely to consist mainly of large investors who are able to take advantage of scale economies involved in international investments and reduce exchange rate risk by diversifying their foreign-asset portfolios. Hence, even if this group is relatively small, the volume of capital flight caused by a coordinated EU tax on interest income may be substantial. This not only reduces the effectiveness of the coordination measure as a revenue-raising device, but it also implies that the tax may be paid primarily by small savers.

6 Factor taxation and income distribution

Chapter 5 has focused on the distributive effects of tax competition and tax coordination *between* different countries, while the effects of capital taxation on the distribution of income *within* each country has been ignored in the representative-agent framework employed. To be sure, in the benchmark case of a small open economy that is perfectly integrated in world capital markets (see section 4.2) the incidence of all taxes is always fully on labour. Hence, in this model there is no equity–efficiency trade-off for capital taxation. However, our further discussion has indicated that perfect capital mobility cannot be assumed, in general. In particular, our review of the empirical evidence in section 4.4 has shown that effective rates of capital taxation have fallen only slightly in the OECD average, and have indeed risen in several countries since the 1980s (cf. table 4.1).

Many observers believe that distributional effects play an important role in explaining these stylised facts. Sørensen (1995), for example, addresses the question of whether source-based corporate taxes will disappear under growing international mobility of capital as follows:

> However, there are several reasons why the corporate income tax will hardly vanish in the long run, despite the growing international mobility of capital. First of all, it may be politically infeasible to impose high explicit taxes on immobile factors, and the government may therefore have to tax these factors indirectly through the source-based corporate income tax, even though this involves a higher efficiency cost. (Sørensen, 1995, p. 290)

In this chapter we analyse the interaction of efficiency and equity effects in determining the optimal mix of capital and wage taxation. To study this trade-off, we introduce positive transaction costs for international capital flows, which limit capital mobility. The distributive concerns of governments arise from their desire to maximise the political support from voters, but it should be stressed at the outset that a conventional analysis of social welfare maximisation would yield formally similar results. It will be shown that such a framework is capable, in principle, of explaining rising rates of capital taxation in one of the competing countries.

One of the first and most widely quoted contributions on the interaction of efficiency and distributive effects of capital taxation in open economies is Persson and Tabellini (1992). Their median voter model is described in some detail in section 6.1. Section 6.2 then presents an alternative approach that is based on governments maximising a political support function. Section 6.3 analyses the Nash equilibrium in this model and section 6.4 derives the comparative static effects of capital market integration. Section 6.5 compares the results to the findings of Persson and Tabellini and other contributions related to our analysis. Finally, section 6.6 reviews some analyses that study the welfare effects of centralised vs. decentralised capital taxation from a political economy perspective.

6.1 Capital taxation in a median voter model

Persson and Tabellini (1992) set up a two-country, two-period model of redistributive capital taxation. In both countries, each individual is given an endowment in the first period and decides how much and where to invest it. Individuals have the same preferences but differ in their first-period endowments. Investment in both countries takes the form of a simple storing technology where each unit not consumed in the first period is transformed into one unit of output in the second period. Hence the interest rate is fixed at zero and there are no decreasing returns to investment. With source-based capital taxes, this technology also implies that any tax differential between the countries would lead to a corner solution, implying that all investment takes place in the low-tax region. To avoid this, international capital flows are subject to convex 'mobility costs', which represent a simple way of covering the extra complications of foreign operations, such as additional information requirements or diverging regulations between countries. At the same time, the imperfect international mobility of capital ensures that a tax on capital will not be fully shifted to labour so that efficiency and equity effects interact in non-trivial ways.

The only tax instrument in the model of Persson and Tabellini (1992) is a source-based tax on the capital stock installed in the second period. The proceeds from the tax are returned as equal lump-sum payments to each individual, implying that the tax is used exclusively for redistributive purposes. The distribution of endowments in each country is skewed to the left so that the median voter receives a net income gain from a positive tax on capital.

The game structure of the model is as follows: in the first stage, the policy-maker (i.e. the government) is elected in each country under majority rule. In the second stage, policy-makers in both countries simultaneously decide on the capital tax rates. In the third stage, private investors make their investment decisions.

Since production technologies and overall capital endowments in both countries are identical, foreign investment will occur only if tax rates differ across countries. Different distributions of endowments are permitted in the Persson and Tabellini model, however, so that capital tax competition will generally be asymmetric and tax rates will differ across countries. In general, there will therefore be counteracting tax base and terms of trade effects from the perspective of the low-tax country, which attracts foreign capital (cf. section 3.1).

Persson and Tabellini analyse the effects that capital market integration, as represented by a reduction in mobility costs, has on the optimal tax rates set by both governments. They find that lower mobility costs unambiguously reduce the tax rate chosen by the high-tax country, for which only the tax base externality is relevant. In contrast, the low-tax country may either raise or lower its tax rate, depending on whether the terms of trade or the tax base externality dominates in the initial equilibrium.

The focus of the analysis is, however, on the first stage of the game. This is best seen for the case of symmetric countries, where increased tax competition (i.e. a higher degree of capital mobility) unambiguously reduces the capital tax rate in both countries. By the sequence of events assumed in this model, the voting majority rationally anticipates the effects that increased tax competition has on the tax policy chosen by the government. Since voters thus do not take the tax rate of the foreign country as given, they delegate tax policy to a government *to the left* of the median voter (i.e. to an individual with a higher preference for redistribution), expecting correctly that the higher domestic capital tax rate set by this government will also induce the foreign government to increase its tax rate. Hence, endogenising the political process serves as a partial solution to the typical prisonner's dilemma situation faced by competing governments, once elected.

In this model, the economic and political effects of capital market integration always work in opposite directions. However, Persson and Tabellini also show that the 'economic effect' of capital market integration (the increased competition for capital, as perceived by elected policy-makers) dominates the 'political effect' (the change in the election behaviour of voters). Hence, provided that tax base effects dominate in both countries, capital tax rates will be unambiguously lowered in both countries as a consequence of capital market integration. Finally, capital market integration generally reduces the capital tax rate of the high-tax country by more than the tax rate of its low-tax neighbour, so that the model predicts a convergence of capital tax rates in response to higher capital mobility.

In the following we will present an alternative approach, which differs from the Persson and Tabellini analysis in two main respects. First, production is modelled explicitly and governments solve a conventional optimal tax problem, choosing between a wage tax and a source tax on capital in order to meet a fixed revenue constraint. This setup allows us to link our analysis more closely to the other chapters in this part of the book, and to most of the other literature on capital tax competition. Second, and more important for our central result, we employ an alternative model of the political equilibrium by assuming that the government maximises a political support function where workers and capitalists are the only two interest groups. In this model, the effects of capital market integration on the distribution of factor incomes are exactly opposed for the capital exporter and the capital importer. In contrast to the findings by Persson and Tabellini, distributive effects may then lead to a capital tax increase in the exporting country, and to diverging rates of capital taxation.

6.2 An alternative model of interest groups

Our analysis is based on a static model of capital tax competition between two countries which produce a homogeneous output good using internationally mobile capital and internationally immobile labour.[1] This model is extended to allow for mobility costs and we distinguish between two income groups, workers and capitalists, in each country. Individuals in each group are homogeneous and workers supply only labour whereas capital owners do not work.[2] Countries are endowed with fixed amounts of labour and capital. All endowments are normalised to unity and hence are equal across countries.

[1] The analysis in sections 6.2–6.4 is revised and adapted from Haufler (1997).

[2] Taken literally, this rigid class structure is clearly not justified from an empirical perspective, nor from a lifecycle savings approach. However, all that is needed in our model is that, for example, a labour tax falls relatively more on one income group ('the poor') than on the other ('the rich'). Assuming that the second group earns no labour income at all is then merely a simplifying device that does not qualitatively affect any results.

Governments have two tax instruments at their disposal, a wage tax and a source tax on capital. In the following, we first describe the production relationships and international arbitrage in the capital market and then turn to the optimal tax problem faced by each country's government.

A standard assumption in the literature on capital tax competition is that production functions are identical across countries. Furthermore, in the present context there is little to be gained from generality with respect to the underlying production structure. We therefore assume a quadratic technology, which leads to several convenient simplifications and allows us to focus more closely on the issues specific to the present two-class model. Denoting countries as usual by superscripts $i \in \{A, B\}$, these assumptions imply

$$f(k^i, 1) = \left(a - bk^i\right)k^i \quad \forall\, i \in \{A, B\}, \qquad a > 0,\;\; b > 0,$$

where the input of labour is fixed at unity and k^i is the amount of capital used in each region (and is equal to the capital–labour ratio). Assuming that the technology parameter a is sufficiently large, relative to b, the quadratic production function exhibits the usual property of a positive but falling marginal productivity of capital

$$f' = a - 2bk^i > 0, \qquad f'' = -2b < 0. \tag{6.1}$$

With the capital endowment of each country normalised to one, the full employment condition for this factor is

$$k^A + k^B = 2. \tag{6.2}$$

Capital exports are subject to convex transaction costs, as in the analysis of Persson and Tabellini (1992). The existence of transaction costs can be motivated by the (albeit mixed) empirical evidence discussed in subsection 4.2.2. In the present setting, transaction costs are required despite the presence of diminishing returns to capital in each location, because the effects of capital market integration will be modelled as an exogenous decrease in the extra costs of foreign investment.[3] Furthermore, as we will see below, specifying convex rather than linear transaction costs will ensure that the responsiveness of the capital tax base to a domestic tax increase will depend on the mobility cost para-

[3] This is a standard procedure in models of international taxation that will be used again in our analysis of cross-border shopping in chapter 8. Note, however, that the costs of foreign investment may themselves be regarded as a policy instrument, as is the case in the literature on capital controls. For analyses of the latter in a political economy context see, for example, Alesina and Tabellini (1989) and Schulze (2000).

meter. This model element thus incorporates in a simple way the idea that the efficiency costs of capital taxation are rising when capital becomes more mobile internationally.

The simplest functional form consistent with these properties specifies transaction costs τ as a quadratic function of the volume of foreign investment

$$\tau = \frac{1}{2}\,\beta(1-k^i)^2, \qquad \beta > 0, \tag{6.3}$$

where we assume that the transaction cost function is identical for both countries (since τ is not indexed) and $(1-k^i)$ are the capital exports of country i. By equating gross and net trade flows, this specification implies that capital flows only in one direction in equilibrium. The derivatives of (6.3) with respect to $(1-k^i)$ are

$$\tau' = \beta(1-k^i), \qquad \tau'' = \beta. \tag{6.4}$$

Arbitrage by capitalists ensures that international differences in the net-of-tax return to capital must be equal to the marginal transaction costs incurred in equilibrium. Assuming again that the tax rates on capital, t^i, are unit taxes,[4] the arbitrage condition is

$$f'(k^i) - t^i = f'(k^j) - t^j - \beta(1-k^i) \quad \forall\, i,j \in \{A,B\},\ i \neq j. \tag{6.5}$$

When country i is the capital exporter, $f'(k^j) - t^j > f'(k^i) - t^i$ must hold in the trade equilibrium. It then follows from the assumption of equal endowments and technologies and the falling marginal productivity of capital that the country with the higher tax rate on capital must always be the capital exporter. This feature, which our model shares with that of Persson and Tabellini (1992), is important for the discussion of whether capital market integration leads to a convergence of capital tax rates between the trading countries.

From the capital market clearing condition (6.2) and the arbitrage condition (6.5), the capital employment in each region can be determined as a function of the two capital tax rates, the technology constant b, and the transaction cost parameter β. Using (6.1) gives after straightforward manipulations

$$k^i(t^i,t^j,\beta) = 1 - \frac{(t^i - t^j)}{4b+\beta} \qquad \forall\, i,j \in \{A,B\},\ i \neq j, \tag{6.6}$$

with first- and second-order derivatives

[4] This implies that transaction costs are not deductible from the capital tax base.

$$\frac{\partial k^i}{\partial t^i} = \frac{-1}{4b+\beta} < 0, \quad \frac{\partial k^i}{\partial t^j} = \frac{1}{4b+\beta} > 0, \quad \frac{\partial k^i}{\partial \beta} = \frac{(t^i - t^j)}{(4b+\beta)^2} \gtreqless 0 \text{ if } t^i \gtreqless t^j,$$
$$\frac{\partial^2 k^i}{\partial t^i\, \partial \beta} = \frac{1}{(4b+\beta)^2} > 0, \quad \frac{\partial^2 k^i}{\partial t^j\, \partial \beta} = \frac{-1}{(4b+\beta)^2} < 0. \tag{6.7}$$

In each country i, an increase in the domestic capital tax rate t^i causes a capital outflow and reduces the amount of capital employed in this country, whereas an increase in the foreign country's tax rate t^j has the opposite effect. An increase in the transaction cost parameter β reduces capital flows for any given tax differential; this increases the capital stock in the capital exporting region and decreases it in the capital importing region.

Note further from the derivative $\partial k^i/\partial t^i$ in (6.7) that the capital outflow caused by a domestic tax increase will be larger if the transaction cost parameter β is small. Hence, owing to the convexity of the transaction cost function, the efficiency costs of capital taxation will increase in the present model as a result of capital market integration.[5]

We assume that governments in both regions face fixed, non-negative revenue constraints T_0^i and have two tax instruments at their disposal. These are the unit tax on capital (t^i) and a tax on wages (t_w^i). Either of the two taxes (but not both) can be negative, as long as the overall revenue requirement is met. Since labour supply in each country is fixed and labour is immobile across countries, the wage tax represents a lump-sum instrument in the present model. To determine the optimal mix of tax rates (t^i, t_w^i) we first derive the comparative static effects of each tax on the consumption levels of workers (denoted by a subscript L) and capitalists (subscript K). Using (6.1) the workers' budget constraint in each country is given by

$$c_L^i = f(k^i, 1) - f'(k^i)k^i - t_w^i = b(k^i)^2 - t_w^i \quad \forall\, i \in \{A, B\}. \tag{6.8}$$

The income of capitalists must be determined separately for the two countries if mobility costs are present. Capitalists in the exporting state own some assets in both jurisdictions whereas capitalists in the importing country invest everything at home. Let us assume – exogenously, for the moment – that country A is the capital exporter whenever capital flows occur in equilibrium.[6] Thus $1 - k^A \geq 0$ and $1 - k^B \leq 0$. We also assume

[5] The reader can easily verify that if transaction costs were linear in the level of capital flows, then the derivative $\partial k^i/\partial t^i$ would depend only on the production parameter b, but not on the degree of capital market integration (β).

[6] In the following section, we will *derive* this equilibrium from differences in the political weights of workers in the two countries. A more general modelling strategy that introduces different regimes will be presented in chapter 8.

that all transaction costs τ (6.3) must be borne by the capital exporter. Then the net income of capitalists in the two countries is

$$c_K^A = k^A\left[f'(k^A) - t^A\right] + (1 - k^A)\left[f'(k^B) - t^B\right] - \tau = f'(k^A) - t^A + \tau,$$
$$c_K^B = f'(k^B) - t^B, \tag{6.9}$$

where the second step in the equation for c_K^A has used the arbitrage condition (6.5) and the transaction cost function (6.3). The effects of the labour tax on the feasible consumption levels of workers and capitalists are determined by differentiating (6.8) and (6.9) with respect to t_w^i. This yields

$$\frac{\partial c_L^i}{\partial t_w^i} = -1 \quad \forall\, i \in \{A, B\}, \tag{6.10}$$

$$\frac{\partial c_K^i}{\partial t_w^i} = 0 \quad \forall\, i \in \{A, B\}. \tag{6.11}$$

Since labour supply is fixed, the wage tax falls exclusively on labour and leads to a one-to-one reduction in the net wage while capital income remains unaffected.

Similarly, the effects of the capital tax are obtained by differentiating (6.8) and (6.9) with respect to t^i. These effects differ for the capital exporter (country A) and the capital importer (country B). Substituting in from (6.1), (6.3) and (6.7) gives

$$\frac{\partial c_L^i}{\partial t^i} = \frac{-2bk^i}{4b + \beta} < 0 \quad \forall\, i \in \{A, B\}, \tag{6.12}$$

$$\frac{\partial c_K^A}{\partial t^A} = \frac{-2b - k^A\beta}{4b + \beta} < 0, \qquad \frac{\partial c_K^B}{\partial t^B} = \frac{-2b - \beta}{4b + \beta} < 0. \tag{6.13}$$

In each country, the imposition of a capital tax is borne jointly by capitalists and workers. The tax reduces wage income by lowering the capital–labour ratio and hence the marginal productivity of labour in the taxing jurisdiction. The net return to capital must also fall in both regions. Note that the two equations in (6.13) coincide when the transaction cost parameter β is zero, or when the equilibrium is symmetric and $k^A = k^B = 1$.

We can now turn to the constrained optimisation problem faced by the two regions. Each government maximises a function $\Pi^i[u_L^i(c_L^i), u_K^i(c_K^i)]$ that depends positively on the utilities of both classes, which in turn are exclusively determined by the consumption levels (or net factor incomes) of each group. In principle, this function can be viewed either as a social welfare function or as a political support function. We adopt the latter interpretation here, in line with most of the literature on redistributive taxation and social insurance under conditions of increasing factor market integration. This implies a view of the government that, in its own self-interest, balances the diverging interests of different groups. While the political process is not modelled explicitly, the political support function provides a simple way to describe how policy responds to exogenous shocks in order to maintain a political equilibrium.[7]

Budget balance in each country requires $T_0^i = t_w^i + t^i k^i$, leading to the Lagrangians

$$\mathcal{L}^i = \Pi^i[u_L^i(c_L^i), u_K^i(c_K^i)] + \lambda^i(t_w^i + t^i k^i - T_0^i) \quad \forall\, i \in \{A, B\}. \tag{6.14}$$

Differentiating with respect to t_w^i and substituting in from (6.10) and (6.11) gives the first-order condition for the wage tax

$$\frac{\partial \mathcal{L}^i}{\partial t_w^i} = -\frac{\partial \Pi^i}{\partial u_L^i}\frac{du_L^i}{dc_L^i} + \lambda^i = 0 \quad \forall\, i \in \{A, B\}. \tag{6.15}$$

Thus the Lagrange parameter λ^i is simply the marginal political support that policymakers derive from an increase in labour income. This is intuitive since the Lagrange parameter gives the shadow price of public revenues, and the wage tax offers an instrument to transfer one unit of income from workers to the government.

The first-order condition for the optimal use of the capital tax is derived analogously. Differentiating (6.14) with respect to t^i gives

$$\frac{\partial \mathcal{L}^i}{\partial t^i} = \frac{\partial \Pi^i}{\partial u_L^i}\frac{du_L^i}{dc_L^i}\frac{\partial c_L^i}{\partial t^i} + \frac{\partial \Pi^i}{\partial u_K^i}\frac{du_K^i}{dc_K^i}\frac{\partial c_K^i}{\partial t^i} + \lambda^i\left(k^i + t^i\frac{\partial k^i}{\partial t^i}\right) = 0 \;\forall\; i \in \{A, B\}. \tag{6.16}$$

In the following analysis, it will be useful to specify the political support function Π^i in more detail. A frequently used formulation is that political support is a weighted average of the utility levels attained by different income groups, and the utility of each group is a concave function of its own level of income (cf. Peltzman, 1976; Hillman, 1982). In the present model this implies $\partial \Pi^i / \partial u_L^i = s_L^i$ and $\partial \Pi^i / \partial u_K^i = s_K^i$, where

[7] As shown by Grossman and Helpman (1994), the political support function can be seen as the 'reduced form' of an explicit political model where each interest group provides a contribution that depends on the chosen policy vector, and the government maximises the sum of contributions and general well-being.

s_L^i and s_K^i represent exogenous political weights of workers and capitalists which may, for example, indicate the size of the two groups. A non-increasing marginal utility of income is represented by a CES function of the form[8]

$$\Pi^i = \frac{1}{\rho}\left[s_L^i \cdot (c_L^i)^\rho + s_K^i \cdot (c_K^i)^\rho\right] \quad \forall \quad i \in \{A, B\}, \quad 1 \geq \rho > -\infty. \tag{6.17}$$

This specification allows us to clearly distinguish between the political weights s_L^i and s_K^i and the elasticity parameter ρ, which is assumed to be equal across countries. The lower is ρ, the more concave is the utility function of each group, and the more difficult is it to substitute political support from workers for that of capitalists, or vice versa. The marginal political impact of each income group is thus determined jointly by this group's exogenous political weight, its income level and the elasticity ρ.

Next, we introduce the government's marginal rate of substitution between the support from workers and capitalists. Differentiating (6.17) with respect to the consumption levels of both income groups, this is given by

$$m^i(c_L^i, c_K^i) \equiv \frac{\partial \Pi^i / \partial c_K^i}{\partial \Pi^i / \partial c_L^i} = \frac{s_K^i}{s_L^i}\left(\frac{c_K^i}{c_L^i}\right)^{\rho-1} \qquad \forall\, i \in \{A, B\}. \tag{6.18}$$

Country-specific first-order conditions for the capital tax are obtained by inserting the partial derivatives from (6.7), (6.12) and (6.13) into (6.16). Furthermore, we can substitute out for λ^i using (6.15) and multiply through by $(4b + \beta)/(\partial \Pi^i / \partial c_L^i)$. The resulting, modified first-order conditions are denoted by F^i. Using (6.18) these are given by

$$F^A(t^A, t^B, \beta) = (2b + \beta)k^A - t^A - m^A(2b + \beta k^A) = 0, \tag{6.19}$$
$$F^B(t^A, t^B, \beta) = (2b + \beta)k^B - t^B - m^B(2b + \beta) = 0. \tag{6.20}$$

The functions F^i in (6.19)–(6.20) depend on the capital tax rate of region j through the terms k^i (cf. (6.6)), and represent best-response functions for the capital exporter and the capital importer, respectively. Incorporated in each country's best response for the capital tax rate is the optimal adjustment of wage taxes in the political equilibrium.

[8] If a graphical representation of this function is drawn in *income* space, then an iso-political support curve is a straight line for $\rho = 1$, but is L-shaped for $\rho \to -\infty$. Note, however, that in terms of the usual classification of social welfare functions (e.g. Atkinson and Stiglitz 1980, pp. 339–40) the entire class of functions considered here is of the Bentham type, since governments always maximize a (weighted) sum of individual *utilities*.

6.3 Nash equilibrium

A general problem in models of tax competition is that reaction functions may not be continuous, and hence a Nash equilibrium may not exist. This problem has not attracted much attention in the literature on capital tax competition, where the continuity of reaction functions is often simply assumed (e.g. Wilson, 1991, p. 433). The literature on commodity tax competition has shown, however, that the issue becomes important in the presence of transaction costs, and a critical point occurs when countries switch from the high-tax to the low-tax regime. We will discuss this point in detail in our analysis of cross-border shopping (section 8.4). For the purposes of our analysis here, it suffices to know that the chosen transaction cost specification ensures that best-response functions are continuous at the switch of regimes. The continuity of reaction functions implies, in particular, the existence of a symmetric Nash equilibrium when countries are identical in all respects. In the symmetric equilibrium $k^A = k^B = 1$ and (6.19)–(6.20) simultaneously reduce to

$$F^i = (2b + \beta)\,(1 - m^i) - t^i = 0 \quad \Leftrightarrow \quad (1 - m^i) = \frac{t^i}{2b + \beta} \quad \forall\, i \in \{A, B\}. \tag{6.21}$$

In the symmetric case both countries choose a positive tax rate on capital if and only if the policy-maker's marginal rate of substituting labour income for capital income is less than unity. In the second formulation of (6.21), the left-hand side gives the marginal gains from using the capital tax instrument, i.e. the increase in political support when one dollar of tax revenue is raised from capitalists as opposed to workers. On the right-hand side are the marginal revenue losses to the economy incurred by levying a tax on internationally mobile capital as opposed to internationally immobile labour. These losses are increasing in the equilibrium capital tax t^i, which gives the wedge between the social return to one unit of capital employed in the home country (the sum of tax revenues and the net return earned by capitalists) and the social return to one unit of capital invested abroad (which is only the net return to domestic investors). In the optimum, each government balances the marginal political gains and the marginal efficiency losses of using the capital tax instrument, as opposed to an exclusive reliance on wage taxation.

To link the condition for a positive capital tax rate to the values of exogenous model parameters we substitute (6.1), (6.8), (6.9) and (6.18) into (6.21) and note that $k^A = k^B = 1$ in the symmetric equilibrium.

Furthermore we assume as a benchmark that the government revenue requirement is exclusively financed by the wage tax ($T_0^i = t_w^i$) and consider the value of m^i at this point. The results are summarised in

Proposition 6.1
Capital tax rates in the symmetric Nash equilibrium are determined by

$$t^i \gtreqless 0 \iff \frac{s_L^i}{s_K^i}\left(\frac{a-2b}{b-T_0^i}\right)^{1-\rho} \gtreqless 1.$$

From proposition 6.1, it is straightforward to identify the conditions for positive tax rates on capital in the non-cooperative equilibrium. Consider first the special case $\rho = 1$, which implies a constant marginal utility of income for each group. This isolates the role of the exogenous political weights s_L^i, s_K^i and the capital tax rate will be positive if and only if workers have the higher weight in each country's political support function. In the special case where the weights of both income groups are just equal (and $\rho = 1$ still holds), the politician simply maximises national income and the optimal source tax on capital is zero. This result has been discussed in section 4.2 for representative-agent models of small open economies under conditions of perfect capital mobility. In the present model, the result holds even for 'large' countries and imperfect capital mobility because of our simplifying assumption that labour supply is fixed and the wage tax is a lump-sum instrument.

In the more general case $\rho < 1$, additional factors enter the analysis. A high marginal productivity of capital (a high value of $(a - 2b)$ in (6.1)) lowers the marginal utility of income for capitalists and tends to increase the optimal tax rate on capital. Furthermore, a high government revenue requirement T_0^i will also tend to raise the tax rate on capital since an exclusive financing by wage taxes reduces labour income and thus increases the marginal political impact of this group. This last factor is not present in models where the revenue from the capital tax is directly redistributed to workers (Persson and Tabellini, 1992; Lopez, Marchand and Pestieau, 1998).

In the following, we assume that exogenous model parameters are chosen such that capital tax rates are positive in the symmetric Nash equilibrium. The next step is to introduce an asymmetry between the trading countries. We focus on the case where the exogenous political weight of workers is higher in country A than in country B. Starting from the symmetric equilibrium, this is modelled as a small increase in s_L^A holding s_L^B constant. From (6.18) we have $\partial m^A/\partial s_L^A < 0$. It then follows from (6.21) that the impact effect of this shock is to raise the capital tax rate in country A. However, the tax rate in country B may also rise in the new Nash equilibrium. Establishing that the tax increase in country A must dominate in the neighbourhood of a symmetric initial equilibrium requires either a stability argument or the assumption that the Nash equilibrium is unique. The result is summarised in

Proposition 6.2
For small differences between the two countries, there exists a Nash equilibrium in which the country with the higher political weight of workers (country A*) levies the higher tax rate on capital.*

Proof: *See the appendix (p. 124).*
Using proposition 6.2 in the arbitrage condition (6.5) shows that the high-tax country must be the capital exporter when endowments and production functions are identical across countries. In this asymmetric Nash equilibrium country A thus exports capital to the low-tax region B and the pattern of trade flows postulated exogenously in our discussion above is now motivated by cross-country differences in the relative political influence of the two income groups.

6.4 Capital market integration

Capital market integration is modelled as an exogenous reduction in the transaction cost parameter β. Since this change increases the elasticity of the capital tax base, it tends to raise the costs of capital taxation in both countries, relative to the non-distortive wage tax. A complication arises from terms of trade effects, which tend to increase the tax rate of the capital importing region and thus counteract the tax base externality in this country. We have already discussed this issue in our presentation of the Persson and Tabellini model in section 6.1. It will be seen, however, that the quadratic specification of the production and mobility cost functions in the present model ensures that tax base effects dominate terms of trade effects in both countries. In representative consumer models, the outcome of capital market integration will then be an unambiguous shift away from capital and towards wage taxation.[9] Furthermore, under these

[9] This result should be intuitive from the combination of our benchmark analyses in sections 4.2 and 4.3. More generally, Bucovetsky and Wilson (1991, section 3) have shown that any increase in the number of (identical) countries engaged in tax competition will reduce the level of capital taxation at source, relative to the level of wage taxation. Increasing the number of regions in a model without mobility costs raises the elasticity of capital supply in a way that is very similar to the reduction of mobility costs in the present two-country framework.

conditions the same result also arises in the analysis of Persson and Tabellini (cf. section 6.1). The issue here is whether efficiency considerations will also necessarily dominate in both countries under our alternative specification of the political equilibrium.

The importance of distributive effects for tax policy depends crucially on the elasticity parameter ρ in the political support function (6.17). A low level of this parameter ($\rho \to -\infty$) leads to a rigid ratio of net labour income to net capital income. This implies that losers from capital market liberalisation will vigorously oppose the income loss suffered, and the distributive effects of market integration will have strong repercussions on optimal tax policy. On the other hand, if ρ is high ($\rho \to 1$), then a given change in the distribution of income has only minor effects on the policy-maker's marginal rate of substitution between the support from different income groups.

We first analyse the effects on workers' and capitalists' consumption in each country induced by changes in the foreign tax rate and the transaction cost parameter, respectively. All these effects are unambiguous and follow directly from the private budget constraints (6.8)–(6.9), the set of partial derivatives (6.7) and proposition 6.2 (which implies $t^A > t^B$):[10]

$$\frac{\partial c_L^A}{\partial t^B} > 0, \quad \frac{\partial c_K^A}{\partial t^B} < 0, \quad \frac{\partial c_L^B}{\partial t^A} > 0, \quad \frac{\partial c_K^B}{\partial t^A} < 0, \tag{6.22}$$

$$\frac{\partial c_L^A}{\partial \beta} > 0, \quad \frac{\partial c_K^A}{\partial \beta} < 0 \quad \frac{\partial c_L^B}{\partial \beta} < 0, \quad \frac{\partial c_K^B}{\partial \beta} > 0. \tag{6.23}$$

Turning first to the terms collected in (6.22), we see that the effects of a foreign tax change are symmetric in the two countries. An increase in country j's capital tax rate causes capital to flow to region i and benefits workers in region i while making capitalists worse off. On the other hand, it can be seen from (6.23) that the direct effects of capital market integration on the incomes of the two classes are directly opposed in the capital exporting and the capital importing region. At unchanged tax rates, a reduction in β increases country A's capital exports to country

[10] Signing the effects in (6.22) and (6.23) is straightforward, except for the derivative $\partial c_K^A / \partial \beta$. Differentiating (6.9) and substituting in for k^A using (6.6) gives after straightforward manipulations

$$\frac{\partial c_K^A}{\partial \beta} = -[2b + \beta(1 - k^A)] \frac{(t^A - t^B)}{(4b + \beta)^2} + \frac{1}{2}(1 - k^A)^2$$
$$= \frac{-(t^A - t^B)}{2(4b + \beta)^3} \{4b[(4b + \beta) - (t^A - t^B)] + \beta(t^A - t^B)\} < 0,$$

which is negative since (6.6) requires $(4b + \beta) \geq (t^A - t^B)$ from $k^A \geq 0$.

Table 6.1 *Effects of capital market integration on income, by group*

$\beta \downarrow$	Capital exporter (country A)	Capital importer (country B)
Workers	$c_L^A \downarrow$	$c_L^B \uparrow$
Capitalists	$c_K^A \uparrow$	$c_K^B \downarrow$

B. This hurts workers in country A and benefits workers in country B. Capitalists in country B are also hurt by the capital inflow whereas capitalists in country A gain from the increased investment opportunities. For further reference, the results given in (6.23) are summarised in table 6.1.

In both countries, the change in the optimal domestic tax rate on capital in response to the exogenous variation in the transaction cost parameter β is given by the following equation, which is derived in the appendix:

$$\frac{dt^i}{d\beta} = \frac{1}{|\mathcal{J}|}\left[-\frac{\partial F^j}{\partial t^j}\frac{\partial F^i}{\partial \beta} + \frac{\partial F^i}{\partial t^j}\frac{\partial F^j}{\partial \beta}\right] \quad \forall \quad i,j \in \{A,B\},\ i \neq j. \quad (6.24)$$

It is also argued in the appendix that the determinant of the Jacobian matrix $\mathcal{J}$ must be positive. For each country i, there are two effects in (6.24): the first term gives the direct response of country i's optimal capital tax rate to the change in the transaction cost parameter, whereas the second effect describes country i's best response to the induced change in the capital tax rate of country j.

From the second-order condition of each country's optimal tax problem we know that $\partial F^j/\partial t^j < 0 \, \forall j \in \{A,B\}$. In the following, we determine the sign of the other partial derivatives in (6.24) in order to evaluate the overall effects. We first turn to the direct effect of the parameter change on the tax rate of the capital exporting country A. Differentiating (6.19) with respect to β and using (6.18) gives

$$\frac{\partial F^A}{\partial \beta} = \underbrace{(1-m^A)k^A + [2b + (1-m^A)\beta]\,\frac{\partial k^A}{\partial \beta}}_{(+)} \\ + \underbrace{(2b + \beta k^A)\,(1-\rho)m^A\,\frac{c_L^A}{c_K^A}\,\frac{\partial (c_K^A/c_L^A)}{\partial \beta}}_{(-,0)}, \quad (6.25)$$

where the first effect is signed with the help of proposition 6.1 ($m^A < 1$) and (6.7), whereas the signing of the last effect has used (6.23).

From our discussion of the optimal tax condition in the symmetric Nash equilibrium (6.21), the interpretation of (6.25) is straightforward. The first effect gives the increase in the efficiency costs of capital taxation as capital exports increase owing to the lower mobility cost parameter. This effect tends to reduce the optimal level of t^A. On the other hand, a reduction in β also increases the political gains from capital taxation from the perspective of country A's government by lowering labour income and raising the income of capitalists (see table 6.1). This increases the marginal political impact of workers, relative to capitalists, and tends to push the capital tax rate upward. Note that this effect is absent, and the second term equals zero, when the marginal utility of income is constant for each group ($\rho = 1$).

Next, we consider the direct effect of the reduction in β on the optimal tax rate in the capital importing country B. Differentiating (6.20) gives[11]

$$\frac{\partial F^B}{\partial \beta} = \underbrace{(1 - m^B) - 2b\,\frac{\partial k^B}{\partial \beta}}_{(+)} + \underbrace{(2b + \beta)\,(1 - \rho)m^B\,\frac{c_L^B}{c_K^B}\,\frac{\partial (c_K^B/c_L^B)}{\partial \beta}}_{(+,0)} > 0. \tag{6.26}$$

As before, the signing of individual effects has used (6.7) and (6.23) while $m^B < 1$ must hold in the neighbourhood of a symmetric equilibrium. A lower level of β leads to increased efficiency costs of capital taxation for the capital importer, despite the fact that a source tax on capital improves country B's terms of trade by reducing its net import demand for capital. However under a quadratic specification of the production and mobility cost functions this terms of trade gain is dominated by the higher tax base loss incurred from capital taxation.[12] In contrast to the capital exporter, a reduction in β also lowers the political benefits of capital taxation in country B (for $\rho < 1$), where capital market integration causes a redistribution of income from capitalists to workers (table 6.1). Hence, economic and political forces work in the same direction for the capital importer and the direct effect of a reduction in β unambiguously leads to a lower tax rate on capital.

[11] To obtain the first effect in (6.26) we expand the initial derivative by adding and subtracting 1, and then substitute in for k^B and $\partial k^B/\partial \beta$ using (6.6) and (6.7).

[12] This result will be demonstrated rigorously in chapter 8 (proposition 8.3).

Whether the positive sign of $\partial F^B/\partial\beta$ tends to increase or reduce country A's optimal capital tax rate through the indirect (second) effect in (6.24) depends on the slope of country A's reaction function. This is given by the derivative

$$\frac{\partial F^A}{\partial t^B} = \underbrace{\frac{2b + (1 - m^A)\beta}{4b + \beta}}_{(+)} + \underbrace{(2b + \beta k^A)(1 - \rho)m^A \frac{c_L^A}{c_K^A} \frac{\partial(c_K^A/c_L^A)}{\partial t^B}}_{(-,0)}, \tag{6.27}$$

where the second effect is signed from (6.22).

The slope of country A's reaction function exhibits a similar ambiguity as the direct effect of a reduction in the mobility cost parameter (6.25). The fall in the tax rate of country B increases the capital outflow from country A and reduces this country's tax base. Thus the efficiency costs of capital taxation are increased for country A as a result of the initial tax response in the low-tax region. However, the capital outflow from country A also causes a redistribution of income from workers to capitalists, and this increases the political benefits of capital taxation.

Finally, we turn to the slope of country B's reaction function, which is given by

$$\frac{\partial F^B}{\partial t^A} = \underbrace{\frac{2b + \beta}{4b + \beta}}_{(+)} + \underbrace{(2b + \beta)\,(1 - \rho)m^B \frac{c_L^B}{c_K^B} \frac{\partial(c_K^B/c_L^B)}{\partial t^A}}_{(-,0)}. \tag{6.28}$$

This partial derivative is also ambiguous: an increase in t^A raises country B's tax base and increases the economic incentive for capital taxation by the first effect. On the other hand, an increase in country A's capital tax rate also redistributes income in country B from capitalists to workers and this reduces the political incentive to raise t^B.

Summarising the effects that capital market integration has on optimal capital tax rates in both countries, it is obvious that the parameter ρ plays a crucial role. The value of this parameter, which measures the degree of 'income stickiness' inherent in the political process, determines the size of the second terms in all partial effects (6.25)–(6.28). In the following, we consider the two benchmark cases where ρ is either at the upper or at the lower end of its permitted range. In both instances, this leads to unambiguous changes in optimal capital tax rates as a result of capital market integration. The results are summarised in

Proposition 6.3

Case 1: *When the political support from workers and capitalists are close substitutes from the government's perspective* ($\rho \rightarrow 1$)*, then capital market integration will reduce optimal tax rates on capital in both countries.*

Case 2: *When it is very difficult for policy-makers to substitute between the political support from workers and capitalists* ($\rho \rightarrow -\infty$)*, then capital market integration will reduce the optimal tax rate on capital in the capital importing country, but increase the capital tax rate in the exporting country.*

Proof: As $\rho \rightarrow 1$, the second effects in (6.25)–(6.28) approach zero and $\partial F^i/\partial\beta > 0, \partial F^i/\partial t^j > 0 \; \forall \, i \in \{A, B\}, \; i \neq j$. Substituting these partial effects into (6.24) gives case 1 of the proposition. For $\rho \rightarrow -\infty$, the second effects in (6.25)–(6.28) become arbitrarily large and dominate the first effects. This gives $\partial F^A/\partial\beta < 0$, $\partial F^B/\partial\beta > 0$, $\partial F^A/\partial t^B < 0$, $\partial F^B/\partial t^A < 0$. Substituting these partial effects in (6.24) gives case 2 of the proposition. ■

To explain these results in some more detail, table 6.2 summarises the partial effects (6.25)–(6.28) for each of the two cases. In case 1 ($\rho \rightarrow 1$), distributive effects of capital market integration do not effectively feed back into the policy-makers' optimal tax problems, and the increased efficiency costs of capital taxation dominate in both countries. The direct effect of a reduction in mobility costs is to intensify the competition for the internationally mobile capital tax base, and this lowers capital tax rates in both countries. In addition, both reaction functions are upward sloping in this case: other things being equal, the initial reduction in each country's tax rate reduces the capital tax base in the other region, and this further weakens the incentive to employ source taxes on capital. Therefore direct and indirect effects work in the same direction and both countries will unambiguously reduce the level of capital taxation.

Table 6.2 *Effects of capital market integration on optimal capital tax rates*

	Capital exporter (country A)	Capital importer (country B)
Case 1: $\rho \rightarrow 1$		
Direct effect $(\partial F^j/\partial t^j) \times (\partial F^i/\partial\beta)$	$t^A \downarrow$	$t^B \downarrow$
Indirect effect $(\partial F^i/\partial t^j) \times (\partial F^j/\partial\beta)$	$t^A \downarrow$	$t^B \downarrow$
Case 2: $\rho \rightarrow -\infty$		
Direct effect $(\partial F^j/\partial t^j) \times (\partial F^i/\partial\beta)$	$t^A \uparrow$	$t^B \downarrow$
Indirect effect $(\partial F^i/\partial t^j) \times (\partial F^j/\partial\beta)$	$t^A \uparrow$	$t^B \downarrow$

In case 2 ($\rho \to -\infty$), distributive effects are central to policy-makers' optimal tax problems since resistance to income changes caused by capital market integration is very high in both countries. In this case, distributive considerations dominate the effects of increased efficiency costs of capital taxation. The initial response to a reduction in mobility costs is then a capital tax reduction in the capital importing country B (where, from (6.23), workers gain from the additional capital inflow while capitalists lose), and a capital tax increase in country A (where the capital outflow hurts labour and benefits capital). Also, both reaction functions are downward sloping in this case and indirect effects again reinforce the direct effects in both countries. The additional capital inflow to country B resulting from the initial tax increase in country A benefits workers and hurts capitalists in the capital importing region. To counteract these income changes, the tax rate on capital must further fall in country B. On the other hand, the initial tax reduction in country B attracts capital to this region, and this hurts workers and benefits capitalists in country A. Therefore, country A's capital tax rate must further rise – and the wage tax can accordingly fall – in order to shield workers from the income loss.

As it stands, proposition 6.3 describes the effects of capital market integration only for the special cases where either efficiency or distributive effects are central for tax policy. However, a more general result is also implicit in our analysis, if we are willing to assume that the direct effect of capital market integration dominates the indirect effect in both countries (cf. (6.24)). With this assumption we can state that the lower is the elasticity parameter ρ, and thus the more important are distributive considerations, the more will capital tax rates in the two countries diverge as a result of capital market integration. Formally, we have to show that $(dt^A/d\beta - dt^B/d\beta)$ must be monotonously rising in ρ. From (6.24) and the above assumption that the direct effects of a change in β dominate, a sufficient condition for this is that $\partial F^A/\partial\beta$ is monotonously rising in ρ, whereas $\partial F^B/\partial\beta$ is monotonously falling. But it is directly seen from (6.25) and (6.26) that this condition is fulfilled. Hence, as the political resistance to income changes is increased (ρ falls), the downward adjustment of tax rates is reinforced in the low-tax country B, but is slowed down and eventually turned around in the high-tax country A.

6.5 Discussion and comparison of results

This section links our results to related findings in the literature and critically discusses their relevance for explaining observed capital tax patterns. Case 1 in proposition 6.3 corresponds to the conventional result that increased capital mobility will lead to a general reduction in the level of capital taxation. This result is typical for one-consumer models of capital tax competition (Bucovetsky and Wilson, 1991; Hoyt, 1991) and is reproduced in the present more general framework when policy-makers can easily substitute increased political support from one income group for the reduced support of the other.

In contrast, case 2 in proposition 6.3 shows that when distributive concerns are predominant, the optimal tax rate on capital *increases* in the capital exporting country. Since the capital exporter is the high-tax country in the present analysis, this result also implies a *divergence* of tax rates as a result of capital market liberalisation. This finding differs not only from one-consumer analyses, but also from the results obtained by Persson and Tabellini (1992). As we have seen in section 6.1, changes in the political equilibrium mitigate the economic effects of capital market integration in their model, but the net effect in both countries is still a reduction in the rate of capital taxation. Furthermore, capital market integration implies a convergence of capital tax rates in their analysis, as it induces a larger tax rate reduction in the high-tax country.

These differences in results can be traced back to different assumptions regarding the political process. The crucial 'political' effect in the Persson and Tabellini model is that the median voter delegates tax policy to a more 'left-wing' agent in response to capital tax competition between governments. But since any 'distance' between the policy-maker and the median voter causes a net income loss to the latter, the median voter clearly cannot have an interest in electing a politician that 'overshoots' the tax rate which was levied before capital market integration occurred.[13] Hence it is intuitive that the political delegation effect cannot dominate the economic efficiency effect in the Persson and Tabellini model.

This constraint on the redistributive repercussions that capital market integration has on tax policy is not present in our interest group model. This is most easily seen in the extreme case where workers in the capital exporting region are able to maintain – through the political process – their after-tax level of income. In this case, the losses in pre-tax wage income induced by the additional outflow of capital must be fully compensated by a reduction in the aggregate tax payments of this group, which in turn requires an increase in the capital tax rate to balance the government budget.

[13] Similar trade-offs for the median voter arise in Perroni and Scharf (2001), whose analysis will be discussed below.

There are several other contributions on capital taxation and income distribution to which some of our results can be compared. Bjerksund and Schjelderup (1998) also study a two-class setting with capitalists and workers, but in a two-period model of a small open economy that is a capital exporter. Importantly, their model considers the case where labour supply is endogenous. The government of the small open economy levies a wage tax and a source tax on capital, and it can additionally impose capital controls. The authors first show that it will be optimal for the small country to impose some constraint on capital exports, even if only capitalists count in the government objective function. In the presence of capital controls the elasticity of the capital tax base is finite and the source tax on capital will accordingly be positive. This result is again obtained for *any* government objective, because the incidence of the wage tax is partly on capitalists owing to the endogenous labour supply response.[14] In contrast, our analysis above has assumed that the labour tax is a lump-sum instrument, and the optimal source tax on capital could be zero or even negative for appropriate specifications of the political support function (proposition 6.1). In general, endogenising the labour supply decision will thus tend to raise the capital tax rate in the Nash equilibrium for a given government objective function.

Lopez, Marchand and Pestieau (1998) also consider a two-class, two-country model of capital tax competition and assume that governments maximise a social welfare function. Their focus is on the Nash equilibrium level of redistributive, source-based capital taxation in the presence of *perfect* capital mobility. Their analysis includes several numerical simulations that study the role of different asymmetries between countries in the Nash equilibrium. When the degree of inequality aversion differs across countries, then the more inequality-averse country will have the higher tax rate in equilibrium. This result compares directly with our proposition 6.2 above. Another scenario studied numerically in the Lopez *et al.* paper considers differences in factor endowments. If technologies are identical and country A has the smaller labour force, but the same level of capital as country B, then capital will flow from country A to country B in the no-tax equilibrium. In this case terms of trade effects dominate tax base effects (in contrast to our analysis of section 6.4) and the capital-exporting country A has an incentive to subsidise the domestic use of capital (cf. section 3.1). The optimal policy

[14] These results generalise the earlier findings of Razin and Sadka (1991b). Razin and Sadka show for a one-consumer economy and in the absence of a residence-based capital tax that it is optimal for a small country to restrict capital exports and simultaneously impose a positive source tax on capital.

then trades off this incentive against the redistributive effects of the capital subsidy.

Huizinga and Nielsen (1997b) consider a median voter model of a small open economy where agents differ systematically both in their (first-period) endowment income and in their (second-period) profit income. The Huizinga and Nielsen paper focuses on the structure of capital taxation (profit tax, residence-based and source-based capital taxes), rather than on the mix of wage and (source-based) capital taxation. The volume of government spending is exogenously fixed in their model and enters the determination of optimal tax rates in a way similar to our proposition 6.1. A special feature of the analysis is that it explicitly compares the results of the median voter model with those obtained in a representative agent framework. This comparison identifies several tax constellations that are possible outcomes only in the median voter model, for example the existence of a negative tax on savings. Similar to our proposition 6.3, this illustrates the general point that the presence of distributive effects leads to a greater variety of tax policy outcomes than a representative agent framework.

Furthermore, there are obvious links to recent contributions on tax-financed social insurance schemes. Gabszewicz and van Ypersele (1996) show in a median voter model that the level of social protection – which takes the form of a minimum wage in their model – always falls when capital mobility is introduced, even if the median voter receives wage income only. This result is derived, however, for the case of symmetric countries. Hence their paper effectively focuses on what we have labelled above the 'efficiency effect' of capital market integration, whereas the distributive effects that arise from asymmetries between countries are excluded in this analysis.

Closer to our approach is Lejour and Verbon (1996) who model two asymmetric countries providing unemployment insurance to risk-averse agents in the presence of imperfect capital mobility. Capital mobility matters because social security payments are partly shifted to firms in the process of wage bargaining. In this model the degree of risk aversion plays a role similar to the elasticity parameter ρ in our framework and hence the distributive effects are similar to ours: if risk aversion is sufficiently high, then capital market integration reduces the level of social insurance in the capital importing country and increases it in the capital exporting country (Lejour and Verbon, 1996, p. 506). However, there are no 'efficiency effects' of capital market integration in the Lejour and Verbon model. This is owing to the fact that the mobility cost function is linear in the volume of international capital flows, implying that the efficiency costs of capital taxation will not increase as a result of capital market integration (cf. n. 5). Hence the effects of capital market integration on social insurance policy are always exactly opposed in the capital exporting and the capital importing country, and the distinction between two different cases that is characteristic for our proposition 6.3 cannot occur.

Finally, we should note two important limitations of our analysis. First, in the above model the different tax responses to capital market integration have been exclusively tied to the net trade position of the two countries. One problem with this approach is that tax policy is generally a long-run concern, whereas the net trade position of many countries fluctuates over time. Moreover, the above model has isolated the shocks to the distribution of income as a result of capital market integration. In practice these shocks will overlap with other exogenous disturbances to either wage or capital income, and possibly also with exogenous policy shifts as a result of changes in the political balance of power.[15]

A second important limitation that our model shares with most of the related work (including Persson and Tabellini, 1992) is that capital flows are exclusively determined by tax differentials. This assumption is particularly relevant for the question of tax rate convergence. If the high-tax country is also the capital exporter, then distributive effects tend to cause diverging rates of capital taxation in the present model as a result of capital market integration. The same need not be the case, however, if production-related differences across countries are the main reason for international trade. The problem for any analytical treatment of this issue is that differences in technologies or factor endowments significantly complicate the model, relative to the specification of demand-side differences. It is therefore quite likely that an analysis of this case requires the use of simulation methods, as in Lopez, Marchand and Pestieau (1998).

To summarise, the simple model used here clearly cannot claim to 'explain' the cross-country differences in the development of effective rates of capital taxation, as summarised in table 4.1. However it may nevertheless indicate how distributive effects can counteract the clear-cut predictions derived from conventional one-consumer models of capital tax competition.

[15] An econometric study by Hallerberg and Basinger (1996) argues, for example, that the number of 'veto players' (institutions whose approval is required for tax reform) can help in explaining why capital tax reforms have been carried in most, but not all, OECD countries. In particular, they attribute the absence of capital tax reform in Italy to the fact that governments are often formed by large and changing coalitions of parties.

6.6 Political economy and the welfare effects of tax coordination

In the analysis of this chapter, we have so far been concerned almost exclusively with a positive analysis of tax policy. However, there are also a number of analyses which are primarily concerned with the normative implications of capital tax competition in the presence of different agents or interest groups.

Lorz (1998) argues that capital tax competition may be socially beneficial when interest groups engage in wasteful lobbying for redistributive capital taxation. He studies a setting of symmetric regions and models increased capital mobility as an exogenous increase in the number of competing countries (cf. n. 9). Lorz's paper shows that increased tax competition will make lobbying for redistribution less worthwhile and leads to a reduced level of wasteful lobbying activities in equilibrium. This counters the welfare loss through a less efficient tax system and implies that increased tax competition may actually benefit consumers in all countries.

This contribution can be seen as a complement to the study by Edwards and Keen (1996), which we have already discussed in section 3.5. In the Edwards and Keen model, there are gains from tax competition even in a one-consumer framework, because governments partly act in their own self-interest and derive utility from expenditures that do not benefit the representative citizen. In this setting, tax coordination will be welfare improving if and only if the marginal excess burden of the tax system exceeds the policy-makers' 'marginal propensity to waste'. Fuest (2000) links the analyses of Lorz (1998) and Edwards and Keen (1996) by considering the effects of tax coordination in a model with politicians, bureaucrats and lobbying groups. In Fuest's model, consumer welfare enters the utility function of politicians, but not that of bureaucrats. In this setting it can be shown that – for any given set of parameters in the Edwards and Keen (1996) framework – the consumer is the more likely to lose from tax coordination, the greater is the bargaining power of bureaucrats *vis-à-vis* politicians in the political process. Intuitively, if bureaucrats dominate political decision-making, then the additional tax revenue gained from a coordinated capital tax increase will primarily be used to satisfy interest groups, rather than consumers.

Perroni and Scharf (2001) advance a further argument for tax competition when jurisdiction size is endogenous. They consider a model with a large number of individuals and as many varieties of local public goods. Each individual prefers a different variety, but only one variety is chosen in each region by the median voter. Jurisdiction size in this model is endogenously determined by the trade-off that exists for a 'border individual' between the scale economies in public good provision and the welfare costs that arise for this individual from the distance between her own preferred variety of the local public good and that chosen by the median voter. In this model the lack of coordination between the median voter and the border individual results in a suboptimally small jurisdiction size. Interjurisdictional tax competition results in larger jurisdictions, because the downward pressure on taxation reduces the gap between the median voter's choice and the variety that is preferred by the border individual. Hence tax competition partly corrects for the original distortion and may raise welfare for all members of a jurisdiction, even in the absence of compensating transfers.

Finally, Lockwood (1998b) adopts a public choice approach to study the costs and benefits of decentralised taxation in the tradition of the original fiscal federalism literature. The cost of centralisation in his model are political inefficiencies generated by agenda-setting and the voting procedure in the national legislature. This model element replaces the cost of policy uniformity in the framework of Oates (1972) and constitutes an alternative – and arguably more realistic – specification to capture the notion that central governments are less responsive to citizens' preferences than lower levels of government. This benefit of decentralisation is traded off against the inefficiencies generated by interregional spillovers between jurisdictions.

In sum, it should be obvious that these analytical models do not aim to give a general answer to the 'grand question' whether tax competition benefits or hurts consumers, in general. Instead they identify alternative channels for tax competition to improve social welfare, which can be set against the well-known inefficiencies of decentralised tax policy in the presence of fiscal externalities. As Edwards and Keen (1996) have shown, the gains from coordination can be approximated by the marginal excess burden of the tax system, for which empirical estimates exist. It is far more difficult to obtain a satisfactory and quantifiable measure of the (political) gains from decentralisation. The above models provide an enriched representation of the political process, as compared to the monolithic government assumed by Edwards and Keen (1996). In doing so, they go at least some way in meeting the criticism by Frey and Eichenberger (1996) that the 'possibility frontier' relating economic and political distortions is not static, but will shift under different political institutions. Whether such a 'realistic' description of the political process will also lead to a quantifiable measure of the political gains from tax competition is a question that cannot yet be answered.

APPENDIX

Proof of proposition 6.2 The general form of the best-response functions (6.19)–(6.20) is

$$F^A(t^A, t^B, \theta^A) = 0, \qquad F^B(t^A, t^B, \theta^B) = 0. \tag{6A.1}$$

Totally differentiating (6A.1) and inverting gives

$$\begin{bmatrix} dt^A \\ dt^B \end{bmatrix} = \frac{1}{|\mathcal{J}|} \begin{bmatrix} -\dfrac{\partial F^B}{\partial t^B} & \dfrac{\partial F^A}{\partial t^B} \\ \dfrac{\partial F^B}{\partial t^A} & -\dfrac{\partial F^A}{\partial t^A} \end{bmatrix} \begin{bmatrix} \dfrac{\partial A^A}{\partial \theta^A} & d\theta^A \\ \dfrac{\partial F^B}{\partial \theta^B} & d\theta^B \end{bmatrix}, \tag{6A.2}$$

where the determinant of the Jacobian must be positive from the argument given in the appendix to chapter 8 (8A.5).

To analyse the effects of an increase in the political weight of workers in country 1, we substitute $d\theta^A = ds_L^A$ and $d\theta^B = 0$ in (6A.2). Since the initial equilibrium is symmetric, (6.21) and (6.18) can be used to obtain

$$\frac{\partial F^A}{\partial s_L^A} = -(2b + \beta) \frac{\partial m^A}{\partial s_L^A} = (2b + \beta) \frac{m^A}{s_L^A} > 0. \tag{6A.3}$$

Using $|\mathcal{J}| > 0$, (6A.3) and the second-order conditions $\partial F^i / \partial t^i < 0 \; \forall \, i \in \{A, B\}$ in the first line of (6A.2) gives $dt^A / ds_L^A > 0$. Combining this with the change in t^B [the second line in (6A.2)] gives

$$\frac{\partial F^B}{\partial t^A} \frac{dt^A}{ds_L^A} = - \frac{\partial F^B}{\partial t^B} \frac{dt^B}{ds_L^A}. \tag{6A.4}$$

From the symmetry of the initial equilibrium ($\partial F^A / \partial t^A = \partial F^B / \partial t^B$ and $\partial F^A / \partial t^B = \partial F^B / \partial t^A$) and $|\mathcal{J}| > 0$ it follows that $dt^A / ds_L^A > dt^B / ds_L^A$, no matter whether dt^B / ds_L^A is positive or not. Since tax rates are equal initially, this demonstrates the proposition for small deviations from the symmetric equilibrium. ■

Derivation of (6.24)

Equation set (6A.2) simultaneously includes the solution for the more general case when best responses in both countries are altered by shift parameters. Setting $d\theta^A = d\theta^B = d\beta$ yields (6.24) in the main text.

7 Profit-shifting and the corporate tax structure

Our analysis in the preceding chapters has focused on the overall *level* of capital taxation in the presence of international capital mobility. As we have discussed in section 2.1, however, an important feature of the capital tax reforms that have occurred since the 1980s is a change in the tax *structure*. The combination of tax rate cuts with a broadening of the capital tax base has been particularly pronounced for the taxation of corporate income, although similar trends are also visible under personal income tax. The prototype for a corporate tax reform of this type was the 1986 reform in the United States, which partially abolished the accelerated depreciation rules that had been introduced in 1981. However, similar developments have occurred in most other EU and OECD countries, as our policy overview in section 2.1 and the calculation of effective rates of capital taxation summarised in section 4.4 have shown.

In the following we propose an explanation for these developments that is based on the increasing internationalisation of production, and in particular on the growing importance of multinational corporations.[1] Several authors have stressed that this has made corporate tax bases, especially in the OECD countries, more vulnerable to strategic transfer pricing and other profit-shifting activities of multinational corporations (see, e.g., Devereux, 1992; Keen, 1993a). Present international tax rules attempt to eliminate such tax arbitrage activities through the principle that internal transactions within a multinational firm must be valued at 'arm's length' prices (cf. n. 6 in chapter 2). However, there is growing evidence – surveyed in section 7.4 – that the enforcement of this principle becomes increasingly difficult as the globalisation of production proceeds.

[1] Markusen and Venables (1998, table 1) collect data showing that the stock of outward and inward foreign direct investment (FDI), as a share of GDP, is substantially higher in the OECD countries as compared to developing countries. The highest ratios are obtained in Western Europe where the stock of inward (outward) foreign investment, as a share of GDP, was 13 per cent (15.9 per cent) in 1994.

In the following, we pursue this argument in more detail and formally analyse the effects of cross-border profit-shifting on corporate tax systems. Since profit shifting responds primarily to international differences in statutory tax rates, this setting allows us to show that a tax-rate-cut-cum-base-broadening reform of the corporate tax system is an optimal policy adjustment to the rise in FDI.

Section 7.1 describes our basic model and derives optimal government policy in a benchmark scenario where portfolio capital is mobile internationally but there is no FDI. In this setting we restate the basic case for an investment-neutral business tax with an immediate write-off for investment expenditures that is well known from closed economy models. Section 7.2 introduces FDI and hence the possibility of a multinational firm engaging in profit-shifting. We derive the optimal transfer price chosen by the firm and then turn to the optimal corporate tax policy in this setting. Section 7.3 critically discusses our results and compares them to related work. Section 7.4 summarises the empirical evidence and draws policy conclusions for the international coordination of corporate tax bases.

7.1 The benchmark case: cash-flow taxation

7.1.1 The individual's problem

Our analysis uses a standard two-period model of savings and investment in a single homogeneous good.[2] There is a representative consumer–investor in each of two small countries $i \in \{A, B\}$.[3] In period 1 the individual in each country receives an exogenous endowment e^i, which can either be consumed (c_1^i) or saved. Savings ($e^i - c_1^i$) can be invested in the capital stock of either country, or in the world capital market. Arbitrage will then ensure that in each case the investment earns the competitive (net) world rate of return R.

Capital is the only variable factor of production and output in period 2 is given by the production function $f(k^i)$, which is identical across countries and has the usual properties $f'(k^i) > 0,\ f''(k^i) < 0$. Hence there is an implicit fixed factor that gives rise to pure profits and which, for the purposes of our analysis, can be interpreted as entrepreneurial services.

[2] The analysis in sections 7.1–7.2 is revised and adapted from Haufler and Schjelderup (2000).

[3] Restricting the number of countries to two is largely a matter of simplifying the notation and the argument. Analytical results would not change if there were instead a large number of identical countries. In either case, the important assumption is that tax policy in each country has no repercussions on the world interest rate.

The capital stock in both countries depreciates at the same rate δ, so that the user cost of a unit of capital is $R+\delta$. Gross profits in each country are then $f(k^i) - (R+\delta)k^i$. These profits accrue to the representative firm in each country, or alternatively to the owner of the fixed factor (i.e. the entrepreneur). The important assumption in the present section is that the ownership of the firm is entirely in the hands of the domestic resident in each country, even if foreigners finance part of the domestic capital stock. Hence all profits from the firm located in country i accrue to the domestic resident. This assumption will be relaxed in the next section, where we introduce joint ownership of the representative firm operating in each country.

Taxable profits in country i are subject to the corporate tax rate t^i in the source country of the investment. The tax base in each country is the value of output, less a fixed share α^i of the 'true' cost of capital $(R+\delta)$. The tax base parameter α^i may differ across countries and we place no restrictions on the value of α^i so that the deductibility of investment costs for tax purposes can either be above or below its true value. In practice, most existing corporate tax systems have $\alpha^i < 1$ and thus permit only an incomplete deduction of investment costs. This occurs either because investments are partly financed by retained profits and the opportunity costs of this internal financing method are not tax-deductible, or because depreciation allowances – which are generally based on historical rather than replacement costs – are below real economic depreciation in periods of inflation or rapid technological change. Our specification of the corporate tax base incorporates both of these scenarios.[4]

In each country, consumption in period 2 is given by the after-tax profits earned by the firm, plus the principal and the interest earned on the savings made in period 1. The intertemporal budget constraint for the consumer in country i is then

$$c_2^i = \pi^i + (1+R)(e^i - c_1^i) \quad \forall \quad i, \tag{7.1}$$

where net after-tax profits π^i are given by

$$\begin{aligned} \pi^i(k^i) &= f(k^i) - (R+\delta)k^i - t^i\left[f(k^i) - \alpha^i(R+\delta)k^i\right] \\ &= (1-t^i)[f(k^i) - (R+\delta)k^i] - (1-\alpha^i)t^i(R+\delta)k^i. \end{aligned} \tag{7.2}$$

[4] Of course, one could also isolate the role of depreciation allowances, or of an imperfect deductibility of interest in conjunction with a required debt–equity ratio (see Sandmo, 1974). These changes in the definition of the corporate tax base would affect none of our qualitative results.

Hence, for $\alpha = 1$ the corporate tax falls only on pure profits while $\alpha < 1$ implies that a positive tax is also levied on investment (and conversely, investment is subsidised when $\alpha > 1$).[5]

The representative individual in each country maximises a well-behaved utility function $u^i(c_1^i, c_2^i)$, subject to the intertemporal budget constraint (7.1). Setting up the Lagrangian for the private optimisation problem and differentiating with respect to c_1^i and c_2^i, it can immediately be seen that the household's intertemporal consumption decision will be undistorted in this model, because households can always invest in the international capital market. Our focus in the following will be on the first-order conditions for the optimal investment choices. Differentiating the net profit equation (7.2) with respect to k^i gives

$$f'(k^i) = \frac{(1 - \alpha^i t^i)}{(1 - t^i)} (R + \delta) \quad \forall \quad i \in \{A, B\}. \tag{7.3}$$

Condition (7.3) shows that, except for the trivial case $t^i = 0$, investment will be undistorted if and only if $\alpha^i = 1$. In this case, the deductibility of the true costs of capital from the corporate tax base ensures that the marginal return from investment is untaxed and only pure rents or profits are captured by the corporation tax. In contrast, if $\alpha^i < 1$ then the right-hand side of the equation is greater than $(R + \delta)$, implying that the marginal product of capital exceeds its opportunity cost.

7.1.2 *The government's problem*

Each country's government chooses a corporate tax system (t^i, α^i) that secures an exogenously given amount of revenue, denoted by $T_0^i > 0$. Formally, this is a conventional Ramsey-type tax problem that isolates changes in the structure of the corporate income tax. One possible motivation for the fixed revenue assumption is that governments are aware of the politically sensitive distributive implications of reducing the overall level of corporate taxation. In the setting of our analysis in chapter 6, this corresponds to a very low elasticity of substitution between the support from workers and capital owners, respectively. As we have seen in proposition 6.3, optimal tax policy will then not reduce the overall level of

[5] Since the supply of capital is infinitely elastic at the world (net) rate of return, a tax on capital falls fully on domestic profits, even if the capital stock is partly owned by foreigners. Note further that our modelling of the corporate tax system excludes a tax on the capital gains or losses that accrue when depreciation allowances for tax purposes differ from true economic depreciation (i.e. $\alpha \neq 1$).

capital *vis-à-vis* labour taxation, even if increased capital mobility raises the efficiency costs of the capital tax.[6]

Each government maximises the indirect utility function $V^i(t^i, \alpha^i)$ of its representative consumer–investor, subject to the fixed revenue requirement. Setting up the Lagrangian for the government's optimisation problem gives

$$\mathcal{L}_G^i(t^i, \alpha^i, \mu^i) = V^i(t^i, \alpha^i) + \mu^i\{t^i[f(k^i) - \alpha^i(R+\delta)k^i] - T_0^i\} \quad \forall \; i. \tag{7.4}$$

Using the envelope theorem to form the derivatives $\partial V^i/\partial t^i$ and $\partial V^i/\partial \alpha^i$ and normalising the marginal utility of private income to unity, the first-order conditions with respect to the two tax parameters are

$$\frac{\partial \mathcal{L}_G^i}{\partial t^i} = (\mu^i - 1)[f(k^i) - \alpha^i(R+\delta)] + \mu^i t^i \frac{\partial k^i}{\partial t^i}\gamma^i = 0, \tag{7.5}$$

$$\frac{\partial \mathcal{L}_G^i}{\partial \alpha^i} = -(\mu^i - 1)\, t^i\,(R+\delta)\, k^i + \mu^i t^i \frac{\partial k^i}{\partial \alpha^i}\gamma^i = 0, \tag{7.6}$$

where, from the firm's optimal investment choice (7.3)

$$\gamma^i \equiv f'(k^i) - \alpha^i(R+\delta) = \frac{(1-\alpha^i)(R+\delta)}{(1-t^i)} \quad \forall \quad i \in \{A, B\}. \tag{7.7}$$

Implicitly differentiating condition (7.7) further gives

$$\frac{\partial k^i}{\partial t^i} = \frac{(1-\alpha^i)\,(R+\delta)}{(1-t^i)^2 f''(k^i)}, \qquad \frac{\partial k^i}{\partial \alpha^i} = \frac{-t^i\,(R+\delta)}{(1-t^i) f''(k^i)}. \tag{7.8}$$

This solution shows that setting $\alpha^i = 1$ implies $\gamma^i = 0$, and the second terms in both (7.5) and (7.6) disappear. It then follows from the first terms in either (7.5) or (7.6) that $\mu^i = 1$, implying that the shadow price of public revenues equals the private marginal utility of income and there is no excess burden of corporation tax. Hence, in the benchmark case, a first-best optimum can be obtained if investors are allowed to fully deduct the cost of capital from the corporate tax base. This result is summarised in

[6] The implications of endogenising the level of corporate tax revenues will be discussed in section 7.3.

Proposition 7.1
With international capital mobility, but in the absence of foreign direct investment and profit-shifting, the optimal corporate tax system implies a full deduction for the cost of capital ($\alpha^i = 1 \; \forall \; i$).

Proposition 7.1 restates – in a simplified setting, but in the presence of portfolio capital flows – the conventional argument in favour of a complete exemption of investment expenditures from corporation tax. An early theoretical demonstration of the equivalence between a tax on pure economic profits and a tax on the real cash flow of firms has been given by Sandmo (1974).[7] The policy interest in investment-neutral corporation taxes received a major stimulus through the report of the Meade Committee (1978) and later through the flat tax proposal of Hall and Rabushka (1985). While investment neutrality can also be achieved, in principle, through the combination of true economic depreciation and the deductibility of debt interest, the latter has the important disadvantage of distorting the firm's financing decision. A thorough and comprehensive treatment of these issues in a dynamic context is found in Sinn (1987).

Two principal ways to achieve investment neutrality are currently under discussion (cf. Cnossen, 1996). One is to allow an immediate expensing of all investment expenditures, but give no deduction for interest paid. This is a cash-flow tax in the sense used by the Meade Committee (1978), and it also underlies the flat tax proposal of Hall and Rabushka (1985). Alternatively, a tax allowance can be granted for the company's total equity capital, valued at a normal (risk-free) market rate of return. This 'allowance for corporate equity' (ACE) scheme was originally conceived by Boadway and Bruce (1984) and later developed in detail by the IFS Capital Taxes Group (1991). A variant of this scheme has been employed in the tax reform of Croatia and some elements of the proposal have also been incorporated in the corporate tax reforms of Italy and Austria (see subsection 2.1.2).

As we have emphasised earlier, however, capital tax reforms in most OECD countries have increased, rather than reduced, the corporate tax base. To be sure, domestic factors cannot be neglected in this process. Empirical cost of capital comparisons in King and Fullerton (1984) and subsequent studies have shown very clearly that one of the most important distortions caused by corporation tax lies in the differential treat-

[7] As Sandmo (1979) has pointed out, the investment neutrality of the cash-flow tax breaks down if the tax rate changes over time, and this change is anticipated by investors. The policy relevance of this caveat is stressed, for example, by Alvarez, Kanniainen and Södersten (1999). We will return to this issue in our analysis of the transitional effects of a switch from destination- to origin-based commodity taxation in chapter 9.

ment of alternative forms of financing. These distortions have generally been reduced through the 'tax-rate-cut-cum-base-broadening' reforms carried out since the 1980s. However, the first-best solution in this case would be to treat all forms of financing alike by switching either to a cash-flow tax (with immediate expensing of real investments, but no deduction for any costs of finance), or to an allowance for corporate equity scheme (with full deductibility of all costs of finance). Hence, by focusing on the distortion of the firm's financing decision, one is not able to explain the failure of corporate tax reforms in most OECD countries to move towards investment-neutral tax systems.

7.2 Corporate taxation under profit-shifting

7.2.1 Joint ownership and transfer pricing

Based on our benchmark analysis above, this section offers a simple explanation for the observed changes in the structure of corporation tax that is based on the growth of FDI. We now assume that the representative individual in each country i also owns a share of the fixed factor 'entrepreneurial services' in country j. The important difference to the analysis in section 7.1 is that joint ownership establishes a nexus between the two firms, which allows them to engage in tax arbitrage activities through profit-shifting. In the following we assume that the two firms collude and jointly take their investment and transfer-pricing decisions to maximise global net profits.[8]

Profit-shifting in our model takes the following simple form: without loss of generality we assume that the firm located in country A provides one unit of an input good – or, alternatively, an overhead service – to the firm located in country B. The true (arm's length) price of this input must equal unity in our one-good setting, but this price cannot be directly observed by tax authorities. Hence, the transfer price q becomes an additional choice variable for the multinational firm, which may either

[8] Our treatment thus excludes possible conflicts of interests between shareholders, which may arise if they hold different equity shares in the home and in the foreign country. In this case, transfer prices are still used as a tax arbitraging device, but each majority shareholder simultaneously tries to use this instrument in order to change the international distribution of gross profits in their favour. See Gabrielsen and Schjelderup (1999) for an analytical treatment of these issues, and Sinn and Weichenrieder (1997) for an account of the practical relevance of transfer-pricing disputes in the context of FDI in eastern Europe. In the present model it can be shown, however, that conflicts between shareholders do not affect the first-order conditions for the government's optimal tax policy.

overinvoice ($q > 1$) or underinvoice ($q < 1$) in order to reduce aggregate tax payments. To balance trade between the two integrated firms in real terms, the firm located in country B delivers one unit of output, valued at the 'true' price of unity, to country A in order to pay for the inputs received.

To limit the extent of misdeclaration, we assume that transfer pricing involves resource costs to the integrated firm, which are a convex function of the difference between the declared and the true price of exported inputs. This assumption is standard in the literature on both tax evasion and transfer pricing, and is justified either by an increased probability of detection (see Kant, 1988), or by additional efforts that need to be taken in order to conceal the transfer-pricing activity from tax authorities. In the latter case, the transaction costs incurred by the firm represent a pure waste of resources, and this is the scenario that underlies the present analysis.[9] This concealment (transaction) cost function is denoted by $\theta(q)$. It is modelled in a more general way as compared to our transaction cost function in chapter 6, but possesses the same standard properties. In particular, transaction costs are zero if the 'true' price of unity is reported, but rise more than proportionally for deviations in either direction

$$\theta(1) = \theta'(1) = 0, \quad \text{sign}(\theta') = \text{sign}(q - 1), \quad \theta''(q) > 0. \tag{7.9}$$

With these specifications, global net profits of the multinational firm are, by analogy to (7.2):

$$\begin{aligned} \Pi(k^A, k^B, q) = {} & (1 - t^A)[f(k^A) + (q - 1) - (R + \delta)k^A] \\ & - (1 - \alpha^A)t^A(R + \delta)k^A \\ & + (1 - t^B)[f(k^B) - (q - 1) - (R + \delta)k^B] \\ & - (1 - \alpha^B)t^B(R + \delta)k^B - \theta(q). \end{aligned} \tag{7.10}$$

Differentiating (7.10) with respect to k^i it can immediately be seen that the optimal investment decision in each country corresponds to (7.3) in section 7.1. In each country, the optimal level of investment k^i chosen by the multinational firm thus depends only on the local corporate tax system.

The additional decision variable of the integrated firm is the transfer price q. Differentiating with respect to this variable gives

[9] See, e.g., Huber (1997) for the same assumption in a related setting. We emphasise, however, that our qualitative results would be unchanged if the governments collected fines from the transfer-pricing investor. Intuitively, the important point is that transfer pricing will occur only to the extent that this activity is profitable for the investor, implying conversely that the two countries' tax authorities must lose revenues in the aggregate.

$$\theta'(q) = t^B - t^A. \tag{7.11}$$

Hence overinvoicing (underinvoicing) of inputs will occur when $t^A < t^B$ ($t^A > t^B$); in each case profits are shifted from the high-tax to the low-tax country of the multinational's operations.[10]

In our simple framework, the maximisation problem of the multinational firm thus dichotomises into independent investment and transfer pricing decisions ((7.3) and (7.11)). This is due to the joint assumptions that the only costs associated with profit-shifting are the concealment costs θ, and that these costs depend only on the absolute difference between the true and the declared price of the input traded between the two firms. In section 7.3 we will discuss the implications of introducing a more general specification, under which investment and transfer pricing decisions are interdependent.

It remains to discuss the division of global net profits of the multinational firm. Here we can simplify the notation without affecting any of our results by assuming that the entrepreneur residing in country i owns the same exogenous share s^i in the firms of both countries A and B (where $s^A + s^B = 1$). With these specifications, the intertemporal budget constraint of the consumer in country i is

$$c_2^i = s^i\Pi + (1 + R)(e^i - c_1^i) \quad \forall \quad i, \tag{7.12}$$

where global net profits Π of the multinational firm are given in (7.10).

7.2.2 *Corporate tax policy with foreign ownership and profit-shifting*

The government's maximisation problem is the same as in section 7.1, but both policy instruments (t^i, α^i) have additional effects when there is foreign ownership of the domestic firm and the two firms engage in transfer pricing. Country i's corporate tax base D^i is given by total profits declared in this country[11]

[10] Our treatment of the firm's transfer-pricing decision abstracts from any trade-offs with other levies. (See, e.g., Schulze, 1994, for the interaction between corporate tax payments and tariffs.) The interaction with origin-based commodity taxes will be discussed in more detail in chapter 9.

[11] In principle it is possible in our model that declared profits in one country are negative because of transfer pricing. For arbitrary differences in statutory tax rates this problem can be ruled out only by assuming that the transaction cost schedule $\theta(q)$ is sufficiently steep. Alternatively we can focus on largely symmetric countries, which levy similar capital tax rates in equilibrium. In this case, no or little profit-shifting occurs in equilibrium and the constraint that D^i must be positive will not be binding. Of course, as in all symmetric models of capital tax competition, strategic forces are operative even if there is no profit-shifting in the non-cooperative equilibrium.

$$D^A = f(k^A) - \alpha^A(R+\delta)k^A + \left[q(t^A, t^B) - 1\right],$$
$$D^B = f(k^B) - \alpha^B(R+\delta)k^B - \left[q(t^A, t^B) - 1\right]. \tag{7.13}$$

Hence tax bases are now affected by the transfer price set by the multinational firm. Each government maximises the Lagrangian

$$\mathcal{L}^i_G(t^i, \alpha^i, \mu^i) = V^i(t^i, \alpha^i) + \mu^i\{t^i D^i - T^i_0\}.$$

The effect that each government's tax policy has on the indirect utility of its representative resident is given by the direct effects of a change in the tax parameters on the domestic resident's net profit income $s^i\Pi$. Using the global profit equation (7.10) and implicitly differentiating (7.11), the first-order conditions for the two tax instruments (t^i, α^i) are

$$\frac{\partial \mathcal{L}^i_G}{\partial t^i} = (\mu^i - s^i)\, D^i + \mu^i\, t^i \left[\frac{\partial k^i}{\partial t^i}\, \gamma^i - \frac{1}{\theta''}\right] = 0, \tag{7.14}$$

$$\frac{\partial \mathcal{L}^i_G}{\partial \alpha^i} = -(\mu^i - s^i)\, t^i\, (R+\delta)\, k^i + \mu^i\, t^i\, \frac{\partial k^i}{\partial \alpha^i}\, \gamma^i = 0, \tag{7.15}$$

where γ^i is given in (7.7) and $\partial k^i/\partial t^i$, $\partial k^i/\partial \alpha^i$ are given in (7.8).

Comparing the first-order conditions (7.14)–(7.15) to those of section 7.1 ((7.5)–(7.6)), there are two main differences: (i) with foreign ownership of the domestic firm both corporate tax parameters have additional effects on the international distribution of income; (ii) in the presence of strategic profit-shifting by the firm, the corporate tax rate leads to an additional tax base loss from the perspective of the taxing country. As we will see below, the latter effect changes the optimal tax policy mix towards a broadening of the tax base, and this result is independent of the simultaneous changes in international income distribution. In the following we will develop the intuition for these findings in more detail.

(i) In the first terms of (7.14)–(7.15), the multiplier for the domestic tax base is $(\mu^i - s^i)$, rather than $(\mu^i - 1)$. The reason is that the taxation of profits in the home country will affect the domestic resident only to the extent of her ownership share in the domestic firm (s^i); the remainder is borne by foreigners. Hence, in a setting with cross-ownership of firms, a source-based corporate tax can be used to redistribute income from foreigners to the domestic treasury and the shadow price of public funds may now fall below the private marginal utility of income (which has been normalised to unity). We have discussed this redistributive effect in section 3.1 and have also encountered it in section 5.5. In the present setting it implies that the extra costs of the corporate tax system must now be defined relative to the domestic ownership share in the home firm, rather than in relation to the marginal utility of income of the domestic resident.

(ii) The second term in (7.14) is then the 'modified excess burden' of an increase in the domestic tax rate. In contrast to (7.5) it comprises not only the reduction in domestic investment (the first term in the square bracket), but also a new term that gives the tax base change as a result of changes in the transfer price set by the multinational firm. As is known from section 7.1, the investment distortion can be avoided if the tax base parameter α^i is set equal to one; both the term γ^i and the derivative $\partial k^i/\partial t^i$ will then be zero (cf. (7.7) and (7.8)). However the transfer price set by the multinational firm will be affected by the tax increase even if the corporate tax system does not distort investment decisions. Therefore, even for $\alpha^i = 1$ the square bracket in (7.14) will be negative and the first term must be positive in the tax optimum, implying that the marginal cost of public funds exceeds the domestic ownership share (i.e. $(\mu^i - s^i) > 0$).

With this information we can infer the optimal level of α^i from (7.15). Since the tax rate must be positive to meet the government budget constraint, the first term in (7.15) is negative, implying that the second term must be positive in the government's optimum. Note that from (7.8) we have $\partial k^i/\partial \alpha > 0$ for $t^i > 0$. For the second term in (7.15) to be positive we must then have $\gamma^i > 0$, which in turn requires $\alpha^i < 1$ from (7.7). Hence a cash-flow tax that leaves investment decisions undistorted cannot be optimal in a setting where multinational firms engage in transfer pricing. We summarise this result in

Proposition 7.2
With FDI and cross-country profit shifting, the optimal corporate tax system involves an incomplete deduction for the cost of capital ($\alpha^i < 1 \ \forall \ i$).

Proposition 7.2 is a straightforward application of the general theorem of the second best. Since tax rates cannot be raised without cost in a setting with transfer pricing, the optimal policy is to accept some distortion of the investment decision in order to reduce the incentives to shift profits out of the country.

The last step in the argument is to show that this intuition applies even though each government is able to shift part of the burden of the corporation tax to foreign shareholders of the domestic firm. The reason is that the tax base parameter α^i is an equally effective instrument to perform this task, as is seen from the analogy of the first terms in (7.14) and

(7.15). As α^i is reduced, total investment in the domestic capital stock will fall, and this reduces the rents to the fixed factor entrepreneurial services. Since an increase in t^i and a reduction in α^i affect domestic and foreign shareholders in the same proportions, the optimal trade-off between these two instruments is determined only by the induced substitution effects on the domestic tax base.

Finally, it is straightforward to derive a Nash equilibrium in corporate tax rates from the first-order conditions (7.14)–(7.15). In particular, if countries are fully symmetric, then tax rates will be equal in the non-cooperative equilibrium and no profit-shifting occurs. Hence no country can gain from attracting paper profits, but each is left with the investment distortion caused by the imperfect deductibility of the cost of capital (cf. n. 11). Therefore, non-cooperative corporate tax policy in the present model leads to a conventional prisoner's dilemma situation with tax *rates* being 'too low' from a perspective of global welfare maximisation. The formal derivation of this symmetric Nash equilibrium is largely analogous to the one employed in the previous chapter, and is therefore relegated to the appendix (pp. 142–3).

7.3 Discussion and comparison of results

In this section we first consider two possible extensions of the analysis in this chapter and then compare our results with those of related work.

A first important feature of our analysis has been the requirement that the corporation tax must yield a fixed amount of revenue. This assumption has served to isolate the effects of increased tax competition on the corporate tax structure while excluding simultaneous changes in the level of corporate taxation. For this reason, our results should not be interpreted as an attempt to explain the observed changes in effective marginal tax rates on capital (EMTR). As we have discussed in section 4.4, most empirical studies find a moderate fall in the EMTR for the OECD average since the 1980s. In contrast, according to our model the EMTR would actually rise from zero in the benchmark case to some positive level in the presence of FDI and profit-shifting.[12] Clearly, in a more general model that allowed for some substitutability between different taxes, or for an endogenous level of public good supply, total revenues

[12] In the notation of this chapter, the EMTR is proportional to the difference between the marginal product of capital and the true cost of capital, i.e. $f' - (R + \delta)$. Substituting the optimal levels of the tax base parameter α (which differ in the benchmark case and in the case with FDI) into the optimal investment condition (7.3), the above result then follows immediately.

from the corporation tax would also change in response to the increased efficiency costs of this tax. We would expect, however, that the simultaneous change in the corporate tax structure, on which the present analysis has focused, would still be present in such an extended framework.

Secondly, our analysis of transfer pricing has been simplified by the independence of the firm's investment and transfer-pricing decisions ((7.3) and (7.11)). This implies, for example, that increasing the investment in the low-tax country will not reduce the overall transaction costs of shifting a given amount of profits. Instead it may be argued that profit-shifting into or out of a country becomes easier – or less costly – when the involvement in the firm located in this country is increased. A simple way to incorporate this extension into our model would be to make the transaction cost function (7.9) dependent on the investment volume (or, alternatively, gross profits) in both countries, i.e. $\theta(q, k^i)$ with $\partial\theta/\partial k^i < 0$. For any given set of corporate tax parameters, it is then easily shown that the investment volume in both countries is increased beyond the level implied by (7.3), since the capital location decision in each country now also represents an 'investment in tax avoidance'.

With this extension, the corporate tax rate will distort the investment decision even if depreciation allowances correspond to the true cost of capital ($\alpha^i = 1$). Conversely, an increase in the corporate tax base (i.e. a fall in α^i) will reduce investment and increase the transaction costs of strategic transfer pricing. One can thus argue that considering these additional interdependencies makes a policy of 'tax-rate-cut-cum-base-broadening' even more attractive than in the simpler framework analysed above. In any case, however, it remains true that the corporate tax rate can no longer be a non-distortive instrument in the presence of FDI and transfer-pricing opportunities. Therefore, the qualitative result derived above should still be valid when investment and transfer-pricing decisions interact.

Turning to related work, perhaps closest to our analysis in this chapter is the paper by Gordon and MacKie-Mason (1995) already mentioned in subsection 4.2.2. They model the trade-off for a home and a host government of employing either a corporation tax or a tax on wages. An increase in corporation tax leads to international income-shifting via transfer pricing while a positive tax differential between the tax rates on wages and profits will induce domestic income shifting from labour income to profit income. Hence the Gordon and MacKie-Mason paper does not focus on the structure of corporation tax, but instead on the mix between different factor taxes. A further difference between Gordon and MacKie-Mason (1995) and our analysis is that we allow foreigners to own a fixed share of the domestic firm, and hence incorporate a 'tax exportation' motive for national tax policy. As we have seen, this additional fiscal externality does not affect the optimal structure of corporation tax in our model, but it would affect the mix of factor taxes analysed by Gordon and MacKie-Mason.

The possibility of taxing rents that accrue to foreigners is an important element in the models of Mintz and Tulkens (1996) and Huizinga and Nielsen (1997a). In Mintz and Tulkens (1996) the incentive for each of two small countries to impose source-based taxes on the profits of foreign firms operating within its borders is the main reason why globally optimal residence-based taxation cannot be sustained as an equilibrium. Huizinga and Nielsen (1997a) show that when domestic firms are partly owned by foreigners optimal source taxes on capital levied by a small open economy may become so high that they exceed the fixed revenue requirement, the difference being returned to consumers either as a lump-sum payment or as a savings subsidy. Clearly, the intuition for this last result is that – as in our analysis above – the shadow price of public funds may fall *below* the private marginal utility of income.[13]

Elitzur and Mintz (1996) analyse optimal corporate tax policy in the presence of transfer pricing, but do not endogenise the government's choice of tax base. In their model, the profits made by the foreign subsidiary affect the remuneration of its manager. Hence there is a trade-off for the multinational firm between the minimisation of its worldwide tax payments and the incentives given to the subsidiary's managing partner. Furthermore, Elitzur and Mintz introduce a transfer-pricing rule that separates reported profits for tax purposes from the firm's optimal transfer price. This turns the corporation tax into a sales (or excise) tax and, by the optimal decision of the subsidiary's managing partner, reduces output in the foreign country. Hence, in equilibrium, corporate taxes impose a *negative* fiscal externality on the neighbouring country and are therefore 'too high' from a global perspective.

In other models by Mansori and Weichenrieder (1999) and Raimondos-Møller and Scharf (2001), the transfer-pricing regulation itself – rather than the corporate tax rate – is the strategic variable of governments. As in Elitzur and Mintz, the non-cooperative outcome in both models implies an 'excessive' taxation of the multinational firm; this result is here brought about by a partial double taxation of the firm's profits. In Raimondos-Møller and Scharf (2001) the incentive to overtax

[13] Similar results are also known from the international trade literature. Schweinberger and Vosgerau (1997) show that optimal tariffs can be negative when the gains from the taxation of foreign factor owners dominate the usual terms of trade effect. Since a tariff is equivalent to the combination of a production subsidy and a consumption tax, this result implies a positive tax on production when there is foreign factor ownership.

the firm is further reinforced by the explicit modelling of cross-ownership of firms, which introduces the 'tax exportation' motive discussed above. The authors also show, however, that the harmonisation of transfer pricing rules according to the current 'arm's length principle' is not Pareto improving, relative to the non-cooperative outcome.

Finally, Osmundsen, Hagen and Schjelderup (1998, section 3) endogenise the government's choice of the corporate tax base, but do not consider transfer pricing in their model. Instead, there is a continuum of firms which are imperfectly mobile internationally and the degree of mobility is known only to the individual firm, but not to the taxing government. In this setting a cash-flow tax on pure profits loses its lump-sum character, as firms can move their operations to the region offering the highest net profits.[14] The authors show that the government can implement an optimal revelation mechanism by offering firms a menu of choices combining either high corporate tax rates with favourable depreciation allowances or vice versa. In this setting, mobile firms will self-select more unfavourable depreciation allowances, and thus lower tax rates, as compared to relatively immobile firms. Hence, an imperfect deductibility of the cost of capital serves as a way to reduce the information rents accruing to firms. While this argument is obviously very different from the one made here, it offers a complementary reason why governments may not choose cash-flow corporate tax schemes when production decisions are increasingly made at an international level.

7.4 Profit-shifting and international coordination of corporate tax bases

There is by now substantial, albeit indirect, evidence that multinational corporations engage in profit-shifting and other methods of tax arbitrage.[15] Hines and Rice (1994), for example, analyse the aggregate reported profitabilities of US affiliates in various foreign locations and find that a 1 per cent tax increase in the host country's tax rate is associated with a 2.3 per cent decrease in reported *before-tax* profits in this country. This pattern is incompatible with competitive conditions, under which net-of-tax profits should be equalised across countries, and thus offers strong indirect evidence for tax avoidance. Another study by Collins, Kemsley and Lang (1998) uses a pooled sample of US multinationals and finds that 'normalised' reported foreign profitability exceeds US profitability among those firms which face foreign tax rates

[14] Related settings will be studied in detail in part 4 of this book.
[15] For a comprehensive survey of the empirical evidence reported here, see Hines (1999).

below those in the United States. In principle, this finding could also be due to favourable business conditions in the (low-tax) foreign countries. However, a structural econometric analysis of the activities of US corporations in Puerto Rico finds that income-shifting advantages, rather than investment opportunities, are the predominant reason for US investment in this country (Grubert and Slemrod, 1998).

Within Europe, Weichenrieder (1996) presents similar evidence for profit-shifting by internationally operating German firms. He shows that these firms have taken advantage of the low Irish tax rate in the manufacturing sector by shifting the returns to financial assets ('passive income') to its subsidiaries in Ireland. Subsequent German tax legislation that restricted the ratio of passive to active income earned in a foreign country led to a shift from financial to real investment in Ireland, in order to relax the new constraint. Similar tax arbitrage opportunities opened up in Belgium, Luxembourg and the Netherlands. These countries offered reduced corporation taxes to subsidiaries of multinational firms which provide intra-firm financial services or act as financial holding companies. The growing importance of special tax breaks for multinational corporations is the core reason underlying the 'Code of Conduct' for business taxation signed by the EU member states in 1998 (cf. subsection 2.1.1).

The examples given above indicate that financial transactions now play a far more important role for tax arbitrage activities within integrated firms than the traditional instrument of the (strategic) choice of a transfer price for intermediate inputs. Of particular importance are interest and royalty payments from the subsidiary to the parent company. Hines (1995) demonstrates, for example, that royalty payments from foreign affiliates of American companies exhibit a considerable elasticity with respect to their tax cost. It should be obvious that enforcing the arm's length principle is considerably more difficult for these transactions, as compared to the exchange of intermediate goods.

In response to these challenges, the United States introduced a new transfer pricing regulation in 1994, labelled the 'comparable profits method'.[16] This scheme complements the arm's length principle in the sense that US tax authorities have the right to correct the corporation tax of a firm which has reported a lower profitability than comparable firms in the same industry over a period of several years. This firm will then be taxed on the basis of the average profits made in the industry. It is too

[16] See Horst (1993) for a more detailed description, and Schjelderup and Weichenrieder (1999) for an analysis of the trade effects of this new regulation.

early, however, to evaluate the effectiveness of this complementary method of taxing US multinationals.

A fundamental alternative to the separate accounting of profits in the different countries of a multinational's operation would be the move to a scheme of formula apportionment. Under this approach, the consolidated profit of a multi-jurisdictional firm is allocated between the different states in which the firm operates according to readily measurable indicators such as employment or total sales. Each state then taxes the share of profits allocated to it by the agreed-upon rule using its own, independently chosen tax rate. This scheme is already in place in the United States, Canada and Switzerland for domestic firms operating in several national jurisdictions.[17] Based on this experience, it has also long been advocated for the taxation of multinational corporations (P. Musgrave, 1987).

A systematic evaluation of formula allocation rules at a worldwide level is provided by Mintz (1999). According to his analysis, the efficiency case for formula apportionment is by no means obvious. On the one hand, tax base flight and hence the tax base externality is likely to be weakened as firms trying to reduce tax payments in high-tax countries will find it more difficult and costly to manipulate the weights in the formula allocation rule, as compared to the manipulation of reported profits under the present separate accounting system. On the other hand, an increase in the tax rate of one jurisdiction raises the average tax rate faced by the firm for *any* investment that it undertakes, so that the burden of a change in the domestic tax rate is partly shifted to other jurisdictions. This may increase the incentive for competing governments to tax the profits accruing to non-residents and thus engage in tax exportation.[18]

Mintz (1999) also points out, however, that a major drawback of the separate accounting system lies in high administrative and compliance costs, caused in large part by the increased use of 'exchange of information' agreements to combat tax evasion and of 'competent authority' procedures to settle transfer-pricing disputes between countries.[19] Apart from their costs, these procedures have also effectively reduced national sovereignty over the taxation of multinational firms and have

[17] A detailed review of formula apportionment in the United States is given in Weiner (1996).

[18] Similarly ambiguous conclusions are reached by Nielsen, Raimondos-Møller and Schjelderup (1999) in a formal analysis of tax spillovers under separate accounting vs. formula apportionment rules.

[19] Recall from subsection 2.1.1 that EU member states have addressed the latter issue by signing an arbitration convention that coordinates their arm's length pricing rules.

introduced informal elements of formula allocation. From this perspective, replacing the piecemeal and implicit use of formula allocation rules by an explicit international agreement could offer a more cost-effective way of coordinating the taxation of corporate profits in multinational firms.

APPENDIX

To derive the Nash equilibrium in corporate tax rates, the derivatives $\partial k^i/\partial t^i$ and $\partial k^i/\partial \alpha^i$ from (7.8) are inserted into the first-order conditions (7.14) and (7.15). Using (7.7), $D^i = T^i/t^i$ and rearranging gives in a first step

$$\mu^i \varepsilon = s^i \frac{T_0^i}{t^i}, \quad \varepsilon = \left(\frac{T_0^i}{t^i} + \frac{t^i (\gamma^i)^2}{(1-t^i) f''} - \frac{t^i}{\theta''} \right) \tag{7A.1}$$

$$\mu^i \left[k^i + \frac{t^i \gamma^i}{(1-t^i) f''} \right] = s^i k^i \quad \Longrightarrow \quad \mu^i = \frac{-s^i k^i (1-t^i) f''}{k^i (1-t^i) f'' + t^i \gamma^i}. \tag{7A.2}$$

In a second step we substitute (7A.2) in (7A.1) and add and subtract $\beta\varepsilon$ to the resulting equation, where

$$\beta^i \equiv \frac{-t^i \gamma^i}{k^i (1-t^i) f'' + t^i \gamma^i} > 0. \tag{7A.3}$$

Note that $\beta^i > 0$ follows from (7A.2) for $\mu^i > 0$ and $\gamma^i > 0$ for $\alpha^i < 1$ (cf. (7.7) and proposition 7.2). Collecting terms and rearranging then gives the following best response function for the corporate tax rate in each country

$$F^i(t^i, t^j) \equiv (1 + \beta^i) \left[\frac{t^i (\gamma^i)^2}{(1-t^i) f''} - \frac{t^i}{\theta''} \right] + \beta^i \frac{T_0^i}{t^i} = 0, \tag{7A.4}$$

where $\gamma^i \geq 0$ is given in (7.7). The first term in (7A.4) is then unambiguously negative while the second term is positive.

The reaction function of country i depends on the tax rate of country j through the tax base terms $(T_0^i/t^i) = D^i$, which are a function of both t^i and t^j (see (7.13)). To ensure that the implicitly defined best-response functions $F^i(t^i, t^j)$ yield a utility maximum for each country, the second-order conditions $\partial^2 \mathcal{L}_G^i / \partial (t^i)^2 = \partial F^i / \partial t^i < 0$ must be fulfilled. We assume that these conditions are met.

It is then straightforward to show that best-response functions will be upward sloping. Applying the implicit function theorem to (7A.4) we get

$$\frac{\partial t^i}{\partial t^j} = -\frac{\partial F^i/\partial t^j}{\partial F^i/\partial t^i} \Longrightarrow \text{sign}\left(\frac{\partial t^i}{\partial t^j}\right) = \text{sign}\left(\frac{\partial F^i}{\partial t^j}\right).$$

Differentiating F^i with respect to t^j and recalling that $T_0^i/t^i = D^i$ gives, using (7.11) and (7.13)

$$\frac{\partial F^i}{\partial t^j} = \frac{\beta^i}{\theta''} > 0 \quad \forall \quad i,j,\ i \neq j, \tag{7A.5}$$

since $\beta^i > 0$ from (7A.3). Equation (7A.5) shows that country i's tax base and hence the adjustment in its optimal tax rate will be a continuous function of t^j. In particular, the properties of the transaction cost function (7.9) and the fact that the transfer price q responds symmetrically to tax differentials between the two countries ensure that there is no discrete jump in country i's best response when country i switches from being the high-tax region to being the low-tax region as t^j is continuously increased. Since best-response functions are continuous and strictly quasi-concave in the present model, a Nash equilibrium must exist. In particular, if the model is entirely symmetric there will be a symmetric Nash equilibrium with identical corporate tax systems (t^i, α^i), and no transfer pricing occurs in equilibrium.

Part 3

Commodity taxation

8 The problem of cross-border shopping

Part 3 of this book deals with issues of commodity taxation in open economies. Here it is the international mobility of consumers, who can purchase goods in different jurisdictions, which may give rise to tax competition between countries. As we have discussed in section 2.2, this problem is of particular policy relevance in the European Union, where border controls have been abolished in the internal market. However, similar problems arise in federal economies with independent taxing powers of lower-level jurisdictions, or at international borders where the destination principle cannot be effectively enforced.

Chapter 8 analyses commodity tax competition between two neighbouring countries under a mixed system of destination-based producer trade and cross-border shopping by final consumers. It also explores how different measures of tax coordination and tax harmonisation affect the welfare level in each of the competing countries. Based on these results, chapter 9 addresses the question whether tax rate harmonisation can be avoided by taxing all traded commodities in the country of origin. This policy question has a long tradition in the European Union, but a number of new issues have recently been raised in connection with increasing international capital mobility. Hence, in this chapter the importance of an integrated treatment of commodity and factor taxation is already visible – a theme that will be addressed in detail in part 4 of the book.

The present chapter focuses on the optimal tax response to cross-border shopping in two neighbouring jurisdictions, which are distinguished by their preferences for public goods. One of the fundamental questions will be whether different measures of tax coordination can benefit both countries simultaneously and thus whether a low-tax country, which is able to enlarge its commodity tax base by cross-border shopping, has an incentive to agree to coordinated policies. Hence, there are obvious parallels to the analysis of chapter 5, where similar policy questions have been raised in the context of capital tax competition between countries of different size. At the same time, there are also close analytical similarities with chapter 6, which will be pointed out as the analysis proceeds.

This chapter is organised as follows: section 8.1 introduces alternative schemes of international commodity taxation, including a mixed commodity tax principle which gives rise to cross-border shopping. Section 8.2 briefly summarises the two fundamental analyses of commodity tax competition, the contributions by Mintz and Tulkens (1986) and Kanbur and Keen (1993). Section 8.3 introduces a model that combines important features of both analyses. Section 8.4 discusses the existence and the properties of a Nash equilibrium in this model. Section 8.5 then turns to the analysis of two alternative tax coordination measures, a mandatory minimum tax rate and a tightening of the rules that govern cross-border shopping. Section 8.6 summarises the literature on the welfare effects of indirect tax harmonisation and compares our results with those obtained in related analyses. Section 8.7 concludes with a brief summary of the policy problem posed by present rules of international commodity taxation in the European Union.

8.1 Principles of international commodity taxation

In a way analogous to the taxation of international factor incomes (cf. subsection 4.1.1), internationally traded goods can be taxed either in the country where they are consumed (*destination principle*), or where they are produced (*origin principle*). These parallels are stressed, for example, in the introduction to alternative commodity and factor tax principles by Frenkel, Razin and Sadka (1991, ch. 2). The following brief introduction deviates from their treatment in two respects. First, we emphasise the distinction between uniform and differentiated taxation of traded commodities in the discussion of both tax principles. Second, we introduce a 'mixed tax principle' – relevant in an internal market like the European Union – where the taxation of internationally traded goods depends on whether the purchaser is a VAT-registered trader or a final consumer. Both of these features will play an important role in the following analysis.

Destination principle

Under GATT rules, world trade is generally taxed under the destination principle. Under this scheme, all commodity taxes levied in the country of production are rebated when the good is exported. At the same time, commodity taxes are levied on imports in the country of final consumption, with tax revenue also accruing to this country. Furthermore, in each country the tax rate on imported goods equals the commodity tax rate levied on domestic products.

We denote by p_k^i the producer prices of two traded goods $k \in \{1, 2\}$ in countries $i \in \{A, B\}$. We allow for commodity tax rates t_k^i to be differentiated across products and countries. Then the following arbitrage conditions must hold under the destination principle, from the perspective of country A's consumers:

$$\begin{aligned} (1 + t_1^A)\, p_1^A &= (1 + t_1^A)\, p_1^B \qquad \Longrightarrow p_1^A = p_1^B, \\ (1 + t_2^A)\, p_2^A &= (1 + t_2^A)\, p_2^B \qquad \Longrightarrow p_2^A = p_2^B. \end{aligned} \tag{8.1}$$

It follows from (8.1) that consumer arbitrage under the destination principle will always equalise both absolute and relative producer prices across countries. Hence, international production efficiency will be maintained even in the presence of differentiated commodity taxation and international differences in tax rates. The robust property of the destination principle to ensure undistorted production patterns is one of the core advantages of this tax principle in international trade relations.

To discuss the efficiency of international consumption, two cases must be distinguished. In the first case, each country levies a uniform tax rate $t_1^i = t_2^i$ on both traded goods. Relative consumer prices will then equal relative producer prices in each country. Hence, marginal rates of substitution between the two traded goods will also be equalised across countries, even if tax rates differ internationally. In this case neither production nor consumption decisions are thus distorted internationally.[1]

In the second case, tax rates are differentiated within each country. A frequently analysed scenario assumes that one of the two traded goods – good 2, for example – remains untaxed in both countries ($t_2^A = t_2^B = 0$). In this case, international differences in the remaining tax rate on good 1 will imply that relative consumer prices and hence marginal rates of substitution differ between countries

$$\frac{\partial u^A / \partial c_1^A}{\partial u^A / \partial c_2^A} = (1 + t^A)\frac{p_1}{p_2} \neq (1 + t^B)\frac{p_1}{p_2} = \frac{\partial u^B / \partial c_1^B}{\partial u^B / \partial c_2^B} \qquad \textit{if } t^A \neq t^B, \tag{8.2}$$

[1] Distortions may still arise, however, from an endogenous labour supply choice. International differences in tax rates will then lead to cross-country differences in the marginal rate of substitution between leisure and commodity consumption (cf. Frenkel, Razin and Sadka, 1991, p. 39).

where p_1/p_2 is the common relative producer price in the two countries. In this case the international consumption pattern for traded commodities is thus distorted by commodity tax differentials.

Origin principle

Under the origin principle, commodity taxes levied in the country of production are not rebated upon export, and no import tax is levied in the country of final consumption. This implies consumers will compare international prices on a gross-of-tax basis. In our two-commodity framework, the following arbitrage conditions will then hold:

$$\begin{aligned} (1+t_1^A)\,p_1^A &= (1+t_1^B)\,p_1^B \\ (1+t_2^A)\,p_2^A &= (1+t_2^B)\,p_2^B. \end{aligned} \qquad (8.3)$$

Equation (8.3) shows that international efficiency in consumption will always be obtained under origin-based commodity taxation. In contrast, the distinction between uniform versus differentiated commodity taxation is now crucial for the efficiency of international production patterns.

If $t_1^i = t_2^i$ holds in each country, but tax rates differ internationally, then it is seen from (8.3) that producer price levels will differ across countries. However, *relative* producer prices will not be affected by taxes and production patterns are undistorted under a general origin-based commodity tax. In each country, producer prices and thus factor returns fall by the level of the domestic tax, implying a real devaluation in the high-tax country.[2] Furthermore, since overall trade is balanced, tax bases are the same under a general consumption and a general production tax. These are the basic equivalence properties between a general destination principle and a general origin principle first mentioned in the Tinbergen Report (1953) (see subsection 2.2.1). It has been shown by Lockwood, de Meza and Myles (1994a) that these equivalence results carry over to more general classes of models including, for example, transportation costs for consumers and imperfect competition by firms. In any case, the crucial condition for the equivalence between the destination and origin principles is that the commodity tax is applied uniformly on all goods.

[2] Alternatively the devaluation in the high-tax country can be brought about by a change in the nominal exchange rate. In general, it is sufficient for the price level adjustment to occur if *either* exchange rates *or* factor prices are flexible (see Berglas, 1981; Lockwood, de Meza and Myles, 1994a).

In contrast, if tax rates are differentiated within each country, then the adjustment of exchange rates or factor prices will not be sufficient, in general, to offset international tax differentials and the equivalence between destination- and origin-based commodity taxation no longer holds. Assuming again that good 2 remains untaxed in both countries, equation set (8.3) can be rearranged to give

$$\frac{p_1^A}{p_2^A} = \frac{(1+t^B)}{(1+t^A)} \frac{p_1^B}{p_2^B}. \tag{8.4}$$

Hence, when $t^A \neq t^B$, relative producer prices in the two countries differ and international production patterns are distorted under a non-general origin principle. The distinction between a uniform and a selective origin-based commodity tax will play an important role in our analyses of chapters 9–11.

Mixed tax principle

In an internal market like the European Union a general destination principle cannot be administered since border tax adjustments cannot be enacted for purchases by final consumers. The European Union has nevertheless decided to maintain the destination principle for all purchases between VAT-registered traders. Under the current 'transitional system' border tax adjustments are implemented 'in the books': exporters are required to report the VAT identification number of their customer when claiming the tax rebate, allowing tax authorities to check whether importers have lawfully paid tax to their government for all imports from other EU member states (cf. subsection 2.2.1). However, neither this method nor the international tax credit scheme envisaged by the European Commission can be applied to direct across-the-border purchases by final consumers, which can effectively be taxed only in the country of origin.

Under these conditions international arbitrage will depend on whether the purchaser of an internationally traded good is a registered trader or a final consumer. The first group compares international prices on a net-of-tax basis while gross-of-tax prices are relevant for the latter group:

$$\begin{aligned} p_k^A &= p_k^B \quad \forall \; k \qquad \text{for traders,} \\ (1+t^A)\, p_k^A &= (1+t^B)\, p_k^B \quad \forall \; k \qquad \text{for final consumers.} \end{aligned} \tag{8.5}$$

Two observations follow immediately from (8.5). First, producer prices are *not* distorted under this tax scheme, since all producer trade occurs at net-of-tax prices. Second, the set of arbitage conditions (8.5) is inconsistent with international tax differentials, unless there are transportation costs for cross-border shopping. In the absence of such costs, consumers in the high-tax country would make *all* their purchases in the neighbouring region, and tax revenue in the high-tax region would be zero. In the presence of transportation costs, countries nevertheless have an incentive to lower the domestic commodity tax rate in order to attract cross-border shopping from residents of the neighbouring jurisdiction and thus increase the domestic tax base. The resulting commodity tax competition, and the effects of alternative coordination measures, will be discussed in detail in the remainder of this chapter.

8.2 Two benchmark analyses

To discuss the issue of cross-border shopping, the literature on commodity tax competition has taken two rather different approaches. The first rigorous analysis of the issue is provided by Mintz and Tulkens (1986), who set up a general equilibrium model with a private consumption good, an untaxed numeraire good (labour services) and a public consumption good. Consumer purchases are taxed under the origin principle so that the arbitrage conditions are the same as under the mixed tax principle above (8.5). Cross-border shopping by consumers is subject to a general convex transportation cost function, which may differ across countries. Hence, each consumer will purchase the taxed good in the jurisdiction where the price, gross of taxes and transportation costs, is lower. Governments maximise the utility of the representative consumer and set the domestic commodity tax rate optimally, given the preferences for the public good and the constraints imposed by the open border. Trade between the two countries is balanced; when consumers of region i purchase the taxed good in region j, this is paid for by the untaxed labour services that region i's residents perform in region j.

Within this framework, Mintz and Tulkens identify two fiscal externalities, a *public consumption effect* (tax base effect) and a *private consumption effect* (terms of trade effect). They can show that the tax importing country (whose residents cross-border shop) always sets its tax rate inefficiently low in the Nash equilibrium. For the tax exporting country, however, public and private consumption effects work in opposite directions and the tax rate in the Nash equilibrium may either be above or below its benchmark level in the closed economy (cf. section 3.1). Hence a small, coordinated increase in both tax rates is not necessarily Pareto improving in this model, but a more detailed discussion of tax coordination measures is precluded by the complexity of the framework used. Furthermore, a core feature of the Mintz and Tulkens (1986) analysis is that best-response functions are discontinuous, so that a Nash equilibrium need not exist in all cases.

This is the starting point for the analysis of Kanbur and Keen (1993), who set up a spatial partial equilibrium model with a single taxed good and fixed producer prices. They introduce a basic asymmetry between countries by assuming that regions differ in population size. In each country, the population is uniformly distributed and transportation costs are an increasing function of the distance that each individual has to travel to the border. Effectively, this yields a special case of the convex transportation cost function assumed in Mintz and Tulkens (1986).

An important assumption in the Kanbur and Keen analysis – already stressed in section 3.5 – is that governments behave as revenue maximisers. This assumption eliminates the private consumption effect of the Mintz and Tulkens analysis since it neglects the welfare losses that cross-border shoppers suffer from an increase in the foreign tax rate. As a consequence, both countries now undersupply the public good in the Nash equilibrium, given the objective of revenue maximisation. Furthermore, even though the best-response function of the small country (but not of the large) also exhibits a discontinuity in their model, Kanbur and Keen are able to show that a unique Nash equilibrium exists. They further demonstrate that the smaller country strictly sets the lower tax rate in the Nash equilibrium, reflecting the fact that it perceives a higher elasticity of its domestic tax base. These results are familiar from our analysis in chapter 5 and show the close similarities between capital and commodity tax competition when countries differ in size.

Kanbur and Keen also consider various policies of tax coordination in their model. These include a harmonisation of tax rates towards a common average and a minimum tax rate that is binding for the small (low-tax) country. A strong and important result of their analysis is that the latter policy turns out to be strictly Pareto improving, i.e., it benefits both countries simultaneously. The intuition for this result is that a mandatory rise in the small country's tax rate relaxes the external constraint faced by its high-tax neighbour, leading to a tax increase in the large country that is sufficiently strong to overcompensate the small country for the forced increase in its own tax rate. Analogous results with a similar intuition are also derived for an exogenous increase in transport costs, which can be interpreted as any coordinated policy that raises the costs of cross-border shopping. The setting of Kanbur and Keen thus leads to rather optimistic predictions regarding the prospects of tax coordination measures. In the following, we will examine whether these results continue to hold in a more general framework that re-introduces some of the effects operating in the original Mintz and Tulkens (1986) analysis.

8.3 A simple general equilibrium model with cross-hauling

The model presented here combines elements of both analyses just introduced.[3] While it builds on the general equilibrium model of Mintz and Tulkens (1986), two main simplifying assumptions are made. First, we restrict the shape of transaction cost functions for cross-border shopping. With this modification necessary conditions for the continuity of best responses can be stated, and a Nash equilibrium can be shown to exist. Second we dispense with the second, untaxed good (labour). Instead, trade occurs in a single private good which is simultaneously imported by consumers of the high-tax country and exported by its producers. Thus cross-hauling of a homogeneous commodity takes place in the present model, ensuring that trade is balanced and income effects are incorporated in our framework. This is a simple way to capture the conditions under the mixed tax principle in the EU internal market, where arbitrage conditions differ depending on whether the purchaser of the good is a final consumer or a VAT-registered trader (cf. (8.5)).[4]

There are two countries A and B, which will later be identified as the high-tax and the low-tax country (or region). However, for the description of the Nash equilibrium in this section it is important that each country can, in principle, have the higher or the lower tax rate. Therefore we employ a general notation and introduce country indices $i \in \{A, B\}$ and $j \in \{A, B\}$ $(i \neq j)$. In each country there is a single representative consumer, which is given the same exogenous endowment of x units of output. Output can either be used for private consumption c^i or for local public consumption g^i so that the marginal rate of transformation between these two goods is equal to one. Preferences are described by the strictly quasi-concave utility function

$$u^i(c^i, g^i) \quad \forall \quad i \in \{A, B\}. \tag{8.6}$$

To provide the public good the government of country i purchases some fraction of total output, which is financed by a tax on private

[3] Sections 8.3–8.5 are a revised and adapted version of Haufler (1996a).

[4] In practice cross-hauling occurs, for example, in the so-called 'Channel trade' where British producers export spirits and tobacco to France while British consumers re-import the same goods via the ferry trade in order to save taxes.

consumption. Interdependencies between the two countries' tax choices arise through international trade in the private commodity. Producer trade follows the destination principle and we assume that there are no transportation costs for producers. Producer arbitrage will then equalise net-of-tax prices in the two countries, which can jointly be normalised by $p^A = p^B \equiv 1$ (cf. (8.5)). In contrast, cross-border purchases by final consumers are taxed at the rate of the origin country. Therefore, residents of the high-tax country have an incentive to purchase at least part of their demand for the private good abroad. This leads to a trade deficit in the high-tax country, which is balanced by producer exports. In the aggregate, each country will then import and export the same (homogeneous) good as a result of different tax arbitrage conditions for producers on the one hand and consumers on the other.

Overall private consumption in country i consists of domestic purchases, c_i^i, and cross-border purchases, c_j^i (where $i,j \in \{A, B\}$ and $i \neq j$). If country i is the low-tax country its residents have no incentive to shop abroad so that

$$c^i \equiv c_i^i + c_j^i, \quad c_j^i > 0 \quad \text{if} \quad t^i > t^j \\ c_j^i = 0 \quad \text{if} \quad t^i \leq t^j. \tag{8.7}$$

There are obvious constraints on consumer purchases abroad since residents of the high-tax country must either physically cross the border or place mail-orders in order to take advantage of the lower tax rate. As in chapters 6 and 7, these constraints are captured by a strictly convex transaction (transportation) cost function $\tau_i(c_j^i)$. The convexity assumption can either be rationalised by assuming heterogeneous consumers, who live at varying distances from the border (Kanbur and Keen, 1993; Christiansen, 1994) or by thinking of a continuum of goods, some of which are more easily transported across borders than others.[5]

An important further assumption is that the marginal costs of purchasing the first unit abroad are zero for residents of each country so that any tax differential will lead to positive levels of cross-border shopping. Assuming transaction cost functions to be continuously differentiable, these properties are summarised by

[5] Note, however, that this conventional justification for convex transportation costs implicitly assumes the transaction size of each individual to be fixed. In contrast, Scharf (1999) endogenises the optimal transaction size of an individual when there are scale economies in cross-border shopping on the one hand and storage costs on the other. In this setting she derives optimal tax rules for differentiated commodity taxation in a multi-good framework.

$$\tau_i'(c_j^i) > 0, \tau_i''(c_j^i) > 0 \quad \text{if} \quad c_j^i > 0,$$
$$\tau_i(0) = \tau_i'(0) = 0, \quad \tau_i''(0) > 0 \quad \forall\, i, \tag{8.8}$$

where the index i shows that we initially allow for country-specific transaction cost schedules.

Since producer prices are equal to one in both countries, residents of the high-tax country will cross-border shop until the tax savings are just offset by the marginal transportation cost incurred. Therefore the following consumer arbitrage condition must hold in equilibrium

$$\tau_i'(c_j^i) = t^i - t^j \quad \text{if} \quad t^i > t^j. \tag{8.9}$$

Given the marginal transaction cost schedule, (8.9) implicitly defines the level of cross-border shopping. Inverting gives

$$c_j^i(t^i - t^j) = (\tau_i')^{-1} \quad \text{if} \quad t^i > t^j, \tag{8.10}$$

where the tax differential in $c_j^i(.)$ is a functional argument. Cross-border shopping thus depends exclusively on the international *difference* in tax rates, but not on the level of taxes in the two countries.

There are two possible regimes from the perspective of each country: we define regime I by the condition $t^i \geq t^j$ so that residents of country i cross-border shop in the neighbouring country j. In contrast $t^i \leq t^j$ holds in regime II and residents of country j purchase goods directly in country i. The boundary case $t^i = t^j$ is an element of both regimes with zero cross-border shopping and zero transaction costs from (8.7) and (8.8). This is the first important difference to the general transaction cost function in Mintz and Tulkens (1986), which includes fixed costs of cross-border shopping. Together with the assumption that the marginal costs of purchasing the first unit abroad are zero [$\tau_i'(0) = 0$], this turns out to be a crucial condition for the continuity of reaction functions.

Budget constraints for country i depend on whether its tax rate is higher or lower than that of the union partner. The regime-specific constraints for *private* consumption are given by

$$RI: \quad (1 + t^i)\, c_i^i + (1 + t^j)\, c_j^i + \tau_i(c_j^i) = x, \tag{8.11a}$$

$$RII: \quad (1 + t^i)\, c^i = x, \tag{8.11b}$$

where x denotes the exogenous endowment. In regime I, total expenditures by residents of country i include the resources used up in the process of cross-border shopping. These constitute a 'pure waste' from a global efficiency point of view since producer trade has zero transportation costs by assumption.[6] However, the private budget constraint faced by country i's residents is relaxed through cross-border shopping: from the convexity of the transaction cost function the sum of country j's taxes and transaction costs is always less in an arbitrage equilibrium than if the same amount of goods were purchased in country i. In contrast, if country i is in regime II then its residents have no incentive to shop abroad and all private purchases occur in country i.

The *government* budget constraints are easily derived: in regime I, the tax base of country i is given by the domestic purchases of its own residents, which equals total private consumption less the amount purchased abroad. In regime II country i's tax base consists of domestic purchases plus cross-border shopping by residents of country j

$$RI: \quad g^i = t^i c^i_i = t^i \,(c^i - c^i_j), \tag{8.12a}$$

$$RII: \quad g^i = t^i \,(c^i + c^j_i). \tag{8.12b}$$

In contrast to the Mintz and Tulkens (1986) analysis, where consumers simultaneously decide on private consumption and labour supply, the consumer optimum is fully described by the spatial arbitrage condition (8.10) in the present model. For this reason the comparative static effects of tax changes on the components of private consumption can be directly inferred from (8.10)–(8.11b). Using the inverse function rule and $\tau'_i = t^i - t^j$ to differentiate (8.10), the results are summarised by

$$RI: \frac{\partial c^i_j}{\partial t^i} = \frac{1}{\tau''_i} > 0, \quad \frac{\partial c^i_i}{\partial t^i} = \frac{-c^i_i}{(1+t^i)} - \frac{1}{\tau''_i} < 0, \quad \frac{\partial c^i}{\partial t^i} = \frac{-c^i_i}{(1+t^i)} < 0,$$

$$\frac{\partial c^i_j}{\partial t^j} = \frac{-1}{\tau''_i} < 0, \quad \frac{\partial c^i_i}{\partial t^j} = \frac{-c^i_j}{(1+t^i)} + \frac{1}{\tau''_i} <> 0, \quad \frac{\partial c^i}{\partial t^j} = \frac{-c^i_j}{(1+t^i)} < 0,$$

$$RII: \frac{\partial c^i}{\partial t^i} = \frac{-c^i}{(1+t^i)} < 0, \quad \frac{\partial c^i}{\partial t^j} = 0. \tag{8.13}$$

In regime I, a tax rise in country i increases cross-border shopping so that purchases in country i fall by more than overall consumption. In contrast, a rise in t^j reduces both cross-border shopping and overall private consumption. Therefore, an ambiguity arises for the derivative $\partial c^i_i / \partial t^j$, which determines the change in country i's tax base in regime I. This effect is further discussed below. If country i is in regime II, a tax

[6] Similar efficiency losses arise in more conventional multi-good models when selective tariffs cause a substitution of suppliers with higher (transportation) costs for low-cost suppliers (e.g. Melvin, 1985). Cf. also our specification of the concealment cost function in chapter 7 (n. 9).

rise in country j has no effect on private consumption since no purchases are made in this country.

Given the effects of taxes on private consumption, welfare-maximising governments decide simultaneously on public good supply and the domestic tax rate. These decision variables are linked by the government budget constraint. Since each country $i \in \{A, B\}$ may, in equilibrium, be either in regime I or in regime II and optimisation problems differ across regimes, we first solve each government's problem conditional on a particular regime. In a second step the regime-specific solutions are compared to obtain the unconstrained solution to each country's optimisation problem.

In regime I country i is constrained to set its tax rate at least as high as the exogenously fixed tax rate of country j. Incorporating the regime-specific government budget constraint (18) it maximises the indirect utility function[7]

$$\max_{t^i} v_I^i(t^i, t^j) \equiv u^i[c^i(t^i, t^j),\ t^i c^i(t^i, t^j) - t^i c_j^i(t^i - t^j)] \quad \text{s.t.} \quad t^i - t^j \geqslant 0. \tag{8.14a}$$

If country i is in regime II it is constrained to set its tax rate below or equal to t^j. Incorporating (8.12b) its optimisation problem is

$$\max_{t^i} v_{II}^i(t^i, t^j) \equiv u^i[c^i(t^i),\ t^i c^i(t^i) + t^i c_i^j(t^j - t^i)] \quad \text{s.t.} \quad t^i - t^j \leqslant 0. \tag{8.14b}$$

To solve the problems (8.14a) and (8.14b) we differentiate v^i with respect to t^i and use (8.13). The resulting first-order conditions implicitly define the optimal tax rate t^{i*} for any given level of t^j. Note, however, that these tax rates are a solution to the regime-specific problems only if they fulfil the inequality constraints $t^i \geqslant t^j$ and $t^i \leqslant t^j$, respectively. Denoting marginal utilities by subscript letters, the solution to (8.14a) is thus given by

$$\frac{\partial v_I^i}{\partial t^i} \equiv F_I^i(t^{i*}, t^j) = \begin{cases} \dfrac{-t^{i*}}{\tau_i''} + \dfrac{c_i^i}{(1+t^{i*})}\left(1 - \dfrac{u_c^i}{u_g^i}\right) = 0 & \text{if } t^{i*} \geqslant t^j \\ t^{i*} = t^j & \text{otherwise.} \end{cases} \tag{8.15a}$$

Similarly, the solution to (8.14b) is

[7] Recall from (8.10) that the tax differential in $c_j^i(t^i - t^j)$ is the argument of the consumer's import function, not a multiplication.

$$\frac{\partial v_{II}^i}{\partial t^i} \equiv F_{II}^i(t^{i*}, t^j) = \begin{cases} \dfrac{-t^{i*}}{\tau_j''} + c_i^j + \dfrac{c^i}{(1+t^{i*})}\left(1 - \dfrac{u_c^i}{u_g^i}\right) = 0 \text{ if } t^{i*} \leqslant t^j \\ t^{i*} = t^j \quad \text{otherwise.} \end{cases} \tag{8.15b}$$

The optimality conditions (8.15a)–(8.15b) implicitly define country i's regime-specific reaction functions. Let us first interpret the terms in the upper branches of (8.15a)–(8.15b). Following Mintz and Tulkens (1986, p. 148) we denote the first terms in (8.15a) and (8.15b) as a *public consumption effect*, or tax base effect. It isolates the reduction in country i's tax base owing to changes in the level of cross-border shopping. In both regimes this effect is negative for an increase in t^i by the convexity of the transaction cost function. Note, however, that in regime I it is the response of country i's own residents and thus the marginal transportation cost schedule $\tau_i'(c_j^i)$ which determines the size of this effect, while country j's marginal cost schedule matters in regime II. In regime I the sign of the last term is thus unambiguously determined: in a non-cooperative equilibrium, the marginal rate of substitution (of g^i for c^i) must be less than one and public goods will be undersupplied in the high-tax country. A second fiscal externality, the *private consumption effect*, occurs in regime II only: if residents of country j shop in country i and $c_i^j > 0$, there is an incentive for country i's government to raise its tax rate in order to extract more revenue from foreigners. Therefore, public goods may be undersupplied or oversupplied in the low-tax country, depending on whether the public or the private consumption effect dominates in equilibrium.

8.4 Existence and properties of the Nash equilibrium

In this section we analyse the conditions for the existence of a Nash equilibrium in the present model. This issue has played an important role in the analyses of commodity tax competition by Mintz and Tulkens (1986) and Kanbur and Keen (1993) and we will link our discussion to both of these papers. In addition, the detailed treatment here fills a gap of our analysis in part 2 and shows that the model assumptions made there were indeed consistent with the existence of a non-cooperative tax equilibrium.

In the context of the present model a Nash equilibrium must exist if the overall (regime-independent) objective functions v^i are continuous and quasi-concave in the strategies t^i. We assume that each of the regime-specific payoffs v_I^i, v_{II}^i has these properties, i.e., the second-order conditions of the constrained maximisation problems (8.14a)–

(8.14b) are fulfilled. These conditions are derived and discussed in the appendix (p. 182). It is also easily checked from (8.14a)–(8.14b) that the regime-specific objective functions coincide for $t^i = t^j$ so that the function v^i is continuous in this point. The critical issue for the concavity of v^i is then whether the relevant branches of the first-order conditions (8.15a)–(8.15b) coincide for $t^{i*} = t^j$, and best responses are continuous at the switch of regimes.

We determine the limits of the upper branches of (8.15a)–(8.15b) as t^i approaches t^j. This gives

$$\begin{aligned}
\lim_{t^i \to t^j} F_I^i(t^{i*}, t^j) &= \frac{-t^{i*}}{\tau_i''(0)} + \frac{c^i}{(1+t^{i*})}\left(1 - \frac{u_c^i}{u_g^i}\right) = 0, \\
\lim_{t^i \to t^j} F_{II}^i(t^{i*}, t^j) &= \frac{-t^{i*}}{\tau_j''(0)} + \frac{c^i}{(1+t^{i*})}\left(1 - \frac{u_c^i}{u_g^i}\right) = 0.
\end{aligned} \tag{8.16}$$

As the tax differential approaches zero, cross-border shopping goes to zero and the private consumption effect is eliminated. Furthermore, tax bases in both regimes are then identical. The only difference between the two limits in (8.16) then lies in the second derivatives of the country-specific transaction cost functions, evaluated at $c_j^i = c_i^j = 0$. Two cases must now be distinguished:

(a) $\tau_i''(0) > \tau_j''(0)$. Here it is seen from (8.16) that moving from regime I to regime II must lead to a discrete *downward* adjustment ('jump') in the optimal tax rate of country i. The intuition for this is straightforward. If, in the immediate vicinity of the border, the slope of country i's marginal transaction cost function is steeper than that of country j, then a given (small) tax differential causes less cross-border shopping by residents of country i, relative to country j. From the perspective of country i's government this implies that the gain from marginally undercutting t^j is larger in absolute terms than the loss of setting t^i slightly above t^j. Since the trade-off between domestic efficiency and a favourable international distribution of tax revenues changes discretely at the switch of regimes, there must be a critical level of t^j for which country i's overall best-response correspondence is multi-valued, i.e., there exist different optimal tax rates in regimes I and II.[8]

[8] Similar discontinuous trade-offs for government policy also arise in models of capital tax competition when one part of the domestic capital tax base is internationally mobile while another is not. When governments are constrained to tax both parts of the capital tax base at the same rate, then there will be a critical level of t^j where country i's government cedes the mobile part of the tax base to country j, and is then unconstrained in the taxation of the immobile part of its tax base. See, for example, Schulze and Koch (1994); Janeba and Peters (1999).

(b) $\tau_i''(0) < \tau_j''(0)$. By the same argument as above, the move from regime I to regime II would now imply a discrete *upward* adjustment in the optimal tax rate of country i since residents of country j respond less elastically to tax arbitrage opportunities. This, however, is not compatible with country i being in regime II and the constraint in problem (8.14b) will be binding in some intermediate segment of the overall best-response function. In this range the optimal tax policy for country i is thus to set $t^{i*} = t^j$. Since the upper branches in (8.15a)–(8.15b) are never relevant simultaneously for a given level of t^j, no discontinuity need occur in this case.

These results can be applied to the case of differences in country size, as analysed by Kanbur and Keen (1993). Case (a) above corresponds to the perspective of the small country, whereas case (b) is relevant from the viewpoint of the large economy. Each of these cases will apply to one of the two trading countries as long as marginal transaction cost schedules have different slopes for a zero level of cross-border shopping. When these slopes are identical, both the downward jump in case (a) and the intermediate regime in case (b) are eliminated. The overall best response for both countries then consists only of the upper branches in (8.15a) and (8.15b), and these imply the same optimal tax rate $t^{i*} = t^j$ at their common boundary from (8.16). We summarise this discussion in

Proposition 8.1

Best responses for both countries can be continuous only if the slopes of the country-specific marginal transaction cost schedules are equal when the volume of cross-border shopping is zero, i.e., $\tau_i''(0) = \tau_j''(0)$.

Proposition 8.1 contrasts directly with the result by Mintz and Tulkens (1986, proposition 5) that best responses *cannot* be continuous as country i moves from one regime to another. This can be traced to our assumption that there are no fixed costs of cross-border shopping and hence a 'double autarky' regime, where no cross-border shopping occurs in either direction, cannot arise. If there are positive costs of purchasing the first unit abroad, as in Mintz and Tulkens (1986), no tax competition occurs within the range $|t^i - t^j| \leq \tau_i'(0)$ and the negative tax base effect disappears in this range. As a consequence the optimal tax problem in country i changes discretely as t^j reaches a level where residents of country j start to cross-border shop in country i, and the best-response correspondence exhibits a downward jump at this point (cf. (A.13) in Mintz and Tulkens, 1986, p. 166). In contrast, a tax increase in country i always causes a negative tax base effect in the present model, either by increasing country i's purchases in country j (regime I) or by reducing country j's purchases in country i (regime II). Together with the symmetry condition discussed in proposition 8.1 and the fact that the private consumption effect is zero when tax rates are equal this ensures that best responses are single-valued and continuous at the common boundary of the two regimes.

In the remainder of this chapter we assume identical transaction cost functions in both countries. This is sufficient but not necessary for the continuity of best responses in $t^i = t^j$ since proposition 8.1 requires equal second derivatives only if the volume of cross-border shopping is zero. However, the assumption is also necessary in the special case of quadratic transaction costs, where $\tau_i'' =$ const. This assumption has already been made in chapter 6, and it will also be introduced below.

Assumption 8.1
Transaction cost functions are identical in both countries so that $\tau_i'(c_j^i) = \tau'(c_j^i) \quad \forall \ i,j \in \{A,B\}, \ i \neq j.$

Next, we briefly discuss the uniqueness of the Nash equilibrium. In the model of Kanbur and Keen (1993), uniqueness follows immediately from the fact that reaction functions are linear. In contrast, figure 8.1

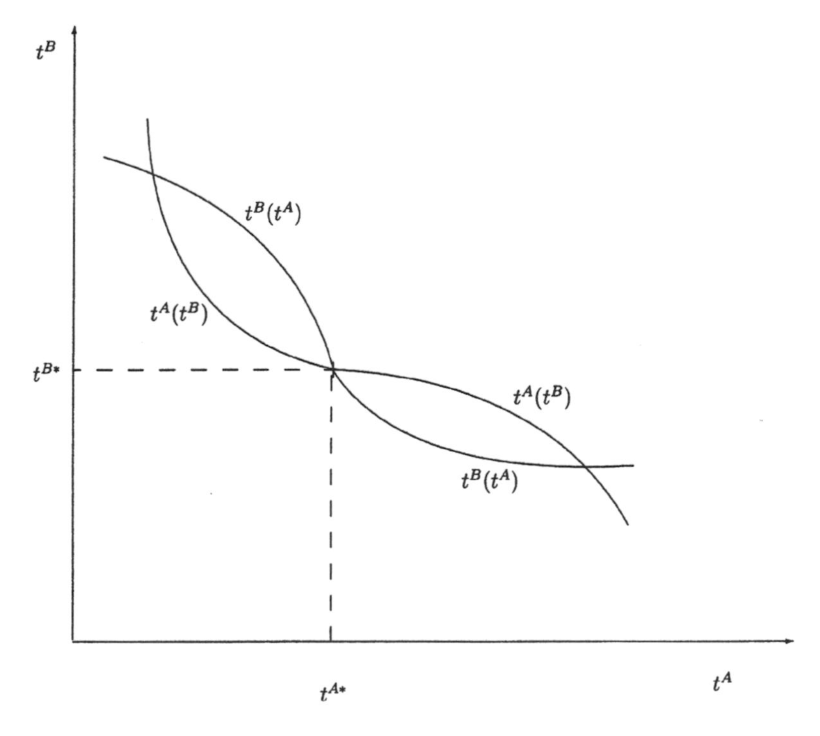

Figure 8.1 Multiple Nash equilibria

shows that the existence of multiple equilibria cannot generally be ruled out when reaction functions are continuous, but non-linear.

The intuition for the existence of multiple equilibria is best gained if we consider the special case of a fixed government revenue constraint. As will be discussed below, this leads to downward sloping reaction functions in both countries. Apart from the symmetric equilibrium with no cross-border shopping (where tax rates are denoted by an asterisk), both countries' revenue constraints can also be met if one country has a low tax rate and a high tax base (by attracting purchases of foreign residents) while the reverse is true in the other country. While we will not further explore the possibility of multiple equilibria in this work, it is important to bear in mind that uniqueness of the equilibrium must often be assumed, rather than rigorously proven, even in simple models of tax competition.[9]

The next step in the analysis is to introduce an asymmetry into the present model. Similar to the shock introduced in chapter 6, we assume that preferences for public goods are higher in country A as compared to country B. Starting from a symmetric equilibrium this can be modelled as a downward shift in country A's marginal rate of substitution, $\partial(u_c^A/u_g^A)/\partial\alpha < 0$, while preferences in country B are unchanged. It is then straightforward to derive

Proposition 8.2
If differences between the countries' preferences for the public good are small, then there exists a Nash equilibrium in which the country with the higher preference for the public good has the higher tax rate.

Proof: *See the appendix (pp. 183–4).*
It is shown in the appendix that the proof of proposition 8.2 requires us to assume either uniqueness or stability of the initial Nash equilibrium. Given the possibility just discussed that multiple Nash equilibria exist in this model, we must thus draw on stability arguments in all the comparative static analyses carried out in this and other chapters. This, however, is a customary assumption in models of strategic interaction (see Dixit, 1986). Furthermore, the assumption that the exogenous shock to country A's preferences is small ensures that, in response to the shock, the economy will not 'adjust globally' by jumping to a different equilibrium (see Wilson, 1991, section 4, for a similar argument).

[9] Bucovetsky (1991, section 6), for example, is unable to prove uniqueness of the Nash equilibrium in a conventional model of capital tax competition (see chapter 5), despite the simplifying assumption that production functions are quadratic.

Keeping these restrictions in mind, proposition 8.2 gives us an asymmetric Nash equilibrium where country A is the high-tax country (and is in regime I) while country B is in regime II. The next step is to determine the effects of a change in one country's tax rate on welfare in the other country. Differentiating the objective functions v^i in (8.14a) and (8.14b) with respect to t^j and using the partial derivatives in (8.13) gives

$$\frac{\partial v^A}{\partial t^B} = u_c^A \left[\frac{-c_B^A}{(1+t^A)}\right] + u_g^A\, t^A \left[\frac{-c_B^A}{(1+t^A)} + \frac{1}{\tau''}\right] <> 0, \tag{8.17}$$

$$\frac{\partial v^B}{\partial t^A} = u_g^B t^B \left(\frac{1}{\tau''}\right) > 0. \tag{8.18}$$

By (8.18) a tax increase in the high-tax country unambiguously increases welfare in the neighbouring low-tax region. Private consumption in country B is unaffected while tax revenues rise as a result of increased cross-border shopping by residents of country A. Matters are more complicated for a tax increase in country B. As shown in (8.17) private consumption unambiguously falls while the tax base in country A, and thus the consumption of public goods, may rise or fall following the increase in t^B. The last effect depends on the elasticity with which cross-border shopping reacts to the reduced tax differential, and thus on the transportation cost schedule. To sign this effect we introduce

Assumption 8.2

The transaction cost function is quadratic in the volume of cross-border shopping and given by $\tau = (1/2)\beta(c_B^A)^2$.

As we have discussed in chapter 6, a quadratic transaction cost function is a simple and frequently assumed specification in models of both capital and commodity tax competition. It implies that cross-border shopping is a linear function of the tax differential and $\tau'' = \beta$ is a constant. Using assumption 8.2 in (8.10) and (8.11a) gives

$$c_B^A = \frac{(t^A - t^B)}{\beta}, \tag{8.19}$$

$$c_A^A = \frac{1}{(1+t^A)}\left[1 - \frac{(t^A - t^B)}{\beta} - \frac{(t^A)^2 - (t^B)^2}{2\beta}\right], \tag{8.20}$$

$$c^A = c_A^A + c_B^A = \frac{1}{(1+t^A)}\left[1 + \frac{(t^A - t^B)^2}{2\beta}\right]. \tag{8.21}$$

Inserting c_A^A from (8.20) into (8.17) yields after some manipulations

$$\frac{\partial v^A}{\partial t^B} = \frac{u_g^A}{\beta(1+t^A)}\left[(t^A - t^B)\left(1 - \frac{u_c^A}{u_g^A}\right) + t^B(1+t^A)\right] > 0, \quad (8.22)$$

which must be positive since country A undersupplies the public good in equilibrium. Under a quadratic transaction cost schedule an increase in t^B thus raises the tax base and public consumption in country A, as is seen from (8.20). Furthermore, this gain overcompensates the representative consumer in country A for the fall in her private consumption. These results are summarised in

Proposition 8.3

In an asymmetric Nash equilibrium the low-tax country gains from a tax increase in the high-tax country. If the transaction cost schedule is quadratic, then the high-tax country also gains from a tax increase in the low-tax country.

Put differently, proposition 8.3 states that a quadratic specification of transaction costs ensures that public consumption effects (tax base effects) dominate private consumption effects (terms of trade effects) in the present model. This result extends to the model of capital tax competition in chapter 6, where production and transaction costs were both specified as quadratic functions (cf. n. 12 in chapter 6). The formal similarities between the model of chapter 6 and the one used here will also be obvious in the following discussion of comparative static results.

8.5 Tax coordination

We are now ready to discuss the effects of alternative tax coordination measures when governments care about the consumption of both private and public goods. Assumptions 8.1 and 8.2 are maintained throughout the analysis in this section. With a quadratic transportation cost function private consumption in country A is given by (8.19)–(8.21). For convenient reference we summarise here the effects of changes in t^j and the transportation cost parameter β on the levels of public and private consumption in country i:

$$\frac{\partial c_A^A}{\partial t^B} > 0, \quad \frac{\partial g^A}{\partial t^B} = t^A\,\frac{\partial c_A^A}{\partial t^B} > 0, \quad \frac{\partial c^A}{\partial t^B} < 0, \quad \frac{\partial c^B}{\partial t^A} = 0, \quad \frac{\partial g^B}{\partial t^A} = t^B\,\frac{\partial c_B^A}{\partial t^A} > 0, \quad (8.23)$$

$$\frac{\partial c_B^A}{\partial \beta} < 0, \quad \frac{\partial c_A^A}{\partial \beta} > 0, \quad \frac{\partial g^A}{\partial \beta} > 0, \quad \frac{\partial c^A}{\partial \beta} < 0, \quad \frac{\partial c^B}{\partial \beta} = 0, \quad \frac{\partial g^B}{\partial \beta} < 0. \quad (8.24)$$

A final assumption is needed to sign the change in the marginal rate of substitution (u_c^i/u_g^i) in response to changes in the ratio of public over private consumption (g^i/c^i). This effect must always be positive along an indifference curve but ambiguities arise when the change in g^i/c^i simultaneously affects country i's utility. A sufficient condition to rule out income effects that may work in the opposite direction is that preferences are homothetic. In this case the elasticity of substitution between the public and the private good depends only on the ratio, but not on the levels of public and private consumption.

Assumption 8.3
Preferences are homothetic in both countries. If σ^i denotes the elasticity of substitution between the public and the private good, then its inverse is

$$\frac{1}{\sigma^i} \equiv \frac{\partial[u_c^i/u_g^i(g^i/c^i)]}{\partial(g^i/c^i)} \frac{(g^i/c^i)}{(u_c^i/u_g^i)} > 0 \quad \forall \quad i \in \{A, B\}.$$

A low value of σ^i implies that country i's government prefers a largely fixed ratio of public over private consumption. In contrast, if σ^i is large then g^i/c^i will change substantially in response to exogenous shocks. Stepping outside the confines of our model, σ^i can also be interpreted as the elasticity of substitution between alternative sources of tax revenue. A low value of σ^i then indicates that the revenue requirement from *commodity* taxation is inflexible since other taxes (e.g. income taxes) cannot readily be adjusted. Alternatively, if σ^i is high then the changes in g^i/c^i derived from the model can be interpreted as changes in the relative reliance on commodity taxes *vis-à-vis* other sources of government revenue.

8.5.1 Minimum tax rates

A first coordination measure, which has been implemented in the European Union, is a minimum tax requirement imposed on the low-tax country (cf. subsection 2.2.1). If this constraint is binding, and if transportation costs are quadratic, then country A will gain from this measure by proposition 8.3. If the required tax increase is small for the low-tax country then the change in t^B will not affect country B's utility since the tax was set optimally in the initial equilibrium. By proposition 8.3 the welfare change in country B then depends on whether its tax increase lowers or raises the optimal tax rate in country A, and thus on the slope of the high-tax country's best-response function. Of course, if the required increase in t^B is discrete rather than marginal then country

B will, on impact, lose from the change in its *own* tax rate, which forces it to move away unilaterally from the non-cooperative Nash equilibrium.

Applying the implicit function theorem to the first-order conditions $F^i(t^i, t^j) = 0$ gives

$$\text{sign}\left(\frac{dt^i}{dt^j}\right) = -\ \text{sign}\left(\frac{\partial F^i/\partial t^j}{\partial F^i/\partial t^i}\right) = \text{sign}\ (\partial F^i/\partial t^j), \tag{8.25}$$

from the second-order condition $\partial F^i/\partial t^i < 0$. To determine the derivatives $\partial F^i/\partial t^j$ we differentiate (8.15a)–(8.15b) with respect to the tax rate of the union partner. This gives for country A (which is in regime I)

$$\frac{\partial F^A}{\partial t^B} = \underbrace{\frac{(1 - u_c^A/u_g^A)}{(1+t^A)}\frac{\partial c_A^A}{\partial t^B}}_{(1)\ (+)} + \underbrace{\frac{-c_A^A}{(1+t^A)}\frac{1}{\sigma^A}\frac{(u_c^A/u_g^A)}{(g^A/c^A)}\frac{\partial(g^A/c^A)}{\partial t^B}}_{(2)\ (-)} <> 0, \tag{8.26}$$

where individual effects are signed using (8.23). Similarly we get for country B (which is in regime II)

$$\frac{\partial F^B}{\partial t^A} = \underbrace{\frac{\partial c_D^A}{\partial t^A}}_{(1)\ (+)} + \underbrace{\frac{-c^B}{(1+t^B)}\frac{1}{\sigma^B}\frac{(u_c^B/u_g^B)}{(g^B/c^B)}\frac{\partial(g^B/c^B)}{\partial t^A}}_{(2)\ (-)} <> 0. \tag{8.27}$$

In general, both countries may thus raise or lower their own tax rate in response to a tax increase in the other region. By assumption 8.2 the second derivative of the transaction cost function is a constant so that, for each country i, the size of the negative public consumption effect (the 'marginal costs' of a domestic tax increase) is independent of the other country's tax rate. This allows us to focus on how a change in t^j alters the 'marginal benefits' of a tax increase in country i. For country A, the first effect is positive since it undersupplies the public good and its tax base increases from (8.23). Intuitively a higher level of t^B increases the amount of extra revenue that country A can collect from marginally raising its tax rate. The second effect is negative, however, since the increase in t^B raises government revenue in country A while reducing private consumption. By assumption 8.3 this will unambiguously raise the marginal rate of substitution (of g^A for c^A) and reduce the marginal benefits from redistributing purchasing power towards the public sector. For country B, the first effect is also positive since a rise in t^A increases the role of the private consumption effect, thus giving an incentive to country B to raise its own tax rate at the (partial) expense of foreigners.

However, an increase in t^A simultaneously raises g^B from (8.23) so that the second effect is negative.

Note that if governments behave as revenue maximisers the marginal utility of private consumption is zero and the negative second effects are eliminated in (8.26)–(8.27). Both best responses will then be upward sloping and a small mandated rise in country B's tax rate will benefit both countries. This corresponds to proposition 12 in Kanbur and Keen (1993). The same result is obtained when the elasticity of substitution is very high in both countries and the second effect is negligible. The other limiting case is when governments have to raise a fixed level of revenues from commodity taxation so that $\sigma^i \to 0$. In this case the negative second effect always dominates and country i's optimal tax rate unambiguously falls as t^j rises. This is summarised in

Proposition 8.4
If the elasticity of substitution is very large (small) in the high-tax country A, then a small mandated increase in t^B raises (lowers) welfare in the low-tax country B.

Proposition 8.4 can, informally, be extended to determine the effects of a *discrete* tax increase in country B. We have argued above that, for a *given* level of t^A, this policy must hurt the low-tax country B since it is forced to set a higher tax rate than it would otherwise wish. For country B to gain from a discrete increase in its own tax rate the induced tax rise in country A must then be sufficiently large to compensate the negative impact effect. We turn now to a formal analysis of this more complex case in the context of a different coordination policy.

8.5.2 Tightening rules of destination

A second coordination policy consists of legal or administrative measures which tighten the enforcement of the destination principle. Such measures may include stricter controls and penalties for illegal smuggling or the closing of loopholes as in the mail-order industry. They are especially important when central governments do not have the legal powers to impose tax rate harmonisation, as is the case for retail sales taxes set by US states. As we have discussed in subsection 2.2.1, the European Union has also tried to maintain rules of destination for consumers wherever this was compatible with the abolition of border controls (mail-ordering, purchases of new cars).

A tighter enforcement of the destination principle can be represented by raising the transaction cost parameter β for private consumer purchases abroad. Hence, the policy measure discussed here is the *reverse* of increasing market integration, as analysed in chapter 6. It has been shown by Kanbur and Keen (1993, proposition 6) that this measure strictly benefits both countries when revenue maximisation is the objective. In the present framework the national welfare effects of a change in the transaction cost parameter β can be decomposed into an impact effect, at unchanged tax rates, and the induced change in the tax rate of the other union country. Algebraically, this is given by (cf. Dixit, 1986)

$$\frac{dv^i}{d\beta} = \left.\frac{\partial v^i}{\partial \beta}\right|_{t^A,\, t^B=\text{const.}} + \frac{\partial v^i}{\partial t^j}\frac{dt^j}{d\beta} \quad \forall\ i,j \in \{A,B\},\ i \neq j. \tag{8.28}$$

It is straightforward to sign the impact effect for each country.

Proposition 8.5(a)

At unchanged tax rates a rise in the marginal transaction cost schedule increases welfare in the high-tax country and lowers welfare in the low-tax country:

$$\left.\frac{\partial v^A}{\partial \beta}\right|_{t^A,\, t^B=\text{const.}} > 0, \qquad \left.\frac{\partial v^B}{\partial \beta}\right|_{t^A,\, t^B=\text{const.}} < 0.$$

Proof: *See the appendix (p. 184).*

The intuition for this result is obvious for the low-tax country: an upward shift in the marginal transaction cost schedule reduces cross-border shopping by country A's residents and thus the tax base of country B. For the high-tax country, there are counteracting effects similar to the ones discussed in proposition 8.3. Private consumption falls as residents of country A are redirected towards their more expensive home market. However, with a quadratic transaction cost function this effect is dominated by a positive public consumption effect from the expansion of country A's tax base.

It follows that for country B to gain from a coordinated rise in marginal transaction costs, the tax rate in country A must rise by enough to overcompensate the negative impact effect. The changes in optimal tax rates in response to a variation in β are derived in the appendix (p. 184) and are given by

$$\frac{dt^i}{d\beta} = \frac{1}{\Delta}\left[-\frac{\partial F^j}{\partial t^j}\frac{\partial F^i}{\partial \beta} + \frac{\partial F^i}{\partial t^j}\frac{\partial F^j}{\partial \beta}\right] \quad \forall i,j \in \{A,B\},\ i \neq j, \tag{8.29}$$

where $\Delta > 0$ follows from (8A.5) in the appendix. The first effect in (8.29) gives the direct response of country i's optimal tax rate to the parameter change, whereas the second effect describes the response to the induced change in the optimal tax rate of country j. Since $\partial F^i/\partial t^j$ has already been determined in (8.26)–(8.27) it remains to differentiate the first-order conditions (8.15a)–(8.15b) with respect to β. This gives for country A (regime I)

$$\frac{\partial F^A}{\partial \beta} = \underbrace{\frac{t^A}{\beta^2}}_{(1)\,(+)} + \underbrace{\frac{(1 - u_c^A/u_g^A)}{(1+t^A)} \frac{\partial c_A^A}{\partial \beta}}_{(2)\,(+)} + \underbrace{\frac{-c_A^A}{(1+t^A)} \frac{1}{\sigma^A} \frac{(u_c^A/u_g^A)}{(g^A/c^A)} \frac{\partial (g^A/c^A)}{\partial \beta}}_{(3)\,(-)} <> 0, \tag{8.30}$$

and for country B (regime II)

$$\frac{\partial F^B}{\partial \beta} = \underbrace{\frac{t^B}{\beta^2}}_{(1)\,(+)} + \underbrace{\frac{\partial c_B^A}{\partial \beta}}_{(2)\,(-)} + \underbrace{\frac{-c^B}{(1+t^B)} \frac{1}{\sigma^B} \frac{(u_c^B/u_g^B)}{(g^B/c^B)} \frac{\partial (g^B/c^B)}{\partial \beta}}_{(3)\,(+)} <> 0, \tag{8.31}$$

where individual effects have been signed using (8.24). The first effect in both (8.30) and (8.31) is positive: a higher β makes cross-border shopping less responsive to tax changes, thus lowering the marginal costs of a domestic tax increase in both countries. This effect will be strong when the initial value of β is low – indicating intense tax competition through cross-border shopping – but tax rates must remain relatively high because of inflexible revenue requirements. The induced changes in the marginal benefits of a domestic tax rise are again ambiguous in both countries. For country A the reasoning is essentially the same as given in (8.26). The second effect is positive, but the rise in β reallocates domestic purchasing power from the private to the public sector and the third effect tends to reduce the optimal tax rate. For country B the signs of the last two effects are now reversed in comparison to (8.27) because a rise in β *lowers* cross-border shopping by residents of country A. Thus the private consumption effect becomes less important and tends to reduce the optimal tax rate, whereas the reduction in government revenues makes the third effect positive.

Equations (8.26)–(8.27) and (8.30)–(8.31) provide all the information needed to evaluate (8.29). Since each of these effects is ambiguous, general results – which hold for all parameter values – can clearly not be expected. However, when substitution elasticities are very low or very large in both countries, best responses to the parameter change can be signed. This is summarised in the following proposition and in table 8.1.

Table 8.1 *Optimal tax responses to a change in transaction costs*

		$\partial F^i/\partial\beta$ (8.30)–(8.31)	$\partial F^i/\partial t^j$ (8.26)–(8.27)	$dt^i/d\beta$ (8.29)
Case 1	Country A	+	+	+
(high σ^i)	Country B	+	+	+
Case 2	Country A	−	−	−
(low σ^i)	Country B	+	−	+

Proposition 8.5(b)
Case 1: *If substitution elasticities are very high in both countries and the low-tax country undersupplies the public good initially, then an increase in β raises the optimal tax rate in both countries.*
Case 2: *If substitution elasticities are very low in both countries, then an increase in the transaction cost parameter β lowers the optimal tax rate in the high-tax country and raises it in the low-tax country.*

Proof: *See the appendix (pp. 184–5).*
In case 1 the last effects in both (8.30) and (8.31) are small owing to very high substitution elasticities, and the other effects dominate. This is sufficient to sign $\partial F^A/\partial\beta > 0$ in (8.30). For country B, it is shown in the appendix that the positive first effect dominates the negative second effect, if country B undersupplies the public good initially. In this case $\partial F^A/\partial\beta > 0$ and the direct effect of a rise in β is to raise both optimal tax rates. Intuitively, both countries wish to increase public good supply in response to the fall in its marginal cost. Furthermore, both best responses (8.26) and (8.27) are upward sloping in this case. Thus indirect effects are also positive in both countries, reinforcing the direct effects. Note that this case necessarily applies under the assumption of revenue-maximising governments. With $u_c^i = 0$ country B always undersupplies the public good, relative to its objective, and the partial effects given in (8.26)–(8.27) and (8.30)–(8.31) are all positive.

In case 2 the last effects in (8.30)–(8.31) are very large owing to low substitution elasticities and determine the signs of $\partial F^A/\partial\beta < 0$ and $\partial F^B/\partial\beta > 0$. The direct effect of the increase in transportation costs (the first term in (8.29)) is therefore to lower t^A and to raise t^B. This is intuitive since the tax base of country A expands and the tax base of country B shrinks following the rise in β, and tax rates adjust to meet largely fixed revenue requirements. Furthermore, from proposition 8.4 both reaction functions (8.26)–(8.27) are downward sloping in this case. Therefore, optimal tax responses to the induced change in the other country's tax rate (the second term in (8.29)) further reduce t^A (in response to the initial rise in t^B) and further increase t^B (in response to the initial fall in t^A).

Using (8.28), the partial results in propositions 8.5(a) and 8.5(b) can be combined to give the overall effect of an increase in β on welfare in each country:

Proposition 8.5(c)

Case 1: *If substitution elasticities are very high in both countries and the low-tax country undersupplies the public good initially, then an increase in β raises welfare in the high-tax country. Welfare in the low-tax country rises if the gain from the induced tax increase in the high-tax country overcompensates the negative impact effect, and falls otherwise.*

Case 2: *If substitution elasticities are very low in both countries, then an increase in the transaction cost parameter β raises welfare in the high-tax country and reduces welfare in the low-tax country.*

The individual effects underlying this proposition are shown in table 8.2. The high-tax country unambiguously gains from the coordination measure in both cases. In case 1, the overall welfare change in country *B* is ambiguous, in general. The low-tax country will gain from tax coordination if the induced rise in t^A is strong enough to compensate the negative impact effect. In this case, the two countries will thus have a common interest in raising the costs of cross-border shopping. In case 2, however, the low-tax country unambiguously loses from a coordinated rise in β since both the impact effect and the effect of the induced change in t^A are negative. Therefore, there is a clear conflict of interest in this case.

To summarise, the analysis in this section has worked out the conditions under which the mutual gains from reduced tax competition are likely to dominate redistributive effects. Tax coordination tends to benefit

Table 8.2 *Welfare effects of a rise in transaction costs*

		Impact effect (t^A, t^B const.) $\partial v^i/\partial\beta$	Induced change in t^j $(\partial v^i/\partial t^j)(\partial t^j/\partial\beta)$	Overall effect $dv^i/d\beta$
Case 1	Country *A*	+	+	+
(high σ^i)	Country *B*	–	+	?
Case 2	Country *A*	+	+	+
(low σ^i)	Country *B*	–	–	–

both countries if the governments' tax choices respond elastically to the marginal costs of public good supply in the presence of cross-border shopping (σ is high). Many observers of both EU and North American conditions have argued, however, that governments are price-insensitive owing to rigid revenue requirements and lack of flexibility to adjust other taxes. In this case the low-tax country stands to lose not only from a minimum tax requirement (proposition 8.4), but also from a coordinated effort to increase the costs of cross-border shopping (proposition 8.5).

Finally, we have already indicated that close analytical similarities exist between this chapter and our discussion of redistributive capital taxation in chapter 6. In both analyses there is a seemingly counterintuitive scenario – the second cases in propositions 6.3 and 8.5(b) – under which increasing (reduced) market integration does not lead to a general reduction (increase) in tax rates. Note that this result is *not* caused by terms of trade effects (private consumption effects). The fact that terms of trade effects and tax base effects work in opposite directions for one of the trading countries is well known (see section 3.1) and this ambiguity has been excluded in both analyses by assuming a quadratic transaction cost function.

Instead the critical issue is the substitutability between different arguments in the government objective function. In the analysis of labour vs. capital taxation in chapter 6 these arguments were the consumption levels of the two different income groups, whereas the government's objective in this chapter included the private and public consumption levels of a representative individual. The common and central point in both analyses is that, with asymmetries between the two countries, market integration will affect the allocation of resources even in the absence of tax responses. Therefore, if the *ratio* of the different consumption levels is largely fixed in the government's optimum, then the response of tax policy will not be driven by the changed excess burden of taxation in the presence of increased consumer or capital mobility, but by the desire to maintain the status quo ante with respect to either the distribution of incomes between individuals, or the distribution of national output between public and private consumption.

8.6 Welfare effects of commodity tax harmonisation: a comparison with related literature

Our above analysis of tax competition for cross-border shopping has assumed that there is only a single tax rate, levied uniformly on all consumer goods. As a result, the focus of the analysis has been on the overall *level* of commodity taxation in the competing countries. In subsection 8.6.1 we survey a number of related analyses of cross-border shopping and compare our results with those obtained in this literature. Another set of papers analyses the welfare effects of indirect tax harmonisation when commodity taxes can be differentiated and the focus is thus on the efficient *structure* of commodity taxation. This literature, summarised in subsection 8.6.2, yields a complementary perspective on the issue whether harmonising commodity tax reforms are able to improve welfare in each of the trading countries.

8.6.1 Tax competition for cross-border shopping

The two benchmark analyses introduced in section 8.2 have somewhat different implications for the direction of welfare improving commodity tax reforms. In the analysis of Kanbur and Keen (1993), only a tax base externality is operating and governments engaged in tax competition always undersupply the public good, relative to the objective of revenue maximisation. In contrast, there is a second fiscal externality, the private consumption effect, in the analysis of Mintz and Tulkens (1986). If, starting from an asymmetric Nash equilibrium, the tax rate of the high-tax region is increased, then only the public consumption externality is effective and this region must thus undersupply the public good. In contrast, a tax increase in the low-tax region affects the (gross-of-tax) price paid by foreign cross-border shoppers and thus has counteracting public and private consumption externalities. Mintz and Tulkens (1986, proposition 10) cannot sign the net effect of this tax increase on welfare in the high-tax country, implying that the non-cooperative tax rate set by the low-tax country may either be too high or too low from a perspective of global efficiency.

In a follow-up paper, de Crombrugghe and Tulkens (1990) obtain the stronger result that, in the model of Mintz and Tulkens (1986), the public consumption effect must always dominate in the Nash equilibrium. Hence both countries' tax rates are set 'too low' in the Nash equilibrium and a small, coordinated increase in both tax rates is strictly Pareto improving (1990, proposition 1). This result is obtained without any restrictions on the government objective function, or on the shape of the transaction cost function for cross-border shopping. It thus seems to be more general than our proposition 8.3, which has required the assumption that the transaction cost function is quadratic (assumption 8.2). Since our model also simplifies the Mintz and Tulkens (1986) analysis in other respects, there is a clear conflict of results between the above analysis and that of de Crombrugghe and Tulkens (1990), as they seem to obtain the stronger result in a more general setting.

However, de Crombrugghe and Tulkens introduce the additional assumption that the (regime-specific) objective function of country A is concave in the tax rate of the *other* region B. This is very different from the standard assumption that each country's objective is concave in its *own* tax rate, which ensures the second-order condition for a maximum to hold. In particular, it implies under the restrictions of the Mintz and Tulkens (1986) model that welfare in country A is a *monotonously* rising function of country B's tax rate for all relevant initial equilibria where $t^A > t^B$. If this assumption is relaxed, then it can be shown that proposition 1 in de Crombrugghe and Tulkens (1990) no longer holds, in general, and the private consumption effect dominates the tax base externality in some initial Nash equilibria (see Haufler, 1998). To exclude this possibility it is thus either necessary to restrict the government objective to the maximisation of tax revenues, in which case terms of trade effects are eliminated entirely (as in Kanbur and Keen, 1993), or one has to restrict the elasticity of the transaction cost schedule for cross-border shopping as we have done in our analysis of sections 8.4 and 8.5.

The interaction between different fiscal externalities is also of central importance in the analysis of Lockwood (1993), who compares the incentives for strategic commodity taxation under the destination and origin principles. In the large-country case a selective destination-based tax causes only a terms of trade effect and this will tend to push tax rates upward, relative to their level in the closed economy. Under the origin principle, however, the 'strategic effect' consists of both the public and private consumption externalities of the Mintz and Tulkens model. As in their analysis, the public consumption effect tends to reduce the optimal commodity tax rate while the private consumption effect tends to increase it, the net effect being ambiguous, in general (1993, pp. 155–6).

Our comparative static analysis in section 8.5 has considered two coordination measures, a mandated tax increase in the low-tax country and a policy-induced increase in the costs of cross-border shopping. Kanbur and Keen (1993) have shown that these tax coordination measures unambiguously benefit both countries when governments behave as revenue maximisers. However, as we have argued above, this result depends crucially on the simplified government objective. When governments care about both private and public consumption, then the tax response in the high-tax region is no longer ambiguous and there is a distinct possibility that the low-tax country loses from tax coordination.[10]

[10] In contrast, the result that the small country underbids the large region in the Nash equilibrium is robust with respect to the introduction of a more conventional utility function defined over public and private consumption (Trandel, 1994). Trandel further shows that this result still applies in the presence of imperfect competition.

Other papers have analysed the welfare effects of tax coordination under imperfect competition. Trandel (1992) considers the welfare effects of use tax evasion in the United States, which has many similarities with the issue of cross-border shopping (cf. subsection 2.2.2). Trandel employs a model of spatial competition where four firms are located symmetrically around a circle, consumers are distributed uniformly and a state border cuts the circle in two equal halves. In contrast to Kanbur and Keen (1993) and our earlier analysis in this chapter the model is thus completely symmetric. If firms behave perfectly competitively in this framework, then use tax evasion is unambiguously welfare reducing: it induces individuals to travel to more distant stores and it also gives strategic incentives to governments to pursue globally inefficient beggar-thy-neighbour policies. Both of these factors have also been present in the above analysis. However, when firms charge a markup over marginal costs, then use tax evasion will induce them to set lower prices and this benefits consumers. If the markup is sufficiently high – and competition between firms is thus sufficiently weak – then use tax evasion will actually be welfare improving for both regions (Trandel, 1992, theorem 2). Vice versa, coordinated efforts to reduce tax evasion will then be welfare reducing in this model. This shows that the global efficiency effects of tax coordination measures strongly depend on the assumption that there are no distortions in product markets.

Note, however, that the question whether governments maximise welfare or tax revenues is again critical in this context. Wrede (1994) considers the case of spatial competition between two firms in the Kanbur and Keen model. Each firm may choose the optimal place of production *within* its home country, but is not permitted to locate in the other jurisdiction. Wrede retains, however, the assumption of revenue-maximising governments. In this framework tax coordination increases tax revenues in both jurisdictions, as in the analysis of Kanbur and Keen (see Wrede, 1994, proposition 6). Furthermore, Wrede shows that if the number of firms within each country is (exogenously) increased, then revenue-maximising governments respond to the increasingly competitive behaviour of firms by lowering their optimal tax rates (proposition 9). Implicit in this result is that revenue-maximising governments prefer monopolistic over competitive market structures, since monopoly profits are easier to tax. This suggests that the distinction between welfare- and revenue-maximising governments becomes even more critical when firms have price-setting power in product markets.

Optimal commodity taxation in the presence of cross-border shopping and monopoly firms is also discussed in Christiansen (1994) from the perspective of a single country. Christiansen assumes welfare-maximising governments and distinguishes two cases, depending on whether the monopoly is owned by domestic or foreign residents. In the latter case, the optimal tax rate is greater than in the benchmark model of competitive suppliers if and only if the tax is not fully shifted into consumer prices by the foreign monopolist. As Christiansen notes, this is essentially an optimal tariff argument since the tax is able to reduce the *producer* price charged by the foreign-owned firm.

A model by Nielsen (1998) modifies the analysis of Kanbur and Keen in a different way by focusing on differences in the geographical extent of the two countries, rather than on differences in the density of their population. It turns out that this model is even simpler than that of Kanbur and Keen and eliminates the discontinuous trade-off that exists for the small country at the switch of regimes (cf. section 8.4). The qualitative results for tax coordination are largely unchanged from the Kanbur and Keen analysis, but the simple setting allows Nielsen to incorporate further model elements, such as transportation costs for the commercially traded goods, or border inspections to discover illegal cross-border shopping.

Finally, Wang (1999) has reconsidered the Kanbur and Keen (1993) analysis when government's tax choices are sequential rather than simultaneous and the large country behaves as the Stackelberg leader in the tax game. He shows that the Stackelberg equilibrium strictly dominates the Nash equilibrium in the sense that each country collects higher tax revenues. We are mostly interested here in the implications that the Stackelberg equilibrium has for the welfare effects of tax coordination. It turns out that both a strategy of tax harmonisation towards a common average and a minimum rate strategy lower the welfare of the small, low-tax country. In particular, a mandatory tax increase in the low-tax country will *reduce* the tax rate set by the large region, if this country is a Stackelberg leader. We know from our discussion in subsection 8.5.1 that this must imply a welfare loss for the small country, whose welfare level is monotonously rising in the large country's tax rate. Hence Wang's (1999) results show that the two countries will also have conflicting interests with respect to tax coordination measures when the underlying game structure in the model of Kanbur and Keen (1993) is changed.

8.6.2 *Pareto improving indirect tax harmonisation*

A second strand in the literature on commodity tax harmonisation focuses on the efficiency of the tax structure when commodity taxes are differentiated. Most of these models assume a pure destination principle without cross-border shopping. Hence, tax competition – where it occurs – works primarily through terms of trade externalities. In addition, there are several papers in this field which do not assume that countries will maximise national welfare, but instead analyse the welfare effects of harmonising tax reforms starting from an arbitrary initial equilibrium. Finally, some papers have addressed the welfare effects of indirect tax harmonisation under the origin principle. These will also be covered here, even though the origin principle is discussed in more detail in chapter 9.

As shown in the initial contribution to this literature by Keen (1987), international differences in the tax structure yield a simple, yet general, argument for tax rate harmonisation under the destination principle. A first intuition for this result can already be gained from the two-good framework employed in section 8.1, where we have seen that international differences in tax rates cause inefficiencies in consumption when tax rates in each country are differentiated (cf. (8.2)). More generally, the welfare gains from tax harmonisation derive from the fundamental property that the deadweight loss of taxation rises more than proportionally when the tax rate is increased. Hence, starting from arbitrary tax vectors in the initial equilibrium, a harmonising tax reform that moves tax rates in each country towards the common average will reduce the global welfare losses from taxation when producer prices remain unchanged. A *potential* Pareto improvement, i.e., an increase in aggregate world welfare, thus results from this reform under rather general conditions.

Keen (1989) analyses the conditions under which this reform also represents an *actual* Pareto improvement, i.e., a welfare increase in each country. One particularly interesting case arises when initial tax rates are set at their Nash equilibrium levels and certain additional 'independence conditions' hold (1989, proposition 4).[11] In this case each country tries to improve its terms of trade through national commodity taxation (see section 3.1) and tax harmonisation leads to similar welfare gains as a multilateral tariff reduction in international trade policy (cf. Dixit, 1985).

Under the destination principle, these results also carry over to at least some forms of imperfect competition. As shown by Keen and Lahiri (1993), the conditions for both a potential and an actual Pareto improvement are precisely the same as in the competitive case, when there is only a single firm in each country and the two firms engage in quantity com-

[11] These conditions are that either cross-price effects must be absent, or local demand responses must be identical in the initial equilibrium. See Keen (1989, pp. 10–11).

petition (Cournot duopoly). The reason for this result is that the demand-side gains from tax rate convergence under the destination principle do not interact with the production distortions arising from imperfect competition.

One important assumption in all these analyses is, however, that tax revenues are returned to the consumer as a lump sum. A number of recent contributions has analysed the welfare effects of harmonising tax reforms when governments use tax revenues to supply public goods. Delipalla (1997) focuses on potential Pareto improvements and shows that, in comparison to Keen (1987), additional – and strict – conditions are required for harmonising tax reforms to be Pareto improving. These are that the tax reform is revenue-neutral for the world as a whole and either transfers between governments are possible, or revenues increase in the country with the higher marginal social cost of public funds (1997, propositions 2 and 3). Lahiri and Raimondos-Møller (1998) concentrate on tax harmonisation in small open economies in large parts of their analysis. In this setting they show that different harmonisation rules must be devised for tax reforms to be potentially Pareto improving, depending on whether both countries undersupply or oversupply the public good in the initial equilibrium.

Lockwood (1997) uses a simpler Ricardian model of trade to derive a general rule for Pareto improving tax reforms when producer prices are endogenous and governments provide a public good. He assumes that taxes in the initial equilibrium are at their Nash equilibrium levels and shows that a necessary and sufficient condition for the reform to improve welfare in each country is that it raises the compensated demand for imports in each country. In other words, tax rate harmonisation is beneficial if and only if it offsets the strategic incentive in each country to improve the domestic terms of trade.

Finally, some papers have analysed the welfare effects of commodity tax harmonisation under a selective origin principle. As shown by Lopez-Garcia (1996), the analysis of Pareto improving tax reforms in Keen (1987, 1989) is largely parallel under the origin principle, as long as production occurs under conditions of perfect competition. Instead of demand-side gains, tax harmonisation now improves international production efficiency, since it leads to a convergence of relative producer prices in the trading countries (cf. (8.4)).

When imperfect competition is introduced, however, the difference between destination- and origin-based commodity taxation becomes crucial. This is shown by Keen, Lahiri and Raimondos-Møller (2000) who find that harmonising welfare reforms that are Pareto improving under the destination principle can be welfare reducing under the origin principle when competition is imperfect. The results are derived in a Cournot duopoly model where the two firms have different costs of production. In this setting the globally optimal policy is to shift production to the more efficient firm. In the non-cooperative equilibrium the production tax imposed by the country with the high-cost firm exceeds the tax that is levied by the country hosting the low-cost firm. Hence an international alignment of production taxes increases the output of the high-cost firm, reducing global welfare. This is just one example of how international commodity tax differentials under the origin principle interact with existing production distortions, leading to seemingly counterintuitive second-best results. In chapter 9 (subsection 9.7.1) we will see that the choice between destination- and origin-based commodity taxation can also be critically affected by the introduction of imperfect competition.

8.7 Summary: deficiencies of the current system

This chapter has analysed the effects of a mixed scheme of commodity taxation, which subjects producer and consumer purchases to different international tax rules. The core problem of such a scheme is that it provides an incentive for consumers to cross-border shop in neighbouring jurisdictions, leading to commodity tax competition for mobile consumers. If countries differ either in size or through different preferences for public goods, tax competition will create winners and losers who need not agree on the desirability of alternative tax coordination measures. In particular, we have argued that conflicting interests are likely to emerge when elasticities of substitution between private and public consumption (or, equivalently, between alternative sources of tax revenues) are low owing to largely fixed revenue requirements. For the present situation in the European Union, for example, this condition seems by no means unrealistic. If this conjecture is correct, it may explain the insistence of the European Commission on achieving an agreement on coordination measures *before* the opening of internal borders.

In any case, commodity tax harmonisation under the current mixed tax principle faces the fundamental trade-off that existing distortions can be reduced only at the cost of sacrificing national autonomy over the fiscally important VAT base. The importance of national revenue constraints for the feasibility of Pareto improving tax harmonisation has been stressed in the theoretical literature summarised in subsection 8.6.2. It is also at the heart of conflicting views among international tax specialists with respect to the desirability of further tax rate harmonisation in Europe.[12]

Most empirical surveys of cross-border shopping were conducted before the opening of internal borders, partly in preparation for the introduction of a Community-wide minimal tax rate in 1992 (see subsection 2.2.1). Consumer surveys from the late 1980s and early 1990s show that cross-border shopping at sensitive borders with relatively high VAT differentials (Ireland and the United Kingdom; Germany and Denmark) has reached 5–10 per cent of expenditure in the relevant border region, but this translates to only 1–2 per cent of national expenditure in the high-tax countries (Bode, Krieger-Boden and Lammers, 1994; FitzGerald, Johnston and Williams, 1995). A qualitative survey conducted at the level of retail traders suggests that cross-border shopping for goods that are subject to VAT, but not excise taxes, has not increased significantly after 1992 (Ratzinger, 1998). In contrast, differences in excise tax rates, in particular for cigarettes and spirits, have led to significant tax revenue losses in Britain as a result of increased Channel trade (London Economics, 1994; Price Waterhouse, 1994).

While these results suggest that the distortions induced by cross-border shopping are still limited, it is likely that the pressure on the system of value added taxation in the Union will increase in the longer run. One reason lies in continuing market integration through the monetary union and – perhaps even more important – technological innovations such as electronic commerce. These developments are likely to increase the sensitivity with which final consumers in EU member states respond to international tax differentials.[13] Another reason is that the current scheme of taxing intra-Community trade differentiates between domestic transactions and transactions across EU borders. This runs counter to the establishment of a single European market and may lead traders that operate across national borders to challenge current tax regulations before the European Court of Justice (ECJ). These longer-run challenges are summarised by Keen and Smith (1996, p. 386) as follows:

> It is important to recognise, nevertheless, that the transitional system is sustainable only to the extent that there are impediments to the free movements of goods and services; to the extent that reducing these impediments is itself an

[12] Cnossen (1990), for example, vigorously opposes any measures of tax harmonisation, emphasising the importance of national sovereignty in the setting of VAT rates. In contrast, Sinn (1990a) argues that the harmonisation of VAT rates is needed as European integration proceeds, in order to prevent severe revenue shortfalls and protect the European welfare state.

[13] See the empirical study by Goolsbee (2000), relating sales taxation and Internet use in the United States (subsection 2.2.2).

object of policy, there is an important sense in which the transitional system is sustainable only for as long as the single market fails to be realised.

Against this background it is not surprising that there has been a renewal of interest in the fundamental alternative of switching to a general origin principle for the taxation of trade within the European Union. The main advantage of this scheme is that it allows governments to tax purchases by VAT-registered traders and by final consumers in the same way, thus reducing or even eliminating the incentives for cross-border shopping. Whether this alternative can indeed be expected to represent an improvement over the current set of tax rules is the subject of chapter 9.

APPENDIX

Second-order conditions of (8.14a)–(8.14b)

The second-order derivatives of (8.14a)–(8.14b) with respect to t^i are given by

$$\frac{\partial^2 v_I^i}{\partial t^{i2}} \equiv \frac{\partial F_I^i(t^{i*}, t^j)}{\partial t^i} = \frac{-\tau_i'' + (t^i \tau_i'''/\tau_i'')}{(\tau_i'')^2} - \frac{2c_i^i}{(1+t^i)^2}\left(1 - \frac{u_c^i}{u_g^i}\right) - \frac{c_i^i}{(1+t^i)} \frac{\partial(u_c^i/u_g^i)}{\partial(g^i/c^i)} \frac{\partial(g^i/c^i)}{\partial t^i}, \tag{8A.1}$$

$$\frac{\partial^2 v_{II}^i}{\partial t^{i2}} \equiv \frac{\partial F_{II}^i(t^{i*}, t^j)}{\partial t^i} = \frac{-\tau_j'' - (t^i \tau_j'''/\tau_j'')}{(\tau_j'')^2} - \frac{2c^i}{(1+t^i)^2}\left(1 - \frac{u_c^i}{u_g^i}\right) - \frac{c^i}{(1+t^i)} \frac{\partial(u_c^i/u_g^i)}{\partial(g^i/c^i)} \frac{\partial(g^i/c^i)}{\partial t^i}. \tag{8A.2}$$

Most of the conditions which ensure that (8A.1) and (8A.2) are negative are introduced in the analysis of this chapter: the first effect in both (8A.1) and (8A.2) is negative if the transaction cost function is quadratic in the volume of cross-border shopping, i.e., $\tau''' = 0$ (assumption 8.2). The second effect is negative if country i undersupplies the public good in the Nash equilibrium. This is always the case in regime I but need not be so in regime II. However, it is likely to be fulfilled even in regime II if differences in preferences are small (proposition 8.2). Finally, homothetic preferences (assumption 8.3) ensure $\partial(u_c^i/u_g^i)/\partial(g^i/c^i) > 0$ so that the third effects in (8A.1) and (8A.2) are negative.

Proof of proposition 8.2 Let F be an equation system which consists of the two implicitly defined best responses

$$F^A(t^{A*}, t^B, \theta^A) = 0,$$
$$F^B(t^A, t^{B*}, \theta^B) = 0, \tag{8A.3}$$

where θ^i are exogenous shift parameters. Totally differentiating (8A.3) and inverting gives

$$\begin{bmatrix} dt^A \\ dt^B \end{bmatrix} = \frac{1}{|\mathcal{J}|}\begin{bmatrix} -\dfrac{\partial F^B}{\partial t^B} & \dfrac{\partial F^A}{\partial t^B} \\ \dfrac{\partial F^B}{\partial t^A} & -\dfrac{\partial F^A}{\partial t^A} \end{bmatrix}\begin{bmatrix} \dfrac{\partial F^A}{\partial \theta^A} & d\theta^A \\ \dfrac{\partial F^B}{\partial \theta^B} & d\theta^B \end{bmatrix}, \tag{8A.4}$$

where the Jacobian is

$$\mathcal{J} = \begin{bmatrix} \partial F^A/\partial t^A & \partial F^A/\partial t^B \\ \partial F^B/\partial t^A & \partial F^B/\partial t^B \end{bmatrix}.$$

Let the set N contain all tax combinations (t^{A*}, t^{B*}) which solve (8A.3). Then, given the boundary behaviour of F, the index theorem states $\sum_{(t^{A*}, t^{B*})\in N} \text{sign}\, |-\mathcal{J}(t^{A*}, t^{B*})| = 1$ if all equilibria are regular (Mas-Colell, 1985, pp. 201–4). From the properties of determinants $|-\mathcal{J}| = |\mathcal{J}|$ in the 2×2 case. Therefore, if the Nash equilibrium is unique, the index theorem unambiguously signs

$$|\mathcal{J}| = \frac{\partial F^A}{\partial t^A}\frac{\partial F^B}{\partial t^B} - \frac{\partial F^A}{\partial t^B}\frac{\partial F^B}{\partial t^A} \equiv \Delta > 0. \tag{8A.5}$$

If multiple Nash equilibria exist $\Delta > 0$ can alternatively be obtained as a 'stability condition' (cf. Dixit, 1986, p. 110). For a symmetric initial equilibrium this stability requirement is equivalent to the familiar condition that the slope of best response functions must be less than one in absolute value.

To analyse the effects of a change in preferences $\partial(u_c^A/u_g^A)/\partial\alpha^A < 0$ we substitute $d\theta^A = d\alpha^A$ and $d\theta^B = 0$ in (8A.4). If the initial equilibrium is symmetric (8.16) can be used to obtain

$$\frac{\partial F^A}{\partial \alpha^A} = \frac{-c^A}{(1+t^A)}\frac{\partial(u_c^A/u_g^A)}{\partial \alpha^A} > 0. \tag{8A.6}$$

Using (8A.5)–(8A.6) and the second-order conditions $\partial F^i/\partial t^i < 0\ \forall\, i \in \{A, B\}$ in the first line of (8A.4) gives $dt^A/d\alpha^A > 0$. Combining this with the change in t^B (the second line in (8A.4)) gives

$$\frac{\partial F^B}{\partial t^A}\frac{dt^A}{d\alpha^A} = -\frac{\partial F^B}{\partial t^B}\frac{dt^B}{d\alpha^A}. \tag{8A.7}$$

From $\Delta > 0$ in (8A.5) and the symmetry of the initial equilibrium $(\partial F^A/\partial t^A = \partial F^B/\partial t^B$ and $\partial F^A/\partial t^B = \partial F^B/\partial t^A)$ it follows that $dt^A/d\alpha^A > dt^B/d\alpha^A$. Since tax rates are equal initially this demonstrates the proposition. ■

Proof of proposition 8.5(a) As a preliminary step, differentiating (8.19)–(8.21) with respect to β gives (cf. (8.24) in the main text)

$$\frac{\partial c_B^A}{\partial \beta} = \frac{-(t^A - t^B)}{\beta^2} < 0,$$

$$\frac{\partial c_A^A}{\partial \beta} = \frac{2(t^A - t^B) + (t^A)^2 - (t^B)^2}{2\beta^2(1+t^A)} > 0,$$

$$\frac{\partial c^A}{\partial \beta} = \frac{-(t^A - t^B)^2}{2\beta^2(1+t^A)} < 0. \tag{8A.8}$$

Differentiating the payoff functions in (8.14a)–(8.14b) with respect to β and using (8A.8) gives

$$\frac{\partial v^A}{\partial \beta} = \frac{u_g^A}{2\beta^2(1+t^A)}\left[(t^A - t^B)\left(1 - \frac{u_c^A}{u_g^A}\right) + 2(t^A)^2 - 2(t^B)^2\right] > 0, \tag{8A.9}$$

$$\frac{\partial v^B}{\partial \beta} = -u_g^B t^B \frac{(t^A - t^B)}{\beta^2} < 0, \tag{8A.10}$$

which demonstrates the proposition. ■

Derivation of (8.29)

Equation set (8A.4) simultaneously includes the solution for the more general case when best responses in both countries are altered by shift parameters: setting $d\theta^A = d\theta^B = d\beta$ yields (8.29) in the main text.

Proof of proposition 8.5(b): The right-hand side of (8.26), (8.27) and (8.30) are all monotonously falling in $(1/\sigma^i)$ whereas (8.31) is monotonously increasing in $(1/\sigma^B)$. Therefore, there exist lower bounds $\underline{\sigma}^A$ and $\underline{\sigma}^B$ such that for all $\sigma^A < \underline{\sigma}^A$ and $\sigma^B < \underline{\sigma}^B$ it must be true that $\partial F^A/\partial t^B < 0$, $\partial F^B/\partial t^A < 0$, $\partial F^A/\partial \beta < 0$ and $\partial F^B/\partial \beta > 0$. Substituting this combination of partial derivatives into (8.29) gives case 1 of proposition 8.5(b).

Similarly there exist upper bounds $\overline{\sigma}^A$ and $\overline{\sigma}^B$ such that for all $\sigma^A > \overline{\sigma}^A$ and $\sigma^B > \overline{\sigma}^B$ it must be true that $\partial F^A/\partial t^B > 0$, $\partial F^B/\partial t^A > 0$ and $\partial F^A/\partial \beta > 0$. It remains to show that $\partial F^B/\partial \beta > 0$ if country B undersupplies the public good initially. Inserting $\partial c_B^A/\partial \beta$ from (8A.8) into (8.31) in the main text shows that the sum of the first two effects in (8.31) is positive if and only if $2t^B - t^A > 0$. Similarly, using (8.19) in (8.15b) shows that $2t^B - t^A > 0$ implies $(1 - u_c^B/u_g^B) > 0$. Thus, if country B undersupplies the public good in the initial equilibrium $\partial F^B/\partial \beta > 0$ follows, since the last effect in (8.31) is negligible for very high σ^B. Substituting these results into (8.29) gives case 2 of proposition 8.5(b). ■

9 Switching to the origin principle?

The fundamental equivalence between a general commodity tax levied under the destination and origin principles has already been mentioned in subsection 2.2.1 and section 8.1. It was first stated in the Tinbergen Report (1953) for the European Coal and Steel Community (ECSC). The Neumark Report (1963) recommended a switch to the origin principle for the internal trade in the European Economic Community (EEC), arguing that the existence of border tax adjustments – as required for the implementation of the destination principle – was incompatible with the integration goals set by the Community. In an influential contribution, Biehl (1969) argued that for a multi-stage tax like VAT, border tax adjustments can be dispensed with, if the country of destination credits taxes paid in the exporting country in the same way as tax crediting occurs within a single country (*common market principle*). Another important issue, pioneered by Shibata (1967), concerns the interaction of internal and external trade relations when a group of countries switches to the origin principle for their internal trade while the destination principle is maintained in the rest of the world (*restricted origin principle*).

While the EEC decided in 1967 to maintain the destination principle for its internal trade, the debate on the proper scheme of commodity taxation in Europe has re-opened again with the completion of the internal market and the abolition of border controls within the Community. In comparison to the debate in the 1960s, the basic new aspect was the mobility of factors of production, in particular capital. For this reason, the issues raised by capital mobility in connection with a possible switch to the origin principle are at the centre of the analysis in this chapter. However, there have also been a large number of contributions that deal with other aspects of a switch to origin-based commodity taxation. These developments will also be summarised here.

Our procedure in this chapter is as follows: section 9.1 addresses an important preliminary issue, which is the administration of an origin-based multi-stage tax like VAT. Section 9.2 sets up a simple two-period model with investment decisions and international capital mobility and studies the equivalence between destination- and origin-based commodity taxation in this setting. Section 9.3 extends the analysis to a three-period model, where a switch to the origin principle can also have (short-run) anticipation effects. Section 9.4 presents a dynamic model that analyses this issue in more detail. The effects of an anticipated switch to the origin principle on macroeconomic variables and welfare are discussed in section 9.5. Section 9.6 compares the results of our dynamic analysis with related contributions in the literature. Section 9.7 addresses a number of other critical issues for a switch to the origin principle, including the problem raised by the Community's external trade relations, imperfect competition and an incomplete coverage of VAT, and the possibility of transfer pricing under the origin principle. Section 9.8 evaluates the arguments presented in this chapter.

9.1 The administration of an origin-based VAT

The discussion here draws on our introduction to a general origin-based commodity tax in section 8.1, which corresponds to the case where $t_1^i = t_2^i \; \forall \; i$ in (8.3).[1] The arbitrage conditions under a general origin-based commodity tax can then be summarised as

$$(1 + t^A)p_k^A = (1 + t^B)p_k^B \quad \forall \quad k. \tag{9.1}$$

Clearly, it is crucial for the allocative neutrality of a general origin-based consumption tax that this condition holds not only for final consumer goods but also for internationally traded intermediate goods and capital inputs, since these purchases are deductible from the base of a VAT of the consumption type. To ensure that (9.1) is indeed enforced by arbitrage for inputs as well as outputs, we have to look at the precise implementation of an origin-based VAT in some more detail.

For a producer in country A purchasing intermediate inputs from a domestic supplier the tax credit method applies and the taxation of international trade is irrelevant. If she buys inputs m at a producer price of p_m^A and sells final output x at a producer price of p_x^A her VAT bill is

$$VAT = t^A p_x^A x - t^A p_m^A m,$$

and she earns a net cash flow of

[1] The analysis in sections 9.1–9.2 is revised and adapted from Genser, Haufler and Sørensen (1995).

$$p_x^A(1+t^A)x - p_m^A(1+t^A)m - VAT = p_x^A x - p_m^A m. \tag{9.2}$$

Alternatively, the producer can purchase intermediate inputs from a supplier in country B at a tax-inclusive price of $p_m^B(1+t^B)$. There are now two different ways to implement the effective taxation of internationally traded intermediate goods in the country of production. The first scheme is the so-called 'international subtraction method' (e.g. Sinn, 1990a, p. 496). Under this method gross-of-tax imports can be deducted from the tax base and the VAT liability is calculated as

$$\begin{aligned} VAT &= \frac{t^A}{(1+t^A)}\left[p_x^A(1+t^A)x - p_m^B(1+t^B)m\right] \\ &= t^A p_x^A x - \frac{t^A}{(1+t^A)} p_m^B(1+t^B)\, m, \end{aligned} \tag{9.3}$$

where the tax rate is discounted by the domestic tax factor to express it as a percentage of consumer prices. This implies that the producer's net cash flow is equal to

$$p_x^A(1+t^A)x - p_m^B(1+t^B)m - VAT = p_x^A x - p_m^B \frac{(1+t^B)}{(1+t^A)} m. \tag{9.4}$$

Comparing (9.2) and (9.4), we see that producers will not be indifferent between purchasing their inputs at home or abroad, unless the condition $p_m^A(1+t^A) = p_m^B(1+t^B)$ holds for all intermediates and capital goods. Thus, under the international subtraction method, (9.1) will be enforced for all transactions by international arbitrage.

The international subtraction method raises potentially severe administrative problems, however, since it represents a break in the tax credit chain that applies to domestic transactions. As an alternative, it has therefore been proposed to apply a 'notional tax credit' which is compatible with the tax credit scheme applicable to domestic transactions in a single country (Krause-Junk, 1990). Under this scheme the purchase of intermediate goods is treated for VAT purposes as if it had borne the domestic tax rate t^A rather than the foreign rate (hence the term 'notional'). The tax credit is calculated by applying the domestic tax rate, deflated by the domestic tax factor $(1+t^A)$, to the gross-of-tax import expenditure $p_m^B\,(1+t^B)\,m$. Hence the domestic VAT liability becomes

$$VAT = t^A p_x^A x - \frac{t^A}{(1+t^A)} p_m^B(1+t^B)\, m,$$

which is equivalent to (9.3) above. To summarise, either the international subtraction method or the notional credit method of implementing the origin principle ensure that imported goods effectively bear the tax rate of the exporting country, even if they enter further stages of production in the destination country.

9.2 A basic equivalence result with mobile capital

In this section we introduce a simple two-period model of a small open economy to study the (long-run) equivalence of a general destination and a general origin principle in a setting with intertemporal savings and investment decisions and international capital mobility. In principle, capital mobility can be introduced in a one-period framework where two countries trade capital for a homogeneous output good. This is the so-called MacDougall–Kemp model, which is widely used in international trade models with factor mobility (see Ruffin, 1988). As we will see, however, an intertemporal framework is needed in order to explicitly account for the fact that all existing schemes of value-added taxation are of the *consumption type*. In all other respects we make the simplest possible assumptions. The small open economy produces a single internationally traded good which can be used for consumption as well as investment. This implies, in particular, that the commodity tax is levied at a *uniform* rate on all goods. Furthermore, we assume in this section that foreigners do not own part of the initial capital stock in the home country, and that the policy switch is not anticipated.

Destination principle

Under a destination-based consumption tax, the producer price in the small country (p) must equal the world price (cf. (8.1)) and is thus fixed exogenously. The representative domestic consumer lives for two periods and maximises a well-behaved utility function of the form

$$u = u(c_1, c_2), \tag{9.5}$$

where c_1 is consumption during the first period of her life, and c_2 is consumption during the second period.

The consumer is the owner–manager of a domestic competitive firm. At the beginning of period 1, this firm is endowed with a predetermined, initial stock of capital k_1, whereas the capital stock in period 2, k_2, is a decision variable. Output is assumed to depreciate fully in each period. Production in each period is a function of the physical capital stock existing at the beginning of the period and of the consumer's fixed labour supply, which is subsumed in the production function $f(k)$. In addition to her earnings from the firm – which include wage income, the normal return to investment and above-normal profits – the consumer receives a lump-sum government transfer T in each period.

The consumer may use part of the cash inflow in period 1 to purchase an internationally traded financial asset a, which pays the exogenous world interest rate R in period 2. Allowing for the resale of this asset at the end of period 2, the consumer then faces the period-specific budget constraints

$$p(1+t)c_1 + a = [pf(k_1) - pk_2] + T_1, \tag{9.6}$$

$$p(1+t)c_2 = [pf(k_2)] + T_2 + (1+R)a, \tag{9.7}$$

where the terms in square brackets represent the net cash flows from the firm after payment of commodity taxes. The term pk_2 in (9.6) indicates expenditure on physical investment during period 1. This is valued at producer prices because investment expenditure is deductible from the base of a VAT of the consumption type. Similarly, the term $pf(k_2)$ in (9.7) is the value of output from this capital stock in period 2. Since this revenue is taxable, the net cash flow to the consumer is again determined by the producer price p.

When she has access to an international capital market, the consumer may reallocate consumption over time along the international capital market line, and her budget equations collapse into a single intertemporal constraint. Eliminating a from (9.6)–(9.7) yields

$$p(1+t)\left[c_1 + \frac{c_2}{(1+R)}\right] = pf(k_1) - pk_2 + T_1 + \frac{[pf(k_2) + T_2]}{(1+R)}, \tag{9.8}$$

stating that the present value of (tax-inclusive) consumption expenditure must equal the present value of the payments received from the firm and from the government. To close the model, we finally have to specify tax revenues and hence transfer payments. Under the destination principle, the tax base is final consumption and tax revenues are given by

$$T_1 = tc_1, \qquad T_2 = tc_2. \tag{9.9}$$

We maximise the utility function (9.5) with respect to c_1, c_2 and k_2, subject to the budget constraint (9.8). The optimality conditions for consumption and investment are then given by

$$\frac{\partial u/\partial c_1}{\partial u/\partial c_2} = 1 + R, \qquad f'(k_2) = 1 + R. \tag{9.10}$$

Equation (9.10) shows that the value of consumption equals the value of output, net of investment, in present value terms. Since the tax does not appear in either of these equations, neither the consumption nor the investment decisions in the small country will be distorted.[2] The consumer will reallocate consumption over time until her marginal rate of substitution between present and future consumption equals the (constant) marginal rate of transformation $(1+R)$ offered by the international capital market. At the same time, the firm will carry physical investment to the point where the marginal product of capital equals its replacement value plus the opportunity costs of forgone investments in international financial assets.

In a second step, we substitute (9.9) to eliminate T_1 and T_2 from the intertemporal budget constraint.[3] This gives

$$c_1 + \frac{c_2}{(1+R)} = f(k_1) - k_2 + \frac{f(k_2)}{(1+R)}, \tag{9.11}$$

which shows that the value of consumption equals the value of output, net of investment, in present value terms. This, of course, is precisely the intertemporal budget constraint in the absence of taxes, showing that the destination-based tax also causes no income effects. Hence our analysis yields the expected result that the neutrality properties of the destination principle carry over to a setting with international capital mobility.

Origin principle

Under the origin principle, commodity price arbitrage implies that the domestic producer price p will be governed by

$$p\,(1+t) = P \equiv 1, \tag{9.12}$$

where we have normalised the producer price level in the rest of the world (P) to unity. In contrast to the destination principle, the producer price in the small open economy is now an endogenous variable. However, the temporal budget contraints (9.6) and (9.7) – and thus also the intertemporal budget constraint (9.8) – remain unchanged if we switch from a destination- to an origin-based tax. In particular, the investment expenditure in period 1 remains tax-deductible under an

[2] Note that the optimal investment condition in (9.10) is a special case of the more general condition (7.3) derived in chapter 7. The assumptions made here are that investment expenditures are fully deductible under a consumption-based VAT (i.e. $\alpha = 1$) and that output depreciates fully in each period ($\delta = 1$).

[3] Note that the transfer payments in each period are exogenous from the viewpoint of the representative consumer so that their values must be inserted only *after* the optimisation problem has been solved.

origin-based tax of the consumption type and hence the *producer* price of capital goods remains relevant for the investment decision (cf. (9.2)). Since the maximisation problems under the destination and the origin principle are identical, the first-order conditions for the consumption and investment decisions are again given by (9.10) and an origin-based consumption tax causes no efficiency losses. The intuition for the investment neutrality of an origin-based VAT can be further strengthened if we rewrite the intertemporal budget constraint (9.8) as

$$p\left[c_1 + \frac{c_2}{(1+R)}\right] = \frac{1}{(1+t)}\left[pf(k_1) + T_1 + \frac{p[f(k_2) - (1+R)k_2] + T_2}{(1+R)}\right]. \tag{9.13}$$

In conjunction with the optimal investment condition in (9.10) this shows that the deductibility of investment expenditures in period 1 is equivalent in present value terms to not taxing the equilibrium return to capital in period 2. As is seen from (9.13), an origin-based consumption tax thus falls on the entire value of the *initial* capital and labour endowments $[pf(k_1)]$, and on above-normal profits and wage income in the second period $[p\{f(k_2) - (1+R)k_2\}]$. Apart from the taxation of the initial capital stock, the origin-based commodity tax is thus equivalent to a combination of a tax on wage income and a cash-flow tax on the firm's profits, both levied at the same rate. The neutrality of a cash-flow tax for the investment decision of firms has been discussed in detail in our analysis in chapter 7.

Finally, tax revenue under the origin principle and hence transfer payments in the two periods are given by

$$T_1 = t[pf(k_1) - pk_2], \qquad T_2 = t[pf(k_2)]. \tag{9.14}$$

Substituting (9.14) in (9.8) shows that an origin-based VAT also has no income effects. As in the framework with commodity trade only, it is the equivalence in present value terms of consumption expenditures and factor incomes that is responsible for this result. If – as we have assumed here – the small country's *initial* capital stock is fully owned by domestic residents, then both the origin- and the destination-based tax are exclusively borne by domestic residents and effects on the international distribution of income are absent.[4] Our results are summarised in the following proposition.

[4] This point is familiar from our analysis in chapter 7 where we have differentiated between the case where pure economic rents accrue fully to the domestic individual (section 7.1), and where there is joint ownership of rent-generating entrepreneurial services (section 7.2). We will return to this issue in subsection 9.5.3, where we allow for foreign ownership of the initial capital stock.

Proposition 9.1
In the long run, a switch from a general destination to a general origin principle causes neither investment nor consumption distortions in the presence of capital mobility. If the capital stock is entirely owned by domestic residents, then the switch will also not affect the international distribution of income.

In proposition 9.1 we have emphasised that the results in this section should be seen as the long-run effects of a switch in the commodity tax system. The two-period framework employed here has assumed that the producer price adjustment required under the origin principle (9.12) occurs instantaneously, and that there is no lag between the announcement and the implementation of the policy switch. The latter assumption is relaxed in the analysis of the following two sections.

9.3 Anticipation effects in a three-period model

In the two-period model of section 9.2 we have assumed that the capital stock was fixed in period 1, when the switch to the origin principle occurred. This feature of the model ensured that capital flight from the small country did not take place *before* the fall in the world market price of the small country's capital goods (cf. (9.12)). The simplest way to extend this model is to consider an initial period 0 where the destination-based system is still in place but the switch to the origin principle in period 1 becomes known to all agents. This framework allows some first insights into how intertemporal decisions may be distorted in the short run by the switch in the tax principle. All other simplifying features of the previous analysis are retained in this section.

Assume then that the destination principle is in place in period $s = 0$, but the origin principle applies for international trade in periods $s = 1, 2$. The world price of the homogeneous good is normalised to unity in all periods.[5] From the international arbitrage conditions under the destination and origin principles, this implies the following path of producer prices in the small open economy:

$$p_0 = 1, \quad p_1 = \frac{1}{(1+t)}, \quad p_2 = \frac{1}{(1+t)}. \tag{9.15}$$

[5] Hence we normalise the 'current' world price of the commodity in each time period and express relative prices over time by the (constant) world interest rate R. Alternatively, one could normalise the price of the commodity at period 0 only. Relative prices over time would then be reflected in a declining sequence of 'discounted' prices, without explicitly introducing an interest rate. Of course, these two approaches yield identical results and the choice between them is merely a matter of exposition.

The utility function of the representative consumer in the small country is given by

$$u(c_0, c_1, c_2), \tag{9.16}$$

where c_s denotes the consumption level in period s. The initial capital stock of the economy, which is entirely owned by the representative domestic agent, is given by k_0. Output in period s is given by the time-invariant production function $f(k_s)$ and capital depreciates fully in each period. The output produced in each period can be consumed, invested in the home country, or invested in the world capital market at the fixed and time-invariant interest rate R. All international bonds mature after one period.

Since investment is fully deductible from the base of either the destination- or the origin-based consumption tax, its price equals the domestic producer price of output in each period. With tax revenues in each period given by T_s and investments in the world capital market denoted by a_s, the budget constraints in each period are

$$\begin{aligned} p_0(1+t)c_0 &= p_0 f(k_0) - p_0 k_1 - a_0 + T_0, \\ p_1(1+t)c_1 &= p_1 f(k_1) - p_1 k_2 - a_1 + (1+R)a_0 + T_1, \\ p_2(1+t)c_2 &= p_2 f(k_2) + (1+R)a_1 + T_2, \end{aligned} \tag{9.17}$$

where all outstanding debt is paid back and all income is consumed in the last period. As in section 9.2, the period-specific budget constraints can be consolidated to a single intertemporal budget constraint by eliminating the variables a_0 and a_1. Furthermore, we substitute world prices for domestic prices using (9.15). This gives

$$(1+t)c_0 - f(k_0) + k_1 - T_0 + \frac{1}{(1+R)}\left[c_1 - \frac{1}{(1+t)}f(k_1) + \frac{1}{(1+t)}k_2 - T_1\right]$$

$$+\frac{1}{(1+R)^2}\left[c_2 - \frac{1}{(1+t)}f(k_2) - T_2\right] = 0. \tag{9.18}$$

The problem for the representative consumer in the small country is to maximise (9.16) subject to the constraint (9.18), where the choice variables are the three consumption levels and the domestic capital stocks in periods 1 and 2 (corresponding to real investment decisions in periods 0 and 1). Using the marginal utility of consumption in period 0 to eliminate the Lagrangian multiplier, the optimal consumption and investment plans are given by

$$\frac{\partial u/\partial c_0}{\partial u/\partial c_1} = (1+t)(1+R), \tag{9.19}$$

$$f'(k_1) = (1+t)(1+R), \tag{9.20}$$

$$\frac{\partial u/\partial c_1}{\partial u/\partial c_2} = (1+R), \tag{9.21}$$

$$f'(k_2) = (1+R). \tag{9.22}$$

These results show that an anticipated reduction in the domestic producer price level in period 1 distorts *both* the savings and the investment decision in period 0. From (9.19) we see that the marginal rate of substitution between consumption in periods 0 and 1 exceeds the marginal rate of transformation $(1+R)$. Similarly, from (9.20) the marginal product of capital in period 1 exceeds the costs of financing the investment through the world capital market.

The intuition for these results is straightforward. In period 0 both consumers and producers expect a fall in the domestic price level, as measured in world prices. For consumers this implies that domestic consumption becomes cheaper in period 1 when expressed in terms of assets held (or issued) in foreign currency. Thus consumers substitute away from relatively expensive consumption in period 0 and increase their investment in the world capital market. This raises the marginal utility of consumption in period 0 above its value in subsequent periods. By a similar reasoning, the anticipated fall in the domestic producer price in period 1 reduces investments in the small open economy made in period 0. This translates into an inefficiently high marginal (physical) product of capital in period 1, compensating investors for the simultaneous capital loss through the reduced producer price. Thus both the consumption and the investment effects of an anticipated switch to the origin principle work in the direction of a trade surplus and a higher investment in international capital markets in the period prior to the tax reform. This is summarised in

Proposition 9.2
For a small open economy that unilaterally switches to the origin principle, anticipation effects lead to inefficiently low levels of consumption and investment in the period before the switch occurs.

However, and corresponding to our discussion in section 9.2, neither consumption nor investment decisions are distorted once the origin principle has been introduced in period 1. This is seen from (9.21) and (9.22), which imply that both the marginal rate of substitution between consumption in periods 1 and 2 and the marginal product of capital in period 2 equal the opportunity costs of funds in the world capital market. After the switch in the tax principle, consumption is taxed at the same rate in each period whereas new investment in the home country bears an effective tax rate of zero through the deduction of all capital expenditures for VAT purposes.

The three-period model in this section represents an intermediate step in our analysis. It offers some first insights into the distortionary short-run effects of an anticipated switch to the origin principle while confirming the long-run efficiency result derived in the two-period model of section 9.2. In the following the adjustment processes of consumption and investment will be studied in more detail by considering the switch to the origin principle in a fully dynamic setting.

9.4 A dynamic model of investment and savings

The dynamic analysis is carried out in an infinite-horizon model with a single, representative consumer.[6] We consider again a small, open economy which faces fixed world prices in both goods and capital markets. The world price of the homogeneous consumption–investment good is normalised to unity at each instant in time (cf. n. 5) and the time-invariant international interest rate is here denoted by r (which equals R, since there are no source taxes on capital in the small economy). To describe the model we separately discuss the dynamic optimisation problems faced by producers and consumers in the small country and then discuss the precise form that the regime switch takes in this dynamic setting.

9.4.1 Firms

In the basic model, the representative firm is owned exclusively by domestic households, which act as producer–consumers. The firm produces output under the time-invariant production function $f(k_s)$, where k_s is the capital stock at time s. The production function has the usual properties of positive but diminishing returns to capital ($f' > 0, f'' < 0$). The firm invests an amount i_s in each period. For convenience we introduce a separate variable for the firm's *relative* investment $h_s \equiv i_s/k_s$. An additional element in models of small open economies is a convex installation cost function, which depends on the firm's relative investment. Without these installation costs the adjustment of the capital stock to an exogenous shock would be instantaneous, as the small open economy faces an infinitely elastic supply of savings (cf. Blanchard and Fischer,

[6] The analysis in sections 9.4–9.5 is revised and adapted from Haufler and Nielsen (1997).

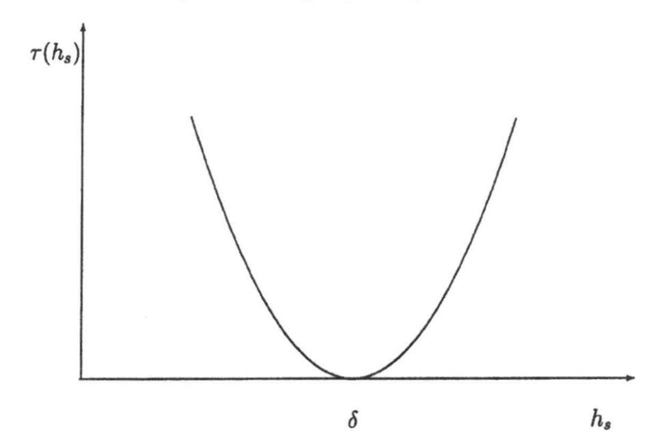

Figure 9.1 Convex installation costs

1989, ch. 2.4; Nielsen and Sørensen, 1991). The installation cost function, denoted by $\tau(h_s)$, thus has a similar role in excluding corner solutions as in previous chapters that focused on the spatial allocation of capital and consumer purchases. When h_s equals the exogenous depreciation rate δ, then both total and marginal installation costs are zero. For all other investment levels there are positive installation costs and marginal costs increase as the deviation from δ increases. The installation cost function is shown in figure 9.1 and its properties are summarised by

$$\tau(h_s) > 0 \text{ for } h_s \neq \delta, \quad \tau(\delta) = 0, \quad \tau'(\delta) = 0, \quad \tau''(h_s) > 0. \tag{9.23}$$

Installation costs consume real resources. To effectively install the investment i_s, the firm must thus incur total costs of $i_s(1 + \tau(h_s))$. These investment costs are valued at the *producer* price p_s since all investment costs are tax-deductible under a VAT of the consumption type (cf. section 9.2). Using $i_s = h_s k_s$ from the above definition, the firm's cash flow in period s can be written as[7]

$$\pi_s = [f(k_s) - k_s h_s(1 + \tau(h_s))]p_s. \tag{9.24}$$

The firm chooses the relative investment level h_s so as to maximise the discounted sum of its cash-flow profits

[7] Note that the cash flow terms in (9.6)–(9.7) of section 9.2 are identical to the expression here, except for the installation cost component.

$$\max_{h_s} \int_0^\infty e^{-rs}[f(k_s) - k_s h_s(1+\tau(h_s))]p_s \; ds,$$

subject to the capital accumulation constraint

$$\dot{k}_s = i_s - \delta k_s = (h_s - \delta)k_s. \tag{9.25}$$

The current-value Hamiltonian for this problem is thus

$$\mathcal{H}_F = [f(k_s) - k_s h_s(1+\tau(h_s))]p_s + \mu_s(h_s - \delta)k_s,$$

where μ_s gives the current value of the co-state variable, i.e. the shadow price of the capital stock. For relative investment h_t, the necessary condition for an optimum implies

$$\frac{\partial \mathcal{H}_F}{\partial h_s} = 0 \quad \Rightarrow \quad \mu_s = [1 + \tau(h_s) + h_s\tau'(h_s)]p_s \equiv \psi^{-1}(h_s)p_s. \tag{9.26}$$

The first-order condition (9.26) shows that investment behaviour is governed by the relative co-state variable (μ_s/p_s). The latter gives the shadow price of the capital stock, relative to the market price of capital, and plays the role of 'Tobin's q' in the present context. Inverting the function $(\psi)^{-1}(h_s)$ defined in (9.26) gives the investment function

$$h_s = \psi\left(\frac{\mu_s}{p_s}\right), \quad \psi(1) = \delta, \quad \frac{\partial \psi}{\partial(\mu_s/p_s)} > 0. \tag{9.27}$$

Since there is no (long-run) growth in the present model, only replacement investments are undertaken in the steady state, where the shadow price and the market price of capital coincide ($\mu_s = p_s$). Relative investment will be above (below) the exogenous depreciation rate if and only if the shadow price of capital is above (below) its market price. Substituting $\psi(.)$ in the equation of motion (9.25) gives the adjustment of the capital stock as a function of the (relative) shadow price of capital

$$\dot{k}_s = \left[\psi\left(\frac{\mu_s}{p_s}\right) - \delta\right]k_s. \tag{9.28}$$

The optimality condition with respect to the state variable k_s implies[8]

[8] See, e.g., Feichtinger und Hartl (1986, p. 18) and Sinn (1987, p. 25). Alternatively, if the *present value* Hamiltonian is used and is denoted by $\mathcal{H}'_F$, then the first-order condition with respect to the state variable is given by

$$\frac{\partial \mathcal{H}'_F}{\partial k_s} = -\dot{\mu}'_s,$$

where μ'_s is the associated co-state variable and $\mu_s = \mu'_s e^{rs}$.

$$\frac{\partial \mathcal{H}_F}{\partial k_s} = -\dot{\mu}_s + r\mu_s \quad \Rightarrow \quad [f'(k_s) - h_s(1+\tau(h_s))]p_s + \dot{\mu}_s = \mu_s(r + \delta - h_s). \tag{9.29}$$

This condition can be simplified by substituting $h_s(1+\tau(h_s))p_s = h_s\mu_s - h_s^2\tau'(h_s)p_s$ from the first-order condition (9.26), giving

$$[f'(k_s) + h_s^2\tau'(h_s)]p_s + \dot{\mu}_s = \mu_s(r+\delta). \tag{9.30}$$

Equation (9.30) implicitly defines the firm's optimal investment path. On the left-hand side of the equation are the marginal benefits of installing an additional unit of capital in the small country. These consist of three elements: capital's marginal product, the marginal savings on adjustment costs (both valued at the producer price p_s) and the capital gains from a change in the nominal shadow price of capital. On the right-hand side are the marginal costs of using capital from one instant to the next, which are composed of the instantaneous interest rate r and the exogenous depreciation rate δ. In the steady state ($\mu_s = p_s$) this implies that $f' - \delta = r$, i.e., the net marginal product of capital must equal the international interest rate. This, of course, is just our long-run neutrality result from section 9.2 (9.10), where we have assumed that the capital stock fully depreciates in each period ($\delta = 1$). The equation of motion (9.28) and the optimal investment condition (9.30) summarise the dynamic evolution of the capital stock in the small open economy.

9.4.2 *Households*

As before, there is a representative, infinitely-lived consumer in the small country, which owns all domestic factors of production. In addition, the household can borrow and lend freely in the international capital market, with a_s denoting the net foreign asset position in period s. The accumulation constraint for foreign assets is given by

$$\dot{a}_s = ra_s + \pi_s + T_s - q_s c_s, \tag{9.31}$$

where household income consists of interest income ra_s on the outstanding foreign asset position, the firm's cash flow π_s, and lump-sum transfers from the government T_s (which are defined below). The consumption level in period s is denoted by c_s and consumption expenditures are valued at the domestic consumer price q_s.

The consumer maximises the discounted sum of instantaneous utilities $u(c_s)$. To avoid the well-known problems that exist when a small open economy accumulates or decumulates foreign assets in the steady state we assume that the household's pure rate of time preference equals the world rate of interest. The optimisation problem is thus described by

$$\max_{c_s} \int_0^{\infty} e^{-rs} u(c_s) \, ds,$$

subject to the accumulation constraint (9.31) and a transversality ('No-Ponzi-game') condition

$$\lim_{s \to \infty} a_s e^{-rs} = 0. \tag{9.32}$$

The transversality condition states that the present value of the consumer's asset holdings in the steady state must be zero. The condition thus prevents both the infinite postponement of consumption and the accumulation of debt at a rate that exceeds the world interest rate (cf. Blanchard and Fischer, 1989, p. 49).

The current value Hamiltonian of the household's optimisation problem is

$$\mathcal{H}_H = u(c_s) + \lambda_s(ra_s + \pi_s + T_s - q_s c_s).$$

From the first-order condition with respect to c_s, the current value of the co-state variable λ_s is determined as

$$\frac{\partial \mathcal{H}_H}{\partial c_s} = 0 \quad \Rightarrow \quad \lambda_s = \frac{u'(c_s)}{q_s}. \tag{9.33}$$

The first-order condition with respect to the state variable a_s implies

$$\frac{\partial \mathcal{H}_H}{\partial a_s} = -\dot{\lambda}_s + r\lambda_s \quad \Rightarrow \quad \dot{\lambda}_s = 0. \tag{9.34}$$

According to (9.34), the shadow price of foreign assets (or the marginal utility of wealth) remains constant over time. In conjunction with (9.33) this implies that after period zero the consumption level will change if and only if the consumer price changes in period s. This, of course, is the conventional result that consumption smoothing will be complete in a small open economy when capital markets are perfect and the interest rate is constant over time. It is important to note, however, that the shadow price λ may jump at $s = 0$ in response to new information like news on a future tax reform. This initial adjustment will be analysed in the following section.

9.4.3 Government

The dynamic analysis carried out below is confined to *marginal* changes in tax rates. To analyse a switch in the tax principle from destination- to origin-based commodity taxation in this framework, we proceed as follows. The analysis allows for both types of commodity taxes, a destination-based tax at rate t_d, and an origin-based tax at rate t_o. The destination tax increases the consumer price q_s in the small country, whereas the origin tax reduces the producer price p_s. Hence, given the world price of unity, we have

$$q_s = 1 + t_d, \qquad p_s = \frac{1}{(1 + t_o)}. \tag{9.35}$$

To close the model we have to specify the government budget constraint. Government revenues in period s are given by the sum of tax receipts from the destination-based tax and the origin-based tax on the firm's cash flow (the value of production minus gross investment costs). For simplicity we assume again that tax revenues are fully returned to the representative consumer as a lump-sum transfer; in fact, this has already been incorporated in the private budget constraint (9.31). With lump-sum redistribution of revenues we can assume without further loss of generality that the government's budget is balanced in each period

$$T_s = t_d c_s + t_o \pi_s. \tag{9.36}$$

From (9.35), origin- and destination-based taxes can be combined to give the total tax wedge between producer and consumer prices in the small country

$$q_s = (1 + t_d)(1 + t_o)p_s \equiv \theta p_s.$$

The policy change analysed below is a marginal switch from destination- to origin-based consumption taxes which leaves the aggregate tax wedge θ unchanged. As in the preceding sections this implies that when the small open economy switches to the origin principle, the rest of the world does not. Totally differentiating gives $dt_d = -(1 + t_d)/(1 + t_o)\, dt_o < 0$, i.e., a small, exogenous increase in the origin-based tax rate t_o is compensated by a reduction in the destination-based tax rate t_d. Using (9.35), the price effects of a compensated increase in t_o in period s are derived as

$$dq_s = dt_d = -\frac{q_s}{(1 + t_o)}\, dt_o < 0, \qquad dp_s = -\frac{p_s}{(1 + t_o)}\, dt_o < 0. \tag{9.37}$$

Hence both consumer and producer prices in the small country will fall in response to the change in the tax scheme. In the long run, these price adjustments ensure that there are no real effects of a switch from the destination to the origin principle.[9] In the short run real effects occur, however, when agents anticipate the switch in the tax principle. These adjustment processes are analysed in detail in section 9.5.

9.5 Short-run effects of a switch in the tax regime

9.5.1 The investment path

We linearise the two dynamic equations (9.28) and (9.30) around the initial steady state.[10] As a preliminary step, we define the parameter κ to denote the first derivative of the investment function (9.27), evaluated in the steady state. Using the properties of the installation cost function (9.23) and the first-order condition (9.26), we can employ the inverse function rule to get

$$\kappa \equiv \psi'(1) = \left(\frac{\partial(\psi^{-1})}{\partial h_s}\right)^{-1} = \frac{1}{\delta\tau''(\delta)} > 0. \tag{9.38}$$

Totally differentiating the equation of motion (9.28), using (9.38) and the properties of the initial steady state gives[11]

$$\hat{\dot{k}} = \kappa\,(\hat{\mu} - \hat{p}), \tag{9.39}$$

where we have introduced the 'hat' notation to describe percentage changes in variables from their steady state values. Thus $\hat{\mu} = d\mu/\mu$, $\hat{p} = dp/p$ and $\hat{\dot{k}} = d(\dot{k})/k$.[12] Similarly, we can totally differentiate the optimal investment condition (9.30) to get in a first step

$$f'(k)dp + p[f''(k)dk + h^2\tau''dh] + d(\dot{\mu}) = (r + \delta)d\mu.$$

From the capital accumulation constraint (9.25) and (9.39) we get $dh = d(\dot{k}/k) = \hat{\dot{k}} = \kappa\,(\hat{\mu} - \hat{p})$. Using this and the properties of the initial steady state gives[13]

9 However, we will see in the following section that the level of steady-state consumption will change when the switch in the tax principle affects savings decisions during the adjustment process, and thus the net foreign asset position in the steady state. For a more detailed discussion of this 'path dependence' property, see Nielsen (1991).

10 For the basic mathematical tools underlying the analysis in this section, cf. Chiang (1984, ch. 18).

11 From now on we drop the time subscript s when no confusion is possible.

12 Noting that $\dot{k} = 0$ in the initial equilibrium, the last result follows from

$$\hat{\dot{k}} \equiv \frac{\partial(dk/k)}{\partial s} = \frac{k(\partial dk/\partial s) - dk\dot{k}}{k^2} = \frac{1}{k}\frac{\partial(dk)}{\partial s} = \frac{d(\dot{k})}{k}.$$

13 We use (9.38) and $h = \delta$ in the initial steady state to get $h^2\tau''dh = \delta(\hat{\mu} - \hat{p})$. Inserting this and observing that $f' = r + \delta$ initially (from (9.30)) and $d(\dot{\mu}/\mu) = \hat{\dot{\mu}}$ (cf. n. 12), we can finally divide by $p = \mu$ (which holds in the initial steady state from (9.26)) to get (9.40).

$$\dot{\hat{\mu}} = r(\hat{\mu} - \hat{p}) + \alpha(r + \delta)\hat{k}, \tag{9.40}$$

where we have introduced the elasticity of the marginal productivity of capital

$$\alpha \equiv -\frac{f''(k)k}{f'(k)} > 0.$$

Equations (9.39) and (9.40) jointly determine the time path for the capital stock k and the nominal shadow price of capital μ. In matrix form, the dynamic investment system is given by

$$\begin{bmatrix} \dot{\hat{k}} \\ \dot{\hat{\mu}} \end{bmatrix} = \mathcal{J} \begin{bmatrix} \hat{k} \\ \hat{\mu} \end{bmatrix} + \begin{bmatrix} -\kappa \\ -r \end{bmatrix} \hat{p}, \qquad \mathcal{J} = \begin{bmatrix} 0 & \kappa \\ \alpha(r+\delta) & r \end{bmatrix}. \tag{9.41}$$

The determinant of the coefficient matrix $|\mathcal{J}| = -\kappa\alpha(r + \delta)$ is negative, thus ensuring saddle-point stability. To determine the general solution to (9.41) we set up the characteristic equation

$$|\eta I - \mathcal{J}| = \begin{vmatrix} \eta & -\kappa \\ -\alpha(r+\delta) & \eta - r \end{vmatrix} = \eta^2 - \eta r - \kappa\alpha(r+\delta) = 0,$$

where I is the identity matrix and η denotes the *eigenvalues*, or characteristic roots, of the matrix $\mathcal{J}$. Solving the quadratic equation, the eigenvalues are

$$\begin{aligned} \eta_1 &= \frac{r}{2} - \sqrt{\left(\frac{r}{2}\right)^2 + \kappa\alpha(r+\delta)} < 0, \\ \eta_2 &= \frac{r}{2} + \sqrt{\left(\frac{r}{2}\right)^2 + \kappa\alpha(r+\delta)} > 0. \end{aligned} \tag{9.42}$$

They show how the speed of stable, resp. unstable movement of the dynamic investment system depends on the exogenous model parameters. For instance, stable adjustment is fast if κ is large, which in turn implies from (9.38) that marginal adjustment costs rise only slowly around the initial steady state ($\tau''(\delta)$ is small). Similarly, a new equilibrium will be reached quickly if the production function is strongly concave (α is large), and if the depreciation rate δ is high.

Let the time at which the policy switch occurs be denoted by s^*. We then have to consider two regimes in the following analysis.[14] Regime I $(0, s^*)$ describes the dynamic evolution of the capital stock and its shadow price from the announcement of the policy change in period 0 to its

[14] The methods involved in analysing anticipated policy shocks are summarised by Turnovsky (1995, pp. 137–41).

actual implementation in period s^*. Regime II (s^*, ∞) traces out the time path of the endogenous variables after the policy switch has been enacted. The crucial link between the two regimes is the condition that both $\hat{k}$ and $\hat{\mu}$ must change continuously at the time of the policy implementation, the latter since there is no new and unforeseen information at time s^*. This also implies that the variables k and μ must follow an unstable path in regime I, moving away from the initial steady-state equilibrium, whereas they will be on a stable path in regime II in order to reach a new steady-state equilibrium in the long run.

Section 9A.1 in the appendix (pp. 224–5) demonstrates in detail how to obtain expressions for the dynamic development of the capital stock and its shadow price in regimes I and II. Letting $\hat{p}_{s^*}$ stand for the (one-time) relative change in the producer price at time s^*, when the switch to origin-based commodity taxation is implemented, we find for regime I

$$\hat{k}_s^I = \frac{\hat{p}_{s^*}\,\kappa}{\eta_1 - \eta_2}\, e^{-\eta_2 s^*}\left(e^{\eta_1 s} - e^{\eta_2 s}\right) < 0, \tag{9.43}$$

$$\hat{\mu}_s^I = \frac{\hat{p}_{s^*}}{\eta_1 - \eta_2}\, e^{-\eta_2 s^*}\left(\eta_1 e^{\eta_1 s} - \eta_2 e^{\eta_2 s}\right) < 0, \tag{9.44}$$

where the signing of the effects has used $\eta_1 < 0, \eta_2 > 0$ from (9.42), and $\hat{p}_{s^*} < 0$ for a switch to origin-based commodity taxes (9.37).

In the initial steady state, the shadow price of capital μ_s coincides with the producer price p_s. In regime I, p_s is unchanged throughout, whereas μ_s jumps down on impact and declines further towards time s^*. At time s^*, investment goods become available at a reduced producer price owing to the commodity tax switch, giving an incentive to firms to postpone investment until s^*. Since capital installed right at time s^* competes with capital installed just before s^*, the latter must have a value close to the reduced producer price of capital plus installation cost at time s^*. At earlier dates within regime I, it is more costly to wait until the producer price falls; hence the value of the capital stock tends to be higher at dates early on in regime I than thereafter.

Overall, the dynamic evolution of the shadow price of capital in regime I thus comprises a downward jump at time 0 and a gradual decline thereafter. From the investment function $\psi(\mu_s/p_s)$ (9.27), the decline in the shadow price of capital will reduce investment below its steady-state level and lead to a reduction in the domestic capital stock between time 0 and s^*. This corresponds to the results of our three-period model in section 9.3, where the marginal product of capital in period 1 was pushed above the opportunity cost of capital in the world market (9.20).

It is interesting to look in more detail at the impact change in the nominal value of the capital stock when the tax regime switch is announced at time 0. From (9.44) this follows by setting $s = 0$ to give

$$\hat{\mu}_0 = \hat{p}_{s^*} \, e^{-\eta_2 s^*} < 0. \tag{9.45}$$

This shows that the downward jump in the nominal shadow price of capital in period 0 will be the more pronounced, the lower is the adjustment speed of investment (cf. (9.42)) and the shorter is the time period that elapses between the announcement and the implementation of the policy switch. Only in the special case where the 'lead period' is infinitely long ($s^* \to \infty$) will the impact effect of the announcement on the shadow price of capital be negligible.

Turning to regime II (s^*, ∞), we get from the appendix

$$\hat{k}_s^{II} = \frac{\hat{p}_{s^*} \, \kappa}{\eta_1 - \eta_2} \, e^{\eta_1 s} \left(e^{-\eta_2 s^*} - e^{-\eta_1 s^*} \right) < 0, \tag{9.46}$$

$$\hat{\mu}_s^{II} = \hat{p}_{s^*} \left[1 + \frac{\eta_1}{\eta_1 - \eta_2} e^{\eta_1 s} \left(e^{-\eta_2 s^*} - e^{-\eta_1 s^*} \right) \right] < 0. \tag{9.47}$$

While the *nominal* shadow price of capital μ_s does not jump at $s = s^*$, the *real* value of capital jumps upward in period s^* because the producer price falls at the time of the policy switch. From (9.47) it is seen that the reduction in μ_s is less than the fall in the producer price, since the second term in the square bracket is negative. Since $\mu_s = p_s$ in the initial equilibrium this must also imply that the relative co-state variable (μ_s / p_s) exceeds unity in regime II. Hence, from (9.27), relative investment will exceed the depreciation rate and the capital stock gradually rises throughout this regime. The adjustment process is completed when the drop in the shadow price of the capital stock equals the percentage fall in the small country's producer price (i.e. the second term in the square bracket of (9.47) is zero) and the capital stock has returned to its steady-state level.

Figure 9.2 illustrates the dynamic evolution of the variables μ and k in both regimes. The initial steady-state equilibrium is given by point E. At the time of the policy announcement, the temporary equilibrium jumps downward to point A. In regime I the system follows an unstable path until it reaches point B at time s^*. In regime II the system then follows the stable trajectory corresponding to the new saddle-point equilibrium E'. Our analysis of the investment effects of an anticipated switch in the commodity tax principle is summarised in

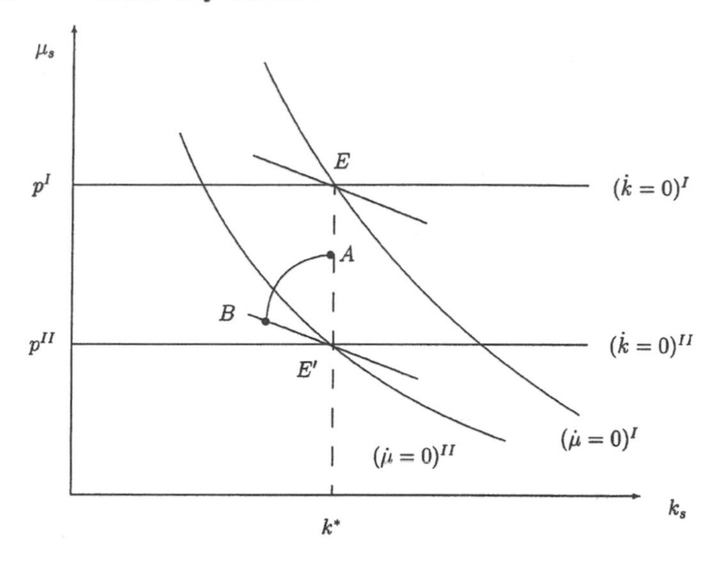

Figure 9.2 The response of the capital stock and its shadow price

Proposition 9.3

In a dynamic model with convex installation costs an anticipated switch to the origin principle leads to a gradual reduction in the capital stock between the announcement and the implementation of the policy change. After the policy change has been enacted, the capital stock rises again and returns to its initial level in the steady-state equilibrium.

Finally, it is easy to show that our analysis of an unanticipated policy change in section 9.2 is included here as a special case. When the announcement and implementation of the switch coincide ($s^* = 0$), then the reduction in the firm's nominal cash flow is immediately and fully capitalised in the nominal value of the capital stock (cf. (9.45)). However the real shadow price of capital (μ/p) remains constant because the producer price p falls by the same amount at time $s^* = 0$. Hence the new steady state will be reached immediately. In the absence of announcement effects, the switch to origin-based commodity taxes will thus reduce the value of 'old' capital by the arbitrage condition (9.12), but will not affect investment decisions and the capital stock at any point in time.

9.5.2 *International asset accumulation*

We have already seen in section 9.3 that, in addition to the effects on investment and production, an anticipated switch in the commodity tax regime also affects the time path of consumption. To analyse these effects in our dynamic model we assume for simplicity that the domestic household holds no foreign assets in the initial steady state ($a_0 = 0$). International asset accumulation is driven by the equation of motion (9.31) and the first-order condition of the consumer's optimisation problem (9.33). Differentiation of (9.33) gives

$$\hat{\lambda} \equiv \frac{d\lambda}{\lambda} = \frac{u''(c)dcq - u'(c)dq}{q^2} \frac{q}{u'(c)} = -\left[\left(-\frac{u''(c)c}{u'(c)}\right)\hat{c} + \hat{q}\right].$$

Noting that $\hat{q} = \hat{p}$ under the policy change considered here (cf. (9.37)) and introducing the elasticity of the marginal utility of consumption gives

$$\hat{c} = -\frac{(\hat{\lambda} + \hat{p})}{\varepsilon}, \qquad \text{where} \quad \varepsilon \equiv -\frac{u''(c)c}{u'(c)} > 0. \tag{9.48}$$

Linearisation of (9.31) around the initial steady state and inserting from (9.24) and (9.36) yields in a first step

$$\dot{a} = d(\dot{a}) = rda + [kf'(k)]\hat{k} - kdh - hk\hat{k} - dc.$$

Using (9.48), $dh = \kappa(\hat{\mu} - \hat{p})$ from (9.39), $h = \delta$ in the initial steady state and recalling that the net foreign asset position is zero initially ($a_0 = 0$), this can be rewritten as

$$\dot{a} = ra + k[r\hat{k} - \kappa(\hat{\mu} - \hat{p})] + \frac{c}{\varepsilon}(\hat{\lambda} + \hat{p}). \tag{9.49}$$

The next step is to incorporate the regime-specific changes in $\hat{k}$ and $\hat{\mu}$. As in the case of the investment path analysed in subsection 9.5.1, the two regimes are linked by the condition that the foreign asset position a must change continuously around s^*. It is demonstrated in appendix 9A.2 (pp. 225–7) that this requirement, together with the transversality condition (9.32), allows to derive an expression for the impact change in the marginal utility of wealth λ:

$$\hat{\lambda} = -e^{-rs^*}\hat{p}_{s^*}, \tag{9.50}$$

which is *positive* for a combined fall in producer and consumer prices at time s^*. From (9.33) this implies that the marginal utility of consumption must rise in regime I – and the level of consumption must thus fall – as a result of the policy announcement. Intuitively, an anticipated fall in the consumer price level at time s^* will cause households to postpone consumption until the price reduction has been realised. This result corresponds to our analysis in section 9.3 (9.19). It is also seen from (9.50) that for a very distant implementation time $s^* \to \infty$ we have $\hat{\lambda} \to 0$, so that the 'postponement effect' on consumption will be negligible. On the other hand, for an unanticipated switch to the origin principle ($s^* = 0$) we have $\hat{\lambda} = -\hat{p}$, and the shadow price of foreign asset holdings rises by the full amount of the price change. However, since the price of consumption is simultaneously reduced, there is no change in the consumption and savings behaviour of the individual. This is seen from (9.48), which implies $\hat{c} = 0$ in this case. Once again, for the special case of an unanticipated switch to the origin principle, our model reproduces the neutrality result derived in section 9.2.

Figure 9.3 shows the time path of consumption in both regimes for the general case where $0 < s^* < \infty$. In regime I, the consumption level is given by c^I, which is below the level that would be realised in the absence of the policy shock ($\bar{c}$). In regime II, households can conversely afford a higher level of consumption (c^{II}) as a result of the increased savings made during the first regime (cf. n. 9). As we have already seen in subsection 9.4.2, consumption smoothing must be complete *within* each regime, since the small open economy can borrow or lend in the international capital market at no extra cost. Our analysis of consumption effects is summarised in

Proposition 9.4

An anticipated switch to the origin principle reduces the level of consumption in the period between the announcement and the implementation of the policy change. After the switch has occurred, consumption jumps upward and exceeds its initial level in the steady-state equilibrium.

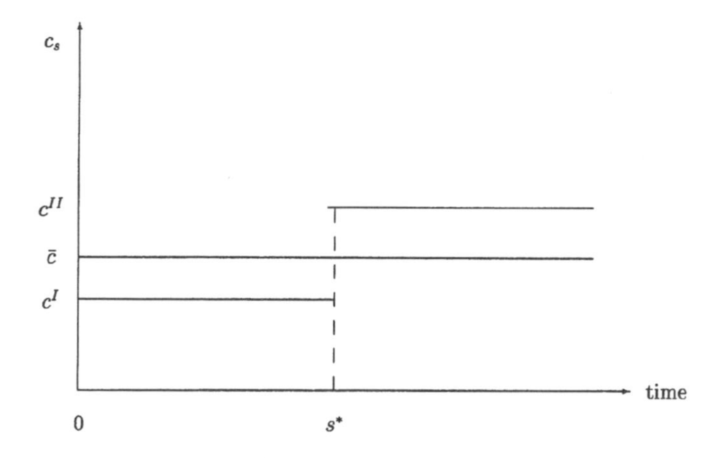

Figure 9.3 The response of consumption

Combining the dynamic effects that an anticipated switch to the origin principle has on investment and savings behaviour, we can trace out the development of the trade balance and the net foreign asset position. The trade balance in period s is equal to output minus absorption

$$TB_s \equiv f(k_s) - h_s k_s[1 + \tau(h_s)] - c_s, \tag{9.51}$$

where all values are measured in international prices. If the net foreign asset position is zero initially (as we have assumed earlier), then the trade balance is also zero in the initial steady state equilibrium and $c_0 = f(k_0) - k_0\delta$.

Drawing on (9.49), the change in the trade balance can generally be written as

$$dTB = k[r\hat{k} - \kappa(\hat{\mu} - \hat{p})] + \frac{c}{\varepsilon}(\hat{\lambda} + \hat{p}). \tag{9.52}$$

For regime I, using (9A.8) in the appendix yields

$$dTB_s^I = \frac{c}{\varepsilon}\hat{\lambda} + \frac{k\kappa\hat{p}_{s^*}e^{-\eta_2 s^*}}{(\eta_1 - \eta_2)}[\eta_2 e^{\eta_1 s} - \eta_1 e^{\eta_2 s}] > 0, \tag{9.53}$$

where we have used $\eta_1 + \eta_2 = r$ from (9.42). Both terms in the expression are clearly positive, indicating that in the period between the announcement and the implementation of the commodity tax switch the trade balance will unambiguously improve. Of course, this is due to the simultaneous fall in consumption and investment in regime I.

For regime II we get from (9A.11) in the appendix

$$dTB_s^{II} = \frac{c}{\varepsilon}\left(\hat{p}_{s^*} + \hat{\lambda}\right) - \frac{k\kappa\hat{p}_{s^*}\left(e^{-\eta_1 s^*} - e^{-\eta_2 s^*}\right)}{(\eta_1 - \eta_2)}\eta_2 e^{\eta_1 s} < 0. \tag{9.54}$$

In line with the upsurge in investment and consumption after the implementation of the tax reform at time s^*, the trade balance deteriorates and becomes negative. It stays below zero even in the new steady state ($s \to \infty$), since the first term in (9.54) will be negative for any strictly positive implementation lag $s^* > 0$ (cf. (9.50)). As discussed earlier this long-run effect on the trade balance arises from the improvement in the net foreign asset position during the anticipation phase, which finances a permanent rise in the level of consumption.

9.5.3 *Welfare analysis*

Finally, we turn to the welfare consequences of an anticipated switch in the commodity tax principle. We first demonstrate that the 'marginal switch' analysed above is not able to influence domestic welfare when, as assumed, the economy's capital stock is entirely owned by domestic residents initially. Later we show, however, that both a non-zero foreign ownership share of domestic capital and a non-marginal tax switch will entail welfare consequences.

The welfare of the household is given by the present value of its consumption stream

$$W = \int_0^\infty e^{-rs} u(c_s) \; ds.$$

The change in welfare induced by the policy switch can be calculated as

$$dW = \int_0^\infty e^{-rs} u'(c_s) \; dc \;\; ds = \int_0^\infty e^{-rs} \frac{u'(c)c}{\varepsilon} \left(e^{-rs^*} \hat{p}_{s^*} - \hat{p} \right) \; ds,$$

where the second step has used (9.48) and (9.50). This expression must be decomposed since $\hat{p} = 0$ in regime I, but $\hat{p} = \hat{p}_{s^*}$ in regime II. Thus

$$\begin{aligned} dW &= \int_0^{s^*} \frac{u'(c)c\hat{p}_{s^*}}{\varepsilon} \; e^{-r(s+s^*)} \; ds + \int_{s^*}^\infty \frac{u'(c)c\hat{p}_{s^*}}{\varepsilon} \left(e^{-r(s+s^*)} - e^{-rs} \right) ds \\ &= \frac{u'(c)c\hat{p}_{s^*}}{\varepsilon} \left[\int_0^\infty e^{-r(s+s^*)} \; ds + \int_{s^*}^\infty -e^{-rs} \; ds \right] = 0. \end{aligned} \tag{9.55}$$

Hence, in the basic model, the preannounced switch to origin-based commodity taxation will not yield any welfare changes for the representative consumer in the small open economy. Efficiency effects are absent because a marginal policy switch will neither cause 'excess' installation costs when marginal costs are zero in the initial equilibrium, nor distort the allocation of capital or the time pattern of consumption. Furthermore, redistributive effects are absent since the capital stock is entirely owned by domestic residents and thus none of the capital losses associated with the switch to the origin regime can be shifted to foreigners.

It is then easy to see how foreign holdings of domestic equity capital will affect the welfare results. If α_F denotes the share of the capital stock owned by foreigners in the initial steady state, then the total value of assets owned by foreigners is $\Omega_F = \mu_0 \alpha_F k_0$. The impact effect of an announced switch to the origin principle will then change the value of these assets by

$$d\Omega_F = \hat{\mu}_0 \mu_0 \alpha_F k_0.$$

It is straightforward to incorporate this additional effect into (9.49), which gives the change in the small country's foreign asset position.

The calculations in the appendix change accordingly, leading to a new impact change in the marginal utility of wealth ($\hat{\lambda}^*$). This is given by

$$\hat{\lambda}^* = -e^{-rs^*}\hat{p}_{s^*} + \mu_0 \alpha_F k_0 \hat{\mu}_0 \frac{\varepsilon r}{c} = -e^{-rs^*}\hat{p}_{s^*}\left(1 - \mu_0 \alpha_F k_0 \frac{\varepsilon r}{c} e^{(r-\eta_2)s^*}\right), \tag{9.56}$$

where the second step has used (9.45) to substitute out for $\hat{\mu}_0$. Comparing (9.50) and (9.56) shows that the impact change in λ is reduced if foreigners own part of the capital stock initially. Intuitively, the small country's net foreign asset position improves discretely at the time of the policy announcement. This represents an increase in lifetime income which raises consumption both before and after the switch in the commodity tax regime, relative to the case where there are no foreign asset holdings initially.

In fact, it is possible now that $\hat{\lambda}^*$ is *negative*, and hence consumption rises, despite the relatively high price of consumption in regime I. It is readily inferred from (9.56) that this is more likely when the share of foreign ownership of domestic capital (α_F) and the share of the return to capital in domestic income (and hence consumption) are high. Furthermore, foreigners will be more effectively 'expropriated' when the speed of adjustment is low owing to high transaction costs (the absolute value of $(r - \eta_2)$ is small) and when the lead period s^* is relatively short. Finally, for any given level of lifetime income, consumption in regime I will be higher when ε is large, implying a high preference for a smooth consumption path over time (and hence a low price elasticity of consumption).

The last step in this analysis is to incorporate the changed value of $\hat{\lambda}^*$ in the welfare expression (9.55). This gives

$$dW^* = -u'\hat{p}_{s^*}\mu_0 \alpha_F k_0 e^{-\eta_2 s^*} > 0. \tag{9.57}$$

To discuss (9.57) consider first the case of a surprise tax reform ($s^* = 0$). The adjustment speed η_2 is then irrelevant and only the extent of initial foreign ownership matters for the international distribution effect. When the policy change is anticipated, however, the welfare changes also depend – via η_2 – on the entire set of parameters of the investment system. Furthermore, since η_2 is positive from (9.42), the welfare gain from taxing foreigners is the smaller, the longer is the time period that elapses between the announcement and the implementation of the regime switch.

So far our analysis has been based on a marginal policy change, thus neglecting any efficiency losses that may arise from a discrete pre-announced switch to the origin principle. As a final step, we present

Table 9.1 *Welfare effects of an anticipated switch to the origin principle*

Transaction cost parameter β	0	10	20	∞
Consumption (regime I) per cent	−11	−10	−10	−10
Capital stock (at time s^*) per cent	−54	−10	−5	0
Equivalent variation (per cent)	−0.97	−0.53	−0.47	− 0.42

$u_s = ln(c_s), f(k_s) = 3.5k_s^{0.5}, r = 0.1, \delta = 0.25$

below some simulation results for a complete, and anticipated, change-over from a destination-based to an origin-based commodity tax. To isolate the efficiency effects of this policy experiment we return to our assumption that there is no foreign ownership of domestic capital. The tax rate in the small country is assumed to be 20 per cent; this implies that a switch to the origin principle entails a 20 per cent devaluation of the domestic currency *vis-à-vis* the rest of the world. The lead period is taken to be $s^* = 5$.

Our simulation experiment focuses on the role of adjustment costs for the efficiency losses involved in the policy change. Following a standard empirical specification, we assume a quadratic installation cost function of the type

$$\tau(h_s) = \frac{\beta}{2}(h_s - \delta)^2,$$

where – as in section 8.5 – β is the parameter to be varied. In the empirical literature this parameter is often taken to be $\beta = 10$ (Auerbach and Kotlikoff, 1987; Fehr, 2000) but we are also interested in the effects of either very high or very low adjustment costs. The results of our simulation experiments are summarised in table 9.1.

With the parameters selected, the announcement of the future tax reform leads to a drop in consumption of about 11 per cent, which is reversed to an increase of almost the same order upon implementation of the reform. The effects on the size of the capital stock in the small open economy at the time just prior to the implementation of the reform depend heavily on the chosen value of β. For the 'central case' value $\beta = 10$, the capital stock is cut back about 10 per cent from its initial level. For very high levels of β it is immediately intuitive that transaction costs prohibit any temporary changes in the capital stock. At the other extreme, the complete absence of installation costs may cause a temporary outflow of capital that exceeds 50 per cent of the initial stock. Taking due account of the simplicity of our empirical model, the results nevertheless suggest that the short-run effects of an anticipated switch to the origin principle on consumption and investment patterns may be rather pronounced for a wide range of installation cost parameters β.

As regards the welfare effects of the anticipated tax reform, they generally stem from variations in the levels of consumption and investment (and thereby the capital stock and production) before and after the implementation of the reform. Note first that the efficiency costs of a pre-announced switch in the tax regime are *declining* as adjustment costs rise. This result should be quite intuitive given our previous finding that high installation costs dampen the inefficiency-creating swings in investment and production activity. In the extreme case of infinitely high transaction costs (and thus zero capital movements) efficiency losses arise only from a consumption distortion as the household anticipates – and responds to – the reduction in the consumer price of output after period s^*. More generally, our simulation results indicate that welfare losses from temporary investment distortions and excess installation costs are quite limited and – together with the costs of the consumption distortion – remain below 1 per cent of the benchmark utility level in all the cases analysed.

9.6 Discussion and comparison of results

In the preceding sections we have focused on the switch from a destination- to an origin-based commodity tax system under conditions of capital mobility. The analysis has first shown – in section 9.2 – that a switch to a general origin principle does not cause any distortions in the long run, even in the presence of capital mobility. The reason for this result is that an origin-based commodity tax falls only on capital that is already installed at the time of the switch, whereas new investment remains untaxed under a consumption-type VAT. In the short run, however, there will be effects of the regime switch, if the reform is anticipated (sections 9.3–9.5). Upon announcement of the switch to the origin principle, investment and consumption will temporarily fall, rising again when the reform is finally implemented. A preliminary numerical analysis has indicated that these macroeconomic ramifications may be quite significant. In contrast, the efficiency losses arising from the temporary distortion of consumption and investment decisions may not be very large.

In the following, we first compare our results with some contributions to the literature that analyse related issues in different policy settings. In a second step we then turn more specifically to other analyses of the switch from a destination- to an origin-based tax regime.

Short-term distortions similar to the ones analysed here will arise even from an *unanticipated* switch in the tax principle, if the price adjustment to the regime change is not instantaneous and exchange rates are fixed, as in the European monetary union (cf. n. 2 in chapter 8). Clearly, there are close analogies between this setting and the real effects of an exchange rate adjustment in the presence of wage stickiness, as analysed by Nielsen (1991). Nielsen assumes that, owing to fixed nominal contracts, it takes some time until wages respond at all to an exchange rate change, but after this time period has elapsed the wage adjusts fully to clear the labour market. The two regimes that arise in this framework – before and after the adjustment of the nominal wage – correspond closely to our discussion in section 9.5.

There are also close links between an anticipated switch to the origin principle and the analysis of time-variant tax rates on capital income. To see this, note that measured in *international* prices, the reduction in the producer price at the time of the regime change has the same effect as if a zero tax rate were applicable before the switch occurs (cf. (9.15)). Hence, from the perspective of capital owners, the anticipated change in the tax principle has the same effect as an anticipated increase in the tax rate on capital income.

The analogy to capital income taxation is closest under a cash-flow tax, since investment expenditures are fully deductible under an origin-based VAT (cf. (9.10) and n. 2). As first shown by Sandmo (1979) in a closed economy setting, a cash-flow tax is non-neutral with respect to investment decisions when the tax rate is subject to change.[15] If, for example, the cash-flow tax rate is expected to increase in the future, then this implies that the tax credit given for the purchase of capital goods will be less in present value terms than the tax imposed on the normal returns to this investment. Hence, as in the present model, investment will fall below its efficient level in the period prior to the tax policy change. Based on this fundamental effect, Howitt and Sinn (1989) have compared the intertemporal distortions that arise from anticipated tax rate changes under alternative schemes of capital income taxation, showing, for example, that a cash-flow tax can in fact be more distortionary than a conventional income tax of the Schanz–Haig–Simons type.

Nielsen and Sørensen (1991) have applied the intertemporal analysis of capital tax reform to a growing open economy. Their analysis shows,

[15] Cf. n. 7 in chapter 7.

among other results, that an anticipated future increase in the rate of an investment tax credit may have contractionary effects on investment in the short run. Again, this is very similar to the setting we have discussed above, since the effective tax credit that capital receives prior to the commodity tax switch is zero in our analysis. These comparisons shows that the investment path traced out in section 9.5 is not specific to an anticipated switch to the origin principle. What is specific to the change in the commodity tax regime is, however, that the pattern of consumer prices is simultaneously and directly affected by the reform.

Turning to other analyses of a switch to an origin-based commodity tax under factor mobility, the first contribution of which we are aware is Krause-Junk (1992). Krause-Junk derives the result that a switch to the origin principle is allocatively neutral in the long run, since 'old' capital is trapped in the high-tax country at the time of the switch (cf. section 9.2). However, his analysis uses a static model without capital accumulation so that the treatment of investment expenditures under a consumption-type VAT cannot be modelled explicitly in his framework.

Bovenberg (1994) provides a comprehensive analytical account of the dynamic effects of an unanticipated switch to the origin principle. His analysis allows for overlapping generations and foreign ownership of domestic equity. Since the switch is unanticipated it causes no allocative distortions in Bovenberg's framework, but it affects both the intergenerational and the international distribution of income. Intergenerational effects arise as the generations alive at the time of the policy change bear the impact of the switch on the value of the domestic capital stock, whereas the capital income of generations born after the switch has occurred remains untaxed. Effects on the international distribution derive from foreign ownership of the initial capital stock, as we have discussed in subsection 9.5.3. Bovenberg's analysis (1994, pp. 258, 263–4) corresponds closely to our discussion in this section, but considers only the special case of a surprise tax reform (implying that $s^* = 0$ in (9.57)). As we have seen, this represents an upper limit of this redistributive effect for any given share α that foreigners own of the initial capital stock.

Bovenberg's analysis of intergenerational and international welfare effects also forms the starting point for the computable general equilibrium (CGE) analysis in Fehr (2000). The additional elements in Fehr's analysis are an endogenous labour–leisure choice and the incorporation of terms of trade effects in a two-country world. Of particular interest with respect to our previous discussion is the analysis of an anticipated switch to the origin principle (Fehr, 2000, section 5.2). The more detailed empirical model confirms that the macroeconomic ramifications of an expected regime change are indeed likely to be significant, leading to a strong improvement in the trade balance of the high-tax country. In fact, Fehr's analysis shows that an endogenous labour supply will even amplify the shocks to the trade balance since workers in the high-tax country anticipate that their wage rate will be reduced in *international* prices after the policy reform has occurred. Hence they increase their labour supply prior to the reform and this effect – together with reduced consumption and reduced investment in the home country – further widens the gap between domestic production and absorption.

With respect to welfare effects, Fehr's analysis confirms that the *world-wide* efficiency losses of temporary consumption and investment distortions tend to be quite small (cf. table 9.1). However, he also shows that distributional effects both between generations and countries may be significantly increased if the policy switch is anticipated. According to this analysis the intergenerational effects, in particular, represent one of the quantitatively most important disturbances of a switch to an origin-based commodity tax.

9.7 Further issues of a switch to the origin principle

Several other aspects of a switch to origin-based commodity taxation in the European Union have been discussed in the literature. These include (i) the problem raised by the EU's external trade relations; (ii) the existence of split VAT rates in most EU member states; (iii) imperfect competition in conjunction with a non-comprehensive coverage of VAT; (iv) the possibility of transfer pricing under an origin-based VAT. In the following we briefly address each of these distinct issues.

9.7.1 Trade with third countries

It has already been emphasised by Shibata (1967) that a switch to an origin-based VAT within a common market will not change tax relations with non-member countries, where border tax adjustments will be maintained in accordance with GATT rules. Therefore a change in the tax treatment of intra-union trade will lead to a 'restricted origin principle' with the union's internal trade taxed according to the origin principle while its external trade with the rest of the world follows the destination principle. In contrast to either a pure destination or a pure origin principle, a geographically restricted origin principle has been shown to cause efficiency losses when tax rates are not harmonised (Whalley, 1979, 1981; Berglas, 1981). The relative price distortion is intuitive from the arbitrage conditions under the destination principle (8.1) and the origin principle (9.1), since consumer prices will be equalised for goods traded within the union, whereas producer prices are equalised for trade with non-members. Furthermore, tax revenues will be redistributed from countries with an *intra-union* trade deficit (and thus a trade surplus with the rest of the world) to countries with the opposite trade pattern. Since a domestic tax increase systematically worsens the intra-union trade balance of the taxing country, commodity taxation under the restricted origin principle tends to lead to a process of downward tax competition (Haufler, 1994).[16]

These distortionary effects can be removed, however, by giving up the condition of bilateral reciprocity, under which any two countries always apply the same tax principle for their bilateral trade. The alternative is that the union countries apply a worldwide origin principle, whereas countries in the rest of the world apply a worldwide destination principle for their trade. This scheme has been proposed by Lockwood, de Meza and Myles (1994b, 1995) and has been labelled a 'non-reciprocal restricted origin principle'. The union countries levy no tax on imports, regardless of their country of origin, so that exports from the rest of the world into the union remain untaxed. If countries A and B are union members while country C represents the rest of the world, arbitrage implies

$$(1+t^A)p_k^A = (1+t^B)p_k^B = p_k^C \quad \forall \quad k. \tag{9.58}$$

On the other hand, since the rest of the world applies a uniform tax on both imported and domestically produced goods, exports from union members to the rest of the world are taxed in *both* the exporting and the importing country. Consumer prices in country C are thus given by

$$(1+t^C)p_k^C = (1+t^C)[(1+t^A)p_k^A] = (1+t^C)[(1+t^B)p_k^B] \quad \forall \, k, \tag{9.59}$$

[16] The analyses of Whalley (1979), Berglas (1981) and Haufler (1994) are carried out in a conventional multi-good trade model which excludes the re-export of goods. In this setting the distortion arising from tax differentials is given by cross-country differences in relative producer prices. Georgakopoulos and Hitiris (1992) have shown that if trade deflection – i.e., the re-export of imported goods – is allowed in this model, then relative producer prices will always be equalised. This corresponds to our discussion of the mixed tax principle in section 8.1. As we have seen there, the resulting set of arbitrage conditions is incompatible with international tax differentials, unless transportation costs are assumed. For a more detailed critique of the analysis by Georgakopoulos and Hitiris, see Haufler (1996b).

which reduces to (9.58) because the tax factor $(1 + t^C)$ cancels out. Hence, relative producer and consumer prices will be unaffected by taxes in all parts of the world.

While the neutrality property of this scheme may not be intuitive at first sight, its economic rationale is fully in line with our earlier discussion. The double taxation of the union's exports to the rest of the world ensures that factor returns in each union state fall by the full amount of the domestic tax, so that border prices (prior to the imposition of destination-based taxes in the rest of the world) are equalised worldwide. Since country C levies VAT on both domestic and imported goods, consumer prices remain unchanged in this country. The same is true in each member state of the union, where the fall in factor prices equalises the consumer prices of domestically produced goods on the one hand and of untaxed imports from either the union partners or the rest of the world on the other. Real income effects also do not arise because the tax base for each union country is the value of domestic production, which equals the value of domestic consumption by the condition of multilaterally balanced trade.

The application of the non-reciprocal restricted origin principle requires that in each union state the price level – measured in international prices – falls by the full amount of the domestic tax. In fact, this is precisely the setting that has been assumed in our small country analysis of sections 9.2–9.5. We have seen there that this downward adjustment can cause short-run distortions and macroeconomic imbalances if either the tax switch is anticipated or exchange rates are fixed and there is some (downward) rigidity of nominal wages. Genser (1996b) has argued, however, that these short-run effects of a switch to the origin principle can be reduced if a unified border tax rate t^U is applied by all union members on their imports from the rest of the world. With this border tax the arbitrage condition for imports into the union changes to

$$(1 + t^A)p_k^A = (1 + t^B)p_k^B = (1 + t^U)p_k^C \quad \forall \quad k, \tag{9.60}$$

which leaves relative prices undistorted and reduces the required price level adjustment in the union countries *vis-à-vis* the rest of the world. The non-reciprocal restricted origin principle discussed by Lockwood, de Meza and Myles (1994b) thus corresponds to a special case of this more general tax principle with a border tax rate of zero.[17]

[17] As noted by Genser (1996b), the common border tax or 'common external tax' is discussed in Shibata's (1967) original analysis of the restricted origin principle. This element of Shibata's discussion has, however, been neglected in most subsequent work.

9.7.2 *Multiple tax rates*

The standard equivalence result between a destination- and an origin-based VAT relies on the assumption of one single national VAT rate for each country and breaks down if countries apply multiple VAT rates for traded goods. It has been shown, however, that harmonising the *relation* between the tax-inclusive prices of the goods bearing the standard and reduced VAT rates, respectively, is sufficient to restore aggregate production efficiency under the origin principle (Fratianni and Christie, 1981). If good 1 bears the regular VAT factor $(1 + t^i)$ while good 2 carries a reduced tax factor $\gamma\,(1 + t^i)$ (where $1 > \gamma > 1/(1 + t^i)$), international arbitrage conditions are summarised by

$$\begin{aligned} (1 + t^A)\, p_1^A &= (1 + t^B)\, p_1^B, \\ \gamma\,(1 + t^A)\, p_2^A &= \gamma\,(1 + t^B)\, p_2^B. \end{aligned} \tag{9.61}$$

This shows that relative prices are undistorted as long as the ratio of reduced and regular tax factors, γ, is equal across union countries. While this allows governments to choose the regular VAT rate in each country autonomously, the rate structure must thus be harmonised across union countries. This implies, for example, that traditional VAT patterns like zero-rates or semi-rates are not compatible with condition (9.61). Furthermore, even if relative prices are undistorted, non-uniform VAT rates will generally involve a redistribution of tax revenues from countries running a trade deficit in the goods that are taxed at the regular rate to the countries that are net exporters of these goods (Keen and Smith, 1996, p. 397).[18]

9.7.3 *Incomplete VAT coverage and imperfect competition*

The above analysis of split VAT rates has shown that relative producer prices *must* be distorted when the coverage of the VAT is incomplete. The present VAT system in Europe and elsewhere excludes a number of services from the tax base, such as banking, insurance or health care. While the effective tax rate on these sectors is not zero, because VAT paid on inputs cannot be deducted,[19] numerical estimates show that the

[18] The last result is closely related to the redistributive effects that arise under the restricted origin principle when bilateral trade is not balanced. It is worth noting, however, that neither relative price distortions nor redistributive income effects arise when reduced VAT rates apply only to non-tradables.

[19] Technically, these services are 'exempt' from VAT, whereas a good or a service is 'zero-rated' if the VAT paid on inputs is also credited.

effective tax rate is quite low. As an example, Gottfried and Wiegard (1991) obtain an effective tax rate of 2.7 per cent for the banking and insurance sector in Germany based on 1984 data, as compared to a general VAT rate at this time of 14 per cent. While methods have been proposed to systematically incorporate the banking and insurance sector into the VAT system, it is unclear whether these schemes will actually be implemented in the EU or elsewhere.[20]

If the coverage of VAT is not comprehensive, then VAT effectively turns into a selective tax. From our discussion in section 8.1 we know that, under a *selective* origin-based tax, relative price distortions fall on factor markets (8.4), whereas they fall on consumer markets under the destination principle (8.2). The production efficiency theorem (see section 4.1) then establishes a clear ranking of the two alternatives in favour of the destination principle, a point to which we will return in detail in the following chapter.

The restrictive assumptions underlying the production efficiency theorem are critical in this context, however, and the argument against the origin principle will not hold when there is imperfect competition in product markets. As we have already discussed in chapter 8 (subsection 8.6.1), origin-based commodity taxes can actually improve global welfare in this case by lowering the mark-up that producers charge over marginal costs (Trandel, 1992).

A more general comparison between selective taxes imposed under the destination versus the origin principle is carried out in Keen and Lahiri (1998). Using a Cournot duopoly model where the two firms differ in their costs of production, they show that the origin principle is likely to dominate the destination principle under both cooperative and non-cooperative tax setting. One core argument is that each country can use the production tax to directly target the (differential) distortion of domestic production. At the same time, consumption efficiency is always guaranteed by consumer arbitrage, even if tax rates differ between countries. Hence, non-strategic tax policy under the origin principle can achieve the first best, whereas the same is not true under the destination principle when production distortions differ in the two countries (Keen and Lahiri, 1998, proposition 2). Under strategic tax setting, the argument in favour of the origin principle is instead closely related to the argument *against* tax rate harmonisation discussed in subsection 8.6.2. When taxes are levied on production, the country hosting the high-cost firm will choose the higher tax, implying that the global market share of

[20] For a discussion of these alternatives and problems of their implementation, see Cnossen (1998, pp. 406–8).

the more efficient firm is increased. This corrective effect is absent when taxes are instead levied in the country of consumption.

9.7.4 *Transfer pricing*

Another issue which has received attention in connection with a possible switch to the origin principle concerns the transfer-pricing incentives offered to multinational firms. Since we have already dealt with this problem in the context of corporate income taxation in chapter 7, the interaction of corporate taxes and origin-based commodity taxes[21] is of particular interest for the overall theme of this study.

Under the origin principle the effective tax rate on the final product is a weighted average of the statutory tax rates in the exporting and importing countries, where the weights are given by the value added in each country. It can therefore be argued that the origin principle gives an incentive to internationally integrated firms to overstate (understate) the value of imported goods, if the tax rate in the destination country is higher (lower) than the tax rate in the country of origin. This transfer pricing incentive is regarded as a potentially serious disadvantage of an origin-based commodity tax system (see Cnossen and Shoup, 1987, p. 73; Cnossen, 1998, p. 411).

The argument has been countered by Genser and Schulze (1997), who emphasise that transfer-pricing incentives already exist through international differences in corporate tax rates, and that any transnational shifts of value added will also affect the aggregate profit tax burden of a multinational firm. The total effect of manipulating the price of an intermediate good on the firm's net-of-tax profits then consists of two components, a corporate income tax effect and a VAT effect. The sign of each effect is determined by the tax differential between the importing and the exporting country. The authors provide empirical evidence on bilateral trade patterns in the Union, showing that in the majority of cases the introduction of origin-based commodity taxes tends to moderate, rather than reinforce, the transfer-pricing incentives that arise from differences in corporate tax rates.[22] This implies that existing incentives to use transfer prices as a way to minimise the corporate tax burden of

[21] Cf. n. 10 in chapter 7.

[22] A first approximation for this result can be obtained from the comparison of statutory corporate tax rates and standard VAT rates in tables 2.2 and 2.3. This shows that the deviations of the two tax rates from the EU average are negatively correlated in seven of the fifteen EU countries, while a positive correlation obtains only for five countries. In three countries the correlation is zero because the corporate tax rate is (roughly) equal to the EU average.

multinational firms may be *reduced*, on average, if commodity taxation follows the origin principle.

Keen and Smith (1996, p. 401) have, however, raised some counter-arguments to the analysis of Genser and Schulze. First, the database underlying their analysis relates to the tax rates under the current destination principle, whereas a regime switch to the origin principle might alter strategic incentives sufficiently to lead to a different tax pattern. Perhaps more importantly, companies may have more than one instrument available for transfer pricing, for example royalty or interest payments from the subsidiary to the parent. This would allow them to separately exploit differences in corporation tax rates on the one hand, and VAT differentials under the origin principle on the other.

9.8 A preliminary evaluation of the arguments

We have discussed several – though by no means all – issues that are relevant for the question whether a tax union like the European Union could benefit from switching to the origin principle, given that a general destination principle is infeasible in the absence of border controls. The focus of our analysis has been on the dynamic effects that a switch to the origin principle has in a world characterised by international capital mobility. In a setting with capital mobility, but with a uniform tax rate levied on all goods, the switch to the origin principle has no long-run effects. However, under the realistic assumption that the switch is anticipated by economic agents, savings and investment decisions will be distorted in the short run, leading to potentially significant disturbances in macroeconomic aggregates. Similar short-run effects can arise even in the absence of anticipation effects, if exchange rates between countries are fixed and wages adjust only slowly to the regime switch. Finally, it is important to emphasise that short-run effects also occur whenever one country adjusts its VAT rate after the origin principle has been put in place. In sum, these highly visible short-run disturbances are likely to be seen as an important obstacle to the introduction of an origin-based commodity tax regime.

Our survey of the overlapping generation models of Bovenberg (1994) and Fehr (2000) has shown that these temporary imbalances will not only affect macroeconomic aggregates, but they will also cause potentially large capitalisation effects that change the distribution of the tax burden across generations. Changes in the intergenerational distribution of income are also known to be a core problem of the transition to a cash-flow income tax (Keuschnigg, 1991) and have been stressed by Bradford (1996) in his evaluation of a possible switch to a consumption-based tax system in the United States (cf. subsection 2.1.2). These distributional effects clearly represent an additional and potentially strong argument against switching to the origin principle.

From a dynamic perspective, there are further aspects that favour the destination over the origin principle (see Bovenberg, 1996). First, owing to intertemporal consumption smoothing by far-sighted agents, consumption is likely to be the *more stable* tax base over time, as compared to output, when the economy is hit by supply shocks. Second, as the European population ages, consumption is also likely to be the *larger* tax base in the coming decades as retirees finance their consumption from accumulated savings, leading to a trade deficit for the EU *vis-à-vis* the rest of the world.

In other parts of our discussion, we have seen – perhaps surprisingly – that trade relations with non-member states which continue to operate the destination principle do not raise new and independent problems, if a non-reciprocal restricted origin principle is applied by the EU. A caveat must be added here, however, since the neutrality of such a scheme must also be *perceived* by economic agents. Even if a common border tax is introduced to minimise the necessary price adjustments, it may be difficult to persuade producers in high-tax countries of the Community that they are *not* put at a disadvantage with their competitors from low-tax member states or the rest of the world.

Finally, we have also addressed the implications of an incomplete coverage of the VAT or, alternatively, of a split and non-harmonised rate structure. This added piece of realism introduces an argument against the origin principle if perfectly competitive product markets dominate in the economy, whereas it may offer an argument in favour of the origin principle if monopolistic and oligopolistic market structures are pervasive. Similarly, an incentive for transfer pricing by multinational firms is opened up by the introduction of an origin-based commodity tax, but this may in fact counteract a pre-existing incentive to minimise the aggregate corporate tax burden. Hence there are similar second-best arguments for the origin principle in each of the last two cases discussed. However, it is not clear how robust these second-best results are and for most commentators the possible new distortions introduced by a switch to the origin principle seem to weigh heavier than the potential to correct existing ones.

The picture that emerges from these heterogeneous aspects is not entirely clear-cut, but the overall tendency is that a switch to the origin principle is likely to cause more severe drawbacks than does the present problem of cross-border shopping under an imperfect destination principle. This conclusion is preliminary because one important argument is still missing. We have seen in section 9.2 that an origin-based commodity tax is essentially a tax on wages and pure profits. These tax bases, however, can also be targeted by direct taxes, whereas consumption can be targeted only by a commodity tax. This argument is just one example of the more general notion that the desirability of a particular tax policy depends crucially on the set of tax instruments underlying the analysis (see section 3.3). This issue has already been analysed in part 2 of this book, but there the discussion has been confined to different sets of factor taxes. In part 4, we will focus explicitly on the interaction between factor taxes on the one hand and commodity taxes on the other. The specific analysis which allows us to state precise conditions under which a destination-based commodity tax dominates an origin-based tax is postponed until chapter 11.

APPENDIX

9A.1 The investment system

This section of the appendix explains in detail the derivation of the dynamic development of the capital stock and its shadow price in regimes I and II. Cf. Turnovsky (1995, pp. 137–41) for a brief introduction to the methods employed here.

Regime I $(0, s^*)$

In this regime, both the stable and the unstable root are needed to describe the evolution of $\hat{k}$ and $\hat{\mu}$. The general solution to the dynamic system (9.41) is

$$\begin{aligned} \hat{k}_s^I &= 0 + d_1 e^{\eta_1 s} + d_2 e^{\eta_2 s}, \\ \hat{\mu}_s^I &= 0 + m_0 d_1 e^{\eta_1 s} + m_0 d_2 e^{\eta_2 s}, \end{aligned} \tag{9A.1}$$

where $(0, 0)$ is the equilibrium point for the dynamic system in regime I, the two eigenvalues η_1 and η_2 are given in (9.42), and d_1 and d_2 are the constants to be determined. The multiplier m_0, which links the multiplicative constants in the two equations, can be derived from the matrix equation $\mathcal{J} \times [d, m_0 d]' = 0$. The first row of this equation determines

$$m_0 = \frac{\eta}{\kappa}. \tag{9A.2}$$

At time 0 the capital stock is fixed, thus linking d_1 and d_2 by

$$\hat{k}_0 = d_1 + d_2 = 0 \quad \Rightarrow \quad d_2 = -d_1. \tag{9A.3}$$

For the instantaneous change in μ we get

$$\hat{\mu}_0 = d_1 \frac{\eta_1}{\kappa} + d_2 \frac{\eta_2}{\kappa} = d_1 \left(\frac{\eta_1 - \eta_2}{\kappa} \right). \tag{9A.4}$$

At the time s^* of the actual policy implementation, the changes in the endogenous variables are given by

$$\begin{aligned} \hat{k}^I_{s^*} &= d_1 \left(e^{\eta_1 s^*} - e^{\eta_2 s^*} \right), \\ \hat{\mu}^I_{s^*} &= d_1 \left(\frac{\eta_1}{\kappa} e^{\eta_1 s^*} - \frac{\eta_2}{\kappa} e^{\eta_2 s^*} \right). \end{aligned} \tag{9A.5}$$

Regime II (s^*, ∞)

The variables $\hat{k}, \hat{\mu}$ follow a stable path in this regime and only the negative eigenvalue is needed. Thus

$$\begin{aligned} \hat{k}^{II}_s &= 0 + d_3 e^{\eta_1 (s - s^*)}, \\ \hat{\mu}^{II}_s &= \hat{p}_{s^*} + d_3 \frac{\eta_1}{\kappa} e^{\eta_1 (s - s^*)}, \end{aligned} \tag{9A.6}$$

where (9A.2) has been inserted and the steady-state change in μ must equal the change in the producer price from (9.26). The latter is denoted by $\hat{p}_{s^*}$ and represents a one-time adjustment at time s^*, when the switch to origin-based commodity taxation is implemented. In regime II the values of $(\hat{k}, \hat{\mu})$ at time s^* are given by

$$\begin{aligned} \hat{k}^{II}_{s^*} &= d_3, \\ \hat{\mu}^{II}_{s^*} &= \hat{p}_{s^*} + d_3 \left(\frac{\eta_1}{\kappa} \right). \end{aligned} \tag{9A.7}$$

We can now employ the condition that $\hat{k}$ and $\hat{\mu}$ must be continuous at time s^*. Equating $\hat{k}^I_{s^*} = \hat{k}^{II}_{s^*}$ and $\hat{\mu}^I_{s^*} = \hat{\mu}^{II}_{s^*}$ in (9A.5) and (9A.7) simultaneously determines the coefficients d_1 and d_3:

$$d_1 = \frac{\hat{p}_{s^*} \kappa}{\eta_1 - \eta_2} e^{-\eta_2 s^*}, \qquad d_3 = \frac{\hat{p}_{s^*} \kappa}{\eta_1 - \eta_2} \left[e^{(\eta_1 - \eta_2) s^*} - 1 \right].$$

Inserting the coefficient d_1 and (9A.2)–(9A.3) in (9A.1) gives (9.43)–(9.44) for regime I. Similarly, substituting d_3 in (9A.6) gives (9.46)–(9.47) for regime II. ■

9A.2 International asset accumulation

Regime I $(0, s^*)$

We substitute (9.43)–(9.44) into (9.49) and note that $\hat{p}$ is still zero in this regime. The evolution of net foreign assets can then be written as

$$\dot{a}_s^I = ra_s + A_1 + A_2[(r-\eta_1)e^{\eta_1 s} - (r-\eta_2)e^{\eta_2 s}], \tag{9A.8}$$

where

$$A_1 = \frac{c}{\varepsilon}\,\hat{\lambda}, \qquad A_2 = \frac{k\kappa\hat{p}_{s^*}e^{-\eta_2 s^*}}{(\eta_1-\eta_2)}. \tag{9A.9}$$

This is a first-order differential equation with constant coefficient and variable term, where the variable term is composed of the two parts denoted by A_1 and A_2. The solution to this equation is (cf. Chiang, 1984, pp. 480–2)

$$a_s^I = m_1\, e^{rs} - \frac{A_1}{r} - A_2(e^{\eta_1 s} - e^{\eta_2 s}), \tag{9A.10}$$

where A_1 and A_2 are given in (9A.9) and $m_1 = A_1/r$ is determined from the condition that $a_0 = 0$ in the initial steady state.

Regime II (s^*, ∞)

We proceed analogously and substitute (9.46)–(9.47) into (9.49). This leads to the differential equation

$$\dot{a}_s^{II} = ra_s + B_1 + B_2(r-\eta_1)\, e^{\eta_1 s}, \tag{9A.11}$$

where

$$B_1 = \frac{c}{\varepsilon}\left(\hat{p}_{s^*} + \hat{\lambda}\right), \qquad B_2 = -\frac{k\kappa\hat{p}_{s^*}\left(e^{-\eta_1 s^*} - e^{-\eta_2 s^*}\right)}{(\eta_1-\eta_2)}. \tag{9A.12}$$

The general solution to this equation is

$$a_s^{II} = m_2\, e^{rs} - \frac{B_1}{r} - B_2\, e^{\eta_1 s}. \tag{9A.13}$$

To determine m_2 we impose the condition that the foreign asset position a must change continuously around time s^*. Setting (9A.10) and (9A.13) equal for $s = s^*$ and using $m_1 = A_1/r$ gives

$$m_2 = \frac{c}{\varepsilon r}\left(\hat{\lambda} + e^{-rs^*}\hat{p_{s^*}}\right).$$

Substituting this in (9A.13) yields

$$a_s^{II} = \frac{k\kappa\hat{p}\left(e^{-\eta_1 s^*} - e^{-\eta_2 s^*}\right)}{(\eta_1-\eta_2)}\, e^{\eta_1 s} + \frac{c}{\varepsilon r}\left[\hat{\lambda}(e^{rs}-1) + \hat{p_{s^*}}\left(e^{r(s-s^*)} - 1\right)\right]. \tag{9A.14}$$

Equation (9A.14) can now be used to determine the change in λ. This is a one-time adjustment in period 0 since we know from (9.34) that λ does not change after this period. The missing element to pin down $\hat{\lambda}$ is the transversality condition (9.32). Applying this to (9A.14) gives

$$\frac{c}{\varepsilon r}\left(\hat{\lambda} + e^{-rs^*}\hat{p_{s^*}}\right) = 0,$$

from which (9.50) in the text follows directly. ■

Part 4

Factor and commodity taxation

10 Optimal taxation with interacting factor and commodity taxes

The final part 4 of this book collects together three analyses which integrate the tax instruments that parts 2 and 3 have studied in isolation. Chapter 10 analyses the interaction of factor and commodity taxes from the perspective of a small open economy. This yields a broader view of the general principles governing optimal taxation in open economies. The remaining chapters 11 and 12 deal with internationally mobile firms, as opposed to mobile capital. Chapter 11 re-addresses the comparison of alternative commodity tax principles and shows that the destination principle dominates the origin principle in a setting where optimal factor taxes can be simultaneously deployed. Finally, chapter 12 analyses profit and commodity tax competition between two countries of different size which are trying to attract a foreign-owned monopolist. We show that several results obtained in conventional models of capital tax competition are reversed when a typical element of the new trade theory, the existence of trade costs, is incorporated into the analysis.

In the present chapter, section 10.1 introduces the interaction between capital taxes and selective commodity taxes in a two-sector trade model with perfect capital mobility. Section 10.2 sets up an optimal taxation framework for a small open economy that can employ both factor and commodity taxes. Section 10.3 analyses the benchmark case where all tax instruments are permitted and production efficiency results. Section 10.4 studies the interaction between commodity taxes and source-based capital taxes under domestic and international constraints on the set of available tax instruments. Section 10.5 relates our analysis to the literature on the production efficiency theorem in open economies, the interaction of production-based taxes and the efficiency of tax competition in the presence of both factor and commodity taxes.

10.1 Integrating capital and commodity taxes

It is well understood that there are many parallels between capital taxation on the one hand and commodity taxation on the other. Keen (1993a), for example, informally argues that the production efficiency theorem – discussed in connection with international capital taxation in chapter 4 – should also create a basic efficiency case for destination- over origin-based commodity taxes. We will return to this issue in detail below. However, there are only relatively few contributions which analyse the interaction of commodity and capital taxes in a common model that allows for distinct economic effects of the different tax instruments. One of the reasons for this lies in the mutually exclusive trade models that are used in the different strands of analysis. Commodity taxation is generally studied in two-good models that do not allow for international capital mobility. In contrast, models of capital income taxation typically assume an aggregate output good, which is traded against capital imports.

One exception to this general pattern is an early analysis of capital tax competition by Wilson (1987). Wilson's model has a large number of identical regions and two sectors with different intensities of the two production factors capital and labour. Capital and labour are perfectly mobile across sectors and capital (but not labour) is also mobile internationally. In this model, each region specialises in the production of a single good in equilibrium, even though all regions are identical. This seemingly counterintuitive result can be explained by noting that the production structure underlying Wilson's model is the same as in the standard Heckscher–Ohlin framework of international trade theory. In the Heckscher–Ohlin model commodity trade equalises *gross-of-tax* factor prices between two countries, as long as production in both countries is diversified. Therefore, any difference in capital tax rates is incompatible with investors' arbitrage, which equalises *net-of-tax* rates of return to capital. This leads to a 'knife-edge' situation in a Heckscher–Ohlin model with factor mobility (see Neary, 1985) where even a minimal departure from a symmetric production point with diversified production leads to discontinuous adjustments in production and hence tax policy.

A Heckscher–Ohlin production structure with international capital mobility also underlies the analysis of Sinn (1990b) which incorporates commodity and capital taxation under alternative international tax principles. Sinn studies the conditions under which selective commodity taxes and taxes on capital are neutral in their joint effects on production and trade flows. The selectivity of the commodity tax is motivated by assuming that the economy produces both consumption and investment goods and a VAT of the consumption type falls on the former but not on the latter category. Hence origin-based commodity taxes change relative producer prices in this model and this feeds back on factor markets through different factor intensities in the taxed and the untaxed sector. The knife-edge property of the Heckscher–Ohlin model in the presence of international capital mobility raises no conceptual problems in this study, as Sinn does not endogenise tax policy and his concern is only with situations of complete tax neutrality.

Concentrating on the interaction of source-based capital taxes and origin-based commodity taxes, two possible scenarios arise from this analysis. If the consumption good sector is capital-intensive, then the origin-based tax will fall more heavily on capital than on labour and thus work in the same direction as a direct tax on capital. In Sinn's terminology, this is the case of '*additive neutrality*' between capital and commodity taxes. In the opposite case, however, where the consumption good sector is labour-intensive, origin-based commodity taxes and source-based capital taxes will be mutually offsetting in their effects on trade and the counterintuitive case of '*subtractive neutrality*' results. Sinn concludes that, in addition to the tax principles applied to international factor and commodity trade, the factor intensities of important commodity aggregates will also be critical for the interaction between the two types of taxes.

The issues taken up in the following analysis are similar to the ones raised by Sinn (1990b), but are approached here from an optimal taxation perspective. From our above discussion, this must inevitably lead to the knife-edge problem, if a Heckscher–Ohlin framework with internationally mobile capital is employed. For this reason, our analysis below is based instead on a mobile-capital version of the specific-factors model, the second major workhorse of international trade theory.

10.2 A specific-factors model with mobile capital

We consider a small open economy which is integrated with the rest of the world through both commodity and capital markets.[1] The trade model used in the analysis is a mobile-capital version of the specific-factors model with two output goods and three factors. The capital endowment of the economy is given exogenously and capital is perfectly mobile both between the two sectors and internationally. In many

[1] The analysis in sections 10.2–10.4 is a revised version of Haufler (1996c).

respects, this analysis is a straightforward extension of the model of optimal factor taxation in a small open economy, as presented in section 4.2.

Production in each sector $i \in \{1, 2\}$ uses capital and a sector-specific factor l_i, which is immobile internationally. These factors will alternatively be interpreted as labour, land, or entrepreneurial services in the course of the analysis. In the general model both factors l_i are supplied elastically, but the special case where the supply of one specific factor is fixed will play an important role in the discussion of optimal tax rules. Equilibrium employment of both specific factors is assumed to be strictly positive, ensuring that the small open economy will produce both goods in a trade equilibrium.

Distributive effects are ignored by assuming that there is a single (representative) household, which owns all factors of production and consumes all goods. The utility function of this individual is strictly quasi-concave and depends positively on the consumption levels c_i and negatively on the factor supplies l_i

$$u = u(c_1, c_2, l_1, l_2). \tag{10.1}$$

The small open economy faces fixed world prices for traded goods and capital. Good 1 is chosen as the numeraire, P gives the world relative price of good 2 and R is the world return to capital. Commodity demands and factor supplies are affected by these prices and five different tax instruments: a source tax on capital (t_k), a selective production tax (t_x), a selective consumption tax (t_c) and taxes on the specific factors (t_{l_i}). All taxes are modelled as unit taxes.

As before, we assume that capital taxation follows the source principle; this allows us to confine the analysis to a one-period framework. With perfect capital mobility, a source-based tax must raise the gross return to capital in the small country by the full amount of the tax

$$r = R + t_k. \tag{10.2}$$

Commodity taxes can be levied as a tax on consumption (*destination principle*) or a tax on production (*origin principle*). Both taxes are assumed to be selective, i.e., they can be levied on only one of the two goods. This may reflect the fact that even under the relatively broad-based European VAT important parts of the tax base are either completely exempt from tax, or are subject to reduced rates (cf. section 9.7). The partial coverage of commodity taxes is also assumed for expository reasons, however, since we will combine the two taxes in subsection 10.4.2.

More specifically, we assume that the production tax falls on the numeraire good while the consumption tax is levied on good 2. Again, this assumption is made purely to save additional notation when the two taxes are combined below. All results would be completely unchanged if the numeraire remained untaxed while both destination- and origin-based commodity taxes were levied on the same good. In particular, it is possible under both specifications that the small country simultaneously uses both types of commodity taxes.[2]

The production tax in sector 1 must lower the producer price p_1, if domestic output is to remain competitive in the world market. In the absence of a domestic consumption tax the consumer price in the small country, q_1, equals the world price of unity. This price may include foreign production taxes that are not rebated for export. Thus

$$p_1 = 1 - t_x, \qquad q_1 = 1. \tag{10.3}$$

In sector 2 the producer price equals the world price of this good, whereas the consumption tax raises the consumer price in the small open economy above the world price

$$p_2 = P, \qquad q_2 = P + t_c. \tag{10.4}$$

Finally, the after-tax return to each specific factor equals the gross return w_i, less the factor taxes t_{l_i}

$$\omega_i = w_i - t_{l_i} \quad \forall \quad i \in \{1, 2\}. \tag{10.5}$$

The relevant prices for the representative consumer in the small open economy are the net returns to specific factors, ω_i, and the consumer price of good 2, q_2. These determine the private budget constraint

$$c_1 + q_2 c_2 = \omega_1 l_1 + \omega_2 l_2 + R\,\overline{k}, \tag{10.6}$$

where $\overline{k}$ is the exogenous capital endowment. Income from this endowment is lump sum since, from (10.2), the net return earned is always the world rate, no matter whether capital is invested at home or abroad.

Maximisation of (10.1) subject to (10.6) yields the individual's indirect utility function $v(q_2, \omega_1, \omega_2)$. By Roy's identity, and setting the marginal utility of private income equal to one for notational simplicity, its derivatives are given by

$$\frac{\partial v}{\partial q_2} = -c_2\,(q_2, \omega_1, \omega_2), \qquad \frac{\partial v}{\partial \omega_i} = l_i(q_2, \omega_1, \omega_2) \quad \forall\, i \in \{1, 2\}. \tag{10.7}$$

[2] What is excluded throughout the analysis in this chapter is a uniform commodity tax levied under a general tax principle. This scenario will be addressed in chapter 11.

Gross returns to specific factors are determined endogenously by the production side of the model. In the general case (l_i variable), we assume a conventional constant returns to scale production function in each sector, $x_i(k_i, l_i)$, with decreasing marginal productivities of each factor and complementarity between capital and the specific inputs. Thus

$$\frac{\partial x_i}{\partial k_i} > 0, \quad \frac{\partial^2 x_i}{\partial k_i^2} < 0, \quad \frac{\partial x_i}{\partial l_i} > 0, \quad \frac{\partial^2 x_i}{\partial l_i^2} < 0, \quad \frac{\partial^2 x_i}{\partial k_i \partial l_i} > 0 \quad \forall \quad i \in \{1, 2\}.$$

Instead, if l_i is fixed in one sector, then returns to scale are decreasing, giving rise to rents accruing to the fixed factor. In either case, the marginal productivity of capital ($\partial x_i / \partial k_i$) depends negatively on the ratio of capital to the specific factor, and this determines capital's gross return by the condition for competitive profit maximisation

$$\frac{\partial x_i}{\partial k_i}\left(\frac{k_i}{l_i}\right) = \frac{r}{p_i} \quad \forall \quad i \in \{1, 2\}. \tag{10.8}$$

Using (10.3) and (10.2) in (10.8), it is immediately seen that production taxes and source taxes on capital are always 'additive' in their effects on the required marginal productivity of capital in sector 1. Hence Sinn's (1990b) case of 'subtractive neutrality' discussed in section 10.1 cannot occur in the present analysis. This is owing to the use of the specific-factors model, which implies that the nominal return to the intersectorally mobile factor will always move in the same direction as the (exogenous) change in the commodity price (Dixit and Norman, 1980, p. 40). The important implication following from this discussion is that the interaction of commodity and factor taxes depends critically on the trade model underlying the analysis.

Gross returns to the specific factors are derived as a function of producer prices and the cost of capital by equating the value of output in each sector to overall factor payments

$$p_i\, x_i[k_i(r, p_i), l_i(r, p_i)] = r k_i(r, p_i) + w_i(r, p_i) l_i(r, p_i) \quad \forall \quad i \in \{1, 2\}. \tag{10.9}$$

If specific factors are supplied endogenously, then they are paid their marginal value product, $w_i = p_i(\partial x_i / \partial l_i)$. If they are in fixed supply, then $l_i = \bar{l}_i$ and their return is derived residually. In both cases, differentiating (10.9) with respect to r and using (10.8) gives the factor price frontiers

$$\frac{\partial w_i}{\partial r} = -\frac{k_i}{l_i} < 0 \quad \forall \; i \in \{1, 2\}. \tag{10.10}$$

Similarly, differentiating (10.9) with respect to the producer price of good 1 and inserting the marginal productivity conditions for factor pricing gives

$$\frac{\partial w_1}{\partial p_1} = \frac{x_1}{l_1} > 0, \qquad \frac{\partial w_2}{\partial p_1} = 0. \tag{10.11}$$

Note from (10.3) that a production tax on good 1 lowers the gross return to the specific factor in this sector. This will also reduce the amount of capital used in sector 1. In contrast to the textbook model without capital mobility, however, the excess capital will flow abroad rather than into sector 2. Hence the return to the specific factor l_2 is unaffected by this change in producer prices.

To derive optimal tax formulae we also need to determine the signs of the second-order derivatives of the gross return functions $w_i(r, p_i)$. These can be inferred directly from the first-order conditions for the optimal use of capital (10.8) and are summarised as follows:

$$\frac{\partial^2 w_i}{\partial r^2} = -\frac{\partial(k_i/l_i)}{\partial r} > 0 \quad \forall \quad i \in \{1, 2\}, \tag{10.12}$$

$$\frac{\partial^2 w_1}{\partial p_1^2} = \frac{\partial(x_1/l_1)}{\partial p_1} > 0, \tag{10.13}$$

$$\frac{\partial^2 w_1}{\partial r \partial p_1} = \frac{\partial^2 w_1}{\partial p_1 \partial r} = \frac{-\partial(k_1/l_1)}{\partial p_1} = \frac{\partial(x_1/l_1)}{\partial r} < 0. \tag{10.14}$$

The government of the small country maximises the indirect utility of the representative consumer, subject to a given revenue requirement T_0. To allow for fixed factor supplies, which turn the taxes t_{l_i} into lump-sum instruments, non-negativity conditions are introduced for the *net* returns ω_i. In this case it is implicitly assumed that the revenue requirement T_0 exceeds the maximum amount that can be collected from the imposition of lump-sum taxes – otherwise, the optimal tax problem would be trivial. The government's problem is thus

$$\begin{aligned} \max \ v(q_2, \omega_1, \omega_2) \ \text{ s.t. } T_0 = t_{l_1} l_1 + t_{l_2} l_2 + t_x x_1 + t_c c_2 + t_k (k_1 + k_2), \\ \omega_1 \geq 0, \qquad \omega_2 \geq 0. \end{aligned}$$

Equations (10.10) and (10.11) are used to substitute out for the amount of capital employed in each sector and the level of production in sector 1. This shows that the capital tax t_k acts as an indirect tax on both specific factors, whereas the production tax is an indirect tax on l_1. The Lagrangian is

$$\begin{aligned}\mathcal{L} &= v(q_2,\omega_1,\omega_2)\\ &\quad+\lambda\Big\{t_c c_2(q_2,\omega_1,\omega_2)+\Big[t_{l_1}-t_k\frac{\partial w_1}{\partial r}(p_1,r)+t_x\frac{\partial w_1}{\partial p_1}(p_1,r)\Big]l_1(q_2,\omega_1,\omega_2)\\ &\quad+\Big[t_{l_2}-t_k\frac{\partial w_2}{\partial r}(r)\Big]l_2(q_2,\omega_1,\omega_2)-T_0\Big\}\\ &\quad+\mu_1(w_1(p_1,r)-t_{l_1})+\mu_2(w_2(r)-t_{l_2}).\end{aligned} \tag{10.15}$$

Using (10.2)–(10.5) and Roy's theorem (10.7), the first-order conditions for the five tax instruments are:

$$\frac{\partial\mathcal{L}}{\partial t_c}=-c_2+\lambda\left[c_2+t_c\frac{\partial c_2}{\partial q_2}+\alpha_1\frac{\partial l_1}{\partial q_2}+\alpha_2\frac{\partial l_2}{\partial q_2}\right]=0, \tag{10.16}$$

$$\frac{\partial\mathcal{L}}{\partial t_{l_i}}=-l_i+\lambda\left[l_i-t_c\frac{\partial c_2}{\partial\omega_i}-\alpha_1\frac{\partial l_1}{\partial\omega_i}-\alpha_2\frac{\partial l_2}{\partial\omega_i}\right]-\mu_i=0\qquad\forall\quad i\in\{1,2\}, \tag{10.17}$$

$$\frac{\partial\mathcal{L}}{\partial t_x}=\frac{\partial w_1}{\partial p_1}\frac{\partial\mathcal{L}}{\partial t_{l_1}}+\lambda l_1\left[t_k\frac{\partial^2 w_1}{\partial r\,\partial p_1}-t_x\frac{\partial^2 w_1}{\partial p_1^2}\right]=0, \tag{10.18}$$

$$\frac{\partial\mathcal{L}}{\partial t_k}=-\frac{\partial w_1}{\partial r}\frac{\partial\mathcal{L}}{\partial t_{l_1}}-\frac{\partial w_2}{\partial r}\frac{\partial\mathcal{L}}{\partial t_{l_2}}+\lambda\left[t_x l_1\frac{\partial^2 w_1}{\partial p_1\,\partial r}-t_k\left(l_1\frac{\partial^2 w_1}{\partial r^2}+l_2\frac{\partial^2 w_2}{\partial r^2}\right)\right]=0. \tag{10.19}$$

Partial differentiation with respect to the Lagrange multipliers yields, in addition

$$T_0=t_{l_1}l_1+t_{l_2}l_2+t_c c_2+t_x x_1+t_k(k_1+k_2), \tag{10.20}$$

$$\mu_i\geq 0,\quad w_i-t_{l_i}\geq 0,\quad \mu_i(w_i-t_{l_i})=0\qquad\forall\, i\in\{1,2\}. \tag{10.21}$$

Finally, the terms α_i introduced in the first-order conditions above are given by

$$\alpha_1=t_{l_1}-t_k\frac{\partial w_1}{\partial r}+t_x\frac{\partial w_1}{\partial p_1},\qquad \alpha_2=t_{l_2}-t_k\frac{\partial w_2}{\partial r}, \tag{10.22}$$

which can be interpreted as effective tax rates on the specific factors l_i.

The first-order conditions (10.16)–(10.21) constitute a system of eight simultaneous equations, which determines the five tax rates and the values of three Lagrangian multipliers λ and μ_i. Since t_x and t_k serve as indirect taxes on the specific factors, the first-order conditions for these instruments fully incorporate (by a multiple) the first-order conditions for the specific factor taxes t_{l_i}. However, by simultaneously affecting the capital intensity of output, the production and capital taxes have additional effects on each other's tax base, as given in the square brackets of (10.18) and (10.19).

The Lagrangian objective function is assumed to be strictly concave in each of its tax instruments, i.e., the second-order conditions for a maximum are assumed to be fulfilled. Constraints on the set of available taxes can be introduced by specifying additional boundaries, or by combining two taxes into a single instrument. In our following analysis this allows us to discuss a variety of institutional settings as special cases of a unified framework.

10.3 The benchmark: production efficiency

We first discuss the benchmark case where all tax instruments introduced in section 10.2 can be chosen freely. Technically, this means that all first-order conditions (10.16)–(10.21) must hold simultaneously. In particular, when the taxes on both specific factors are optimised we can substitute $\partial\mathcal{L}/\partial t_{l_i} = 0$ from (10.17) to simplify the first-order conditions for the taxes t_x and t_k ((10.18)–(10.19)). This gives

$$\left[\frac{\partial\mathcal{L}}{\partial t_x}\right] \qquad t_k\,\frac{\partial^2 w_1}{\partial r\partial p_1} - t_x\,\frac{\partial^2 w_1}{\partial p_1^2} = 0 \tag{10.23}$$

and

$$\left[\frac{\partial\mathcal{L}}{\partial t_k}\right] \qquad t_k\left(l_1\,\frac{\partial^2 w_1}{\partial r^2} + l_2\,\frac{\partial^2 w_2}{\partial r^2}\right) - t_x\,l_1\,\frac{\partial^2 w_1}{\partial r\partial p_1} = 0. \tag{10.24}$$

In a second step, (10.23) is solved for t_x and substituted in (10.24) to obtain

$$t_k\left[l_1\left(\frac{\partial^2 w_1}{\partial p_1^2}\right)^{-1}\mathcal{J} + l_2\,\frac{\partial^2 w_2}{\partial r^2}\right] = 0, \qquad \mathcal{J} = \frac{\partial^2 w_1}{\partial r^2}\,\frac{\partial^2 w_1}{\partial p_1^2} - \left(\frac{\partial^2 w_1}{\partial r\partial p_1}\right)^2. \tag{10.25}$$

$\mathcal{J}$ equals the Jacobian determinant of the two functions $\partial w_1/\partial r$ and $\partial w_1/\partial p_1$. Since these are functionally dependent from (10.10)–(10.11), it follows that $\mathcal{J} = 0$ and the first term in the square bracket cancels in (10.25). The second term, however, is strictly positive from (10.12) so that only $t_k = 0$ satisfies the equation. Substituting this result back into either (10.23) or (10.24) shows that $t_x = 0$ must also be true. This is summarised in

Proposition 10.1
If all tax instruments can be optimised separately, then

$$t_x = 0, \qquad t_k = 0,$$

and production is efficient.

Proposition 10.1 can be seen as a generalisation of proposition 4.1, which states that a zero source tax on capital is optimal for a small open economy, if capital mobility is perfect and the government simultaneously disposes of a wage tax. The intuition for this result is that the capital tax falls exclusively on the internationally immobile factor, but in addition distorts the international allocation of capital. This intuition continues to apply when commodity taxes are simultaneously used, even though capital and production taxes generally interact in equilibrium (see (10.18)–(10.19)). However, the optimal production tax will also be zero in the unconstrained optimum, for reasons that are fully analogous to those given above. The production tax is a combined tax on capital and the specific factor employed in sector 1. When international capital mobility is perfect, this tax is entirely shifted to the specific factor and is therefore dominated by a direct tax on l_1. Finally, we emphasise for our later discussion in subsection 10.5.1 that proposition 10.1 was derived *without* using the first-order condition for the destination-based commodity tax (10.16).

Taking account of these results there are three remaining tax instruments, the consumption tax (t_c) and the taxes on specific factors (t_{l_i}). The first tax distorts the choice between the consumption of different goods, whereas the latter two instruments distort the supply decisions of the specific factors. In general, a balanced use of these tax instruments will minimise the excess burden by spreading the distortions over different margins. However, cross-price effects complicate the picture in the general case where both specific factors are supplied elastically. The following analysis therefore concentrates on the case where only one specific factor (l_i) is in elastic supply, whereas the supply of the other (l_j, $j \neq i$) is fixed. We may interpret the fixed factor as either land or – more relevant in the following – entrepreneurial services. The elastically supplied factor can be thought of as labour, so that ($-l_i$) gives the demand for leisure. This allows us to sign the tax rate of all remaining instruments by

Proposition 10.2
(a) Rents from a fixed factor l_j are fully taxed in the optimum, i.e., $t_{l_j} = w_j$.
(b) If leisure ($-l_i$) and consumption of the taxed good (c_2) are net complements, then

$$t_c > 0 \qquad and \qquad t_{l_i} > 0.$$

Proof: *See the appendix (pp. 254–5).*

The interpretation of proposition 10.2 is familiar from standard optimal tax problems. Taxes on a fixed factor represent lump-sum instruments that will always be used to the fullest possible extent. Since revenues from this tax are insufficient by assumption to meet the government budget constraint, at least one other tax rate must be positive. A sufficient condition for labour and consumption taxes to be *both* positive is that a positive consumption tax on good 2 reduces the factor market distortion introduced by a positive tax on labour. This is the case if and only if the consumption tax reduces the demand for leisure, i.e., the consumption of good 2 and leisure are net complements. Whether this is a realistic assumption is, of course, an empirical matter but it should be stressed that the conditions on cross-price effects stated in proposition 10.2(b) are sufficient, not necessary, for the results. If own-price effects are sufficiently large, then both tax rates t_c and t_{l_i} will be positive, irrespective of the sign of cross-price effects.

10.4 Constraints on tax instruments

While the results of section 10.3 are useful as a reference case, they cannot explain the use of source-based capital taxes in small open economies and do not incorporate the restrictions on commodity taxation imposed by open borders. In the following, positive levels of source-based capital taxation are motivated by domestic constraints on the taxation of specific factors (subsection 10.4.1) while origin-based commodity taxes are derived from international restrictions (subsection 10.4.2). Finally, subsection 10.4.3 briefly takes up the case where internal and external constraints on tax instruments are combined.

10.4.1 Domestic constraints

The assumption that both specific factors can be optimally taxed is a very strong one. This applies in particular when one specific factor is in fixed supply so that the optimal tax rule prescribes that its return must be fully taxed away. Confiscatory taxes are rarely observed in practice, presumably because they violate constitutional property rights. In this section, two different constraints on the taxation of specific factors will therefore be considered. The first is that there are exogenous upper bounds on the taxation of specific factors, whereas the second ties the tax rate imposed on a fixed factor to a distortive tax on capital. In both cases, taxes that affect production will act as instruments that supplement the taxation of specific factors.

We first turn to the case of an exogenous (legally determined) upper bound on the taxation of specific factors. Thus $t_{l_i} \leq \overline{t_{l_i}} \leq w_i \; \forall \, i \in \{1, 2\}$. Let us call the associated Lagrange parameters ϕ_i. As compared to the benchmark case, only the non-negativity constraints are changed and the Lagrangian (10.15) becomes

$$\mathcal{L} = (...) + \phi_1(\overline{t_{l_1}} - t_{l_1}) + \phi_2(\overline{t_{l_2}} - t_{l_2}). \tag{10.26}$$

Note that the benchmark constraints (associated with parameters μ_i) are no longer binding and thus redundant. The optimality conditions for the production and the capital tax can again be simplified by inserting the first-order conditions for the specific factor taxes. We assume that specific factor taxes are chosen optimally, given the new constraints, so that $\partial\mathcal{L}/\partial t_{l_i} = 0$. In contrast to (10.23)–(10.24), the Lagrange parameters ϕ_i now enter the first-order conditions for t_k and t_x:[3]

$$\left[\frac{\partial\mathcal{L}}{\partial t_x}\right] \quad \frac{\partial w_1}{\partial p_1}\phi_1 + \lambda l_1\left[t_k\frac{\partial^2 w_1}{\partial r\,\partial p_1} - t_x\frac{\partial^2 w_1}{\partial p_1^2}\right] = 0, \tag{10.27}$$

$$\left[\frac{\partial\mathcal{L}}{\partial t_k}\right] \quad -\frac{\partial w_1}{\partial r}\phi_1 - \frac{\partial w_2}{\partial r}\phi_2 + \lambda\left[t_x l_1\frac{\partial^2 w_1}{\partial p_1\,\partial r} - t_k\left(l_1\frac{\partial^2 w_1}{\partial r^2} + l_2\frac{\partial^2 w_2}{\partial r^2}\right)\right] = 0. \tag{10.28}$$

From proposition 10.2(a), a sufficient condition for one of the non-negativity constraints to be binding is that the corresponding specific factor is in fixed supply. In this case, the optimal choices of both t_x and t_k must then differ from their benchmark values. Note, however, that a positive shadow price ϕ_i is also compatible with an endogenous supply of factor l_i, as long as the constraint on the level of specific-factor taxation remains binding. The optimal tax rules that emerge under this restriction are summarised in

Proposition 10.3
(a) If the specific factor tax on l_2 is constrained from above, so that $\phi_2 > 0$, then the optimal tax rate on capital is positive and the optimal production tax is negative. (b) If the specific factor tax on l_1 is constrained, so that $\phi_1 > 0$,

[3] The reason is that taxes on specific factors, but not the taxes t_x and t_k, affect the non-negativity constraints in (10.26). The production tax, for example, then has (by a multiple) all the effects of a specific tax on l_1, *except* for the negative term involving the Lagrange multiplier ϕ_1.

then the optimal tax rate on capital is negative and the optimal production tax is positive.

Proof: *See the appendix (pp. 255–6).*

Proposition 10.3 parallels a result that Slemrod, Hansen and Procter (1997) have labelled the 'seesaw principle' in international tax policy (see subsection 10.5.2). In the present context it states that if, owing to constraints on the taxation of specific factors, one of the taxes t_k and t_x is *higher* than in the unconstrained case (i.e. positive rather than zero) then the other of the two taxes will be *below* its unconstrained level (i.e. negative rather than zero). Underlying this inverse relationship are, of course, the cumulative effects that capital and production taxes have on the production inefficiencies generated in sector 1 (10.8).

To interpret these results in some more detail, consider first part (a) of proposition 10.3, where $\overline{t_{l_2}}$ is binding. Since there is no production tax in sector 2 the only way to indirectly increase the tax on l_2 is to levy a positive capital tax $t_k > 0$. This distorts production in both sectors, but the distortion in sector 1 can be counteracted by an appropriate production subsidy. As a side effect of the subsidy, the effective taxation of l_1 is reduced below its optimal level, but this can always be corrected by an appropriate increase in the specific tax on this factor, which is free to adjust. In part (b) of the proposition, where t_{l_1} is constrained, both the production and the capital tax can be employed to increase the effective taxation of l_1. However, it is clear from the principle of targeting in the optimal tax literature that the production tax in sector 1 is the relatively more efficient instrument, since it does not simultaneously distort production in sector 2. A capital subsidy is then used to reduce the production distortion in sector 1 until the marginal gains from this measure are just offset by the additional production distortion introduced in sector 2.

Underlying proposition 10.3 is the model property that both t_x and t_k can raise the effective tax rate on specific factors (cf. the terms α_i in (10.22)). However, it is precisely for this reason that imposing an exogenous ceiling on the tax rates t_{l_i} – rather than on the total effective tax rates α_i – appears somewhat unsatisfactory. An alternative and perhaps more plausible constraint is that it is not possible in practice to distinguish between the return to capital (r) and the return to a specific factor that can be interpreted as entrepreneurial services. This constraint can be seen as an approximation of existing corporation taxes, which generally do not allow a full deduction for the cost of capital (see our detailed discussion in chapter 7). Therefore, corporation taxes can be seen as hybrid instruments that simultaneously tax pure profits or rents and some part of the capital employed by the firm.

Analytically this constraint can be captured by replacing the independent taxes t_k and t_{l_i} through a single instrument that is denoted by $t_{\hat{k}}$ and is referred to as a 'corporation tax' in the following. Its optimal level is determined by the first-order condition

$$\frac{\partial \mathcal{L}}{\partial t_{\hat{k}}} = \frac{\partial \mathcal{L}}{\partial t_k} + \frac{\partial \mathcal{L}}{\partial t_{l_i}} = 0, \tag{10.29}$$

where $t_{\hat{k}} = t_k = t_{l_i}$ in (10.17) and (10.19). It is straightforward to show that $t_{\hat{k}} > 0$ (and $t_x < 0$) holds in the optimum when l_2 is a fixed factor that cannot be taxed by a separate instrument. In this case, there is thus no qualitative difference to proposition 10.3. However, in the reverse case where l_1 is in fixed supply, either the corporation tax or the selective production tax may now be the more efficient instrument to tax the fixed factor, and either $t_{\hat{k}}$ or t_x or both can be positive.[4] To summarise, if the corporation tax is viewed as a combined tax on capital and rents, then positive source-based taxes on capital can be motivated even in the presence of taxes on production.

10.4.2 International constraints

We now incorporate a mixed tax principle for international commodity taxation, similar to the one introduced in chapter 8. As in our previous analysis of cross-border shopping the motivation for this approach derives from the conditions in the EU internal market, where producer trade is taxed under the destination principle, whereas purchases by final consumers are taxed in the country of origin. In contrast to our treatment in section 8.1 (8.5), however, we now assume that transport costs for consumers differ for the two goods. Let good 1 be a category of goods where transport costs are zero for final consumers, so that international arbitrage for this good is based on gross-of-tax prices. In contrast, transaction costs are assumed to be too high to make cross-border shopping worthwhile for good 2, and arbitrage by traders will equalise producer prices for this good. This combination of arbitrage conditions corresponds to the determination of producer and consumer prices in (10.3)–(10.4) and can be modelled as a general commodity tax, which combines a production tax on good 1 with an equal-rate consumption

[4] This is a direct extension of the proof of proposition 10.3 (see the appendix). Intuitively, the combined tax instrument $t_{\hat{k}}$ incorporates a direct tax on the fixed factor whereas t_x can tax l_1 only indirectly. On the other hand, the combined capital tax also distorts production decisions in sector 2, whereas the production tax does not. The choice between the two taxes thus implies trading off these comparative advantages.

tax on good 2. Denoting the new tax instrument by $t_{\hat{x}}$ the constraint is given by

$$\frac{\partial \mathcal{L}}{\partial t_{\hat{x}}} = \frac{\partial \mathcal{L}}{\partial t_x} + \frac{\partial \mathcal{L}}{\partial t_c} = 0, \tag{10.30}$$

where $t_{\hat{x}} = t_x = t_c$ in (10.16) and (10.18). Thus the set of available tax instruments no longer dichotomises into pure consumption and production taxes. The optimal tax policy for the small country is now described by

Proposition 10.4

If leisure is a net complement to commodity consumption and taxes on both specific factors can be optimised, then the introduction of a mixed production–consumption tax leads to

$$t_{\hat{x}} > 0 \qquad \text{and} \qquad t_k < 0.$$

Proof: Under the assumptions made, it follows from propositions 10.1 and 10.2(b) that an isolated consumption tax on good 2 would be positive, whereas an isolated production tax on good 1 and a tax on capital would both be zero. From the concavity of the objective function with respect to each tax instrument we have

$$\frac{\partial \mathcal{L}}{\partial t_x} + \frac{\partial \mathcal{L}}{\partial t_c} = \left.\frac{\partial \mathcal{L}}{\partial t_{\hat{x}}}\right|_{t_{\hat{x}}=t_k=0} > 0, \qquad \left.\frac{\partial \mathcal{L}}{\partial t_k}\right|_{t_{\hat{x}}=t_k=0} = 0.$$

Thus $t_{\hat{x}}$ must be positive to meet the first-order condition. Since tax rates on both specific factors can be optimised, this in turn implies $t_k < 0$ from (10.24) ■

Proposition 10.4 gives another example of the inverse 'seesaw' relationship between the optimal tax rates on capital and production. Within the set of available tax instruments, $t_{\hat{x}}$ is the only possible substitute for the missing consumption tax on good 2. However, this instrument simultaneously taxes the use of capital and the specific factor in sector 1 and forces the marginal productivity of capital in this sector above the world return R. It is then optimal for the small open economy to *subsidise* the capital employed in its jurisdiction, thus trading off a new production distortion in sector 2 against a reduction in the production distortion in sector 1. These production effects are isolated here through the assumption that both specific factors can be taxed optimally; this allows us to increase the specific tax t_{l_2} in response to the implicit subsidisation through the negative tax rate on capital.

10.4.3 Combining domestic and international constraints

In section 10.4.1 we have shown that positive source-based taxes on capital ('corporation taxes') can be explained by the *domestic* constraint that rents on a fixed factor and capital must be taxed at the same rate (10.29). An independent argument for positive production taxes is given by the *international* constraint – introduced in section 10.4.2 – that only mixed commodity tax regimes are feasible under conditions of economic integration (10.30). In these analyses, the corporate tax $t_{\hat{k}}$ acts as a substitute for the missing tax on rents, whereas the mixed commodity tax $t_{\hat{x}}$ acts as a substitute for a missing (pure) consumption tax.

When both constraints are combined, then it is clear from our previous discussion that at least one of the taxes must be positive. Moreover, the corporate tax and the mixed commodity tax will *both* be positive when two conditions are fulfilled. First, neither of the two instruments must be strictly dominated by the other. This will be excluded in the present analysis if the specific factor in sector 2 is in fixed supply. In this case the rents from this factor can be taxed only through the corporation tax, but not through the mixed commodity tax instrument $t_{\hat{x}}$. In our simple two-sector model, the assumption that l_2 is fixed whereas l_1 is flexible may seem like an arbitrary choice, and the opposite case is equally plausible. However, the assumption becomes much less restrictive when a more disaggregated model is considered. All that is needed then for the source-based capital tax and the production tax to fulfil independent second-best roles in optimal tax policy is that there is no perfect overlap between the sectors in which origin-based taxation applies owing to consumer cross-border shopping, and the sectors in which rents accrue to fixed factors.

The second requirement for our second-best model to explain positive source-based taxes on capital and production is that the additive, distortionary effects that the two taxes have on the marginal productivity of capital in sector 1 must not be too large – since it is this effect that underlies the negative relationship between the two taxes in propositions 10.3 and 10.4. Here, the specific modelling of the distortive effects of cross-border shopping becomes important again. In our treatment of section 10.4.2, costless cross-border shopping for good 1 distorts relative producer prices and hence the international allocation of capital. In contrast, if cross-border shopping occurs under increasing marginal costs, as was the case in our analysis of chapter 8, then the distortion induced by cross-border shopping will be given by excess transaction costs, rather than by a distortion of relative producer prices (cf. (8.5)).

Hence in this case there is no interaction with the distortive effects of a source-based tax on capital.

These two approaches can be reconciled if we assume that only a relatively small subset of goods is subject to origin taxation *at the margin*. In the European internal market, for example, intense cross-border shopping is presently restricted to a narrow group of products that bear excise taxes in addition to VAT (cigarettes, alcoholic beverages), as well as some services that are provided through the Internet (cf. section 8.7). While distortions of international producer prices cannot be excluded for this group of goods and services, the interaction with source-based capital taxes is unlikely to be a very strong one for the economy as a whole. In this case positive source-based taxes on capital and a positive production tax for selected sectors of the economy can thus both be part of an optimal tax scheme.

10.5 Discussion and comparison of results

Our above analysis has focused on the optimal mix of factor and commodity taxation when a small open economy faces domestic or international constraints on the set of available tax instruments. With perfect international capital mobility, the small country will choose zero taxes on both production and capital if it is able to tax specific factors of production optimally, and if it can choose freely between alternative schemes of international commodity taxation. Domestic constraints on the direct taxation of rents create a case for a positive source-based tax on capital, whereas origin-based commodity taxes become relevant when border controls are abolished. When only one constraint is effective at a time, then the production inefficiencies caused by the two source-based taxes will tend to create an inverse 'seesaw' relationship between the optimal rates of the two taxes. When both constraints are combined it is possible that both tax rates are positive in the constrained optimum.

Our analysis relates to several strands in the literature. On the one hand, our results provide a suitable starting point for a more detailed discussion of the production efficiency theorem in open economies; this is covered in section 10.5.1. Furthermore, there are several analyses which discuss factor tax interactions that lead to similar results as we have obtained above; this literature is surveyed in section 10.5.2. Finally, section 10.5.3 reviews some contributions that address the efficiency of tax competition and the gains from tax harmonisation in models that incorporate both capital and commodity taxes.

10.5.1 The production efficiency theorem in open economies

As stated in our preliminary discussion of the production efficiency theorem in chapter 4, the result that production taxes should not be part of an optimal tax package depends on two important preconditions: (i) there must be a complete set of consumption tax instruments, and (ii) there must be no untaxed profits. Our analysis in this chapter serves as a background to discuss each of these conditions. While most of the literature on the production efficiency theorem has been confined to the taxation of international capital income, the comparison with the integrated treatment of factor and commodity taxation in the above analysis will outline some more general principles of optimal taxation in open economies.

Turning first to the set of consumption tax instruments, recall that proposition 10.1 was derived *without* using the first-order condition for the destination-based commodity tax (10.16). A parallel result obtains in two-period models of capital taxation with endogenous labour supply, where the set of (distortive) tax instruments includes a wage tax, a residence-based capital tax and a source-based capital tax. However, to show that source taxes are zero in a small open economy, it is sufficient that governments have a wage tax at their disposal and the residence-based capital tax is not needed for the result (Gordon, 1986; Razin and Sadka, 1991a).

These results conflict with the production efficiency theorem in its general form, which requires that a full set of optimal consumption taxes exists, i.e., there must be a separate tax instrument for *each* margin of substitution in the consumer's utility function (Munk, 1980). The intuition for this requirement should be obvious from our analysis above, as production taxes may serve as substitutes for 'missing' consumption taxes and thus will not generally be zero in this case. This implies, however, that the small open economy setting discussed in this section – and in section 4.2 – must represent a special case of a more general open economy version of this theorem.

As we have seen in section 4.2, a simple intuition for the zero source tax on capital in a small open economy is given by the inverse elasticity rule, since the base of the capital tax is infinitely elastic while the elasticity of the labour tax base is finite. The important generalisation offered by the production efficiency theorem is that, in the presence of an optimal commodity tax system, production taxes are zero even though the elasticity of the capital tax base is less than infinity. In an open economy setting this implies that countries have some effect on world market prices and thus are not (infinitely) small. On the other hand, it is well known that countries with some market power in the world economy can use either origin-based commodity taxes or source-based capital taxes to manipulate the terms of trade (see section 3.1). This beggar-thy-neighbour effect will be eliminated, however, when all countries are identical and there is thus no trade in either capital or goods in equilibrium.

This setting is studied in Bucovetsky and Wilson (1991). They consider a two-period, one-sector model with endogenous savings and labour supply and model tax competition between a finite number n of identical countries. Bucovetsky and Wilson (1991) focus on *pairwise* combinations of the three taxes and show that the source-based capital tax will be *non-zero* for any finite number of n, if combined with either a labour tax or a residence-based capital tax. This is precisely the result that the production efficiency theorem would predict in the absence of a full set of tax instruments. A zero source tax on capital will result, however, in the special case of a small open economy ($n \to \infty$).

Within the framework of the Bucovetsky and Wilson (1991) analysis, Eggert and Haufler (1999) have considered the case where the three distortive tax instruments in this model are all permitted simultaneously. In this setting – with a complete set of consumption tax instruments – all countries choose a zero source tax on capital, irrespective of the number of competing (symmetric) countries and thus irrespective of the elasticity that the capital tax base has from the perspective of each individual region. From these results it can be argued that a trade setting with finite elasticities of the capital tax base, but no terms of trade effects, comes closest to an open economy version of the production efficiency theorem.

Note also that a similar argument applies in a dynamic, neoclassical model of capital taxation where one core result is that capital should not be taxed in the steady state (Chamley, 1986). It is tempting to see the intuition for this result in an infinitely high long-run elasticity of capital supply – the dynamic analogue, in a way, to the small open economy case in international taxation. Chamley (1986, p. 613) emphasises, however, that his result also obtains in a model with a finite number of heterogeneous agents where the discount rate in the steady state is endogenous and the interest elasticity of the supply of capital is thus less than infinity in the long run. Furthermore, Correia (1996) has shown that the existence of an optimal commodity tax system is crucial for Chamley's result. In a representative-household framework, she constructs a counterexample where an untaxed factor of production is a complement to capital, and the optimal capital tax rate in the steady state is positive. Hence it is again the existence of an optimal set of commodity taxes, rather than the inverse elasticity rule, which is at the heart of the zero capital tax result in this dynamic setting.

The second well-known condition for taxes on production to be zero is that there must be no pure profits. In section 10.4.1 we have given two justifications why pure profits – if they arise – cannot be fully taxed by an independent instrument.[5] As shown in proposition 10.3(a), this creates a case for positive capital taxation at source, even in a small open economy, as the source-based capital tax acts as a partial substitute for the incomplete profit tax instrument.

Similar constraints on profit taxation have been introduced in a number of studies on optimal capital taxation in open economies. An early contribution is Bruce (1992), who uses a one-sector model of a small open economy where output is produced using capital and labour inputs. Production occurs under decreasing returns to scale, giving rise to pure profits. Bruce shows that the optimal source tax on capital will be positive, if and only if profits cannot be fully taxed by an independent profit tax. Furthermore, if profits can be fully taxed, but the tax on labour income is below its optimal level, then the source tax on capital income will still be positive if capital and labour are complements in production (cf. the result by Correia, 1996). These results show that the absence of untaxed profits and the existence of a complete set of optimised consumption taxes are *both* required for optimal production taxes to be zero.

In chapter 4 we have briefly introduced the contribution by Keen and Piekkola (1997), who link the role of imperfect profit taxation to a general equilibrium extension of Horst's (1980) inverse elasticity rule in international capital taxation (see n. 2 in chapter 4). Keen and Piekkola show that if profits are incompletely taxed, then the globally optimal tax system includes both residence- and source-based capital taxes. Furthermore, the mix of the two taxes is influenced by the restrictions placed on profit taxation, where low exogenous levels of profit taxation increase the weight of the source-based capital tax acting as a substitute. If profits can be fully taxed, the weight of the source tax is zero and only residence-based taxes are used in the global tax optimum.

Huizinga and Nielsen (1997a) study optimal capital income and profit taxation in a small open economy. The additional aspect in their analysis

[5] A further argument has been made by Huber and Krause (1997) who show that with random productivity shocks the rent tax will generally be less than 100 per cent and the source tax on capital will be non-zero, even if independent taxes on capital and the specific factor exist. The intuition for this result is that the two instruments have different risk characteristics and the optimal tax policy trades off an efficient allocation of risk against the production distortions caused by the source-based capital tax.

is that the pure efficiency argument for source-based capital taxes in the presence of incomplete profit taxation is combined with a tax exporting motive. As in Keen and Piekkola (1997), source- and residence-based capital taxes will both be positive if there are constraints on profit taxation, but all profits accrue to domestic residents. Stronger results are obtained, however, when profits accrue partly to foreigners. In this case, the source-based capital tax may become so large that the residence-based capital tax is no longer needed, or even becomes negative (cf. section 7.3).

10.5.2 The interaction of production taxes

When the conditions for the production efficiency theorem are violated, and production taxes are used in the optimum, then familiar second-best considerations will apply when more than one instrument is permitted that does affect production conditions.[6] In the present chapter, these production interactions have arisen from the fact that both a source-based capital tax and a (selective) origin-based commodity tax have been in the set of tax instruments. Since, in the trade model used, these two taxes have additive effects on the required gross rate of return to capital in the small open economy, production distortions are minimised when a positive capital tax rate is accompanied by a negative production tax, or vice versa (propositions 10.3 and 10.4).

A similar inverse relationship between taxes that affect production is obtained in the early analysis of Oates and Schwab (1988, section 3). In their model, production decisions are affected by a direct source tax on capital and an environmental standard. Oates and Schwab assume that the input factor 'environment' is a complement to capital in production, i.e., a rise in the permitted level of emissions raises the marginal product of capital. In this setting the first-best policy is to impose a zero source tax on capital and set an environmental standard that fully internalises the disutility from pollution. If, owing to exogenous contraints, the capital tax is set at a positive level, then the second-best environmental standard will be lower, and the level of emissions will be higher, than in the benchmark. The reduction in the environmental standard thus represents an indirect subsidisation of investment that partly counteracts the distortion caused by the source-based tax on capital.

[6] This argument has similarities with the use of origin-based commodity taxes as an instrument to correct production distortions arising from imperfect competition. See the paper by Keen and Lahiri (1998) discussed in section 9.7.3.

Similar production interactions underlie the analysis of environmental tax reforms in Bovenberg and de Mooij (1998). Similar to Oates and Schwab, the two relevant instruments in their analysis are a source-based capital tax and a pollution tax that increases the price of a 'dirty' input into the production process. Among other results, Bovenberg and de Mooij (1998, pp. 22–3) show that if the capital tax is fixed at an above-optimal level in the initial equilibrium, then an environmental tax reform that substitutes production-based pollution taxes for capital taxes is likely to increase non-environmental welfare, in addition to improving the environment. The reason is that, with sufficient substitution possibilities in production, the overall effect of the reform is to reduce the tax burden on capital and shift it to the internationally immobile factor labour.

Finally, Slemrod, Hansen and Procter (1997) obtain 'seesaw' relationships between taxes in a model of international capital taxation only. They consider a two-country model where one of the two regions ('the North') is large, relative to the other ('the South') and each country is simultaneously an importer and an exporter of (different varieties of) capital. Hence, there are two independent tax instruments in this model which both affect international capital flows. In the absence of constraints, the optimal tax policy for the South is to impose a zero tax on capital imports from the North, and levy the same tax rate on investments in the home country and on the income, net of foreign taxes, that domestic residents receive from investments in the North. The first part of this optimal tax rule is the conventional zero tax result for a capital importing small open economy, whereas the second part restates the optimality of the *deduction method* of double taxation relief from the perspective of a small capital exporting country (cf. n. 3 in chapter 4).

Slemrod, Hansen and Procter analyse how these results change when both problems are linked through the cross-hauling of capital and one of the two instruments is fixed by exogenous constraints. If, for example, the South's tax on capital imports is exogenously constrained to be positive rather than zero, then trade in capital is reduced below its efficient level. This distortion can be (partly) compensated by a trade-promoting reduction in the effective tax rate on capital exports, by granting a more generous tax credit than is implied by the deduction method. Hence it is obvious in this model that optimal tax policy is aimed at maximising the gains from trade, given the exogenous constraints. But the same has also been true in our analysis above, where a trade-restricting source tax on capital imports has been counteracted by a negative production tax that implicitly subsidises domestic investment and hence trade in capital.

10.5.3 Efficient tax competition with factor and commodity taxes

Finally, we turn to the issue whether decentralised decision-making by governments can produce an efficient outcome, given the set of tax instruments. The initial contributions to this literature, summarised in subsection 4.3.2, have focused exclusively on capital taxation. In the following we review some articles that re-address this question in models incorporating both factor and commodity taxes.

Arachi (2001) extends the model of Bucovetsky and Wilson (1991) by considering a two-sector trade model and introducing additional (selective) origin- and destination-based commodity taxes. Arachi's model is thus rather similar to the one used above, but the policy question asked is different. Arachi shows that efficient tax competition in this setting generally requires that all the four possible tax instruments must be available. The intuition for this result is straightforward. In a two-good model there are two international prices – the interest rate and the relative commodity price – that can be affected by tax policies. Hence, in the same way as residence- and source-based capital taxes are needed to insulate the domestic economy from changes in the world interest rate (cf. Bucovetsky and Wilson, 1991, proposition 3), it is necessary to have *both* destination- and origin-based commodity taxes in order to shield the home country from changes in the relative commodity price.

Eggert and Genser (2000) introduce destination- and origin-based commodity taxes into the one-good model of Bucovetsky and Wilson (1991). While the combination of residence- and source-based capital taxes leads to efficient tax competition in the Bucovetsky and Wilson framework, even if a wage tax is absent, Eggert and Genser show that this no longer holds when an origin-based commodity tax is added to the set of tax instruments. In contrast, a destination-based tax is compatible with efficient tax competition in this model, but only if the residence-based capital tax also remains at the disposal of national governments.

The conclusion from these analyses is that the conditions for tax competition to be efficient, as derived in the presence of isolated capital taxation (subsection 4.3.2), become even more stringent when commodity taxes are introduced. In particular, in a two-good model where taxes can affect relative prices, tax competition can be constrained efficient only if capital incomes *and* traded commodities are subject to international double taxation.

While these results strengthen the basic argument for tax coordination, the interaction of different tax instruments may, at the same time, make tax harmonisation less effective. This problem is pursued in the analysis of Fuest and Huber (1999a). Their analysis uses a conventional two-period, one-good model of symmetric tax competition, but incorporates a source-based capital tax, a depreciation parameter for the capital tax base and an origin-based VAT. As in the analyses of Zodrow and Mieszkowski (1986) or Bucovetsky and Wilson (1991), capital is undertaxed in the non-cooperative equilibrium and a coordinated increase in the *effective* tax rate on capital would improve welfare in each country. However, an isolated increase in the *nominal* (statutory) capital tax rate will be completely offset by the competing governments, either through more generous depreciation allowances, or through a reduction in the origin-based commodity tax. In this case, where different tax instruments have completely equivalent effects, inefficient capital tax competition and ineffective tax harmonisation can thus co-exist.

APPENDIX

Proof of Proposition 10.2: Without loss of generality, assume that the fixed factor is l_2 while l_1 is elastically supplied. Uncompensated price effects are decomposed using the Slutsky equations

$$\frac{\partial z}{\partial q_2} = \frac{\partial z^C}{\partial q_2} - c_2 \frac{\partial z}{\partial y}, \quad \frac{\partial z}{\partial \omega_1} = \frac{\partial z^C}{\partial \omega_1} + l_1 \frac{\partial z}{\partial y}, \quad \frac{\partial z}{\partial \omega_2} = l_2 \frac{\partial z}{\partial y} \quad \forall \quad z \in \{l_1, c_2\}, \tag{10A.1}$$

where a superscript C denotes a compensated derivative, y is nominal income and a change in ω_2 causes only income, but no substitution effects. Using (10A.1) in (10.17) and noting that l_2 is a constant gives

$$\frac{\partial \mathcal{L}}{\partial t_{l_2}} = l_2\theta - \mu_2 = 0, \qquad \theta = \lambda\left(1 - t_c \frac{\partial c_2}{\partial y} - \alpha_1 \frac{\partial l_1}{\partial y}\right) - 1, \tag{10A.2}$$

and $\theta > 0$ must hold if the revenue requirement T_0 exceeds the maximal amount that can be collected by the lump-sum tax t_{l_2} (cf. Atkinson and Stiglitz, 1980, p. 373). From (10A.2) it then immediately follows that $\mu_2 > 0$, i.e., the non-negativity constraint on the net income of the fixed factor is binding. From (10.21) then follows $t_{l_2} = w_2$, as stated in part (a) of the proposition.

To show proposition 10.2(b), substituting the Slutsky relationships (10A.1) into (10.16) and (10.17) gives

$$\frac{\partial \mathcal{L}}{\partial t_c} = c_2\theta + \lambda\left(t_c \frac{\partial c_2^C}{\partial q_2} + \alpha_1 \frac{\partial l_1^C}{\partial q_2}\right) = 0,$$

$$\frac{\partial \mathcal{L}}{\partial t_{l_1}} = l_1\theta - \lambda\left(t_c \frac{\partial c_2^C}{\partial \omega_1} + \alpha_1 \frac{\partial l_1^C}{\partial \omega_1}\right) = 0,$$

where θ is given in (10A.2) and α_1 has been reduced to t_{l_1} since $t_x = t_k = 0$ (cf. proposition 10.1). Combining the two equations gives

$$-t_c\left(\frac{1}{c_2}\frac{\partial c_2^C}{\partial q_2} + \frac{1}{l_1}\frac{\partial c_2^C}{\partial \omega_1}\right) = t_{l_1}\left(\frac{1}{c_2}\frac{\partial l_1^C}{\partial q_2} + \frac{1}{l_1}\frac{\partial l_1^C}{\partial \omega_1}\right).$$

Using the assumption that leisure $(-l_1)$ and c_2 are net complements $(\partial c_2^C/\partial \omega_1 = -\partial l_1^C/\partial q_2 < 0)$ shows that both tax rates must have the same sign. From the government budget constraint it then follows that t_c and t_{l_1} must both be positive. ■

Proof of Proposition 10.3: (*a*) We turn first to the case where t_{l_2} is constrained. Since $\phi_1 = 0$, (10.27) reduces to (10.23) as before. Solving for t_x and substituting in (10.28) gives

$$t_k = -\frac{1}{l_2}\left(\frac{\partial^2 w_2}{\partial r^2}\right)^{-1} \frac{\partial w_2}{\partial r}\,\phi_2 > 0, \tag{10A.3}$$

where (10.10) and $\mathcal{J} = 0$ from (10.25) have been used to sign t_k. Using (10.13) and (10.14) it then immediately follows from (10.27) that sign $(t_x) = -\text{sign}\ (t_k) = -1$.

(*b*) The case where t_{l_1} is constrained requires a few more steps. Substituting (10.27) in (10.28) and setting $\phi_2 = 0$ gives

$$t_k\, l_2 \frac{\partial^2 w_2}{\partial r^2} = \phi_1\, \varepsilon, \qquad \varepsilon = \frac{\partial^2 w_1/\partial p_1 \partial r}{\partial^2 w_1/\partial p_1^2}\frac{\partial w_1}{\partial p_1} - \frac{\partial w_1}{\partial r}. \tag{10A.4}$$

Using the zero-profit condition in sector 1 (cf. (10.9)–(10–11))

$$p_1 \frac{\partial w_1}{\partial p_1} - w_1 + r\frac{\partial w_1}{\partial r} = 0$$

and expanding by r gives

$$\varepsilon = \frac{1}{r}\left[\frac{\partial w_1/\partial p_1}{\partial^2 w_1/\partial p_1^2}\left(r\frac{\partial^2 w_1}{\partial r \partial p_1} + p_1 \frac{\partial^2 w_1}{\partial p_1^2}\right) - w_1\right] = -\frac{w_1}{r} < 0, \tag{10A.5}$$

since $\partial w_1/\partial p_1$ is homogeneous of degree zero in r and p_1. From (10A.4) and (10.12) then follows

$$\text{sign}(t_k) = -\ \text{sign}(\phi_1) = -1.$$

Substituting (10A.4) into (10.28) using (10A.5) gives

$$t_x = t_k \left(\frac{\partial^2 w_1}{\partial p_1^2} \right)^{-1} \left[\frac{\partial^2 w_1}{\partial r \partial p_1} - \frac{l_2}{l_1} \frac{r}{w_1} \frac{\partial w_1}{\partial p_1} \frac{\partial^2 w_2}{\partial r^2} \right],$$

which can be signed from (10.11)–(10.14) to give sign $(t_x) = -$sign $(t_k) = 1$. ■

11 Commodity and profit taxation with imperfect firm mobility

Chapters 11 and 12 of this study deal with firm – as opposed to capital – mobility. There are clearly many similarities between these two issues and in many analyses the two concepts are not even separated. We believe, however, that there are at least two reasons why this distinction is relevant.

First, there are taxes which do affect the location of firms, but not the location of capital. This is true for all taxes that fall on pure profits, such as a cash-flow tax on corporate income (chapter 7) and a general origin-based tax on consumption (chapter 9). Hence while our analysis in chapter 9 has concluded that a commodity tax levied under the origin principle does not cause a (long-run) distortion of *capital* flows, the same tax may distort the location decision of internationally mobile *firms*. The distortive role of profit taxes in a setting with internationally mobile firms will be at the centre of the analysis in this chapter.

A second and related reason is that models of capital tax competition should allow us to distinguish between international portfolio investments on the one hand and foreign direct investment (FDI) on the other. One of the main differences between the two types of investment is that portfolio investors generally expect to earn a normal rate of return, whereas foreign direct investment is often associated with pure profits made in imperfectly competitive markets (see Devereux, 2000).[1] This implies that the standard model of capital tax competition, with its assumption of perfectly competitive capital markets, may not be well suited for an analysis of FDI. Instead, there are close links to the new trade theory, where firm mobility in imperfectly competitive markets has played an important role. These issues will be addressed in chapter 12.

[1] Another difference may arise from asymmetric information between foreign and domestic investors. Razin, Sadka and Yuen (1998) argue that the asymmetric information problem discussed by Gordon and Bovenberg (1996) (cf. n. 7 in chapter 4) may be particularly relevant for foreign portfolio equity investment, whereas FDI represents a way to overcome this information problem. Hence the optimal tax policy of the capital importing country will differ for the two types of investment.

In the present chapter, we introduce a model where firms behave competitively but entry to the market is restricted so that pure profits can arise in equilibrium. This model builds on Richter (1994), whose approach is outlined in section 11.1. In section 11.2 we then present our own model which simplifies Richter's analysis in some respects, but also introduces new features. In particular, we incorporate cross-border shopping by final consumers, thus linking our analysis to the earlier discussion of this issue in chapter 8. Section 11.3 derives the optimal tax structure for our problem and supplements the theoretical results with some numerical simulations. Section 11.4 discusses the results and summarises the policy implications of the analysis.

11.1 An efficient tax system with public inputs

Richter (1994) outlines a model where a large number of identical regional governments supply local public inputs and use a combination of profit and land taxation to balance their budget. Each firm uses interregionally mobile capital, immobile land and the local public input to produce a homogeneous output good. The production function exhibits constant returns to scale in the three inputs together and thus decreasing returns in the two factors that must be privately remunerated by the firm. As a result, each firm makes positive gross profits in equilibrium. Entry into the market is excluded, however, by the assumption that existing firms have incurred fixed costs that are just equal to the net profits made in equilibrium. The core distinguishing feature of the model is that existing firms are assumed to be perfectly mobile between jurisdictions. Hence international arbitrage not only equalises net-of-tax returns to the production factor capital, but also the net-of-tax profits of firms producing in different jurisdictions.

The conditions for a first-best optimum in this model are that the Samuelson condition for the provision of local public inputs must be satisfied, and both gross-of-tax returns to capital and the gross profits of firms must be equalised between regions. The last condition ensures that the fixed number of profitable firms is efficiently distributed across jurisdictions. Since an optimal (source-based) tax on capital would be zero in this framework with perfectly mobile capital and small jurisdictions, this tax instrument is not considered and only taxes on profits and land are analysed.

As the discussion in Richter (1994) makes clear, there are two ways of decentralising the first-best allocation. The simplest solution is to use profit taxes in equilibrium only to cover the marginal congestion costs of the local public input. If public goods are pure, then no taxes are levied on the firms' profits and all revenue is raised through the non-distortive land tax. An alternative tax scheme with a greater role for local profit taxation is also outlined, however. This involves a fixed positive profit tax rate, the returns of which are earmarked to finance a fixed proportion – equal to the profit tax rate – of the expenditures for public inputs. The tax on pure profits is thus a benefit tax and the earmarking of the revenue simultaneously ensures an incentive for local governments to supply an efficient level of public inputs. At the same time, each government pays a lump-sum subsidy for the settlement of a firm in its jurisdiction, which just compensates for the profit taxes paid in equilibrium. Hence, in the absence of congestion costs, net profit taxes are again zero and all expenditures for the public input must be covered by taxes on land. In the static framework employed, the two tax schemes are thus equivalent. Richter (1994, pp. 335–6) argues, however, that the second scheme comes closer to explaining existing practices of profit taxation, which aim at taxing the profits of 'old' firms, but leave the profits of 'new' firms tax-free.[2]

11.2 Combining imperfect mobility of firms and consumers

Richter's approach is modified here in order to relate the framework with firm mobility to our previous analyses of destination- vs. origin-based commodity taxation.[3] We simplify the model by ignoring an endogenous supply of local public inputs and instead assume that the government has to meet a fixed revenue constraint. Furthermore there is no independent production factor capital in our model. On the other hand, the inter-regionally immobile factor is here given by elastically supplied labour, making the wage tax a distortive tax instrument. The main extension is that we introduce commodity taxes in addition to factor taxation. A destination-based commodity tax distorts the consumers' decision where to shop, whereas an origin-based tax falls partly on the profits of imperfectly mobile firms.

We consider a small country (the 'home country') with identical individuals that can be treated as a single, aggregate household. Trade occurs in a single output good whose world price is normalised to unity. The small country can tax both the consumption and the production of the aggregate commodity. In the first case, the tax corresponds to

[2] The strategic incentives for governments to pursue such time-inconsistent policies are analysed in detail in the literature on 'tax holidays'. See Doyle and van Wijnbergen (1994); Bond and Samuelson (1986).

[3] The analysis in sections 11.2–11.4 is a revised version of Genser and Haufler (1996b).

a destination-based commodity tax (t_d), whereas in the second case it is an origin-based commodity tax (t_o). The domestic producer price p and the consumer price q are given by

$$p = 1 - t_o, \tag{11.1}$$
$$q = 1 + t_d. \tag{11.2}$$

Since there is no strategic interaction between firms, we can again model all taxes in this analysis as unit taxes without affecting the relevant results. Also, we do not impose any restrictions on the sign of tax rates.

11.2.1 Firms

Production in the small country takes place in n identical firms, where n is a continuous variable. All firms are owned by foreigners, an assumption that eliminates complex repercussions through income effects and to which we will return below. Each firm chooses a labour input l and employs a fixed factor, which need not be reimbursed by the firm. In the present context, this fixed factor is best interpreted as a public intermediate input (as in Richter, 1994). The production function at the firm level, $x(l)$, exhibits decreasing returns to scale in the labour input only and constant returns to scale in both factors together, hence giving rise to pure profits before tax (π).

In addition to the two commodity tax instruments, the government also disposes of a tax on wages (t_w) and a cash-flow tax on the firm's profits (t_p). The wage tax creates a wedge between the gross wage w and the net wage ω

$$\omega = w - t_w. \tag{11.3}$$

Firms producing in the large world market are guaranteed a fixed profit level Π. If international firm mobility were perfect, then net profits earned in the small country would have to equal this level. However, as in several previous chapters, we assume that firms face some mobility costs when they settle in the small country. One possible scenario is that firms locate around a central marketplace, for example a harbour from which exports are shipped. Early entrants will be able to settle close to this market while later entrants have to locate in more distant places, incurring additional transportation costs. A similar argument can be made using setup or development costs which increase for new entrants that are forced to settle in inferior locations.[4] Alternatively, and closer to

[4] An analytically similar approach is followed by Osmundsen, Hagen and Schjelderup (1998), who model firms which differ parametrically in their opportunity costs of relocating and hence exhibit varying degrees of international mobility.

the regional economics tradition, it can be argued that the fixed factor underlying our analysis consists not exclusively of free public inputs or entrepreneurial services. Rather, it partly represents the return to a private factor in limited supply (e.g. land) and an increasing number of firms producing in the small country drives up the land rent to be paid in equilibrium. To exclude the income effects that arise for land owners, this interpretation of mobility costs requires the further assumption – a common one in the local public finance literature – that land is entirely owned by foreigners ('absentee landowners'; cf. Wildasin, 1986; Wellisch, 2000).

Any of these scenarios can be called on to justify an additional mobility (or location) cost element, denoted by $\rho(n)$, that is a rising function of the number of firms operating in the small country. International arbitrage by firms ensures that net profits received in the small country – after the deduction of profit taxes and location costs – are equal to profits in the world market. Hence the gross profit level that must be earned in the small country is determined by

$$\pi - t_p - \rho(n) = \Pi, \qquad \rho'(n) > 0. \tag{11.4}$$

If firm mobility is perfect $[\rho(n) = 0]$, the arbitrage condition (11.4) implies that a reduction in the domestic profit tax t_p leads to an inflow of foreign firms until the level of gross profits has fallen by the full amount of the tax. If, instead, mobility costs are positive, then the inflow of foreign firms induced by a reduction in the domestic profit tax rate will be limited by the additional costs that new entrants face. Hence a given reduction in t_p will not be fully matched in the new equilibrium by a corresponding reduction in the level of gross profits.

From (11.1) the producer price in the small country is directly determined by the world price of unity and the origin-based tax rate chosen by the government. In contrast, both the gross wage w and the gross profit level π in the small country are endogenous variables. Together with the producer price p, they determine the level of employment in each firm, $l(w, p, \pi)$, from the gross profit definition $px(l) - wl = \pi$.

The important point to note is that the gross profit requirement acts like a factor price in a setting with internationally mobile firms. This similarity is exploited in the following when we determine the derivative of the gross wage with respect to changes in the producer price level and the gross profit requirement in a way that is completely analogous to the analysis in chapter 10. From the firm's profit maximisation condition, $p[\partial x/\partial l(w, p, \pi)] = w$, the gross wage can be expressed as $w(p, \pi)$, where the dependence on π represents the 'factor price frontier' in the present context. Hence the gross profit identity can be written as

$$px[l(w(p,\pi),p,\pi)] - w(p,\pi)l[w(p,\pi),p,\pi] - \pi = 0.$$

Labour demand is homogeneous of degree zero in (w, p, π). Since we will need this property in the following it is important to clearly separate the direct effects of tax-induced changes in p and π from the indirect effects that operate through changes in the gross wage. Implicitly differentiating the profit identity and using the property that the wage rate equals the marginal value product of labour in the firm's optimum gives

$$\frac{\partial w}{\partial \pi} = \frac{-1}{l} < 0, \qquad \frac{\partial w}{\partial p} = \frac{x(l)}{l} > 0, \tag{11.5}$$

which are analogous to (10.10)–(10.11) in chapter 10. The interpretation of these derivatives is straightforward: a higher gross profit requirement will reduce the gross wage that firms are paying in equilibrium for any given output price p, whereas a higher output price allows a higher gross wage to be paid for any given level of gross profits. This completes the description of the production side of the model.

11.2.2 Consumers

The representative household supplies an endogenous amount of internationally immobile labour (L) and consumes an aggregate private good (C). Its utility function has the usual properties and is given by

$$u = u(C, -L). \tag{11.6}$$

We model imperfect mobility of consumers in a way that is similar to the treatment of firms. Since – in contrast to the analysis in chapter 10 – there is only a single output good in the present analysis, consumer purchases of this single good are bounded by convex transportation costs (as in chapter 8). Total consumption of the homogeneous private good (C) consists of domestic (c^H) and foreign (c^F) purchases:

$$C = c^H + c^F. \tag{11.7}$$

If the home country levies a consumption tax $t_d > 0$, then its residents shop abroad and purchase goods at the world price of unity, but these purchases are subject to convex transaction costs. In order to allow for the symmetric case where the home country offers a consumption subsidy ($t_d < 0$), the transaction cost function must be specified to allow for negative consumer purchases abroad, $c^F < 0$ (i.e. the small country attracts foreign consumer purchases). In this case, the total amount of goods purchased in the home country (c^H) exceeds the total consumption of the representative individual (C) from (11.7). The relationship

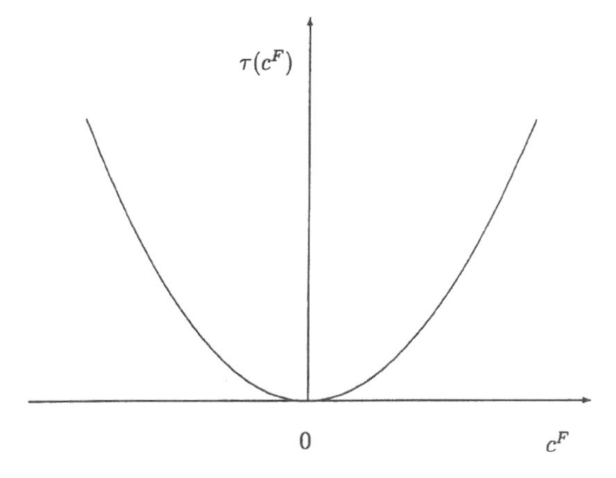

Figure 11.1 Consumer transaction costs

between the level of cross-border shopping (in either direction) and consumer transaction costs is shown in figure 11.1.

Figure 11.1 is already drawn for the case where transaction costs in the cases of positive and negative levels of c^F are symmetric. We will make this assumption in the following in order to ensure a continuous trade-off for the small country's optimal tax policy (cf. proposition 8.1). The properties of the consumer transaction cost function $\tau(c^F)$ are familiar by now and are summarised as follows:

$$\tau(c^F) > 0 \text{ if } c^F \neq 0, \quad \text{sign } (\tau') = \text{sign } (c^F), \quad \tau(0) = \tau'(0) = 0, \quad \tau'' > 0.$$

Consumer arbitrage equates the marginal transaction costs of foreign purchases with the difference in consumer prices between home and foreign goods. From (11.2) this implies $\tau'(c^F) = q - 1$ in the consumer optimum, irrespective of the direction of cross-border shopping. Inverting determines the volume of cross-border shopping as a function of the domestic consumer price

$$c^F(q) = (\tau')^{-1}, \quad c^F(1) = 0.$$

Differentiating with respect to q gives

$$\frac{\partial c^F}{\partial q} = \frac{1}{\tau''} > 0, \tag{11.8}$$

which holds for both positive and negative values of c^F. As in our analysis of chapter 8, consumer transaction costs represent a loss of real resources. These enter the budget constraint for the representative individual in the home country in the case where c^F is positive.

We now return to our assumption that all firms operating in the small open economy are foreign-owned. This assumption ensures that tax policies which affect net profits in equilibrium do not feed back on the individual's commodity demand and labour supply functions through income effects. On the other hand, domestic residents own some share of the profit-making firms that operate in the world market. The domestic profit income accruing abroad represents a lump sum and is denoted by $Z \geq 0$. This procedure is a standard simplification in the regional economics literature, and the neglected effects are likely to be small when the residents of a small country diversify their portfolio and thus hold only a small fraction of their wealth in domestic assets. Finally, on the basis of our discussion in subsection 4.1.2, we assume that it is not possible for the government of the small country to impose residence-based taxes on the foreign profit income Z.

Similar to the analysis in chapter 8, the consumer budget constraint in this model depends on the direction of consumer purchases. If domestic residents shop abroad ($c^F > 0$), then the budget constraint reads $qc^H + c^F + \tau(c^F) = \omega L + Z$, which can be rearranged using (11.7). If instead $c^F \leq 0$, then all domestic income must be spent at home. Hence we get

$$qC = \omega L + Y, \tag{11.9}$$

where

$$\begin{aligned} Y = Z + [(q-1)c^F - \tau] \quad &\text{if} \quad c^F > 0, \\ Y = Z \quad &\text{if} \quad c^F \leq 0. \end{aligned}$$

Therefore, for $c^F > 0$, exogenous income includes the aggregate tax savings that home residents can make by shopping abroad. Maximising (11.6) subject to (11.9) yields the individual's (regime-specific) indirect utility function $v(q, \omega, Y)$. By Roy's identity, and setting the marginal utility of private income equal to one, the derivatives of the indirect utility function are given by

$$\frac{\partial v}{\partial \omega} = L(q, \omega, Y), \tag{11.10}$$

$$\frac{\partial v}{\partial q} = -c^H(q, \omega, Y) \quad \textit{if} \;\; c^F > 0,$$

$$\frac{\partial v}{\partial q} = -C(q, \omega, Y) \quad \textit{if} \;\; c^F \leq 0. \tag{11.11}$$

Production and consumption decisions together determine the last endogenous variable in this model, the number of firms operating in the small country. Since firms are identical by assumption, the labour market clearing condition gives

$$n(p, q, \pi, \omega, Y) = \frac{L(q, \omega, Y)}{l[w(p, \pi), p, \pi]} \ . \tag{11.12}$$

11.2.3 *Government*

The government of the small country maximises the indirect utility of the representative consumer, subject to a given revenue requirement $T_0 > 0$. The problem is thus

$$\max \ v(q, \omega, Y) \quad \text{s.t.} \ T_0 = t_d c^H + t_w L + t_o nx + t_p n,$$

where nx is total output produced in the small open economy and t_p, modelled as a unit tax, acts like a poll tax on firms operating in the home country. Using (11.12) we can eliminate n and set up the Lagrangian

$$\mathcal{L} = v(q, \omega, Y) + \lambda \left\{ t_d \, c^H(q, \omega, Y) + \left[t_w + \frac{t_o x(p, \pi)}{l(p, \pi)} + \frac{t_p}{l(p, \pi)} \right] L(q, \omega, Y) - T_0 \right\}. \tag{11.13}$$

The complexity of this problem derives from the fact that, through the firms' arbitrage condition (11.4), the gross profit level that must be earned in the home country depends on the number of firms in the market. Hence all tax instruments affect π through their effects on either domestic labour supply or the employment level of firms. Differentiating (11.4) and (11.12) with respect to the four tax instruments gives

$$\frac{\partial \pi}{\partial t_p} = 1 - \frac{\rho' \beta}{(1 + \rho' \beta)} \frac{1}{l}, \qquad \frac{\partial \pi}{\partial t_w} = \frac{-\rho'}{(1 + \rho' \beta)} \frac{1}{l} \frac{\partial L}{\partial \omega}, \tag{11.14}$$

$$\frac{\partial \pi}{\partial t_d} = \frac{\rho'}{(1 + \rho' \beta)} \frac{1}{l} \frac{\partial L}{\partial q}, \qquad \frac{\partial \pi}{\partial t_o} = \frac{\rho'}{(1 + \rho' \beta)} \frac{1}{l} \left(n \frac{dl}{dp} - \frac{\partial L}{\partial \omega} \frac{\partial w}{\partial p} \right). \tag{11.15}$$

These equations use

$$\beta = n \frac{dl}{d\pi} - \frac{\partial L}{\partial \omega} \frac{\partial w}{\partial \pi}$$

and

$$\frac{dl}{d\pi} \equiv \frac{\partial l}{\partial w}\frac{\partial w}{\partial \pi} + \frac{\partial l}{\partial \pi} > 0, \qquad \frac{dl}{dp} \equiv \frac{\partial l}{\partial w}\frac{\partial w}{\partial p} + \frac{\partial l}{\partial p} < 0 \tag{11.16}$$

summarise the direct and the indirect effects (via the gross wage w) of changes in p and π on the firm's labour demand. To interpret the derivatives in (11.14)–(11.15) let us assume for concreteness that the labour supply curve is upward sloping ($\partial L/\partial \omega > 0$, $\partial L/\partial q < 0$).[5] First, it is evident that an increase in the profit tax requires a higher level of gross profits to be earned in the small country. In contrast, both the wage tax and the consumption tax reduce labour supply and thus the number of firms operating in the small country. With imperfect firm mobility, the reduced mobility costs then allow a reduction in π in the firm's arbitrage equilibrium. Finally, the production tax also reduces the number of firms in equilibrium since it reduces aggregate labour supply while simultaneously raising the level of firm employment (by lowering the producer price and thus the gross wage).

With these effects in mind, we can now turn to the first-order conditions for the four tax instruments $t_i \in \{t_d, t_w, t_p, t_o\}$ available to the home country's government. We use the price definitions (11.1)–(11.3), the factor price frontier (11.5), Roy's identity (11.10)–(11.11), and the labour market clearing condition (11.12). This gives[6]

$$\frac{\partial \mathcal{L}}{\partial t_w} = -L + \lambda\left(L - t_d\frac{\partial c^H}{\partial \omega} - \alpha\frac{\partial L}{\partial \omega}\right) + \frac{\partial \pi}{\partial t_w}\gamma = 0, \tag{11.17}$$

$$\frac{\partial \mathcal{L}}{\partial t_d} = -c^H + \lambda\left(c^H + t_d\frac{\partial c^H}{\partial q} + \alpha\frac{\partial L}{\partial q}\right) + \frac{\partial \pi}{\partial t_d}\gamma = 0 \quad \text{if } c^F > 0, \tag{11.18a}$$

$$\frac{\partial \mathcal{L}}{\partial t_d} = -C + \lambda\left(c^H + t_d\frac{\partial c^H}{\partial q} + \alpha\frac{\partial L}{\partial q}\right) + \frac{\partial \pi}{\partial t_d}\gamma = 0 \quad \text{if } c^F \leq 0, \tag{11.18b}$$

[5] Note that this assumption is made purely to facilitate the interpretation and is not needed for any of the results.

[6] The system (11.17)–(11.20) is obtained through straightforward differentiation, where all terms involving the derivatives $\partial\pi/\partial t_i$ are collected separately. Note further that $\partial\pi/\partial t_p$ is decomposed in (11.19) using the first equation in (11.14). The effects of the various taxes on the average labour productivity $x(l)/l[w(p,\pi),p,\pi]$ are obtained as

$$\frac{\partial(x/l)}{\partial t_j} = \frac{1}{l}\left(\frac{\partial x}{\partial l} - \frac{x}{l}\right)\frac{\partial \pi}{\partial t_j}\frac{dl}{d\pi} \quad \forall\, t_j \in \{t_d, t_w, t_p\}, \qquad \frac{\partial(x/l)}{\partial t_o} = \frac{1}{l}\left(\frac{\partial x}{\partial l} - \frac{x}{l}\right)\left(\frac{\partial \pi}{\partial t_o}\frac{dl}{d\pi} - \frac{dl}{dp}\right).$$

The derivatives $\partial(1/l)/\partial t_i$ are obtained analogously. Finally, recall from (11.5) that $\partial w/\partial p = x/l$ and $\partial w/\partial \pi = -1/l$.

$$\frac{\partial \mathcal{L}}{\partial t_p} = -\frac{L}{l} + \frac{\lambda}{l}\left(L - t_d \frac{\partial c^H}{\partial \omega} - \alpha \frac{\partial L}{\partial \omega}\right) + \left(\frac{\partial \pi}{\partial t_p} - 1\right)\gamma + n\left[t_o\left(\frac{\partial x}{\partial l} - \frac{x}{l}\right) - \frac{t_p}{l}\right]\frac{dl}{d\pi} = 0, \tag{11.19}$$

$$\frac{\partial \mathcal{L}}{\partial t_o} = -\frac{Lx}{l} + \frac{\lambda x}{l}\left(L - t_d \frac{\partial c^H}{\partial \omega} - \alpha \frac{\partial L}{\partial \omega}\right) + \frac{\partial \pi}{\partial t_o}\gamma - n\left[t_o\left(\frac{\partial x}{\partial l} - \frac{x}{l}\right) - \frac{t_p}{l}\right]\frac{dl}{dp} = 0. \tag{11.20}$$

These conditions incorporate the effects of the different tax rates on the gross profit level given in (11.14)–(11.15). Furthermore,

$$\alpha = t_w + \frac{t_o x}{l} + \frac{t_p}{l} \tag{11.21}$$

can be interpreted as the effective tax rate on labour. Finally $dl/d\pi$ and dl/dp are given in (11.16) and

$$\gamma = -\frac{L}{l} + \lambda\left\{-t_d \frac{\partial c^H}{\partial \omega}\frac{1}{l} - \alpha \frac{\partial L}{\partial \omega}\frac{1}{l} + n\left[t_o\left(\frac{\partial x}{\partial l} - \frac{x}{l}\right) - \frac{t_p}{l}\right]\frac{dl}{d\pi}\right\} \tag{11.22}$$

is the common multiplier for the derivatives $\partial \pi / \partial t_i$.

Two observations should be pointed out in this set of equations. First, note that the first-order condition for the consumption tax t_d (11.18a)–(11.18b) depends on the direction of consumer trade. However, the derivative $\partial c^H / \partial q$ captures the substitution effect from cross-border shopping in *both* regimes, since a rise in q will either increase the purchases of domestic residents abroad, or reduce cross-border shopping by foreigners in the home country (11.8). Second, while the first-order conditions (11.19)–(11.20) are complex, they exhibit many common elements and both can be simplified if they are combined with the optimality condition for the wage tax (11.17). These properties will be exploited below.

11.3 The optimal tax structure

11.3.1 Theoretical results

We rewrite the first-order condition for the profit tax and the production tax (11.19)–(11.20), using the optimality condition for the wage tax (11.17). This yields

$$\frac{\partial \mathcal{L}}{\partial t_p} = \frac{1}{l}\frac{\partial \mathcal{L}}{\partial t_w} - n\,\frac{dl}{d\pi}\left[\frac{\rho'}{(1+\rho'\beta)}\,\frac{\gamma}{l} + \frac{t_p}{l} - t_o\left(\frac{\partial x}{\partial l} - \frac{x}{l}\right)\right] = 0, \tag{11.23}$$

$$\frac{\partial \mathcal{L}}{\partial t_o} = \frac{x}{l}\frac{\partial \mathcal{L}}{\partial t_w} + n\,\frac{dl}{dp}\left[\frac{\rho'}{(1+\rho'\beta)}\,\frac{\gamma}{l} + \frac{t_p}{l} - t_o\left(\frac{\partial x}{\partial l} - \frac{x}{l}\right)\right] = 0. \tag{11.24}$$

This formulation already indicates that the first-order conditions (11.23)–(11.24) are not independent. To show this we add (11.23), multiplied by $(dl/dp)/(dl/d\pi)$, to (11.24) without requiring, for now, that the profit tax rate be optimised. This replaces the square bracket in (11.24) by the derivative $\partial\mathcal{L}/\partial t_p$. Further we use the homogeneity property of the labour demand function. If indirect effects via the induced change in wages are taken into account, then proportional increases in the price of output and the required gross profit level will leave the firms' labour demand unaffected. Recalling the definition of $dl/d\pi$ and dl/dp in (11.16) this is expressed by

$$\pi\,\frac{dl}{d\pi} + p\,\frac{dl}{dp} = 0.$$

Noting further that $px - \pi = wl$ from the definition of gross profits we obtain

$$\frac{\partial \mathcal{L}}{\partial t_o} = \frac{w}{p}\frac{\partial \mathcal{L}}{\partial t_w} + \frac{\pi}{p}\frac{\partial \mathcal{L}}{\partial t_p}. \tag{11.25}$$

Equation (11.25) shows that that the production tax combines the effects of the wage tax and the profit tax in the present model. If both of these taxes can be optimally chosen, then the first-order condition for the production tax (11.24) is necessarily fulfilled and is thus redundant. This in turn implies that the production tax cannot improve welfare in this model when factor taxes are at their optimal levels. This is summarised in

Proposition 11.1

If both wages and profits can be optimally taxed, then a general production tax is not needed as an additional tax instrument and its tax rate can be set equal to zero without welfare loss.

The crucial difference to the analysis in chapter 10 is that the production tax (origin-based commodity tax) is here a general tax, whereas a selective production tax was assumed in chapter 10. Hence, there are no effects on relative producer prices in the present model and only the effects on factor returns remain. These, however, can be duplicated by an appropriate combination of factor taxes.

Using proposition 11.1, we can exclude the production tax in the following without restricting the government's set of independent tax instruments. Next, we turn to the optimal rate of profit taxation. A convenient starting point for this analysis is the modified first-order condition (11.23). If wages can be optimally taxed then $\partial\mathcal{L}/\partial t_w = 0$ and the expression in the square bracket must be zero for optimality. Furthermore, the last term in this bracket disappears for $t_o = 0$. Let us first consider the special case of perfect firm mobility $[\rho(n) = \rho' = 0]$. In this case the first term in the bracket is also zero and (11.23) can be fulfilled only for $t_p = 0$. Hence profits remain entirely untaxed if firms are perfectly mobile internationally. This, of course, directly parallels the results in propositions 4.1 and 10.1, where the mobile tax base is the production factor capital.

In the presence of mobility costs ($\rho' > 0$), the first term in the square bracket of (11.23) is non-zero and depends on the sign of γ. This sign cannot directly be inferred from (11.22), since the slope of the labour supply curve is generally ambiguous and negative tax rates are not excluded in the present analysis. However, γ can be signed from the first-order condition (11.19). If the terms from the derivative $\partial\pi/\partial t_p$ (11.14) are collected, this equation can be condensed to

$$\frac{\partial\mathcal{L}}{\partial t_p} = \lambda n + \gamma\frac{\partial\pi}{\partial t_p} = 0.$$

Since $\lambda > 0$ is the shadow price of the government budget constraint and $\partial\pi/\partial t_p > 0$ from (11.14) this equation can be fulfilled only for $\gamma < 0$.

From $\gamma < 0$ it follows that the first term in the square bracket of (11.23) is negative. Since the third term in the bracket is zero, the second term must be positive, implying a positive profit tax rate t_p. This is summarised in

Proposition 11.2

The optimal profit tax rate t_p is positive when there are positive mobility costs which are rising in the number of firms ($\rho' > 0$). In the special case of zero mobility costs the optimal profit tax is zero.

Proposition 11.2 is easily understood by noting that our setting of imperfectly mobile firms lies in between the two benchmark cases of firms that are either immobile or perfectly mobile internationally. In the first case, the profit tax is a lump-sum instrument and – in the absence of further constraints – profits will be fully taxed away in the optimum. In the perfect mobility case, profits cannot be effectively taxed by the government of a small country and the optimal profit tax rate is zero. In an intermediate setting with positive, but finite, mobility costs, the base of the profit tax is less than perfectly elastic and it will thus be optimal for the government to obtain some fraction of the required tax revenue from this base.

The remaining question is whether the remaining tax rates t_w and t_d can also be expected to be positive. Both of these taxes reduce the net real wage and thus distort the consumer's labour–leisure choice. The fundamental trade-off between the wage tax and the consumption tax is that the latter is able to tax the lump-sum profit income Z, along with wage income, but at the same time causes an additional distortion through cross-border shopping.

The appendix to this chapter (pp. 276–8) shows that if t_d and t_w are both chosen optimally, the Slutsky decomposition and the homogeneity properties of compensated commodity demand and labour supply functions can be used to derive the following regime-specific relationships

$$[Z - c^F - \tau(c^F)]\varphi = qt_d \frac{\partial c^F}{\partial q} \quad \text{if} \quad c^F > 0, \tag{11.26a}$$

$$Z\varphi - qc^F = qt_d \frac{\partial c^F}{\partial q} \quad \text{if} \quad c^F \leq 0, \tag{11.26b}$$

where it is shown in the appendix ((11A.7) and (11A.8)) that $\varphi > 0$.

Equations (11.26a)–(11.26b) isolate the differences between the consumption tax and the wage tax in the two different trade regimes. In both equations, the left-hand side gives the difference in the base of the two taxes while the right-hand side shows the additional distortion through cross-border shopping caused by the destination-based commodity tax.

It is easy to see that a strictly positive level of Z is incompatible with either a negative or a zero rate of t_d, i.e. with a solution in the second trade regime $c^F \leq 0$. The left-hand side of (11.26b) is unambiguously positive for $c^F \leq 0$ whereas the right-hand side has the same sign as t_d since $\partial c^F/\partial q > 0$ from (11.8). Hence $t_d \leq 0$ cannot be optimal in this case. In contrast, $Z > 0$ is compatible with a solution in the first trade regime $c^F > 0$. To see this we start from $t_d = 0$, which implies $c^F = 0$ and $\tau(0) = 0$ from the properties of the consumer transaction cost function and note that in this case the left-hand side of (11.26a) is strictly positive, whereas the right-hand side is zero. As t_d is increased, the left-hand side of the equation becomes smaller while the right-hand side increases; hence, from continuity, there must be a positive tax rate t_d for which the equation is fulfilled.

Similar reasoning applies in the case $Z = 0$. In this case, neither a strictly positive nor a strictly negative tax rate t_d are compatible with (11.26a)–(11.26b), whereas a consumption tax rate of zero (which implies the borderline case $c^F = 0$) satisfies the second equation. Hence we have the following result:

Proposition 11.3
For $Z > 0$, the destination-based commodity tax will be positive in the government's optimum. It is zero if and only if there is no non-wage income.

Intuitively, since the consumption tax is the only instrument that is able to effectively tax the lump-sum profit income Z, this instrument will always be used to some extent. In the present setting with cross-border shopping the optimal level of t_d is reached when the additional distortion caused by this activity just compensates for the benefit of being able to levy a tax on a partly immobile base. It is then also obvious that if non-wage income is zero the consumption tax is strictly dominated by the wage tax and will thus not be used in the optimum.

Finally, note that while we are able to exclude the possibility of a negative consumption tax from optimal tax considerations, a similar argument cannot be made for the wage tax. Technically, the reason is that t_w does not appear in (11.26a)–(11.26b); hence the optimal choice of t_d has no general implications for the sign of t_w. Again the difference from the discussion in chapter 10 (cf. proposition 10.2) is that the consumption tax is here a general one and thus affects the same margin of substitution as the wage tax. Of course, in the special case of zero non-wage income and zero firm mobility costs both t_p and t_d will be zero and the wage tax must be positive to meet the government revenue constraint. In general, however, situations where a wage subsidy is optimal cannot be excluded by means of theoretical analysis alone.

11.3.2 A complementary simulation analysis

To gain a deeper understanding for the optimal tax structure and its dependence on core model parameters, the model can be simulated using a CES utility function of the form

$$u = \left(s_1^{1/\sigma}\, C^{(\sigma-1)/\sigma} + s_2^{1/\sigma}\, (E - L)^{(\sigma-1)/\sigma}\right)^{\sigma/(\sigma-1)},$$

where σ is the elasticity of substitution and E denotes an exogenous time endowment so that $(E - L)$ is the consumption of leisure. The exogenous weights obey the adding-up restriction $s_1^{1/\sigma} + s_2^{1/\sigma} = 1$ and we have chosen the ratio of the weights to be $s_1/s_2 = 4$. This makes commodity

Table 11.1 *Optimal tax rates with imperfectly mobile firms and consumers*

	$\sigma = 0.25$	$\sigma = 1$	$\sigma = 2.0$
$Z = 0 (T_0 = 2)$	$t_d^* = 0.0$ $t_w^* = 0.122$ $t_p^* = 0.122$	$t_d^* = 0.0$ $t_w^* = 0.130$ $t_p^* = 0.117$	$t_d^* = 0.0$ $t_w^* = 0.143$ $t_p^* = 0.110$
$Z = 3 (T_0 = 3)$	$t_d^* = 0.124$ $t_w^* = 0.069$ $t_p^* = 0.122$	$t_d^* = 0.079$ $t_w^* = 0.139$ $t_p^* = 0.112$	$t_d^* = 0.053$ $t_w^* = 0.179$ $t_p^* = 0.108$
$Z = 6 (T_0 = 4)$	$t_d^* = 0.339$ $t_w^* = -0.110$ $t_p^* = 0.122$	$t_d^* = 0.194$ $t_w^* = 0.093$ $t_p^* = 0.108$	$t_d^* = 0.087$ $t_w^* = 0.224$ $t_p^* = 0.105$

$E = 20, \quad \Pi = 0.15, \quad \theta_f = 0.001, \quad \theta_c = 0.5.$

consumption four times as important as leisure in the individual's utility function and corresponds to the specification in chapter 5 (cf. table 5.1). The production function at the firm level has been specified as $x = l^{0.8}$. Finally we have assumed that the firm's mobility cost function, $\rho(n)$, and the marginal transportation cost function for consumers, $\tau'(c^F)$, are linearly increasing in n and c^F, respectively:

$$\rho(n) = \theta_f \, n,$$
$$\tau'(c^F) = \theta_c \, c^F.$$

There are no literature estimates to draw on for the specification of mobility costs and the simulation assumes $\theta_f = 0.001$ and $\theta_c = 0.5$. Based on these values, table 11.1 presents our optimal tax calculations for different values of the elasticity of substitution in consumption (σ) and the amount of lump-sum profit income (Z). Note that optimal tax rates are expressed in *ad valorem* form, i.e., $t_w^* = t_w/w$, $t_p^* = t_p/\Pi$ and $t_d^* = t_d/1 = t_d$. Furthermore, to maintain comparability between cases where exogenous income levels differ, we have simultaneously varied the exogenous revenue requirement T_0, thus maintaining a roughly constant ratio of tax revenues to national income.

The results show that the exogenous parameter variations carried out here have very little influence on the optimal profit tax rate t_p^*, which is determined primarily by the mobility cost parameter θ_f. However, the chosen values of σ and Z are clearly critical for the optimal mix of wage and consumption taxes. As expected from proposition 11.3 of our theoretical discussion, the role of consumption taxes increases when the share of exogenous income rises. It is also seen that a higher elasticity of substitution reduces the role of consumption taxes and increases the role of wage taxation. This can be explained from the fact that the base of the consumption tax is more elastic than the base of the wage tax, since it is reduced by both the increased consumption of leisure and the purchases in the foreign country. For any given level of non-wage income, an increase in the substitution elasticity thus shifts the balance between the two instruments in favour of the wage tax.

Note that there is only one case where the optimal tax rate on wages is negative. This occurs in the lower left corner of table 11.1 where the exogenous income component is high and the substitution elasticity is low. The combination of these factors makes it optimal to put a high indirect tax on all sources of income and partly relieve labour from the tax burden by offering a wage subsidy. Except from such special cases, however, the framework employed in this chapter is able to generate an optimal tax system where profits, wages and consumption are simultaneously taxed at positive rates.

11.4 Discussion of results and policy implications

Our results in this chapter are best summarised on the basis of two basic identities. First, the value of output produced in the small open economy must equal the sum of gross wages paid and profit income earned

$$npx = n(wl + \pi) = wL + n\pi. \tag{11.27}$$

On the other hand, the income of the representative household – which consists of net wage earnings and exogenous income – must be spent either domestically or on cross-border purchases (gross of transportation costs)

$$\omega L + Z = qc^H + c^F + \tau(c^F). \tag{11.28}$$

From these two equations the relationships between the different tax bases are immediately apparent. On the production side (11.27), an origin-based commodity tax (i.e. a tax on output) equals a tax on wages and an equal-rate tax on profits, so that only two of these three taxes can be independent instruments. What cannot be seen from this identity is the optimal rate of profit taxation, which is directly linked to the degree to which profit-making firms are mobile internationally.

On the consumption side (11.28), there are two differences between the tax bases of a wage tax and a destination-based commodity tax (i.e. a consumption tax): the base of the consumption tax (c^H) includes the exogenous income component Z, but falls short of aggregate net income because of cross-border shopping. Because of this trade-off involved in the choice of the tax base, the most likely outcome is a combination of positive tax rates on wage income and domestic consumption in the government's optimum.

The basic equivalences in (11.27) and (11.28) can be used to compare our results with some of the propositions obtained in the related analysis by Richter (2000). In this paper Richter extends the framework presented in section 11.1 by considering perfectly mobile households which cause positive marginal costs ('congestion costs') for the provision of a public consumption good. Symmetrically there are positive marginal costs of providing public inputs to perfectly mobile firms. As in the present model, labour supply is endogenous and households may dispose of an additional, exogenous source of income. The set of tax instruments available to the government consists of a poll tax on households, a profit tax on firms and destination- and origin-based commodity taxes. In contrast to our analysis above, there is no tax on wage income in his model.

The absence of a wage tax in Richter's (2000) model is in turn closely linked to the absence of cross-border shopping. It is seen from the household budget constraint (11.28) that a tax on domestic consumption dominates a wage tax in this case, because it allows the simultaneous taxation of the exogenous income component Z. In the absence of a wage tax, both identities (11.27) and (11.28) must be used to see how a production tax can be replicated. The necessary tax instruments are (i) a tax on profits, (ii) a tax on consumption and (iii) a lump-sum tax (poll tax); this is Richter's (2000) proposition 2. In the special case where lump-sum income is zero, a wage tax and a consumption tax are equivalent in Richter's framework so that a production tax is equivalent to a consumption tax plus a tax on profits (Richter's proposition 4). This proposition is fully compatible with proposition 11.1. If lump-sum income is raised above zero, then the consumption tax becomes partly a lump-sum instrument, and is raised in the optimum (Richter, 2000, corollary 2). This result conforms with proposition 11.3.

Turning to the policy implications of our analysis, let us first briefly mention the role of profit taxation. Positive taxes on profits have been explained in the above analysis by assuming the existence of mobility costs. While such costs are likely to exist in practice, the crucial problem for the government is to obtain information on their *level*. This is difficult, in particular, when the mobility costs differ for firms operating in different sectors and are private information. This issue has been addressed by Osmundsen, Hagen and Schjelderup (1998), who show that a possible revelation mechanism is for the government to offer alternative tax packages that either consist of high lump-sum taxes ('registration fees') and low taxes on investment, or vice versa. As we have discussed in section 7.3, this self-selection mechanism can be implemented within a conventional corporate income tax system where different tax rates on investment are achieved by alternative depreciation allowances.

Of course, the ability of governments to tax corporate profits also depends on the rents that firms can earn by locating in a particular country. These rents have been modelled in the present chapter in a very simple way, by assuming that there is a fixed level of public inputs which does not have to be remunerated by the firm. In chapter 12 we will analyse the interaction between location rents and corporate profit taxation in more detail by explicitly modelling imperfect competition in product markets and introducing an asymmetry between the competing countries through the combination of trade costs and differences in market size.

In the analysis of the present chapter, the more direct policy implications lie in the field of commodity taxation. Our main result has been that a destination-based commodity tax is likely to dominate an origin-based tax in a second-best setting where optimal factor taxation is simultaneously taken into account. This result has been obtained even though the analysis has incorporated cross-border shopping, in a way similar to the treatment in chapter 8.

This overall conclusion can be broken down into two parts. On the one hand, an origin-based commodity tax constitutes no independent instrument when factor taxes can simultaneously be optimised. To demonstrate this result, it has been crucial to switch to a model where firms, rather than capital, are internationally mobile. Since an origin-based consumption tax falls on pure profits and wages, but not on the normal return to capital, destination- and origin-based commodity taxes are equivalent in a setting with capital mobility (see section 9.2). This equivalence breaks down in the presence of mobile firms, however, and an origin-based VAT becomes effectively a tax on production. Even in this case factor taxes will duplicate an origin-based commodity tax only if the latter is levied uniformly on all goods and services. However, as our detailed analysis in part 3 of this book has shown, these are precisely the conditions under which a switch to the origin principle is attractive in isolated models of commodity taxation.

On the other hand, the destination-based commodity tax remains an independent instrument in the government's tax mix whenever some components of national income escape factor taxation. An example of the latter is foreign-earned profit income which often cannot be effectively taxed by a residence-based income tax, even if this instrument is nominally in place. In this case a consumption tax represents the only way to (indirectly) tax these incomes by means of higher consumer prices at home. The incomplete taxation of capital income is therefore an important argument in favour of maintaining destination-based commodity taxes, despite the distortions caused by this tax through cross-border shopping.

APPENDIX

Derivation of (11.26a)–(11.26b)

Exploiting the similarity between the derivatives $\partial\pi/\partial t_d$ and $\partial\pi/\partial t_w$ in (11.14)–(11.15), we can rewrite the first-order conditions for the consumption tax and the wage tax ((11.17), (11.18a)–(11.18b)) as

$$\frac{\partial \mathcal{L}}{\partial t_w} = -L + \lambda\left(L - t_d \frac{\partial c^H}{\partial \omega} - \varepsilon \frac{\partial L}{\partial \omega}\right) = 0, \tag{11A.1}$$

$$\frac{\partial \mathcal{L}}{\partial t_d} = -c^H + \lambda\left(c^H + t_d \frac{\partial c^H}{\partial q} + \varepsilon \frac{\partial L}{\partial q}\right) = 0 \quad \text{if } c^F > 0, \tag{11A.2a}$$

$$\frac{\partial \mathcal{L}}{\partial t_d} = -C + \lambda\left(c^H + t_d \frac{\partial c^H}{\partial q} + \varepsilon \frac{\partial L}{\partial q}\right) = 0 \quad \text{if } c^F \le 0, \tag{11A.2b}$$

where

$$\varepsilon \equiv \alpha + \frac{\rho'}{(1+\rho'\beta)}\frac{1}{l}\frac{\gamma}{\lambda} \tag{11A.3}$$

can be interpreted as an adjusted effective tax rate on labour, and α and γ are given in (11.21) and (11.22). Uncompensated commodity demand and labour supply functions are decomposed using the Slutsky equations. Denoting a compensated derivative by a tilde ($\tilde{}$) and nominal income by y gives

$$\frac{\partial L}{\partial q} = \frac{\partial \tilde{L}}{\partial q} - c^H \frac{\partial L}{\partial y}, \quad \frac{\partial c^H}{\partial q} = \frac{\partial \tilde{c}^H}{\partial q} - c^H \frac{\partial c^H}{\partial y} \quad \text{if } c^F > 0,$$

$$\frac{\partial L}{\partial q} = \frac{\partial \tilde{L}}{\partial q} - C \frac{\partial L}{\partial y}, \quad \frac{\partial c^H}{\partial q} = \frac{\partial \tilde{c}^H}{\partial q} - C \frac{\partial c^H}{\partial y} \quad \text{if } c^F \le 0,$$

$$\frac{\partial L}{\partial \omega} = \frac{\partial \tilde{L}}{\partial \omega} + L \frac{\partial L}{\partial y}, \quad \frac{\partial c^H}{\partial \omega} = \frac{\partial \tilde{c}^H}{\partial \omega} + L \frac{\partial c^H}{\partial y}. \tag{11A.4}$$

Substituting the Slutsky equations (11A.4) into (11A.1) and (11A.2a)–(11A.2b) gives, after division by λ

$$L\varphi = t_d \frac{\partial \tilde{c}^H}{\partial \omega} + \varepsilon \frac{\partial \tilde{L}}{\partial \omega}, \tag{11A.5}$$

$$c^H \varphi = -t_d \frac{\partial \tilde{c}^H}{\partial q} - \varepsilon \frac{\partial \tilde{L}}{\partial q} \quad \text{if } c^F > 0, \tag{11A.6a}$$

$$C\varphi - c^F = -t_d \frac{\partial \tilde{c}^H}{\partial q} - \varepsilon \frac{\partial \tilde{L}}{\partial q} \quad \text{if } c^F \leq 0, \tag{11A.6b}$$

where

$$\varphi = \frac{\lambda - 1}{\lambda} - t_d \frac{\partial c^H}{\partial y} - \varepsilon \frac{\partial L}{\partial y}. \tag{11A.7}$$

To show, for the regime $c^F > 0$, that φ must be positive, we multiply both sides of (11A.6a) by t_d and both sides of (11A.5) by ε. Summing over the two resulting equations gives, in matrix form

$$\varphi(t_d c^H + \varepsilon L) = [t_d \quad \varepsilon] \begin{bmatrix} \dfrac{-\partial \tilde{c}^H}{\partial q} & \dfrac{-\partial \tilde{L}}{\partial q} \\ \dfrac{\partial \tilde{c}^H}{\partial \omega} & \dfrac{\partial \tilde{L}}{\partial \omega} \end{bmatrix} \begin{bmatrix} t_d \\ \varepsilon \end{bmatrix}. \tag{11A.8}$$

The substitution matrix on the right-hand side of (11A.8) is positive semi-definite; hence the right-hand side must be positive, irrespective of the sign of individual tax rates. The bracketed term on the left-hand side of (11A.8) strictly equals the tax revenue collected in the home country when mobility costs are absent ($\rho' = 0$), as can be seen from (11A.3), the Lagrangian (11.13) and (11.21) in the main text. Hence this term must be positive for a positive revenue requirement in the home country, signing $\varphi > 0$. This restates a standard property of the Ramsey optimal commodity tax model (e.g. Myles, 1995, p. 104) in the present context. For the second trade regime $c^F \leq 0$, it is easily checked from (11A.6b) that φ must also be positive.

Next we use $c^H(q, \omega, Y) = C(q, \omega, Y) - c^F(q)$ from (11.7). This gives for both regimes

$$\frac{\partial \tilde{c}^H}{\partial q} = \frac{\partial \tilde{C}}{\partial q} - \frac{\partial c^F}{\partial q}, \qquad \frac{\partial \tilde{c}^H}{\partial \omega} = \frac{\partial \tilde{C}}{\partial \omega}. \tag{11A.9}$$

Multiplying (11A.5) by ω and (11A.6a)–(11A.6b) by q, using (11A.9) and subtracting the two resulting equations gives

$$(qc^H - \omega L)\varphi = -\left(t_d\left[q\frac{\partial\tilde{C}}{\partial q} + \omega\frac{\partial\tilde{C}}{\partial\omega} - q\frac{\partial c^F}{\partial q}\right] + \varepsilon\left[q\frac{\partial\tilde{L}}{\partial q} + \omega\frac{\partial\tilde{L}}{\partial\omega}\right]\right) \quad \text{if } c^F > 0,$$

$$(qC - \omega L)\varphi - qc^F = -\left(t_d\left[q\frac{\partial\tilde{C}}{\partial q} + \omega\frac{\partial\tilde{C}}{\partial\omega} - q\frac{\partial c^F}{\partial q}\right] + \varepsilon\left[q\frac{\partial\tilde{L}}{\partial q} + \omega\frac{\partial\tilde{L}}{\partial\omega}\right]\right) \quad \text{if } c^F \leq 0.$$

But from the homogeneity properties of the compensated commodity demand and labour supply functions, this reduces to

$$(qc^H - \omega L)\varphi = t_d q\frac{\partial c^F}{\partial q} \quad \text{if } c^F > 0, \qquad \text{(11A.10a)}$$

$$(qC - \omega L)\varphi - qc^F = t_d q\frac{\partial c^F}{\partial q} \quad \text{if } c^F \leq 0. \qquad \text{(11A.10b)}$$

The last step is to use the consumer budget constraint (11.9) to transform (11A.10a)–(11A.10b) into equation set (11.26a)–(11.26b) in the main text. ■

12 Country size and the location of monopolists

While the following chapter is also concerned with optimal tax policy in the presence of internationally mobile firms, the focus of the analysis in chapter 11 is changed in several respects. First, firms acted as price-takers in the preceding analysis, quite in line with the competitive paradigm that prevails in most of the literature on capital tax competition. In contrast, we now turn to imperfect competition in product markets. This provides a first link between our analysis and the new trade theory, where imperfectly competitive behaviour of firms plays a central role. We will, however, confine ourselves to the analytically simplest case of a monopoly supplier, thus leaving out strategic interaction at the firm level.

Second, in the analysis below the internationally mobile monopolist will not only service the domestic market of the country in which it chooses to invest, but it will also use this plant as a base from which it supplies consumers in surrounding countries. Hence, the firm will take into consideration both the costs of shipping its products to final consumers and the commodity taxes levied in the country of final consumption. These transport costs are another main model element that we incorporate from the new trade literature. As we will see below, they create a 'home market effect' that critically influences tax competition between countries of different size. The focus on differences in population size allows a direct comparison with the results in chapter 5, where the same asymmetry has been analysed in a standard model of capital tax competition.

The present chapter is organised as follows: section 12.1 describes in some more detail the model elements that we adopt from the new trade literature and briefly summarises some empirical findings on the relevance of taxes and market size effects for international location decisions. The ensuing analysis considers two different settings of tax competition between countries of unequal size trying to attract a foreign-owned monopolist. Section 12.2 describes the basic model, which applies to both policy settings discussed thereafter. Section 12.3 considers the case where exogenously determined trade costs are incurred when goods are shipped between countries. In this case, the only instrument available to each government is a direct profit tax (or subsidy). In section 12.4, the trade costs are replaced by a second policy instrument, which can either be interpreted as a tariff or – closer to a European setting – as a consumption tax. Section 12.5 compares the results of our analysis with related literature. Section 12.6 discusses the policy implications for corporate income tax harmonisation in the European Union.

12.1 Elements of the new trade theory

The traditional analysis of foreign direct investment (FDI) in the trade literature has been carried out in a general equilibrium setting of perfect competition, and it has focused on the role of differences in factor endowments as the underlying reason for international trade.[1] This theory of comparative cost advantages failed, however, to explain the increasing volume of intra-industry trade between countries with similar factor endowments. From this observation, a new paradigm has been developed in international trade theory since the late 1970s, which is based on economies of scale, product differentiation and imperfect competition.

Within this framework of the 'new' trade theory, transport costs play an important role in connection with the existence of scale economies. This is clearly worked out in Krugman's (1980) early model of monopolistic competition with free entry and free mobility of firms. Krugman shows that differences in preferences, rather than differences in factor endowments, determine the direction of trade in this framework. In particular, each of two otherwise identical countries will export the good for which it has the higher domestic demand. The reason for this trade pattern is that there is an incentive to concentrate the production of a good near its largest market, as this will allow firms to realise scale economies while at the same time minimising aggregate transport costs. In the same paper, Krugman also introduces differences in country size and shows that if two countries have the same composition of demand, then the larger country will be a net exporter of the product whose production involves economies of scale (Krugman, 1980, p. 958).

Krugman (1991) later extended these basic ideas to a model of 'economic geography'. In this model the location of monopolistically competitive manufacturing firms is endogenously determined by the

[1] One example for an analysis in this tradition is Bhagwati and Brecher (1980), who establish that international trade can be harmful for a nation in which some of the productive resources are foreign-owned.

migration decisions of workers, whereas an agricultural numeraire good is produced in each region by immobile peasants. Trade costs have two counteracting effects in this framework: on the one hand, they raise the real wage of workers in highly industrialised regions, where many varieties of the manufacturing good are produced. This 'home market effect' offers an incentive to mobile workers in the other (agricultural) region to also move to the industrial core and thus tends to lead to an equilibrium where all firms and workers agglomerate in one region. On the other hand, higher profits can be made in a less populated region, where local competition between manufacturing firms is weaker. Trade costs shield these excess profits from the competition of firms in the densely populated region and this 'competition effect' tends to distribute firms and workers evenly across regions. Depending on the precise combination of parameter values, both an asymmetric agglomeration equilibrium and a symmetric equilibrium are thus possible outcomes in this model.

Another strand in the new trade literature focuses on endogenous changes in the market structure and is applied, in particular, to the decision problems facing multinational firms. Horstman and Markusen (1992) show in a two-firm, two-country setting that three different equilibria can arise in this framework: (i) each firm operates a plant only in its home country and exports its products from there; (ii) only one (monopoly) firm is active in equilibrium and operates in both countries; (iii) both firms operate plants in their home country and also establish a plant in the other market (FDI). Which of these alternative equilibria is realised depends on the combination of unit transport costs and fixed setup costs at the plant and at the firm level. Transport costs are again critical here, as they represent the main argument for setting up a foreign subsidiary and avoiding the costs of shipping goods to final consumers.

Markusen, Morey and Olewiler (1995) have used a similar trade model to study the optimal setting of environmental taxes when production activities cause local pollution and a multinational firm may operate plants in one, both, or none of the competing regions. In this model, the results of tax competition depend mainly on the disutility that consumers derive from the polluting production activity. If this disutility is low, then the two regions will attempt to undercut each other's environmental tax rates, leading to inefficiently low environmental tax rates (or standards) in equilibrium. In the opposite case where the disutility from pollution is high, countries instead compete by increasing their environmental tax rates until the polluting firm is driven from the market. This 'not-in-my-backyard' (NIMBY) scenario can arise only if production causes negative externalities and is thus specific to the analysis of environmental taxation (cf. subsection 3.6.2).

The model used by Markusen, Morey and Olewiler (1995) is too complicated to be solved analytically and the authors simulate special cases to demonstrate their results. For this reason, Rauscher (1995) simplifies the model in two respects: he neglects transport costs and he ignores strategic interaction between firms by focusing on a single monopolist which chooses its place of location among n (not necessarily identical) jurisdictions. Owing to high fixed costs of setting up a plant, the firm will never locate in more than one jurisdiction. In this setting Rauscher compares non-cooperative and cooperative outcomes and obtains analytical results that closely correspond to those derived in the simulation analysis of Markusen, Morey and Olewiler.[2]

In the following, we use a framework similar to that in Rauscher (1995) and model two countries that compete for the location of a single foreign-owned monopolist, which has already opted for FDI rather than exporting from its home base. In contrast to his analysis, however, there are no externalities from local production and the main instrument of the competing governments is a tax on profits. Also, we (re-) introduce trade costs and thus incorporate Krugman's 'home market effect'.

There is empirical evidence that both capital tax rates and market size are important determinants of foreign direct investment.[3] A detailed econometric analysis based on the model of Horstman and Markusen (1992) is performed by Devereux and Griffith (1998). They find that the effective capital tax rate in each of three EU countries covered in their study (France, Germany and the United Kingdom) has a statistically significant negative effect on the decision of a US-based corporation to invest in this country, once the fundamental decision for FDI in Europe has been made. Devereux and Griffith also show that both demand- and supply-based agglomeration indicators have a significant and positive effect on the probability of an EU host country to attract FDI. The latter result conforms with the findings of Cantwell (1994), whose survey of the theoretical and empirical literature on multinational corporations concludes that much of FDI since 1945 has been local-market oriented.

[2] Imperfect competition and agglomeration effects have also been studied in models of public expenditure competition. Walz and Wellisch (1996) set up a model where an agglomeration advantage from the partial non-rivalry of local public inputs interacts with relocation costs for firms. They show that expenditure competition will generally lead to suboptimally high levels of public input provision in this framework, and may also lead to a suboptimal spatial allocation of firms, characterised by excessive agglomeration.

[3] For surveys of the empirical literature on the effects of taxation for inward and outward FDI from a US perspective, see Hines (1997, 1999).

Grubert and Mutti (1996) combine national measures of effective capital taxation with regional dummy variables and show that location decisions within the European Union are more sensitive to a given tax differential than if the same differential arises in other parts of the world. This can be seen as evidence for the general proposition that tax differentials matter more when countries are open to world markets and relatively similar in structure. This proposition is also supported by the elastic response of investment decisions to tax differentials between different US states (see Papke, 1991).

12.2 Description of household and firm behaviour

Households

The following analysis considers a region that is composed of two countries A and B.[4] Two goods are consumed in each country: the numeraire good 2 is produced by competitive firms while good 1 is produced by a monopolist that has already decided to set up a plant in one of the two countries, in order to service the regional market. Preferences in both countries are identical and equal to[5]

$$u^i = \alpha c_1^i - \frac{1}{2}\beta(c_1^i)^2 + c_2^i \quad \forall \quad i \in \{A, B\}, \tag{12.1}$$

where u^i is the utility of a representative household and c_1^i and c_2^i denote the consumption of goods 1 and 2, respectively. We assume that there is a single household in country B, whereas $n > 1$ identical households reside in country A. Therefore, without loss of generality, country A is the large marketplace for good 1 in the region.

Each household supplies one unit of labour and receives a wage rate w, expressed in units of the numeraire good 2. Furthermore, we assume that in each country all government revenue is distributed equally and in a lump-sum fashion across the population. If these revenues are negative, then our treatment implies symmetrically that governments can impose lump-sum taxes on the population. Denoting total tax revenue by T^i, the budget constraints facing a representative household in each region are

$$w + \frac{T^A}{n} = q^A c_1^A + c_2^A, \qquad w + T^B = q^B c_1^B + c_2^B, \tag{12.2}$$

[4] Sections 12.2–12.4 are a revised and adapted version of Haufler and Wooton (1999).

[5] The quadratic utility function in (12.1) is frequently used in the new trade literature because it offers a simple way to compare welfare levels in different market equilibria (cf. Horstman and Markusen, 1992).

where q^i is the consumer price of good 1 in country i. Maximisation of (12.1) subject to the budget constraint (12.2) yields the representative household's inverse demand for good 1

$$\alpha - \beta c_1^i = q^i \quad \forall \quad i \in \{A, B\}.$$

Note that the individual's tax receipts or payments do not enter the demand function for good 1 since, at the margin, income changes affect only the demand for the numeraire good 2. Aggregating over households in country A and rewriting yields the market demand curves for the two countries

$$C_1^A = nc_1^A = \frac{n(\alpha - q^A)}{\beta}$$

$$C_1^B = c_1^B = \frac{\alpha - q^B}{\beta}. \tag{12.3}$$

Figure 12.1 shows that the inverse market demand curve $q^i(C_1^i)$ is steeper in the small country B, as compared to country A. This has immediate implications for the optimal price policy of the monopolist, to which we now turn.

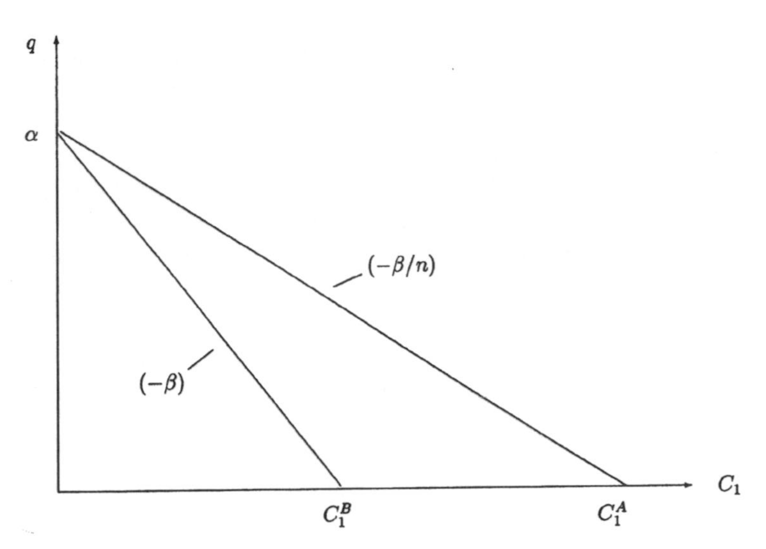

Figure 12.1 Market demand curves when countries differ in size

The firm

We assume that the regional market for good 1 is served by a foreign-owned monopolist intent on establishing production facilities in either country A or country B. The assumption of a monopolistic market structure avoids strategic considerations at the *firm* level and allows us to focus instead on the competition between the two *governments*. It is known from more general models (Horstmann and Markusen, 1992) that monopoly emerges as an equilibrium market structure when firm-specific fixed costs (representing, for example, investments in research and development or R & D) are sufficiently high to render market entry unprofitable for a second firm.

Given this market structure there are, in principle, four options open to the foreign-owned monopoly: it can (i) locate only in country A; (ii) locate only in country B, (iii) set up a plant in both countries A and B; (iv) export to the entire region from its home base. While there are no conceptual difficulties to analysing all the four cases in our framework, the comparison between options (i) and (ii) is the most interesting in a setting of asymmetric country size. We therefore confine our treatment in the main text to these two options. In the appendix (pp. 304–7) we consider options (iii) and (iv) and derive the conditions under which these options will not be chosen in equilibrium.

We assume that the firm cannot price-discriminate between markets and consequently charges the same producer price p (the consumer price net of trade costs), irrespective of the country in which the good is sold. This assumption can be motivated either by the existence of a common competition policy as in the Union, or by international anti-dumping regulations which prohibit price discrimination between markets. The consumer price of good 1 in country i will, however, depend on whether it is locally produced or imported from the other country in the region, as imports incur a trade cost of τ^i per unit.[6] We therefore have to distinguish between the cases of the monopolist setting up in country A and it establishing production facilities in country B. Let q_j^i denote the consumer price of good 1 in country i when it is manufactured in country j. This leads to the following price relations

$$\begin{aligned} &q_A^A = p^A, \qquad && q_A^B = p^A + \tau^B \qquad && \text{for FDI in country } A, \\ &q_B^A = p^B + \tau^A, \qquad && q_B^B = p^B \qquad && \text{for FDI in country } B. \end{aligned} \tag{12.4}$$

[6] In section 12.4 the price wedge between markets will instead take the form of a tariff or a consumption tax. Good 2 is assumed to be freely traded at all times (i.e. without trade costs or tariffs).

We assume a very simple production structure. There is a symmetric fixed cost F of setting up production in either country, which is sufficiently large to ensure that the firm will not choose to operate plants in both countries. Labour is the single factor of production and the production technology has constant returns to scale. The input of one unit of labour is necessary for the production of one unit of good 1, so that marginal cost equals the wage rate w. In order to focus on differences in country size we assume that the wage rate is identical in both countries.

The host country can levy a lump-sum tax (subsidy, if negative) on the firm's profits if it sets up operations within its frontiers. In a stylised form, this tax instrument incorporates both direct investment subsidies paid to firms and (cash-flow) taxes on pure profits.[7] In general, these profit taxes can serve to appropriate any location-specific rent, for example the possession of a natural resource. Our focus in the following will be on the rents generated by savings in aggregate transportation costs.

Let the tax set by host country i be t^i. Net profits of a firm based in country i will be its profits from sales in both countries, less the (symmetric) fixed setup cost F and the country-specific profit tax t^i. This assumes, as before, that profits are taxed under the source principle. Since C_1^i are the firm's aggregate sales in each country, net profits are given by

$$\pi^A = (p^A - w)\left[C_1^A(q_A^A) + C_1^B(q_A^B)\right] - F - t^A \qquad \text{for FDI in country } A,$$
$$\pi^B = (p^B - w)\left[C_1^A(q_B^A) + C_1^B(q_B^B)\right] - F - t^B \qquad \text{for FDI in country } B.$$

Substituting the demand equations (12.3) and the consumer price definitions (12.4) yields

$$\pi^A = \frac{(p^A - w)}{\beta}\left[(\alpha - p^A)(n+1) - \tau^B\right] - F - t^A,$$

$$\pi^B = \frac{(p^B - w)}{\beta}\left[(\alpha - p^B)(n+1) - n\tau^A\right] - F - t^B. \tag{12.5}$$

The optimal price policy of the firm will generally depend on its choice of location. Differentiating each of the profit expressions in (12.5) and solving for the optimal prices yields

[7] Since the taxes modelled here are lump-sum, the difference between (more convenient) unit taxes and (more realistic) proportional taxes does not matter, even under imperfect competition. Cf., however, n. 5 in chapter 4.

$$\hat{p}^A = \frac{1}{2}\left[\alpha + w - \frac{\tau^B}{(n+1)}\right] \quad \text{for FDI in country } A,$$

$$\hat{p}^B = \frac{1}{2}\left[\alpha + w - \frac{n\tau^A}{(n+1)}\right] \quad \text{for FDI in country } B. \tag{12.6}$$

Note that prices are independent of the lump-sum taxes on establishment set by each country, but do depend on the trade cost. If trade costs are the same in both directions ($\tau^A = \tau^B$), then the firm will charge a lower producer price if it settles in the smaller country B. This price policy is linked to the fact that the firm minimises overall trade costs by producing in country A. Hence there is an incentive for the firm to locate in the larger market – the 'home market effect' introduced in section 12.1 – if wages and tax rates are equal in the two countries.

Inserting (12.6) into (12.5) gives the maximum profits attainable from locating in a particular country:[8]

$$\hat{\pi}^A = \frac{[(n+1)(\alpha - w) - \tau^B]^2}{4(n+1)\beta} - F - t^A,$$

$$\hat{\pi}^B = \frac{[(n+1)(\alpha - w) - n\tau^A]^2}{4(n+1)\beta} - F - t^B. \tag{12.7}$$

The firm will be indifferent between locating in country A or country B if $\hat{\pi}^A = \hat{\pi}^B$. We define by $\Gamma \equiv t^A - t^B$ the amount by which country A's tax can exceed that of country B and still leave the firm indifferent between production locations. This 'tax premium' that the firm is willing to pay for locating in country A is given by

$$\Gamma = \frac{[2(n+1)(\alpha - w) - n\tau^A - \tau^B](n\tau^A - \tau^B)}{4(n+1)\beta}. \tag{12.8}$$

Equation (12.8) determines the location decision of the firm for any given set of tax rates t^i and transport costs τ^i. In the following we will consider two different cases. In section 12.3, transport costs are exogenous and assumed to be equal across countries so that tax competition between national governments occurs solely with respect to the lump-sum tax t^i. In section 12.4, the transport costs are re-interpreted as tariffs or – equivalently in the present framework – consumption taxes on good 1. Hence governments have two instruments at their disposal and we will

[8] We assume that gross profits are strictly positive in both countries, i.e., the profit margin implied by the choice of the exogenous parameters α, w and τ is sufficiently large to cover the fixed costs F.

analyse how this affects the outcome of tax competition between the large and the small country.

12.3 Tax competition with symmetric transport costs

In this section we assume that trade costs (transport costs) are exogenous and equal to τ per unit, no matter in which direction good 1 is shipped. In this case (12.8) simplifies to

$$\Gamma = \left[(n-1)\left(\alpha - w - \frac{\tau}{2}\right)\right]\frac{\tau}{2\beta}. \tag{12.9}$$

This expression is zero when countries are of equal size ($n = 1$); the model is then completely symmetric and the firm has no preferences for locating in either country. For $n > 1$, however, Γ must be unambiguously positive since $\alpha - w - \tau/2 > 0$ gives the average of the gross profits earned from selling the *first* unit of output in the two markets. Thus country A can set a higher tax rate than country B, yet still attract the firm. We note that this result is not confined to the case of linear demand functions, but will hold for any downward sloping market demand curve, as long as preferences in the two countries are identical. Furthermore, differentiating (12.9) with respect to τ gives

$$\frac{d\Gamma}{d\tau} = \frac{(n-1)(\alpha - w - \tau)}{2\beta},$$

which is positive for positive sales in the importing region. Hence the tax premium that the firm is willing to pay for locating in country A is larger, the greater are the per-unit trade costs τ.

Each government compares the welfare of its representative household when the country is host to the firm to the welfare level under importing. The income of the representative household in country A arises from the earnings from employment together with its share of any tax revenues collected (and redistributed lump-sum) by the government. Thus the household's budget constraint in country A (cf. (12.2)) is

$$\begin{aligned} q_A^A c_1^A + c_2^A &= w + \frac{t^A}{n} \quad \text{for FDI in country } A, \\ q_B^A c_1^A + c_2^A &= w \quad \text{for FDI in country } B. \end{aligned} \tag{12.10}$$

Substituting (12.10) together with the demand function (12.3), the consumer price definitions (12.4) and the firm's profit-maximising producer prices (12.6) into the utility function (12.1) yields for country A

$$u_A^A = \frac{1}{2\beta}\left[\frac{(n+1)(\alpha - w) + \tau}{2(n+1)}\right]^2 + w + \frac{t^A}{n},$$

$$u_B^A = \frac{1}{2\beta}\left[\frac{(n+1)(\alpha - w) - (n+2)\tau}{2(n+1)}\right]^2 + w. \qquad (12.11)$$

The government of country A (and its citizens) will be indifferent between being the host and importing the good when $u_A^A = u_B^A$. This equality determines the minimal tax rate, or the maximum subsidy, that country A is willing to offer in order to attract the firm. Solving for this tax rate, which is denoted by $\tilde{t}^A$, gives

$$\tilde{t}^A = \frac{-n(n+3)\tau[2(\alpha - w) - \tau]}{8(n+1)\beta} < 0. \qquad (12.12)$$

Thus country A would be prepared to subsidise the firm in order to induce it to locate within its borders. As home production reduces the consumer price for good 1 in country A, relative to importing, a lump-sum subsidy can be paid to the firm that still leaves consumers in country A equally well off than if they had to import good 1 from country B. The gains to consumers in country A arise because q_A^A (the consumer price with home production) is lower than than q_B^A (the consumer price with importing). Note that this result is not trivial because we know from (12.6) that the firm's producer price will be higher if it locates in country A. However, the difference in producer prices will be less than the trade cost per unit; this follows from the well-known textbook result that a monopolist will not find it optimal to fully shift a cost increase into consumer prices, if demand functions are linear (cf. Myles, 1995, p. 361).

Similar calculations can be carried out for country B. The household budget constraint for this country is

$$\begin{aligned} q_A^B c_1^B + c_2^B &= w && \text{for FDI in country } A, \\ q_B^B c_1^B + c_2^B &= w + t^B && \text{for FDI in country } B. \end{aligned} \qquad (12.13)$$

Substituting (12.13) along with (12.3), (12.4) and (12.6) into the utility function (12.1) gives for country B

$$u_A^B = \frac{1}{2\beta}\left[\frac{(n+1)(\alpha - w) - (2n+1)\tau}{2(n+1)}\right]^2 + w,$$

$$u_B^B = \frac{1}{2\beta}\left[\frac{(n+1)(\alpha - w) + n\tau}{2(n+1)}\right]^2 + w + t^B. \qquad (12.14)$$

Setting $u_A^B = u_B^B$ determines the tax rate at which country B is indifferent between having good 1 produced at home or abroad

$$\tilde{t}^B = \frac{-(3n+1)\tau[2(\alpha - w) - \tau]}{8(n+1)\beta} < 0. \tag{12.15}$$

Thus, country B is also ready to offer a subsidy in order to get the FDI and save transportation costs. To see which of the two countries offers the higher subsidy we compare the tax rates in (12.12) and (12.15) and define $\Delta \equiv \tilde{t}^A - \tilde{t}^B$ to be the difference between the profit tax rates at which both countries would be indifferent between being host and importer. This gives

$$\Delta = \frac{-(n^2 - 1)\tau[2(\alpha - w) - \tau]}{8(n+1)\beta} < 0. \tag{12.16}$$

Hence country A is always prepared to offer a bigger subsidy to the firm than would be offered by country B. This result seems surprising at first glance since, from the argument made above, country B not only saves transport costs if it is able to attract the firm, but the producer price (12.6) will also be lower in this case. There is a counteracting effect, however, since the *per capita costs* of the subsidy are smaller in country A, where a larger number of residents share the aggregate tax burden. For the utility specification chosen here, this 'club-good' argument is the dominant effect, and country A offers the higher subsidy.[9]

The next step is to bring together (12.9) and (12.16), which summarise the conditions under which the firm on the one hand and the two governments on the other are indifferent between the two alternative outcomes. From (12.9) we know that the firm is willing to accept a higher tax level in country A and still locate there, whereas (12.16) states that the maximum subsidy country A would be willing to offer is higher than that of country B. Hence it is immediately clear in this setting of exogenous and equal transport costs that the firm will settle in the large country A.

However, to attract the firm, country A need not actually pay the subsidy $\tilde{t}^A$; it suffices to slightly improve (from the perspective of the firm) on the best offer of country B in order to get the investment.[10] Country A's *optimal* tax rate is thus $\hat{t}^A \equiv \tilde{t}^B + \Gamma$. Given country B's best offer, this is the maximum tax that country A can charge while keeping the firm indifferent between locations. Note that the firm will always

[9] With more general utility and demand functions it may not be possible to unambiguously sign the term Δ in (12.16). However, as the following discussion will show, this is also not required for the main argument.

[10] This is a standard result from the theory of auctions: the winner of the auction pays a price equal to the valuation of his last remaining rival and earns some economic rent. (See, e.g., McAfee and McMillan, 1987.)

make positive net profits in equilibrium, because gross profits are positive in country B (cf. n. 8) and country B's best offer involves a subsidy to the firm.

Taking country B's best offer from (12.15) and substituting into (12.9) yields

$$\hat{t}^A = \frac{(2n^2 - 3n - 3)\tau[2(\alpha - w) - \tau]}{8(n+1)\beta}. \tag{12.17}$$

A slightly lower tax (higher subsidy) than given in (12.17) will guarantee that the firm sets up in country A. From the quadratic term in the numerator of the equation, one can establish that country A will actually be able to charge a *positive* profit tax if its market is sufficiently large, relative to that of country B. The critical value at which country A's optimal tax rate turns positive is easily calculated to be $n \approx 2.19$.

Furthermore, we can differentiate $\hat{t}^A$ with respect to relative market size. This gives

$$\frac{d\hat{t}^A}{dn} = \frac{n(n+2)\tau[2(\alpha - w) - \tau]}{4(n+1)^2\beta} > 0.$$

Intuitively, $\hat{t}^A$ balances the firm's gains from locating in country A (as expressed by Γ in (12.8)) and country B's gains from attracting the firm, as incorporated in the negative value of $\tilde{t}^B$ (12.15). Raising n will increase the firm's interest in locating in country A, but leave $\tilde{t}^B$ unchanged; hence country A's optimal tax can unambiguously be raised.[11]

Finally, we can compare the two countries' *per capita* welfare levels in the resulting locational equilibrium. Note that country A's welfare if it is host cannot fall below the level of u_B^A in (12.11), and it will actually be higher since country A does not have to offer the tax rate $\hat{t}^A$ to get the firm. Since, for $n > 1$, u_B^A is in turn greater than u_A^B in (12.14), the *per capita* utility level that country A achieves in equilibrium must exceed the utility level obtained by country B. These results are summarised in

Proposition 12.1

In the presence of exogenous and symmetric trade costs, the large country will be able to attract the foreign-owned monopolist and will achieve a higher welfare

[11] In contrast, a variation in the level of transport costs τ will lead to a proportional increase in the firm's willingness to pay a tax premium in country A *and* in country B's willingness to subsidise the firm. Hence τ represents a 'multiplier' for country A's optimal tax rate, for both positive and negative values of $\hat{t}^A$. In the borderline case $\hat{t}^A = 0$ the two effects net out to zero; this explains why the threshold level at which country A's optimal tax rate turns positive is independent of the level of τ.

level per capita *as compared to the small country. If the size difference between the two countries is sufficiently large, then the large country will charge a positive profit tax rate in the locational equilibrium.*

Note the difference between proposition 12.1 and our earlier analysis of capital tax competition between countries of different size in chapter 5. In the standard tax competition model, the *small* country 'wins' the competition for internationally mobile capital, in the sense that it attracts a higher than proportional share of mobile capital and thus achieves a higher *per capita* utility level than the larger region (proposition 5.1). In contrast, the *large* region 'wins' the competition for FDI in the present model in that it attracts the foreign firm and achieves the higher *per capita* welfare level in the locational equilibrium. The critical difference between the two approaches lies in the existence of trade costs which give the firm an incentive to locate in the larger market, other things being equal.

One caveat to our analysis is that the firm always has the outside option of not locating in the region at all, but rather to export to both countries A and B from its home base. Thus there may be an additional limit to the taxing power of the large country A which is not modelled here. The exporting vs. FDI decision has been extensively discussed in the trade literature, including the studies by Horstman and Markusen (1992) and Markusen, Moley and Olewiler (1995) introduced in section 12.1. In particular, it has been shown by Norman and Motta (1993) and Motta and Norman (1996) that continuing integration within a union makes local production in *one of* the union countries more attractive because it reduces the costs of exporting from this country to its union partners, relative to the costs of exporting from a third (non-member) state. Hence as long as extra-regional trade costs and tariffs are sufficiently high, relative to the fixed cost component F, the firm will have an incentive to invest in country A at all relevant levels of $\hat{t}^A$. The precise conditions under which the firm's exporting option does not constrain the taxing power of country A are derived in the appendix.

12.4 Tax competition with two instruments

We now assume that the wedge between the consumer prices in the two markets arises not from an exogenous trade cost, but from a trade tax chosen optimally by each of the two countries. For simplicity, we will generally refer to this trade tax as a tariff, but emphasise that the additional instrument can equivalently be seen as a consumption tax. The equivalence is strict in the present model because there is no domestic production of good 1 in the importing country.[12] The interpretation of the trade tax as a consumption tax is, of course, especially important in an EU context. As is argued, for example, in Keen (1987, 1989) there is evidence that nationally chosen levels of specific commodity taxation in the Union include a strategic element to improve the terms of trade and thus act as a partial substitute for import tariffs (cf. section 3.1).

The trade tax instrument introduces a third stage into the game played between the two countries in the region. In the first stage, each country sets its profit tax rate t^i. In the second stage, the firm locates in either country A or country B and in the third stage the importing country chooses its optimal tariff. Hence countries commit to profit taxes *before* the firm settles in a particular country, whereas tariffs are chosen *after* the location decision has been made. This sequence can be justified as follows: since the firm knows that each country would like to raise its profit tax rate, once it has settled in their jurisdiction and incurred the fixed cost F, it will insist that the host country commits to an announced profit tax policy or subsidy payment. One example where such a commitment is clearly possible is when the subsidy takes the form of investments in public infrastructure. In contrast, trade or commodity tax policies are less directly tied to the location decision of the firm and are generally subject to change at any point in time, for example because of changing revenue needs. Hence countries will not be able to credibly commit to a given level of tariffs or consumption taxes before the firm makes its location choice.

As usual, the game is solved by backward induction. To incorporate the additional policy instrument, we must first modify the budget constraints to take into account that tariffs – in contrast to transportation costs – represent a source of revenues for the importing country. Hence the budget constraint for country A is now

$$\begin{aligned} q_A^A c_1^A + c_2^A &= w + \frac{t^A}{n} && \text{for FDI in country } A, \\ q_B^A c_1^A + c_2^A &= w + \tau^A c_1^A && \text{for FDI in country } B, \end{aligned} \qquad (12.18)$$

and similarly for country B

[12] If the tax is interpreted as a consumption tax, then this instrument is also available, in principle, to the host country of the investment. However, the only reason for the host country to employ the specific commodity tax is to indirectly tax the profits of the firm. But this can be done directly with the profit tax t^i, which does not distort the consumer's choice between goods 1 and 2. Hence, in the optimum, the host country will always choose *not* to employ the commodity tax, and this is why this instrument can be neglected from the outset.

$$\begin{aligned} q_A^B c_1^B + c_2^B &= w + \tau^B c_1^B && \text{for FDI in country } A, \\ q_B^B c_1^B + c_2^B &= w + t^B && \text{for FDI in country } B. \end{aligned} \tag{12.19}$$

Recall that, owing to our assumption of quasi-linear preferences, this change in the representative individual's budget constraint has no effect on the market demand functions for good 1 (12.3). Furthermore, the profit-maximising price chosen by the firm in each particular location is independent of the source of the trade cost. Hence, the model presented in section 12.2 is completely unchanged when we replace exogenous transportation costs by endogenously chosen tariffs. Note, however, that (12.8) – which summarises the conditions under which the firm is indifferent between locations – now depends on both the tariffs and the profit tax rates chosen by the two governments.

Governments again compare the utility of the representative consumer in the situations where the monopolist locates at home or abroad. Incorporating the budget constraints (12.18)–(12.19) and using (12.3), (12.4) and (12.6) gives for country A

$$\begin{aligned} u_A^A &= \frac{1}{2\beta}\left[\frac{(n+1)(\alpha-w)+\tau^B}{2(n+1)}\right]^2 + w + \frac{t^A}{n}, \\ u_B^A &= \frac{1}{2\beta}\left[\frac{(n+1)(\alpha-w)+n\tau^A}{2(n+1)}\right]^2 + w - \frac{(\tau^A)^2}{2\beta}, \end{aligned} \tag{12.20}$$

and for country B

$$\begin{aligned} u_A^B &= \frac{1}{2\beta}\left[\frac{(n+1)(\alpha-w)+\tau^B}{2(n+1)}\right]^2 + w - \frac{(\tau^B)^2}{2\beta}, \\ u_B^B &= \frac{1}{2\beta}\left[\frac{(n+1)(\alpha-w)+n\tau^A}{2(n+1)}\right]^2 + w + t^B. \end{aligned} \tag{12.21}$$

Comparing (12.20)–(12.21) with the analogous expressions in the case of exogenous transportation costs ((12.11) and (12.14)) shows that the utility expressions are unchanged for the host country, except that they now depend on the tariff in the other region rather than the exogenous transportation cost. In contrast, the utility level for an importing region is changed through the additional revenue collected from the tariff.[13]

[13] In the importing regimes of (12.20)–(12.21), the tariff terms in the square bracket are positive, whereas the corresponding trade cost terms were negative in (12.11) and (12.14). Hence tariff revenue will enter the importing country's utility level with a positive sign, even though the last terms in the importing regimes of (12.20) and (12.21) are negative.

From (12.20) and (12.21) we can now solve for the third stage of the game and determine the optimal tariff that each country will set when it fails to induce the firm to set up local production facilities. The optimal tariff for country A is determined from the second equation in (12.20), whereas country B's optimal tariff is obtained from the first equation in (12.21). Partial differentiation with respect to τ^i yields

$$\hat{\tau}^A = \frac{n(n+1)(\alpha - w)}{(n+2)(3n+2)} > 0,$$
$$\hat{\tau}^B = \frac{(n+1)(\alpha - w)}{(2n+1)(2n+3)} > 0. \tag{12.22}$$

Thus each country will set a positive tariff if it imports good 1. The intuition underlying this result is a conventional terms of trade argument since the tariff reduces the producer price chosen by the monopolist located in the other country (12.6). Furthermore, for $n > 1$ we can see that $\hat{\tau}^A$ must exceed $\hat{\tau}^B$: the numerator is larger, but the denominator is smaller in the optimal tariff formula for country A. Of course, this is because country A, as the larger country, enjoys the greater monopoly power in trade.

The optimal tariffs obtained above can now be used to obtain a condition under which the firm is indifferent between alternative location decisions; this solves the second stage of our game. Given that each country will optimally tax its imports when it cannot attract the firm, the profit tax differential $\Gamma \equiv t^A - t^B$ that leaves the firm indifferent between the two locations is given by inserting (12.22) into (12.8). This yields after tedious, but straightforward manipulations[14]

$$\Gamma = \frac{(\alpha - w)^2 2(n+1)^4 (n-1)}{2\beta\gamma^2}\left[\gamma + 8(n+1)^4 + 16n(n+1)^2 + 3n^2\right], \tag{12.23}$$

where

$$\gamma = (2n+3)(2n+1)(3n+2)(n+2) > 0.$$

Hence the firm is again willing to pay a 'tax premium' for locating in the large market. This premium is now due to two distinct factors: if the firm should locate in country B, then a larger number of its customers face the tariff, and the tariff imposed by country A is higher than the tariff that

[14] Intermediate steps are uninstructive here, and are therefore omitted. A simple way to check the correctness of the results in problems similar to the present one is to use software programs that are able to manipulate algebraic equation systems, such as Maple or Mathematica (see Wolfram, 1999; Varian, 1996).

would be chosen by country B. The first of these two effects is analogous to the case of exogenous transportation costs analysed in section 12.3. The second effect, however, stems from the endogeneity of the trade cost component in a setting where tariffs or consumption taxes are permitted. Overall then, the availability of the new tax instrument tends to further strengthen the incentive for the firm to locate in the large country A.

Turning to the first stage of the game, we now derive the taxes at which governments would be indifferent between importing the good and having local production. Substituting (12.22) into (12.20)–(12.21) gives for country A

$$\hat{u}_A^A = \frac{1}{2\beta}\left[\frac{2(n+1)^2(\alpha-w)}{(2n+3)(2n+1)}\right]^2 + w + \frac{t^A}{n},$$
$$\hat{u}_B^A = \frac{1}{2\beta}\left[\frac{(n+1)^2(\alpha-w)^2}{(3n+2)(n+2)}\right] + w, \tag{12.24}$$

and analogously for country B

$$\hat{u}_A^B = \frac{1}{2\beta}\left[\frac{(n+1)^2(\alpha-w)^2}{(2n+3)(2n+1)}\right]^2 + w,$$
$$\hat{u}_B^B = \frac{1}{2\beta}\left[\frac{2(n+1)^2(\alpha-w)}{(3n+2)(n+2)}\right]^2 + w + t^B. \tag{12.25}$$

Country A is indifferent between being host and being importer when $u_A^A = u_B^A$ in (12.24). This gives the minimum tax (maximum subsidy) that country A is willing to offer the monopolist

$$\tilde{t}^A = \frac{n(n+1)^2(\alpha-w)^2\,\delta^A}{2\beta\,\gamma\,(2n+3)(2n+1)}, \tag{12.26}$$

where $\gamma > 0$ is given in (12.23) and

$$\delta^A = 4n^4 + 8n^3 - 4n^2 - 16n - 7.$$

It is immediately seen that δ^A is negative for $n = 1$ (so that countries are of equal size), but must turn positive for large values of n. To determine the critical value where country A's best offer involves a profit tax of zero, we can either use the mathematical software packages mentioned in n. 14, or an explicit plotting program such as Gnuplot (Williams and Kelley, 1998). With either algebraic or graphical solution methods we can then establish that δ^A (and thus $\tilde{t}^A$) becomes zero for $n \approx 1.40$.

It follows from (12.26) that in contrast to the case of exogenous transportation costs country A will not generally offer a subsidy to attract the firm. The intuition for this result is straightforward: as n increases, country A will set higher tariffs on the import of good 1 and benefit from reduced producer prices forced by its tariff. The existence of the second tax instrument thus increases the bargaining power that country A has *vis-à-vis* the monopolist and will generally enable country A to offer a less favourable tax treatment to the firm.

Analogously, country B is indifferent between being host and being importer when $u_A^B = u_B^B$ in (12.25). This gives country B's best offer to the firm

$$\tilde{t}^B = \frac{(n+1)^2(\alpha - w)^2\, \delta^B}{2\beta\, \gamma\, (3n+2)\, (n+2)}, \tag{12.27}$$

where

$$\delta^B = -7n^4 - 16n^3 - 4n^2 + 8n + 4 < 0.$$

As in section 12.3, country B will thus offer a subsidy to the firm for all values of $n \geq 1$, even though it can set a positive tariff in the case that the firm locates in country A.

Next, we compare the best offers made by countries A and B. Forming $\Delta \equiv \tilde{t}^A - \tilde{t}^B$ and substituting in from (12.26) and (12.27) gives

$$\Delta = \frac{(\alpha - w)^2(n+1)^2(n-1)}{2\beta\gamma^2}\left\{\gamma n + 12(n+1)^4\left[(n+1)^2 + n\right]\right\} > 0. \tag{12.28}$$

Comparing (12.28) with the analogous expression in the case where trade costs were exogenous and symmetric (12.16) shows that country A now offers fewer – rather than more – tax incentives to the firm, relative to country B. This change in the relative tax levels arises because country A now has an improved alternative to local production. If it has to import, it applies a relatively high optimal tariff and collects the tariff revenues.

When trade costs were exogenous, country A was always willing to subsidise the firm's investment more than was country B. Given the preference of the firm for the larger market, this guaranteed that country A was able to induce the firm to set up there. With endogenous tariffs, however, country A is less willing to subsidise FDI, raising the question whether country A will still attract local production. Thus we have to compare $\Gamma - \Delta$ from (12.23) and (12.28). This gives, after straightforward manipulations

$$\Gamma - \Delta = \frac{(\alpha - w)^2 (n+1)^2 (n-1)}{2\beta\gamma^2} \Big\{ (2n^2 + 3n + 2)\, \gamma. + 2(n+1)^2 \Big[2(n+1)^4 + 10n(n+1)^2 + 3n^2 \Big] \Big\} > 0. \tag{12.29}$$

Since this difference is unambiguously positive, country A will still get the firm, even though it imposes the higher profit tax. Hence it is again the efficient solution that prevails in equilibrium – a smaller number of consumers then faces a lower tariff as compared to production in country B. These aggregate efficiency gains can be divided up between the firm and the government of country A, ensuring that the tax premium that the firm is willing to pay for locating in country A exceeds the tax premium implied by country A's best offer.

In the following we assume again that country A is able to appropriate the entire locational rent by offering a tax rate $\hat{t}^A$ that leaves the firm only marginally better off than if it accepted the best offer of country B. Hence $\hat{t}^A = \Gamma + \tilde{t}^B$ and substituting in from (12.23) and (12.27) gives:

$$\hat{t}^A = \frac{(\alpha - w)^2 (n+1)^2}{2\beta\gamma^2} \Big\{ 2(n-1)(n+1)^2 \Big[\gamma + 8(n+1)^4 + 16n(n+1)^2 + 3n^2 \Big] + [4(n+1)^2 - 1]\, \delta^B \Big\}, \tag{12.30}$$

where $\delta^B < 0$ is given in (12.27). To interpret (12.30), let us first consider the benchmark case where countries are of equal size. For $n = 1$ the positive first term in the curly bracket disappears and country A must offer a subsidy to the firm to induce home production. For sufficiently small differences in size, country A's optimal profit tax rate will thus still be negative, even if it has the additional tariff instrument. However, as n increases, the optimal tax rate $\hat{t}^A$ grows more rapidly now than in the case of exogenous transportation costs, and turns positive at a value of $n \approx 1.08$. Hence, in the presence of an additional tariff or consumption tax instrument, even small differences in country size will enable country A to charge a positive profit tax rate in the locational equilibrium.

It is obvious from the above discussion that country A must again have the higher *per capita* welfare level in equilibrium. By an argument analogous to the one made in section 12.3, country A's welfare level as host must be at least as high as u_B^A in (12.24). This in turn can be shown to be greater than u_A^B in (12.25) by comparing the denominators in the two expressions. Our results in this section are summarised in

Proposition 12.2

When countries can impose both profit taxes and tariffs (consumption taxes), the large country will attract the foreign-owned monopolist and will achieve the higher per capita *welfare level. Even for small differences in country size, the large country will charge a positive profit tax rate in the locational equilibrium.*

Proposition 12.2 can again be compared with our analysis in chapter 5. We have seen there that large countries have an advantage with respect to tariff competition (cf. section 5.4), whereas small countries gain from capital tax competition. In the presence of trade costs, however, these effects no longer work in opposite directions. Instead, the large country will win a 'tax war' even if it cannot use its tariff instrument, and the gains will be even larger if this instrument is permitted. Hence, both tax and tariff competition work in favour of the large country.

At the same time, there are also some parallels between the two analyses. In the standard competitive framework of capital tax competition the small country levies the lower tax, since it perceives the higher elasticity of the tax base (cf. section 5.1). In the above model, the small country will also undercut its large neighbour, if both countries have an additional trade tax at their disposal. In this case the weaker monopoly power in trade induces the small country to offer the higher subsidy to the firm, even though the *per capita* cost of a given, aggregate subsidy is higher than in the large region. The small country's higher elasticity of the domestic tax base and its reduced potential to use restrictive trade policies as a bargaining device towards the firm may thus serve as complementary and mutually compatible explanations for the empirical observation that small countries tend to have lower rates of capital taxation.

12.5 Discussion and comparison of results

In the analysis above, trade costs have created a location rent for the large country, allowing this country to extract a positive tax from the monopolist, if the difference in market size is sufficiently high. If exogenous trade costs are replaced by an endogenous tariff or consumption tax instrument, then the bargaining power of the large country *vis-à-vis* the monopolist is further increased and a positive profit tax becomes a likely outcome. Even in this case, however, it is only the size advantage *relative* to the other country which is responsible for the result. If countries were of equal size, then both would offer a lump-sum subsidy for the location of the firm, despite the presence of the tariff instrument.

This brief summary may help to explain the relation between our work and several other contributions on tax competition for internationally mobile firms. Black and Hoyt (1989) consider two cities trying to attract one large and a number of small firms, in order to benefit from scale economies in the provision of public goods. These scale economies thus represent a motive to offer location subsidies, similar to the trade costs above. An asymmetry is introduced into the model by assuming that the firms incur exogenous non-labour costs, which differ between the cities. Black and Hoyt show that under these conditions the *maximum* bid of both countries always involves a subsidy to the firm and the location equilibrium is efficient, as the firm settles in the country with lower exogenous costs. Whether the *equilibrium* profit tax offered by this country is also negative in all cases is not analysed by Black and Hoyt, however.

Another reason for subsidy payments is discussed in Haaparanta (1996). In his analysis the competing countries face different levels of exogenously fixed wages and thus suffer from involuntary unemployment. Haaparanta shows that the high-wage country (with the higher level of unemployment) will always pay the higher subsidy to the firm in equilibrium.[15] As a result, this country may, but need not, attract more capital in the subsidy equilibrium as compared to the case where no subsidy competition occurs. Haaparanta also considers differences in country size, but does not incorporate trade costs into his model. Under these conditions it turns out that model results are driven solely by wage rate differences, whereas differences in market size are inessential for the optimal tax (subsidy) policy.

Fumagalli (2000) considers a model where FDI is associated with positive technological externalities for host countries, and these gains are larger for a 'poor' region. On the other hand, the firm has a profit advantage in the 'rich' region so that it will always locate there when subsidy competition is prohibited. In this model the efficient location of the firm thus depends on the comparison of the differences in technological externalities on the one hand, and the profit advantage of the firm on the other. If the first effect is sufficiently strong, then permitting

[15] The question why countries often use subsidies to capital, rather than labour, is addressed in Fuest and Huber (2000). They set up a model where wages above their market clearing levels arise as an equilibrium outcome from a bargaining process between unions and heterogeneous firms. In this model they show that an investment subsidy, financed by a wage tax, is welfare increasing, since it reduces the bargaining position of unions and raises the number of firms in the economy.

subsidy competition is efficient, because it offers an instrument to the 'poor' region to compete for the internationally mobile firm.

Haaland and Wooton (1999) consider symmetric tax competition for a fixed number of multinational firms. In this model agglomerating forces arise from external economies of scale, which reduce the costs of firms in a region where others have already settled. Counteracting general equilibrium effects arise from rising wages in the region which hosts a large number of firms. Hence, as in Krugman's (1991) model of economic geography (cf. section 12.1), the outcome may either be a concentration of all firms in one region or a symmetric equilibrium with diversified production. Haaland and Wooton find, however, that symmetric subsidy competition will transfer the location rents to multinational firms in *both* of these cases. The intuition is that countries are fully symmetric and even if an agglomeration equilibrium occurs, the absence of trade costs implies that positive rents cannot be extracted by the country hosting the multinational firms.

Kind, Midelfart Knarvik and Schjelderup (2000) explicitly put their model in the economic geography tradition, but change the setting to one where capital is mobile between countries while labour is interregionally immobile. The agglomerating 'home market effect' in Krugman's (1991) framework, which works through the real wage increase of workers in highly industrialised regions, is replaced by a vertical industry linkage that reduces production costs (similar to Haaland and Wooton, 1999). In this model the authors analyse tax competition in each of the two possible equilibria of concentrated or diversified production. In the symmetric equilibrium both countries will again subsidise firms, as the industry linkages offer a benefit to host countries similar to the savings in trade costs in our model, or the economies of scale in Black and Hoyt (1989). In the asymmetric equilibrium, however, the country in which the industry agglomeration takes place will be able to extract some rents from the firms by levying a positive tax rate. This difference from the results in Haaland and Wooton (1999) arises from the incorporation of trade costs, which partly shield the host country from competition by the neighbouring state.

This comparison shows that many results in the literature on tax competition for internationally mobile firms can be explained by two main underlying forces. On the one hand, these models generally incorporate some form of positive externality from FDI. This isolated effect makes each country willing to offer a subsidy to the firm. On the other hand, a country that has some location advantage *vis-à-vis* its competing neighbours will generally be able to extract some rents from the firm, and may also be able to levy a positive tax rate in equilibrium.

This general structure also allows us to explain results in models that seemingly bear little relation to our analysis. Janeba (1998), for example, introduces mobile firms to a symmetric model of strategic trade policy (Brander and Spencer, 1985). In the absence of firm mobility, it is well known from this model that governments engage in a wasteful subsidy race, in an attempt to help their domestic firms secure a higher share in the oligopolistic market. When firms are mobile, however, their profits do not enter the welfare calculations of competing governments and the reason for subsidy payments disappears, given the absence of other (positive) externalities. Hence, as Janeba shows, a second-best efficient zero-tax equilibrium results when tax policy is non-discriminatory. This result, which reverses a highly influential finding in the trade literature, is thus seen to be fully compatible with the analyses above.

Finally, some contributions to this strand of literature also address the interaction of profit taxes and tariffs. An early example is Brander and Spencer (1987), who analyse the optimal tax and tariff policies of a host country towards a foreign-owned firm when there is involuntary unemployment. They show that unemployment induces the host country to attract FDI by setting relatively low rates of capital taxation, but a relatively high tariff. Taken together, these policies lead to a strong 'tariff-jumping' argument and ensure that the foreign firm will locate in the host country, rather than export from its home base.

Raff (2000) studies the effects of preferential trade agreements on tax competition for foreign direct investment. He considers a three-country model where two of the countries (A and B) compete for the location of a firm owned by residents of the third country (C). In the benchmark case, where countries A and B can choose independent tariff policies, the optimal policy in each country is to levy prohibitive tariffs on all imports. This forces the multinational firm to set up a production facility in both countries A and B and eliminates tax competition, allowing each country to fully tax the rents that accrue to the firm in equilibrium. If countries A and B form a free trade area, however, the firm will set up a production facility in only one of the countries in the region, and tax competition will drive the profit tax in the country that obtains the investment below the maximum rate of unity.

12.6 Location rents and corporate taxation in the European Union

Our analysis in this chapter, and the discussion of related work, has pointed out that positive taxes on internationally mobile firms can be levied to the extent that firms obtain rents that are specific to a particular location. If these rents arise at the national level, for example from natural resources or a favourable public infrastructure, then national policy should be able to tax them by means of a corporation tax without causing mobile firms to leave. This may explain why effective tax rates on capital have remained rather stable during the 1980s and the early 1990s (see table 4.1) and corporate tax revenues have even risen in many countries during the same period (see table 2.2). One may then argue, on the basis of this empirical evidence, that individual EU member states still seem to be able to extract a sufficient part of country-specific rents from the firms locating in their jurisdiction.

At the same time, there is at least a theoretical argument that continuing integration in Europe also creates a *common* EU location rent. By this argument, on which the analysis in this chapter has been based, the elimination of internal barriers to trade increases the relevant home market from the perspective of firms outside the Community. Other things being equal, this will increase the incentive of outside firms to build a branch plant in (any) one of the EU countries, in order to gain access to the single European market (cf. Norman and Motta, 1993; Motta and Norman, 1996). Since this rent is shared by all EU members, tax competition between them will imply that the additional profits arising from this rent will remain largely untaxed in equilibrium. If there are positive externalities from FDI, and national location rents are small, tax competition may even lead to subsidies being paid to the firm in equilibrium. In this case there is thus a basic efficiency argument for a harmonised EU corporate tax policy, for example through the introduction of a minimum corporate tax rate (see Keen, 1993a, pp. 33–4).

There are several caveats to this argument, however. One is that an EU-wide minimum corporate tax rate may merely shift competition for the location of internationally mobile firms to other tax instruments, in particular the choice of corporate tax bases (cf. Fuest and Huber 1999a, section 10.5.3). Moreover, the rents earned from locating in Europe will not be the same for all individual firms.[16] Therefore, even an increase in *effective* EU corporation taxes is likely to have two counteracting effects. On the one hand, to the extent that tax competition between EU members currently leads to an undertaxation of corporate profits, the common tax will allow a more effective taxation of those firms which derive relatively high rents from locating in the large European market. On the other hand, the same measure will drive some businesses with low firm-

[16] A related argument, focusing on different transaction costs for individuals, has been made in connection with an EU-wide minimum withholding tax on interest income (section 5.5).

specific EU rents out of production in Europe, and thus impose some extra costs on the Community as a whole. An EU harmonisation measure that is completely free of such trade-offs cannot be expected to exist given that production processes can increasingly be shifted worldwide and 'footloose' industries produce a rising share of national output.

APPENDIX

Section 12A.1 in the appendix analyses the firm's options to export from its home base whereas section 12A.2 considers the case where the firm sets up a plant in *both* countries A and B. We derive conditions under which these options are dominated by the strategies considered in the main text, namely to set up a plant in *either* country A or country B.

12A.1 The firm's exporting option

We index all variables under the exporting option by an index E and denote by s the unit transport costs between the integrated region and the home country of the multinational firm (where $s > \tau$). Consumer prices in countries A and B are then given by

$$q_E^i = p^E + s \quad \forall \quad i \in \{A, B\}. \tag{12A.1}$$

The firm's profits under the exporting option are

$$\pi^E = (p^E - w)[C_1^A(q_E^A) + C_1^B(q_E^B)] = (p^E - w)\left[\frac{(n+1)(\alpha - p^E - s)}{\beta}\right],$$

where w is the going wage rate and we assume that there is no profit taxation in the firm's home country. We assume that price discrimination between the firm's home market and the regional market consisting of countries A and B is possible. The optimal producer price at which to sell in countries A and B is then

$$\hat{p}^E = \frac{1}{2}(\alpha + w - s). \tag{12A.2}$$

Maximised profits are

$$\hat{\pi}^E = \left[\frac{(n+1)(\alpha - w - s)^2}{4\beta}\right]. \tag{12A.3}$$

Quite obviously, the exporting option must become unprofitable for sufficiently high levels of s since, as s approaches $(\alpha - w)$, gross profits under the exporting option will approach zero. In contrast, net profits under FDI will be unambiguously positive under the assumptions made.

More generally, (12A.3) has to be compared with $\hat{\pi}^A$ in the main text (12.7), which is here reproduced for the case of symmetric intra-regional trade costs:

$$\hat{\pi}^A = \frac{[(n+1)(\alpha - w) - \tau]^2}{4(n+1)\beta} - F - t^A.$$

Forming the difference gives:

$$\hat{\pi}^A - \hat{\pi}^E = \frac{[(n+1)(\alpha - w) - \tau]^2 - (\alpha - w - s)^2(n+1)^2}{4\beta(n+1)} - t^A - F. \tag{12A.4}$$

To see under which condition FDI in country A dominates the exporting option, we have to introduce country A's *maximum subsidy* $\tilde{t}^A$ from (12.12) into (12A.4); the condition $\hat{\pi}^A - \hat{\pi}^E > 0$ will then ensure that FDI in country A will actually take place.

A stronger condition must hold if country A's taxing power is not to be constrained by the additional exporting option (see the final paragraph of section 12.3). In this case, country A's *optimal* tax rate $\hat{t}^A$ (12.17) is to be inserted into (12A.4) and $\hat{\pi}^A - \hat{\pi}^E > 0$ must still hold. Inspection of (12A.4) shows immediately that both conditions will be met when the savings in transportation costs $(s - \tau) > 0$ are sufficiently large, relative to the fixed costs F incurred by FDI in country A.

12A.2 Setting up plants in both countries A and B

If the firms sets up a production plant in each of the two regional markets A and B, then it is clear that each plant will serve exactly the local market and there will be no trade in good 1 within the region. This involves zero trade costs and must be cost-minimising since labour costs are w in both countries and plant-specific costs are a fixed sum F. Denoting the two-plant option by an index D, consumer prices in countries A and B are

$$q_D^i = p^D \quad \forall \quad i \in \{A, B\}. \tag{12A.5}$$

Profits under the two-plant option are

$$\pi^D = (p^D - w)[C_1^A(q_D^A) + C_1^B(q_D^B)] - t^A - t^B - 2F,$$

since the firm is now taxed (or subsidised) in both countries A and B, and the fixed plant-specific cost is incurred in both countries. The optimal producer price under this option is

$$\hat{p}^D = \frac{1}{2}\,(\alpha + w), \tag{12A.6}$$

which is higher than for any other option since aggregate trade costs are zero in this case. Maximised profits are then

$$\hat{\pi}^D = \left[\frac{(n+1)(\alpha - w)^2}{4\beta}\right] - t^A - t^B - 2F. \tag{12A.7}$$

For this option to be at least as attractive as settling solely in country A, $\hat{\pi}^D$ in (12A.7) must be equal to $\hat{\pi}^A$ in (12.7). From this we can calculate the maximum tax t_*^B that the firm is willing to pay for setting up a plant in country B *in addition to* its plant in country A:

$$t_*^B = \frac{\tau[2(n+1)(\alpha - w) - \tau]}{4\beta(n+1)} - F. \tag{12A.8}$$

The first term in (12A.8) is positive and gives the gains to the firm of being able to charge a higher producer price (owing to reduced aggregate transport costs) if it maintains plants in both markets in the region. This has to be weighed against the negative second term, which gives the *additional* fixed costs of opening a second plant in country B.

Country B's utility if the firm settles only in country A is given by the expression u_A^B in (12.14) in the main text. Its utility under the two-plant option will differ from u_B^B in (12.14) because the firm's optimal producer price is higher under the two-plant strategy. Substituting (12A.6) along with (12.3), (12.4) and (12.6) in (12.1) gives

$$u_D^B = \frac{(\alpha - w)^2}{8\beta} + w + t^B. \tag{12A.9}$$

Equating u_D^B in (12A.9) with u_A^B in (12.14) gives country B's best offer to attract an additional plant in its own country, given that regional production already occurs in country A. This is

$$\tilde{t}^B = \frac{-(2n+1)\tau}{8\beta(n+1)^2}\,[(2n+1)(\alpha - w - \tau) + (\alpha - w)] < 0, \tag{12A.10}$$

which is unambiguously negative. The conditions under which this offer by country B is *insufficient* to induce the firm to also set up in this country is thus $\Omega \equiv \tilde{t}^B - t_*^B > 0$. Substituting in from (12A.8) and (12A.10) gives

$$\Omega = F - \frac{\tau\omega}{8\beta(n+1)^2}, \qquad (12A.11)$$

where

$$\omega \equiv (2n+1)[(2n+1)(\alpha - w - \tau) + (\alpha - w)] \\ + 2(n+1)[2(n+1)(\alpha - w) - \tau] > 0.$$

It is directly seen from (12A.11) that the option to set up plants in both countries *A* and *B* will not be feasible when *F* is sufficiently high, relative to the intra-regional transport cost parameter τ.

13 Summary and policy conclusions

This study has been concerned with the taxation of commodities and factors of production under conditions of increasing international mobility of capital, consumers, and firms. While most of the literature on international taxation and tax competition has focused on either direct or indirect taxation, we have argued in various parts of this study that there may be important interrelationships between them. These interdependences will also be emphasised below. Before this is done, however, a systematic summary of our main conclusions should clearly distinguish between the positive and normative issues raised by capital taxation on the one hand and commodity taxation on the other.

Capital taxation

Our analysis in this part has proceeded from the basic premise – supported by both theoretical arguments and empirical findings – that the source principle of capital taxation is already dominant in practice and that this trend is likely to become even stronger as capital market integration proceeds. On this basis, the positive part of our analysis has tried to contribute to the understanding of some important stylised facts of capital taxation in open economies.

A benchmark result in the theory of optimal capital taxation is that small countries will find it optimal to set the source-based tax on capital equal to zero if capital mobility is perfect and if they have an alternative wage tax instrument at their disposal. This result suggests that increasing capital mobility should lead to a noticeable shift in the tax burden away from capital and towards labour. While this pattern can be observed, on average, when the development of effective tax rates on capital vs. wage income is compared, it is less pronounced than the theory would suggest, and some countries have even increased the effective rate of capital taxation (chapter 4).

A first explanation for this empirical finding can be based on the combination of imperfect capital mobility and distributive concerns by governments. While capital market integration increases the efficiency costs of capital taxation, it also affects the gross returns to factor owners in different countries. Tax policy may then be directed primarily at compensating the losers from capital market integration, and this implies a shift from labour to capital taxation for a capital exporting country (chapter 6).

A further reason for source-based capital taxes arises when there are pure profits or rents in the economy that cannot be fully taxed by an independent instrument. Existing corporate income taxes can be seen as combined instruments that allow to tax some of these rents, but they also fall partly on investment (chapter 10). This efficiency argument for source-based capital taxes is reinforced by a strategic tax exporting motive when part of the rents accrue to foreigners. Nevertheless, the question remains why the corporation tax is not transformed into a tax on pure profits (cash-flow tax). Instead, corporate tax reforms in most countries have followed a pattern that combines significant reductions in statutory corporate tax rates with less generous depreciation allowances and other measures broadening the tax base.

One explanation for this may lie in the increasing restrictions imposed on governments by the transfer-pricing activities of multinational corporations. In such a setting it can be shown that if the overall revenue requirement from corporate taxation is fixed – for example, for distributive reasons – then a policy that increases the tax base by granting less generous depreciation allowances is a second-best policy to prevent the shifting of paper profits out of the home country (chapter 7).

A further issue in our analysis has been the robust empirical evidence that small countries tend to have lower capital tax rates than their larger neighbours. A simple, yet powerful explanation is that the small country faces the more elastic tax base and hence finds it optimal to use a lower tax. In perfectly competitive markets this implies that the small country will obtain a more than proportional share of capital in equilibrium, raising the possibility that the small country prefers a situation with tax competition to an equilibrium where tax rates are coordinated (chapter 5). This is consistent with the observation that small countries are reluctant to agree to the coordination of taxes on the competitive rate of return to capital.

The competitive model of capital tax competition cannot, however, explain the robust empirical result that foreign direct investment (FDI) tends to concentrate in countries with a large domestic market. To explain this finding we have set up a model where pure profits arise from imperfect competition and there are trade costs for shipping each unit of production to consumers in a foreign country. In this setting the 'home market effect' favours the larger country and allows it to attract an internationally mobile firm, even though its small neighbour offers a lower tax rate on corporate profits (chapter 12).

Turning to policy implications in the field of capital income taxation, the fundamental problem in the area of interest taxation is tax evasion. One proposal for *national* income tax reform to ensure a more effective taxation of interest income is the switch to a dual income tax. The experience with this reform in the Scandinavian countries and Austria has generally been positive and revenues from the taxation of capital income have increased, despite the reduction in statutory tax rates (cf. subsection 2.1.1). From an optimal taxation perspective one core advantage of such a reform is that it offers an additional degree of freedom to respond to differences in the international mobility of the two tax bases.[1] In addition, a reduction in statutory tax rates on capital income may also be attractive from a taxpayer equity perspective, as it reduces the gap between the tax payments of honest taxpayers and those that evade taxation. For these reasons, a dual income tax is considered by several authors to be a promising model for other European states (see, e.g., Cnossen, 1999).

As the experience of the Scandinavian countries shows, however, the taxation of foreign-earned interest income is not rigorously enforced under the dual income tax (cf. table 2.1). Therefore this national reform, even if adopted, does not weaken the case for an international coordination of taxes on interest income. The introduction of an EU-wide notification scheme or a common interest withholding tax in the European Union has to overcome potentially conflicting interests between member states (see above). Moreover, even if a coordinated policy is agreed upon by all EU members, the effectiveness of such a measure is limited in the presence of worldwide capital mobility. A basic efficiency argument for such a policy exists for a large trading bloc like the European Union, and it is reinforced by the existence of differential transaction costs for portfolio investments within and outside Europe. Nevertheless, the gains from this measure are likely to be moderate when it is assumed that per-unit transaction costs for investing in third countries (or in untaxed financial derivatives) are a falling function of the investment volume. In this case, a regionally coordinated interest income tax in Europe will fall primarily on small savers, whereas large investors will be able to escape the tax (section 5.5).

[1] A further, dynamic efficiency argument in favour of this tax reform has been advanced by Nielsen and Sørensen (1997). They argue that investments in human capital (forgone wages) are generally taxed on a cash-flow basis, whereas a positive marginal effective tax rate applies to investments in physical capital. Hence, a reduced tax rate on capital *vis-à-vis* labour income tends to correct for this distortion.

In the field of corporate income taxation, possible international coordination measures encompass both the tax base and the tax rate. There is substantial evidence that the internationalisation of production makes it increasingly difficult to enforce the ruling 'arm's length principle' for the valuation of transfer prices within multinational firms. This leads to strategic profit-shifting into tax havens that erode the corporate tax base in high-tax countries, even if production continues to be carried out there. A systematic approach to this problem would be the introduction of formula apportionment rules, which allocate the profits of multinational corporations between different jurisdictions according to indicators that are less easily manipulated than paper profits. Such rules need to be introduced at a worldwide level, however, in order to avoid either double taxation or new arbitrage opportunities for firms arising from inconsistencies with the existing system of separate accounting (section 7.4).

Meanwhile, the Code of Conduct for business taxation (cf. subsection 2.1.1) may serve to reduce the incentives for individual countries to attract paper profits from internationally mobile firms through discriminatory tax breaks that are not extended to domestic businesses. It can be shown that individual countries always have an incentive to adopt such discriminatory practices, if the domestic tax base is less mobile than the international one.[2] Collectively, this behaviour leads to the complete tax exemption of internationally mobile firms and imposing a worldwide non-discrimination constraint on national governments will unambiguously raise welfare (Janeba and Peters, 1999). However, this argument in favour of tax coordination must again be modified in the presence of third countries that are not part of the agreement. From an EU perspective, the enforcement of non-discrimination rules at an international level, as currently pursued by the OECD, is therefore an important complementary measure to the internal coordination agreement. It remains to be seen whether the relatively informal and vague set of criteria underlying the Code of Conduct, and the means available to the OECD to sanction non-compliant states, will prove to be an effective deterrent for discriminatory business tax policies worldwide.

A further harmonisation proposal in the field of corporate income taxation is the introduction of a minimum corporate tax rate, as recommended in the Ruding Report (1992). Since the ability to tax internationally mobile firms depends critically on the existence of location-specific rents, the case for such a coordination measure is closely tied to the question whether location rents accruing to internationally mobile

[2] This is the same argument, in principle, as made above in favour of the dual income tax.

firms arise primarily at the national or at the EU level. An example of the latter category are location rents that result from access to the single European market (section 12.6). While such rents are likely to exist, countries within Europe still differ widely with respect to the size of local markets, public infrastructure, or labour market conditions. It can be argued from the existing evidence of largely stable effective tax rates on corporate profits that these country-specific rents still dominate the common location rent in Europe. Hence, at this point there seems to be little immediate pressure for the introduction of a minimum EU corporation tax rate. An important precondition for leaving the autonomy over the corporate income tax in the hands of national governments is, however, that cross-country profit-shifting within multinational firms can be effectively reduced by international regulations that complement the ruling arm's length principle.

Commodity taxation

The starting point for our analysis of commodity taxation was the increasing international mobility of consumers. This issue is particularly relevant in – though not confined to – the European internal market, where border controls have been abolished. Maintaining destination-based producer trade under these conditions requires a costly system of monitoring exports to other EU member states, in order to prevent fraudulent claims for tax rebates. Furthermore, intra-EU purchases by final consumers can be taxed only in the country of origin, giving rise to wasteful cross-border shopping by consumers in the high-tax country. These cross-border purchases can in turn provide incentives for national governments to set commodity tax rates strategically, in order to increase the domestic commodity tax base. Finally, when countries are asymmetric and governments face rigid revenue requirements, then coordination measures to reduce cross-border shopping will lead to conflicting interests between high-tax and low-tax countries (chapter 8).

These deficiencies of the mixed commodity tax principle currently in place in the European internal market have formed the basis for our analysis whether a complete switch to origin-based commodity trade within the EU might represent a superior policy solution. This switch raises a variety of different issues, an important one being the implications of international capital mobility. In the presence of capital mobility, the switch to an origin-based commodity tax will be neutral with respect to investment decisions in the long run, but consumption and investment decisions are distorted in the short run if the switch is anticipated. Trade patterns with non-member countries need not be distorted, even if these maintain the destination principle for commodity trade, if the

Union were to accept that their exports to third countries are double-taxed while imports into the Union remain tax-free. In contrast producer price distortions will necessarily result from either a differentiated and non-harmonised rate structure or from an incomplete coverage of VAT (chapter 9).

Perhaps the most important argument against origin-based commodity taxes arises when firms (rather than capital) are internationally mobile and factor taxes can be optimally deployed. In this setting, an origin-based VAT duplicates a tax on wages and a source-based tax on corporate profits and thus plays no independent role in the overall tax system. In contrast, a destination-based commodity tax will complement the direct taxation of factor incomes when a residence-based tax on profit income cannot be enforced. This ensures a welfare increasing role for a consumption-based VAT, even if cross-border shopping is simultaneously incorporated into the analysis (chapter 11).

From these results we have concluded that the current destination-based system of commodity taxation should be maintained in the European Union, despite the distortions caused by this system. The elimination of wasteful cross-border shopping and undesirable revenue shifts between EU member states then constitute an argument in favour of commodity tax harmonisation in the Union. Additional arguments arise when commodity tax rates are differentiated. In this case tax harmonisation has the fundamental merit of equating marginal rates of substitution between consumers in different markets, and it also mitigates the incentive to use commodity taxation as a means to improve the domestic terms of trade (subsection 8.6.2).

The costs of (further) indirect tax harmonisation are likely to be high, however, in particular since national tax autonomy in the field of direct taxation is simultaneously affected by international competition. A more detailed evaluation of the pros and cons then requires that a clear distinction be drawn between value-added taxation on the one hand and excise taxation on the other. For VAT, the empirical evidence suggests that the distortions caused by cross-border shopping are not very severe (cf. section 8.7). Moreover VAT, as a broad-based tax on consumption, cannot systematically be targeted at improving the terms of trade so that the arguments for tax harmonisation in the presence of differentiated commodity taxes have only limited applicability. At the same time, VAT plays an increasingly important role for balancing the government budget. For this tax, therefore, the benefits from further tax rate harmonisation – as pursued by the Commission (European Communities – Commission, 1996a) – seem to be clearly outweighed by the costs. Matters are somewhat different for excises, however, where the distortive effects of international tax differentials are more apparent and the budgetary role is far less important than in the case of value-added taxation.

Capital and commodity taxation

In the final part of this book we have argued that an integrated treatment of factor and commodity taxation in a common analytical framework can improve the understanding of the general rules governing tax policy in open economies. One scenario in which such interactions are relevant arises when origin-based commodity taxes and source-based taxes on capital are levied simultaneously. In most cases, these taxes will have cumulative effects on the distortions caused in capital markets. Therefore, if one of the two instruments is employed for one of the second-best reasons discussed above, this simultaneously creates an argument against levying the other instrument at a positive rate (chapter 10). The interdependence of commodity and capital tax choices is also important when the market power in commodity markets affects the ability of a country to extract positive profit taxes from an internationally mobile firm. In this case a large country can threaten to impose high tariffs or consumption taxes, should the firm decide to locate in a different region. This in turn improves the bargaining power of the government *vis-à-vis* the foreign firm (chapter 12).

More direct policy implications arising from the interaction of factor and consumption taxes have already been mentioned above, in the context of a possible switch to origin-based commodity taxation. It was seen there that it is precisely the difficulty of enforcing residence-based taxes on profit income which makes it important to indirectly tax this income through a destination-based commodity tax. This last result also raises the more general issue whether a shift from direct to indirect taxation could improve the overall performance of national tax systems in the view of increasing international tax base mobility. Some first empirical evidence for possible efficiency gains of such a switch is derived from a study for Denmark, which compares the excess burden of value-added and income taxation caused by international tax avoidance (Gordon and Nielsen, 1997). The study concludes that – despite the high Danish VAT rate and the high tax differential to Germany – the marginal excess burden caused by the avoidance of value-added taxes through cross-border shopping is still substantially below the corresponding marginal excess burden caused by income tax evasion. Hence, from a perspective of minimising international tax avoidance, increased weight should be put on VAT, relative to income taxation.

At the same time, it is obvious that a major policy reform such as a switch from direct to indirect taxation has many aspects that are unrelated to the international mobility of tax bases. One important effect is that such a reform is likely to reduce the overall progressivity of the tax system. This causes important redistributive effects, and it may also *increase* unemployment when labour markets are not cleared.[3] The policy lesson to be derived from these results is that there may be significant and country-specific trade-offs involved in finding the optimal mix of direct and indirect taxation. From an international taxation perspective this underscores the importance of leaving nation states sufficient degrees of freedom in order to pursue their optimal policies.

Furthermore, measures of tax coordination may themselves have unexpected effects when there is involuntary unemployment. It has been shown by Fuest and Huber (1999b) that a coordinated rise in the source tax on capital, which unambiguously raises welfare a model where labour markets are cleared, will reduce employment and may also lower welfare when labour markets are unionised. This corresponds to second-best results that tax rate harmonisation may be welfare-reducing in the presence of imperfect competition in product markets (cf. section 8.6). Taken together, the arguments in favour of national tax sovereignty, the possible second-best distortions caused by tax harmonisation, and the public choice arguments that we have encountered in previous parts of this analysis (section 6.6) stress that, as a general rule, tax harmonisation measures should be confined to those areas where the distortions caused by national policy-making are severe and indisputable.

[3] This seemingly counterintuitive result is a robust finding in alternative models of involuntary unemployment. The intuition is that increasing the *marginal* tax rate on labour, while holding the average tax rate constant, will make it less attractive for either trade unions or employers to increase the wage rate above its market clearing level. See Sørensen (1997) for an overview of the theoretical and empirical literature on this issue.

References

ACIR (Advisory Commission on Intergovernmental Relations), 1994. Taxation of interstate mail order sales. 1994 revenue estimates (Washington, DC)

Alesina, A. and G. Tabellini, 1989. External debt, capital flight, and political risk, *Journal of International Economics* 27, 199–220

Alvarez, L, V. Kanniainen and J. Södersten, 1999. Why is the corporation tax not neutral? Anticipated tax reform, investment spurts and corporate borrowing, *Finanzarchiv* 56, 285–309

Alworth, J., 1998. Taxation and integrated financial markets: The challenges of derivatives and other financial innovations, *International Tax and Public Finance* 5, 507–34

Anderson, J. E. and H. van den Berg, 1998. Fiscal decentralization and government size: an international test for Leviathan accounting for unmeasured economic activity, *International Tax and Public Finance* 5, 171–86

Arachi, G., 2001. Efficient tax competition with factor mobility and trade: a note, *International Tax and Public Finance*, forthcoming

Atkinson, A. B. and J. E. Stiglitz, 1980. *Lectures on Public Economics* (McGraw-Hill, New York)

Auerbach, A. J. and L. J. Kotlikoff, 1987. *Dynamic Fiscal Policy* (Cambridge University Press)

Auerbach, A. J. and J. Slemrod, 1997. The economic effects of the Tax Reform Act of 1986, *Journal of Economic Literature* 35, 589–632

Bacchetta, P. and M. P. Espinosa, 1995. Information sharing and tax competition among governments, *Journal of International Economics* 39, 103–21

2000. Exchange-of-information clauses in international tax treaties, *International Tax and Public Finance* 7, 275–93

Ballard, Ch. and D. Fullerton, 1992. Distortionary taxes and the provision of public goods, *Journal of Economic Perspectives* 6, 117–31

Ballard, Ch., D. Fullerton, J. Shoven and J. Whalley, 1985. *A General Equilibrium Model for Tax Policy Evaluation* (University of Chicago Press)

Baxter, M. and M. J. Crucini, 1993. Explaining saving–investment correlations, *American Economic Review* 83, 416–36

Bayindir-Upmann, T., 1998. Two games of interjurisdictional competition when local governments provide industrial public goods, *International Tax and Public Finance* 5, 471–87

Berglas, E., 1981. Harmonization of commodity taxes, *Journal of Public Economics* 16, 377–87

Bewley, T., 1981. A critique of Tiebout's theory of local public expenditures, *Econometrica* 49, 713–40

Bhagwati, J. N. and R.A. Brecher, 1980. National welfare in an open economy in the presence of foreign-owned factors of production, *Journal of International Economics* 10, 103–15

Bhandari, J. S. and T. A. Mayer, 1990. A note on saving–investment correlations in the EMS, *IMF Working Paper* 97 (Washington, DC)

Biehl, D., 1969, Ausfuhrland-Prinzip, Einfuhrland-Prinzip und Gemeinsamer-Markt-Prinzip. Ein Beitrag zur Theorie der Steuerharmonisierung (Heymanns, Köln)

Bird, R. M. and P.-P. Gendron, 1998. Dual VATs and cross-border trade: two problems, one solution?, *International Tax and Public Finance* 5, 429–42

Bjerksund, P. and G. Schjelderup, 1998. The political economy of capital controls and tax policy in a small open economy, *European Journal of Political Economy* 14, 543–59

Black, D. A. and W. H. Hoyt, 1989. Bidding for firms, *American Economic Review* 79, 1249–56

Blanchard, O. J. and S. Fischer, 1989. *Lectures on Macroeconomics* (MIT Press, Cambridge, Mass.)

Boadway, R. and N. Bruce, 1984. A general proposition on the design of a neutral business tax, *Journal of Public Economics* 24, 231–39

1992. Problems with integrating corporate and personal income taxes in an open economy, *Journal of Public Economics* 48, 39–66

Boadway, R., M. Marchand and M. Vigneault, 1998. The consequences of overlapping tax bases for redistribution and public spending in a federation, *Journal of Public Economics* 68, 453–78

Bode, E., Ch. Krieger-Boden and K. Lammers, 1994. Cross-border activities and the European Single Market (Institut für Weltwirtschaft, Kiel)

Bond, E. W. and L. Samuelson, 1986. Tax holidays as signals, *American Economic Review* 76, 820–26

1989. Strategic behaviour and the rules for international taxation of capital, *The Economic Journal* 99, 1099–1111

Bordignon, M., S. Giannini and P. Panteghini, 1999. Corporate taxation in Italy: an analysis of the 1998 reform, *Finanzarchiv* 56, 335–62

Bordignon, M., P. Manasse and G. Tabellini, 1996. Optimal regional redistribution under asymmetric information, *CEPR Discussion Paper* 1437 (Centre for Economic Policy Research, London)

Boskin, M. J. (ed.) 1996. *Frontiers of Tax Reform* (Hoover Institution Press, Stanford)

Bovenberg, A. L., 1994. Destination- and origin-based taxation under international capital mobility, *International Tax and Public Finance* 1, 247–73

1996. Comment on Genser and Haufler, in R. Holzmann (ed.), *Maastricht: Monetary Constitution without a Fiscal Constitution?* (Nomos, Baden-Baden), 115–19

1999. Green tax reforms and the double dividend: an updated reader's guide, *International Tax and Public Finance* 6, 421–43

Bovenberg, A. L. and R. A. de Mooij, 1998. Environmental taxes, international capital mobility and inefficient tax systems: tax burden vs. tax shifting, *International Tax and Public Finance* 5, 7–39

Bradford, D., 1996. Consumption taxes: some fundamental transition issues, in: M. J. Boskin (ed.), *Frontiers of Tax Reform* (Hoover Institution Press, Stanford), 123–50

Brander, J. A. and B. J. Spencer, 1985. Export subsidies and international market share rivalry, *Journal of International Economics* 18, 83–100

1987. Foreign direct investment with unemployment and endogenous taxes and tariffs, *Journal of International Economics* 22, 257–79

Brennan, G. and J. Buchanan, 1980. *The Power to Tax. Analytical Foundations of a Fiscal Constitution* (Cambridge University Press)

Bretschger, L. and F. Hettich, 2000. Globalisation, capital mobility and tax competition: theory and evidence for OECD countries (University of Greifswald), mimeo

Breyer, F. and M. Kolmar, 1996. Social policy in a common market: labour market, social arbitrage, public finance, in R. Holzmann (ed.), *Maastricht: Monetary Constitution without a Fiscal Constitution?* (Nomos, Baden-Baden), 129–52

Brooke, A., D. Kendrick and A. Meeraus, 1992. GAMS – A user's guide (Scientific Press, San Francisco)

Bruce, N., 1992. A note on the taxation of international capital income flows, *Economic Record* 68, 217–21

Bucovetsky, S., 1991. Asymmetric tax competition, *Journal of Urban Economics* 30, 167–81

Bucovetsky, S. and J. D. Wilson, 1991. Tax competition with two tax instruments, *Regional Science and Urban Economics* 21, 333–50

Bucovetsky, S., M. Marchand and P. Pestieau, 1997. Tax competition and revelation of preferences for public expenditure, *CORE Discussion Paper* 9793 (Université de Louvain)

Burgess, R., S. Howes and N. Stern, 1995. Value-added tax options for India, *International Tax and Public Finance* 2, 109–41

Cantwell, J. (1994). The relationship between international trade and international production, in D. Greenaway and L. A. Winters (eds.), *Surveys in International Trade* (Blackwell, Oxford), 303–28

Chamley, Ch., 1986. Optimal taxation of capital income in general equilibrium with infinite lives, *Econometrica* 54, 607–22

Chennells, L. and R. Griffith, 1997. *Taxing Profits in a Changing World* (Institute for Fiscal Studies, London)

Chiang, A. C., 1984. *Fundamental Methods of Mathematical Economics*, 3rd edn. (McGraw-Hill, New York)

Chipman, J., 1987. International trade, in J. Eatwell, M. Milgate and P. Newman (eds.), *The New Palgrave: A Dictionary of Economics, 2* (Stockton Press, New York), 922–55

Christiansen, V., 1994. Cross-border shopping and the optimum commodity tax in a competitive and a monopoly market, *Scandinavian Journal of Economics* 96, 329–41

Christiansen, V., K. P. Hagen and A. Sandmo, 1994. The scope for taxation and public expenditure in an open economy, *Scandinavian Journal of Economics* 96, 289–309

Cnossen, S., 1990. The case for tax diversity in the European Community, *European Economic Review* 34, 471–9

1996. Company taxes in the European Union: criteria and options for reform, *Fiscal Studies* 17, 67–97

1998. Global trends and issues in value added taxation, *International Tax and Public Finance* 5, 399–428

1999. Taxing capital income in the Nordic Countries: a model for the European Union?, *Finanzarchiv* 56, 18–50

Cnossen, S. and C. S. Shoup, 1987. Coordination of value-added taxes, in S. Cnossen (ed.), *Tax Coordination in the European Community* (Kluwer, Deventer), 59–84

Collins, J. H., D. Kemsley and M. Lang, 1998. Cross-jurisdictional income shifting and earnings valuation, *Journal of Accounting Research* 36, 209–29

Coopers & Lybrand, 1988. *International Tax Summaries* (London)

Correia, I. H., 1996. Should capital income be taxed in the steady state?, *Journal of Public Economics* 60, 147–51

Cremer, H., V. Fourgeaud, M. L. Monteiro, M. Marchand and P. Pestieau, 1996. Mobility and redistribution: a survey, *Public Finance/Finances Publiques* 51, 325–52

Dahlby, B., 1996. Fiscal externalities and the design of intergovernmental grants, *International Tax and Public Finance* 3, 397–412

Daveri, F. and G. Tabellini, 2000. Unemployment, growth and taxation in industrial countries, *Economic Policy* 31, 49–104

de Crombrugghe, A. and H. Tulkens, 1990. On Pareto improving tax changes under fiscal competition, *Journal of Public Economics* 41, 335–50

Delipalla, S., 1997. Commodity tax harmonisation and public goods, *Journal of Public Economics* 63, 447–66

Delipalla, S. and M. Keen, 1992. The comparison between ad valorem and specific taxation under imperfect competition, *Journal of Public Economics* 49, 351–67

Devereux, M. P., 1992. The Ruding committee report: an economic assessment, *Fiscal Studies* 13, 96–107

2000. Issues in the taxation of income from foreign portfolio and direct investment, in S. Cnossen (ed.), *Taxing Capital Income in the European Union* (Oxford University Press), 110–34

Devereux, M. P. and R. Griffith, 1998. Taxes and the location of production: evidence from a panel of US multinationals, *Journal of Public Economics* 68, 335–67

Diamond, P. A. and J. A. Mirrlees, 1971. Optimal taxation and public production, part I: production efficiency, *American Economic Review* 61, 8–27

Dixit, A., 1985. Tax policy in open economies, in A. J. Auerbach and M. Feldstein (eds.), *Handbook of Public Economics, 1* (North-Holland, Amsterdam), 313–74

1986. Comparative statics for oligopoly, *International Economic Review* 27, 107–22

Dixit, A. and V. Norman, 1980. *Theory of International Trade* (Cambridge University Press)

Doyle, C. and S. van Wijnbergen, 1994. Taxation of foreign multinationals: a sequential bargaining approach to tax holidays, *International Tax and Public Finance* 1, 211–25

Due, J. F. and J. L. Mikesell, 1994. *Sales Taxation*, 2nd edn. (The Urban Institute Press, Washington, DC)

Edwards, J. and M. Keen, 1996. Tax competition and Leviathan, *European Economic Review* 40, 113–34

Eggert, W. and B. Genser, 2000. Is tax harmonization useful?, *Center of Finance and Econometrics Discussion Paper 00/23* (University of Konstanz)

Eggert, W. and A. Haufler, 1998. When do small countries win tax wars?, *Public Finance Review* 26, 327–61

1999. Capital taxation and production efficiency in an open economy, *Economics Letters* 62, 85–90

Eijffinger, S., H. Huizinga and J. Lemmen, 1998. Short-term and long-term government debt and nonresident interest withholding taxes, *Journal of Public Economics* 68, 309–34

Elitzur, R. and J. Mintz, 1996. Transfer pricing rules and corporate tax competition, *Journal of Public Economics* 60, 401–22

European Communities, 1988. The economics of 1992. An assessment of the potential economic effects of completing the internal market of the European Community, Study directed by M. Emerson, assisted by M. Aujean, M. Catinat, P. Goybet and A. Jaquemin, *European Economy 35* (Brussels)

1991. Directive 91/680/EEC (Transitional system), *Official Journal of the European Communities L* 376 (16 December 1991)

1992. Directive 92/77/EEC (Tax rate approximation), *Official Journal of the European Communities L* 316 (19 October 1992)

European Communities – Commission, 1996. A common system of value added taxation. A programme for the Internal Market, Document COM (96) 328 (Brussels)

1998a. Proposal for a Council Directive to ensure a minimum of effective taxation of savings income in the form of interest payments within the Community, Document COM (98) 295 (Brussels)

1998b. Electronic commerce and indirect taxation. Communication from the Commission, Document COM (98) 374 (Brussels)

2000. Proposal for a Council Directive amending Directive 77/388/EEC as regards the value added tax arrangements applicable to certain services supplied by electronic mean, Document COM (2000) 349 (Brussels)

European Communities – Council, 1998. Conclusions of the ECOFIN Council meeting on 1 December 1997 concerning taxation policy (including code of conduct for business taxation), *Official Journal of the European Communities* 98/C 2/01 (Brussels)

Fehr, H., 2000. From destination- to origin-based consumption taxation: a dynamic CGE analysis, *International Tax and Public Finance* 7, 43–61

Fehr, H., C. Rosenberg and W. Wiegard, 1995. *Welfare Effects of Value-Added Tax Harmonization in Europe* (Springer, Berlin)

Feichtinger, G. and R. F. Hartl, 1986. *Optimale Kontrolle ökonomischer Prozesse* (de Gruyter, Berlin)

Feld, L., 1997. Exit, voice and income taxes: the loyalty of voters, *European Journal of Political Economy* 13, 455–78

Feldstein, M. and C. Horioka, 1980. Domestic saving and international capital flows, *The Economic Journal* 90, 314–29

FitzGerald, J., J. Johnston and J. Williams, 1995. Indirect tax distortions in a Europe of shopkeepers, *Working Paper* 56 (The Economic and Social Research Institute, Dublin)

Flowers, M. A., 1988. Shared tax sources in a Leviathan model of federalism, *Public Finance Quarterly* 16, 67–77

Frank, M., 1991. Introduction of a common system of interest taxation in the EC member states, *Public Finance* 46, 42–65

Fratianni, M. and H. Christie, 1981. Abolishing fiscal frontiers within the EEC, *Public Finance* 36, 411–29

Frenkel, J., A. Razin and E. Sadka, 1991. *International Taxation in an Integrated World* (MIT Press, Cambridge, Mass.)

Frenkel, J., A. Razin and C.-W. Yuen, 1996. *Fiscal Policies and Growth in the World Economy*, 3rd edn. (MIT Press, Cambridge, Mass.)

Frey, B. S., 1990. Intergovernmental tax competition, in Ch. E. McLure, H.-W. Sinn and R. Musgrave (eds.), *Influence of Tax Differentials on International Competitiveness* (Kluwer, Deventer), 89–98

Frey, B. S. and R. Eichenberger, 1996. To harmonize or to compete? That's not the question, *Journal of Public Economics* 60, 335–49

Friedlaender, A. and A. Vandendorpe, 1968. Excise taxes and the gains from trade, *Journal of Political Economy* 76, 1058–68

Fuest, C., 1995. Interjurisdictional competition and public expenditure: Is tax coordination counterproductive? *Finanzarchiv* 52, 478–96

2000. The political economy of tax coordination as a bargaining game between bureaucrats and politicians, *Public Choice* 103, 357–82

Fuest, C. and B. Huber, 1999a. Can tax coordination work?, *Finanzarchiv* 56, 443–58

1999b. Tax coordination and unemployment, *International Tax and Public Finance* 6, 7–26

2000. Why do countries subsidise investment and not employment?, *Journal of Public Economics* 78, 171–92

Fumagalli, Ch., 2000. On the welfare effects of competition for foreign direct investment, *CEPR Discussion Paper* 2468 (Centre for Economic Policy Research, London)

Gabrielsen, T. and G. Schjelderup, 1999. Transfer pricing and ownership structure, *Scandinavian Journal of Economics* 101, 673–88

Gabszewicz, J. and T. van Ypersele, 1996. Social protection and political competition, *Journal of Public Economics* 61, 193–208

Garrett, G., 1995. Capital mobility, trade, and the domestic politics of economic policy, *International Organization* 49, 657–87

Genser, B., 1996a. Austria's steps towards a dual income tax, in L. Mutén, P. B. Sørensen, K. P. Hagen and B. Genser, *Towards a Dual Income Tax?*

Scandinavian and Austrian Experiences (Foundation for European Fiscal Studies, Rotterdam)

1996b. A generalized equivalence property of mixed international VAT regimes, *Scandinavian Journal of Economics* 98, 253–62

Genser, B. and A. Haufler, 1996a. Tax competition, tax coordination, and tax harmonization: the effects of EMU, *Empirica* 23, 59–89

1996b. On the optimal tax policy mix when consumers and firms are imperfectly mobile, *Finanzarchiv* 53, 411–33

1999. Harmonization of corporate income taxation in the EU, *Aussenwirtschaft* 54, 319–48

Genser, B., A. Haufler and P. B. Sørensen, 1995. Indirect taxation in an integrated Europe: is there a way of avoiding trade distortions without sacrificing national tax autonomy?, *Journal of Economic Integration* 10, 178–205

Genser, B. and G. Schulze, 1997. Transfer pricing under an origin-based VAT system, *Finanzarchiv* 54, 51–67

Georgakopoulos, T. and T. Hitiris, 1992. On the superiority of the destination over the origin principle of taxation for intra-union trade, *The Economic Journal* 102, 117–26

Goolsbee, A., 2000. In a world without borders: the impact of taxes on Internet commerce, *Quarterly Journal of Economics* 115, 561–76

Gordon, R. H., 1983. An optimal taxation approach to fiscal federalism, *Quarterly Journal of Economics* 98, 567–86

1986. Taxation of investment and savings in a world economy, *American Economic Review* 76, 1086–1102

1992. Can capital income taxes survive in open economies?, *Journal of Finance* 47, 1159–80

2000. Taxation of capital income vs. labor income: an overview, in S. Cnossen (ed.), *Taxing Capital Income in the European Union* (Oxford University Press), 15–45

Gordon, R. H. and A. L. Bovenberg, 1996. Why is capital so immobile internationally? Possible explanations and implications for capital income taxation, *American Economic Review* 86, 1057–75

Gordon, R. H. and J. K. MacKie-Mason, 1995. Why is there corporate taxation in a small open economy? The role of transfer pricing and income shifting, in M. Feldstein (ed.), *The Effects of Taxation on Multinational Corporations* (University of Chicago Press), 67–91

Gordon, R. H. and S. B. Nielsen, 1997. Tax avoidance and value-added vs. income taxation in an open economy, *Journal of Public Economics* 66, 173–97

Gordon, R. H. and H. R. Varian, 1989. Taxation of asset income in the presence of a world securities market, *Journal of International Economics* 26, 205–26

Gottfried, P. and W. Wiegard, 1991. Exemption versus zero rating. A hidden problem of VAT, *Journal of Public Economics* 46, 307–28

Goulder, L. H., 1995. Environmental taxation and the 'double dividend': a reader's guide, *International Tax and Public Finance* 2, 157–83

Grossman, G. M. and E. Helpman, 1994. Protection for sale, *American Economic Review* 84, 833–50

Grubert, H. and J. Mutti, 1996. Do taxes influence where US corporations invest?, paper presented at the Trans-Atlantic Public Economics Seminar (TAPES) (Amsterdam, May 1996)

Grubert, H. and J. Slemrod, 1998. The effect of taxes on investment and income shifting to Puerto Rico, *Review of Economics and Statistics* 80, 365–73

Haaland, J. and I. Wooton, 1999. International competition for multinational investment, *Scandinavian Journal of Economics* 101, 631–49

Haaparanta, P., 1996. Competition for foreign direct investment, *Journal of Public Economics* 63, 141–53

Haaparanta, P. and H. Piekkola, 1998. Taxation and entrepreneurship, *Working Paper* 200 (Helsinki School of Economics and Business Administration)

Hall, R. E. and A. Rabushka, 1985. *The Flat Tax* (Hoover Institution Press, Stanford)

Hallerberg, M. and S. Basinger, 1996. Why did all but two OECD countries initiate tax reform from 1986 to 1990?, *CES Working Paper* 119 (Center for Economic Studies, Munich)

Hamada, K. 1966. Strategic aspects of taxation on foreign investment income, *Quarterly Journal of Economics* 80, 361–75

Haufler, A., 1994. Unilateral tax reform under the restricted origin principle, *European Journal of Political Economy* 10, 511–27

1996a. Tax coordination with different preferences for public goods: conflict or harmony of interest?, *International Tax and Public Finance* 3, 5–28

1996b. Tax differentials and external tariffs in a trade deflection model, *Finanzarchiv* 53, 47–67

1996c. Optimal factor and commodity taxation in a small open economy, *International Tax and Public Finance* 3, 425–42

1997. Factor taxation, income distribution, and capital market integration, *Scandinavian Journal of Economics* 99, 425–46

1998. Asymmetric commodity tax competition – comment on de Crombrugghe and Tulkens, *Journal of Public Economics* 67, 135–44

Haufler, A. and S. B. Nielsen, 1997. Dynamic effects of an anticipated switch from destination- to origin-based commodity taxation, *Journal of Economics/Zeitschrift für Nationalökonomie* 66, 43–69

Haufler, A. and G. Schjelderup, 2000. Corporate tax systems and cross country profit shifting, *Oxford Economic Papers* 52, 306–25

Haufler, A. and I. Wooton, 1999. Country size and tax competition for foreign direct investment, *Journal of Public Economics* 71, 121–39

Hausman, J. A., 1985. Labour supply, in A. J. Auerbach and M. S. Feldstein (eds.), *Handbook of Public Economics*, 1 (North-Holland, Amsterdam), 213–63

Hettich, F. and C. Schmidt, 2001. Die deutsche Steuerbelastung im internationalen Vergleich, *Perspektiven der Wirtschafts-politik* 2, 45–60.

Hillman, A., 1982. Declining industries and political-support protectionist motives, *American Economic Review* 72, 1180–87

Hines, J. R., 1995. Taxes, technology transfer, and the R&D activities of multinational firms, in M. Feldstein, J. R. Hines and R. G. Hubbard (eds.), *The Effects of Taxation on Multinational Corporations* (University of Chicago Press), 225–48

1997. Tax policy and the activities of multinational corporations, in A. Auerbach (ed.), *Fiscal Policy: Lessons from Economic Research* (MIT Press, Cambridge, Mass), 401–45

1999. Lessons from behavioral responses to international taxation, *National Tax Journal* 52, 304–22

Hines, J. R. and E. M. Rice, 1994. Fiscal paradise: foreign tax havens and American business, *Quarterly Journal of Economics* 109, 149–82

Hinnekens, L., 1998. The challenges of applying VAT and income tax territoriality concepts and rules to international electronic commerce, *Intertax* 26, 52–70

Hoel, M., 1997a. Environmental policy with endogenous plant locations, *Scandinavian Journal of Economics* 99, 241–59

1997b. International coordination of environmental taxes, in C. Carraro (ed.), *New Directions in the Economic Theory of the Environment* (Cambridge University Press), 105–46

Holzmann, R., 1992. Tax reform in countries in transition: central policy issues, in P. Pestieau (ed.), *Public Finance in a World of Transition*, Supplement to *Public Finance/Finances Publiques* 47, 233–55

Homburg, S., 1999. Competition and co-ordination in international capital income taxation, *Finanzarchiv* 56, 1–17

Horst, T., 1980. A note on the optimal taxation of international investment income, *Quarterly Journal of Economics* 94, 793–98

1993. Comparable profit method analyzed, *Tax Notes International* 6, 1443–58

Horstman, I. J. and J. R. Markusen, 1992. Endogenous market structures in international trade (natura facit saltum), *Journal of International Economics* 32, 109–29

Howitt, P. and H.-W. Sinn, 1989. Gradual reforms of capital income taxation, *American Economic Review* 79, 106–24

Hoyt, W. H., 1991. Property taxation, Nash equilibrium, and market power, *Journal of Urban Economics* 30, 123–31

Huber, B., 1997. Optimal capital income taxes and capital controls in small open economies, *International Tax and Public Finance* 4, 7–24

Huber, B. and G. Krause, 1997. The taxation of capital income and rents in a small open economy under uncertainty, *Finanzarchiv* 54, 151–68

Huizinga, H., 1994. International interest withholding taxation: prospects for a common European policy, *International Tax and Public Finance* 1, 277–91

Huizinga, H. and S. B. Nielsen, 1997a. Capital income and profits taxation with foreign ownership of firms, *Journal of International Economics* 42, 149–65

1997b. The political economy of capital income and profit taxation in a small open economy, *EPRU Working Paper* 1997–01 (Economic Policy Research Unit, Copenhagen Business School)

2000a. The taxation of interest in Europe: a minimum withholding tax?, in S. Cnossen (ed.), *Taxing Capital Income in the European Union* (Oxford University Press), 135–60

2000b. Withholding taxes or information exchange: the taxation of international interest flows, *EPRU Working Paper* 2000-19 (Economic Policy Research Unit, University of Copenhagen)

Hussein, K. A., 1998. International capital mobility in OECD countries: the Feldstein–Horioka 'puzzle' revisited, *Economics Letters* 59, 237–42

IFS Capital Taxes Group, 1991, Equity for companies: a corporation tax for the 1990s, *Commentary* 26 (Institute for Fiscal Studies, London)

Inman, R. P. and D. L. Rubinfeld, 1996. Designing tax policy in federalist economies: an overview, *Journal of Public Economics* 60, 307–34

International Bureau of Fiscal Documentation, 1998. *European Tax Handbook 1998* (Amsterdam)

International Monetary Fund, 1990, 1999. *Balance of Payments Statistics Yearbook*, part 2 (Washington, DC)

Janeba, E., 1995. Corporate income tax competition, double taxation, and foreign direct investment, *Journal of Public Economics* 56, 311–25

1997. *International Tax Competition* (Mohr Siebeck, Tübingen)

1998. Tax competition in imperfectly competitive markets, *Journal of International Economics* 44, 134–53

Janeba, E. and W. Peters, 1999. Tax evasion, tax competition and the gains from nondiscrimination: the case of interest taxation in Europe, *The Economic Journal* 109, 93–101

Jansen, W. J. and G. Schulze, 1996. Theory-based measurement of the saving–investment correlation with an application to Norway, *Economic Enquiry* 34, 116–32

Johnson, H. G., 1953/4. Optimum tariffs and retaliation, *Review of Economic Studies* 21, 142–53

Kanbur, R. and M. Keen, 1993 Jeux sans frontières: Tax competition and tax coordination when countries differ in size, *American Economic Review* 83, 877–92

Kant, C., 1988. Endogenous transfer pricing and the effects of uncertain regulation, *Journal of International Economics* 24, 147–57

Keen, M., 1987. Welfare effects of commodity tax harmonization, *Journal of Public Economics* 33, 107–14

1989. Pareto-improving indirect tax harmonization, *European Economic Review* 33, 1–12

1993a. The welfare economics of tax co-ordination in the European Community: a survey, *Fiscal Studies* 14, 15–36

1993b. Structure of the fiscal and social charges according to their degree of mobility. Draft Final Report to the European Commission

1997. Vertical tax externalities in the theory of fiscal federalism, *IMF Working Paper* 97/173 (Washington, DC)

Keen, M. and S. Lahiri, 1993. Domestic tax reform and international oligopoly, *Journal of Public Economics* 51, 55–74

1998. The comparison between destination and origin principles under imperfect competition, *Journal of International Economics* 45, 323–50

Keen, M., S. Lahiri and P. Raimondos-Møller, 2000. Commodity tax harmonization under destination and origin principles: a cautionary example (Economic Policy Research Unit, University of Copenhagen), mimeo

Keen, M. and M. Marchand, 1997. Fiscal competition and the pattern of public spending, *Journal of Public Economics* 66, 33–53

Keen, M. and H. Piekkola, 1997. Simple rules for the optimal taxation of international capital income, *Scandinavian Journal of Economics* 99, 447–61

Keen, M. and S. Smith, 1996. The future of value-added tax in the European Union, *Economic Policy* 23, 375–420

Keen, M. and D. Wildasin, 2000. Pareto efficiency in international taxation, *CESifo Working Paper* 371 (University of Munich)

Kemp, M., 1962. Foreign investment and the national advantage, *Economic Record* 38, 56–62

Kennan, J. and R. Riezman, 1988. Do big countries win tariff wars?, *Journal of International Economics* 29, 81–5

Keuschnigg, Ch., 1991. The transition to a cash-flow income tax, *Swiss Journal of Economics and Statistics* 127, 113–40

Kind, H. J., K. H. Midelfart Knarvik and G. Schjelderup, 2000. Competing for capital in a 'lumpy' world, *Journal of Public Economics* 78, 253–74

King, M. A. and D. Fullerton, 1984. *The Taxation of Income from Capital. A Comparative Study of the United States, the United Kingdom, Sweden and West Germany* (University of Chicago Press)

Kirchgässner, G. and W. W. Pommerehne, 1996. Tax harmonization and tax competition in the European Union: lessons from Switzerland, *Journal of Public Economics* 60, 351–71

Koch, K.-J. and G. Schulze, 1998. Equilibria in tax competition models, in K. Jäger and K.-J. Koch (eds.), *Trade, Growth and Economic Policy in Open Economies. Essays in Honour of Hans-Jürgen Vosgerau* (Springer, Berlin), 281–311

Kolmar, M., 1999. *Optimale Ansiedlung sozialpolitischer Entscheidungskompetenzen in der Europäischen Union* (Mohr, Tübingen)

Konrad, K. and G. Schjelderup, 1999. Fortress building in global tax competition, *Journal of Urban Economics* 46, 156–67

Krause-Junk, G., 1990. Ein Plädoyer für das Ursprungslandprinzip, in F. X. Bea and W. Kitterer (eds.), *Finanzwissenschaft im Dienste der Wirtschaftspolitik* (Mohr, Tübingen), 253–65

1992. Die europäische Mehrwertsteuer und das Ursprungslandprinzip, *Finanzarchiv* 49, 141–53

Krugman, P., 1980. Scale economies, product differentiation, and the pattern of trade, *American Economic Review* 70, 950–9

1991. Increasing returns and economic geography, *Journal of Political Economy* 99, 483–99

Lahiri, S. and P. Raimondos-Møller, 1998. Public good provision and the welfare effects of indirect tax harmonization, *Journal of Public Economics* 67, 253–67

Lejour, A., 1995. Integrating or disintegrating welfare states? A qualitative study to the consequences of economic integration on social insurance (Center for Economic Research Publication, Tilburg University)

Lejour, A. and H. Verbon, 1996. Capital mobility, wage bargaining and social insurance policies in an economic union, *International Tax and Public Finance* 3, 495–514

1997. Tax competition and redistribution in a two-country endogenous growth model, *International Tax and Public Finance* 4, 485–97

Lockwood, B., 1993. Commodity tax competition under destination and origin principles, *Journal of Public Economics* 53, 141–62

1997. Can international commodity tax harmonisation be Pareto-improving when governments supply public goods?, *Journal of International Economics* 43, 387–408

1998a. Tax competition and tax co-ordination under destination and origin principles: A synthesis (University of Warwick), mimeo

1998b. Distributive politics and the benefits of decentralisation, Centre for the Study of Globalisation and Regionalisation (CSGR), *Working Paper* 10/98 (University of Warwick)

1999. Inter-regional insurance, *Journal of Public Economics* 72, 1–37

Lockwood, B., D. de Meza and G. Myles, 1994a. When are origin and destination regimes equivalent?, *International Tax and Public Finance* 1, 5–24

1994b. The equivalence between destination and non-reciprocal restricted origin tax regimes, *Scandinavian Journal of Economics* 96, 311–28

1995. On the European Union VAT proposals: the superiority of origin over destination taxation, *Fiscal Studies* 16, 1–17

London Economics, 1994. The cross-border purchase of excise products – evidence from Europe and North America (London)

Longo, C., 1990. The VAT in Brazil, in M. Gillis, C. S. Shoup and G. P. Sicat (eds.), *Value Added Taxation in Developing Countries* (The World Bank, Washington, DC)

Lopez, S., M. Marchand and P. Pestieau, 1998. A simple two-country model of redistributive capital income taxation, *Finanzarchiv* 55, 445–60

Lopez-Garcia, M. A., 1996. The origin principle and the welfare gains from indirect tax harmonization, *International Tax and Public Finance* 3, 83–93

Lorz, O., 1997. Standortwettbewerb bei internationaler Kapitalmobilität, *Kieler Studien 284* (Mohr, Tübingen)

1998. Capital mobility, tax competition, and lobbying for redistributive capital taxation, *European Journal of Political Economy* 14, 265–79

Lucas, R. E., 1990. Supply-side economics: an analytical review, *Oxford Economic Papers* 42, 293–316

MacDougall, G. D. A., 1960. The benefits and costs of private investment abroad, *Economic Record* 36, 13–35

Mansori, K. S. and A. J. Weichenrieder, 1999. Tax competition and transfer pricing disputes (University of Munich), mimeo

Markusen, J. R., E. R. Morey and N. D. Olewiler, 1995. Competition in regional environmental policies when plant locations are endogenous, *Journal of Public Economics* 56, 55–77

Markusen, J. R. and A. Venables, 1998. Multinational firms and the new trade theory, *Journal of International Economics* 46, 183–203

Markusen, J. R. and R. M. Wigle, 1989. Nash equilibrium tariffs for the United States and Canada: the roles of country size, scale economies, and capital mobility, *Journal of Political Economy* 97, 368–86

Mas-Colell, A., 1985. *The Theory of General Economic Equilibrium* (Cambridge University Press)

McAfee, R. P. and J. McMillan, 1987. Auctions and bidding, *Journal of Economic Literature* 25, 699–738

McLure, Ch. E., 1991. Tax policy for economies in transition from socialism, *Tax Notes International* 3, 3, 347–53

1999. Electronic commerce and the state retail sales tax: a challenge to American federalism, *International Tax and Public Finance* 6, 193–224

Meade Committee, 1978. *The Structure and Reform of Direct Taxation* (Institute for Fiscal Studies, London)

Melvin, J. R., 1985. The regional economic consequences of tariffs and domestic transportation costs, *Canadian Journal of Economics* 18, 237–57

Mendoza, E., A. Razin and L. Tesar, 1994. Effective tax rates in macroeconomics: cross-country estimates of tax rates on factor incomes and consumption, *Journal of Monetary Economics* 34, 297–323

Mennel, A. and J. Förster, 1999. *Steuern in Europa, Amerika und Japan* (Verlag Neue Wirtschaftsbriefe, Berlin)

Mintz, J., 1994. Is there a future for capital income taxation?, *Canadian Tax Journal* 42, 1469–1503

1999. Globalization of the corporate income tax: the role of allocation, *Finanzarchiv* 56, 389–423

Mintz, J. and H. Tulkens, 1986. Commodity tax competition between member states of a federation: equilibrium and efficiency, *Journal of Public Economics* 29, 133–72

1996. Optimality properties of alternative systems of taxation of foreign capital income, *Journal of Public Economics* 60, 373–99

Motta, M. and G. Norman, 1996. Does economic integration cause foreign direct investment?, *International Economic Review* 37, 757–83

Munk, K. J., 1980. Optimal taxation with some non-taxable commodities, *Review of Economic Studies* 47, 755–65

Musgrave, P. B., 1969. United States taxation of foreign investment income: issues and arguments (Harvard Law School, Cambridge, Mass.)

1987. Interjurisdictional coordination of taxes on capital income, in S. Cnossen (ed.), *Tax Coordination in the European Community* (Kluwer Law and Taxation Publishers, Deventer), 197–225

Musgrave, R. A., 1959. *The Theory of Public Finance* (McGraw-Hill, New York)

Musgrave, R. A. and P. B. Musgrave, 1989. *Public Finance in Theory and Practice*, 5th edn. (McGraw-Hill, New York)

Mutén, L., 1996. Dual income taxation: Swedish experience, in L. Mutén, P. B. Sørensen, K. P. Hagen and B. Genser, *Towards a Dual Income Tax? Scandinavian and Austrian Experiences* (Foundation for European Fiscal Studies, Rotterdam)

Myers, G. M., 1990. Optimality, free mobility, and the regional authority in a federation, *Journal of Public Economics* 43, 107–21

Myles, G. D., 1995. *Public Economics* (Cambridge University Press)

1996. Imperfect competition and the optimal combination of ad valorem and specific taxation, *International Tax and Public Finance* 3, 29–44

2000. Taxation and economic growth, *Fiscal Studies* 21, 141–68

Neary, J. P., 1985. International factor mobility, minimum wage rates, and factor price equalization: a synthesis, *Quarterly Journal of Economics* 100, 551–70

Neumark Report, 1963. *The EEC Reports on Tax Harmonization. The Report of the Fiscal and Financial Committee and the Reports of the Sub-groups A, B and C,* unofficial translation by H. Thurston (International Bureau of Fiscal Documentation, Amsterdam)

Nielsen, S. B., 1991. Current account effects of a devaluation in an optimizing model with capital accumulation, *Journal of Economic Dynamics and Control* 15, 569–88

1998. A simple model of commodity taxation and cross-border shopping, *EPRU Working Paper* 1998-18 (Economic Policy Research Unit, University of Copenhagen)

Nielsen, S. B., P. Raimondos-Møller and G. Schjelderup, 1999. Tax spillovers under separate accounting and formula apportionment (Copenhagen Business School and Norwegian School of Economics and Business Administration), mimeo

Nielsen, S. B. and P. B. Sørensen, 1991. Capital income taxation in a growing open economy, *European Economic Review* 34, 179–97

1997. On the optimality of the Nordic system of dual income taxation, *Journal of Public Economics* 63, 311–29

Nöhrbaß, K.-H. and M. Raab, 1990. Quellensteuer und Kapitalmarkt. Eine theoretische und empirische Untersuchung, *Finanzarchiv* 48, 179–93

Norman, G. and M. Motta, 1993. Eastern European economic integration and foreign direct investment, *Journal of Economics and Management Strategy* 2, 483–507

Oates, W., 1972. *Fiscal Federalism* (Harcourt Brace Jovanovich, New York)

1985. Searching for Leviathan: an empirical study, *American Economic Review* 75, 748–57

1989. Searching for Leviathan: a reply and some further reflections, *American Economic Review* 79, 578–83

Oates, W. and R. Schwab, 1988. Economic competition among jurisdictions: efficiency enhancing or distortion inducing?, *Journal of Public Economics* 35, 333–54

OECD, 1977. *Model Double Taxation Convention on Income and on Capital* (Paris)

1996. *Revenue Statistics of OECD Member Countries* (Paris)

1998a. *Harmful Tax Competition: An Emerging Global Issue* (Paris)

1998b. *Electronic Commerce: Taxation Framework Conditions* (Paris)

1999. *Revenue Statistics 1965/98* (Paris)

2000. *Towards Global Tax Co-operation. Progress in Identifying and Eliminating Harmful Tax Practices* (Paris)

OECD (SOPEMI), 1994, 1997. *Trends in International Migration, Annual Reports 1993 and 1996* (Paris)

Osmundsen, P., K. Hagen and G. Schjelderup, 1998. Internationally mobile firms and tax policy, *Journal of International Economics* 45, 97–113

Papke, L. E., 1991. Interstate business tax differentials and new firm location, *Journal of Public Economics* 45, 47–68

2000. One-way treaty with the world: the US withholding tax and the Netherlands Antilles, *International Tax and Public Finance* 7, 295–313

Peltzman, S., 1976. Toward a more general theory of regulation, *Journal of Law and Economics* 19, 211–40

Perroni, C. and K. A. Scharf, 2001. Tiebout with politics: capital tax competition and constitutional choices, *Review of Economic Studies*, forthcoming

Perroni, C. and J. Whalley, 2000. The new regionalism: trade liberalization or insurance?, *Canadian Journal of Economics* 33, 1–24

Persson, T. and G. Tabellini, 1992. The politics of 1992: fiscal policy and European integration, *Review of Economic Studies* 59, 689–701

Portes, R. and H. Rey, 2000. The determinants of cross-border equity flows, *Centre for Economic Performance Discussion Paper 446* (London School of Economics and Political Science)

Price Waterhouse, 1994. VAT and excise duties: changes in cross-border purchasing patterns following the abolition of fiscal frontiers on 1 January 1993 (Final report to the Commission of the European Communities, DGXXI/C-3)

Quinn, D., 1997. The correlates of change in international financial regulation, *American Political Science Review* 91, 531–51

Raff, H., 2000. Preferential trade agreements and tax competition for foreign direct investment (University of Kiel), mimeo

Raff, H. and J. D. Wilson, 1997. Income redistribution with well-informed local governments, *International Tax and Public Finance* 4, 407–27

Raimondos-Møller, P. and K. Scharf, 2001. Transfer pricing rules and competing governments, *Oxford Economic Papers*, forthcoming

Ratzinger, J., 1998. Die Bedeutung privater Direktimporte für die Güterbesteuerung in der Europäischen Union, *ifo-Studien zur Finanzpolitik 65* (ifo-Institut für Wirtschaftsforschung, Munich)

Rauscher, M., 1995. Environmental regulation and the location of polluting industries, *International Tax and Public Finance* 2, 229–44

Razin, A. and E. Sadka, 1991a. International tax competition and gains from tax harmonization, *Economics Letters* 37, 69–76

1991b. Efficient investment incentives in the presence of capital flight, *Journal of International Economics* 31, 171–81

Razin, A., E. Sadka and C. Yuen, 1998. A pecking order theory of capital inflows and international tax principles, *Journal of International Economics* 44, 45–68

Razin, A. and C. Yuen, 1996. Capital income taxation and long-run growth: new perspectives, *Journal of Public Economics* 59, 239–63

Richter, W. F., 1994. The efficient location of local public factors in Tiebout's tradition, *Regional Science and Urban Economics* 24, 323–40

2000. An efficiency analysis of consumption and production taxation with an application to value-added taxation, *International Tax and Public Finance* 7, 23–41

Richter, W. F. and D. Wellisch, 1996. The provision of local public goods and factors in the presence of firm and household mobility, *Journal of Public Economics* 60, 73–93

Rodrik, D., 1997. Has globalization gone too far? (Institute for International Economics, Washington, DC)

1998. Why do more open economies have bigger governments?, *Journal of Political Economy* 106, 997–1032

Rose, M. and R. Wiswesser, 1998. Tax reform in transition economies: experiences from the Croatian tax reform process in the 1990s, in P. B. Sørensen (ed.), *Public Finance in a Changing World* (Macmillan, London), 257–78

Rubinfeld, D. L., 1987. The economics of the local public sector, in A. J. Auerbach and M. S. Feldstein (eds.), *Handbook of Public Economics* 2, (North-Holland, Amsterdam), 571–645

Ruding Report, 1992. *Report of the Committee of Independent Experts on Company Taxation* (Brussels and Luxembourg)

Ruffin, R., 1988. International factor movements, in R. W. Jones and P. B. Kenen (eds.), *Handbook of International Trade*, 1 (North-Holland, Amsterdam), 237–88

Sandmo, A., 1974. Investment incentives and the corporate income tax, *Journal of Political Economy* 82, 287–302

1979. A note on the cash flow corporation tax, *Economics Letters* 4, 173–6

Schaden, B., 1995. *Effektive Kapitalsteuerbelastung in Europa. Eine empirische Analyse aus deutscher Sicht* (Physica, Heidelberg)

Scharf, K. A., 1999. Scale economies in cross-border shopping and commodity taxation, *International Tax and Public Finance* 6, 89–99

Schjelderup, G. and A. Weichenrieder, 1999. Trade, multinationals, and transfer pricing regulations, *Canadian Journal of Economics* 32, 817–34

Schlesinger, H., 1990. Capital outflow and taxation – the case of the Federal Republic of Germany, in H. Siebert (ed.), *Reforming Capital Income Taxation* (Mohr, Tübingen), 101–9

Schulze, G., 1994. Misinvoicing imports: the interdependence of tax and tariff evasion, *Public Finance Quarterly* 22, 335–65

2000. *The Political Economy of Capital Controls* (Cambridge University Press)

Schulze, G. and K. J. Koch, 1994. Tax competition in a Bertrand model, *Journal of Economics/Zeitschrift für Nationalökonomie* 59, 193–215

Schulze, G. and H. Ursprung, 1999. Globalisation of the economy and the nation state, *The World Economy* 22, 295–352

Schweinberger, A. G. and H. J. Vosgerau, 1997. Foreign factor ownership and optimal tariffs, *Review of International Economics* 5, 1–19

Shibata, H., 1967. The theory of economic unions: a comparative analysis of customs unions, free trade areas and tax unions, in: C. S. Shoup (ed.), *Fiscal Harmonization in Common Markets* (Columbia University Press, New York), 145–264

Shoup, C. S., 1969. *Public Finance* (Aldine, Chicago)

Shoven. J. B. and J. Whalley, 1992. *Applying General Equilibrium* (Cambridge University Press)

Siebert, H. and M. J. Koop, 1993. Institutional competition versus centralization: quo vadis Europe?, *Oxford Review of Economic Policy* 9, 15–30

Sinn, H.-W., 1987. *Capital Income Taxation and Resource Allocation* (North-Holland, Amsterdam)

1990a. Tax harmonization and tax competition in Europe, *European Economic Review* 34, 489–504

1990b. Can direct and indirect taxes be added for international comparisons of competitiveness?, in H. Siebert (ed.), *Reforming Capital Income Taxation* (Tübingen, Mohr), 47–65

1997. The selection principle and market failure in systems competition, *Journal of Public Economics* 66, 247–74

Sinn, H.-W. and A. Weichenrieder, 1997. Foreign direct investment, political resentment and the privatization process in eastern Europe, *Economic Policy* 24, 179–210

Sinn, S., 1992. The taming of Leviathan: competition among governments, *Constitutional Political Economy* 3, 177–96

Slemrod, J., C. Hansen and R. Procter, 1997. The seesaw principle in international tax policy, *Journal of Public Economics* 65, 163–76

Smith, S., 1993. Subsidiarity and the coordination of indirect tax rates in the European Community, *Oxford Review of Economic Policy* 9, 67–94

Sørensen, P. B., 1991. Welfare gains from international fiscal coordination, in R. Prud'homme (ed.), *Public Finance with Several Levels of Government* (Foundation Journal Public Finance, The Hague/Koenigstein), 329–42

1994. From the global income tax to the dual income tax: recent tax reforms in the Nordic countries, *International Tax and Public Finance* 1, 57–79

1995. Changing views of the corporate income tax, *National Tax Journal* 48, 279–95

1997. Public finance solutions to the European unemployment problem?, *Economic Policy* 24, 223–64

(ed.), 1998. *Tax Policy in the Nordic Countries* (Macmillan, London)

2000. The case for international tax coordination reconsidered, *Economic Policy* 31, 429–72

Tanzi, V., 1995. *Taxation in an Integrating World* (The Brookings Institution, Washington, DC)

1999. Is there a need for a World Tax Organization?, in A. Razin and E. Sadka (eds.), *The Economics of Globalization* (Cambridge University Press), 173–86

Tiebout, C., 1956. A pure theory of local expenditures, *Journal of Political Economy* 64, 416–24

Tinbergen Report, 1953. *Bericht über die durch die Umsatzsteuer aufgeworfenen Probleme auf dem gemeinsamen Markt* (Europäische Gemeinschaft für Kohle und Stahl-Hohe Behörde)

Trandel, G. A., 1992. Evading the use tax on cross-border sales. Pricing and welfare effects, *Journal of Public Economics* 49, 313–31

1994. Interstate commodity tax differentials and the distribution of residents, *Journal of Public Economics* 53, 435–57

Turnovsky, S. J., 1995. *Methods of Macroeconomic Dynamics* (MIT Press, Cambridge, Mass.)

United Nations, 1996. *National Accounts Statistics: Main Aggregates and Detailed Tables* (New York)

Vanberg, V., 2000. Globalization, democracy and citizens' sovereignty: can competition among governments enhance democracy?, *Constitutional Political Economy* 11, 87–112

Van den Tempel Report, 1971. *Körperschaftsteuer und Einkommensteuer in den Europäischen Gemeinschaften.* Kollektion Studien, Kommission der Europäischen Gemeinschaften, Reihe Wettbewerb – Rechtsangleichung, Nr. 15 (Brussels)

Varian, H., 1996. *Computational Economics and Finance: Modeling and Analysis with Mathematica* (Springer, The Electronic Library of Science, Santa Clara, Cal.)

Volkerink, B. and J. de Haan, 2000. Tax ratios: a critical survey (University of Groningen), mimeo

Wagener, A., 1996. Corporate finance, capital market equilibrium, and international tax competition with capital income taxes, *Finanzarchiv* 53, 480–514

Walz, U. and D. Wellisch, 1996. Strategic provision of local public inputs for oligopolistic firms in the presence of endogenous location choice, *International Tax and Public Finance* 3, 175–89

Wang, Y.-Q., 1999. Commodity taxes under fiscal competition: Stackelberg equilibrium and optimality, *American Economic Review* 89, 974–81

Weichenrieder, A., 1996, Fighting international tax avoidance: the case of Germany, *Fiscal Studies* 17, 37–58

Weiner, J. M., 1996. Using the experience in the US states to evaluate issues in implementing formula apportionment at the international level, *Tax Notes International* 9, 2113–44

Wellisch, D., 2000. *Theory of Public Finance in a Federal State* (Cambridge University Press)

Whalley, J., 1979. Uniform domestic tax rates, trade distortions and economic integration, *Journal of Public Economics* 11, 213–21

1981. Border adjustment and tax harmonization: comment on Berglas, *Journal of Public Economics* 16, 389–90

Whalley, J. and I. Trela, 1986. *Regional Aspects of Confederation* (University of Toronto Press)

Wiegard, W., 1980. Distortionary taxation in a federal economy, *Journal of Economics/Zeitschrift für Nationalökonomie* 40, 183–206

Wildasin, D. E., 1986. *Urban Public Finance* (Harwood Academic Publishers, Chur)

1988. Nash equilibria in models of fiscal competition, *Journal of Public Economics* 35, 229–40

1991. Some rudimentary 'duopolity' theory, *Regional Science and Urban Economics* 21, 393–421

1997. Income distribution and redistribution within federations, *Annales d'économie et de statistique* 45, 291–313

Williams, T. and C. Kelley, 1998 Gnuplot. An interactive plotting program, online manual for version 3.7 <http://www.gnuplot.org>

Wilson, J. D., 1986. A theory of interregional tax competition, *Journal of Urban Economics* 19, 296–315

1987. Trade, capital mobility, and tax competition, *Journal of Political Economy* 95, 835–56

1991. Tax competition with interregional differences in factor endowments, *Regional Science and Urban Economics* 21, 423–51

1999. Theories of tax competition, *National Tax Journal* 52, 269–304

Wolfram, S., 1999. *The Mathematica Book, Version 4*, 4th edn. (Cambridge University Press)

Wrede, M., 1994. Tax competition, locational choice, and market power, *Finanzarchiv* 51, 488–516

1996. Vertical and horizontal tax competition. Will uncoordinated Leviathans end up on the wrong side of the Laffer curve?, *Finanzarchiv* 53, 461–79

2000. Shared tax sources and public expenditure, *International Tax and Public Finance* 7, 163–75

Zodrow, G. and P. Mieszkowski, 1986. Pigou, Tiebout, property taxation and the underprovision of local public goods, *Journal of Urban Economics* 19, 356–70

Index